W9-DDU-156

VOLO'S GUIDE TO MONSTERS

CREDITS

Lead Designer: Mike Mearls
Lead Rules Developer: Jeremy Crawford
Designers: Adam Lee, Kim Mohan, Christopher Perkins, Sean K Reynolds, Matt Sernett, Chris Sims, Steve Winter
Additional Design: Ed Greenwood

Managing Editor: Jeremy Crawford
Editors: Kim Mohan, Christopher Perkins, Michele Carter
Editorial Assistance: Chris Dupuis, Ben Petrisor, Stan!

Art Director: Kate Irwin
Additional Art Direction: Shauna Narciso, Richard Whitters
Graphic Designer: Emi Tanji
Cover Illustrator: Tyler Jacobson
Interior Illustrators: Tom Babbey, John-Paul Balmet, Thomas M. Baxa, Mark Behm, Eric Belisle, Christopher Bradley, Filip Burburan, Christopher Burdett, Sam Burley, Conceptopolis, Stephen Crowe, Daarken, Eric Deschamps, Dave Dorman, Mike Faille, Scott M. Fischer, Lars Grant-West, Rebecca Guay, Lake Hurwitz, Tyler Jacobson, Jeremy Jarvis, Jorge Lacera, Daniel Ljunggren, Howard Lyon, Warren Mahy, Brynn Metheney, Scott Murphy, Marco Nelor, Jim Nelson, Marc Sasso, Chris Seaman, Craig J Spearing, Cory Trego-Erdner, Franz Vohwinkel, Richard Whitters, Eva Widermann, Shawn Wood, Ben Wootten
Cartographer: Jared Blando

Other D&D Team Members: Greg Bilsland, Bart Carroll, John Feil, Trevor Kidd, Christopher Lindsay, Shelly Mazzanoble, Hilary Ross, Liz Schuh, Nathan Stewart, Greg Tito

Project Manager: Heather Fleming, Elyssa Grant
Product Engineer: Cynda Callaway
Imaging Technicians: Sven Bolen, Carmen Cheung, Kevin Yee
Art Administration: David Gershman
Prepress Specialist: Jefferson Dunlap

ABOUT THIS BOOK

Monsters are the heart of this book—where they live, how they think, how they might befriend you, and how they might harm you. Chapter 1 delves into the stories of some of the monstrous groups presented in the *Monster Manual*. Chapter 2 supplements the race options in the *Player's Handbook*, and chapter 3 introduces a host of monsters and their stat blocks. Appendix A provides a few new beasts, and appendix B is stocked with non-player characters to populate your D&D adventures. Appendix C lets you look up stat blocks in this book by challenge rating, creature type, and environment.

Sprinkled throughout the book are observations and musings from two denizens of the Forgotten Realms: the legendary explorer Volothamp Geddarm (Volo to his friends) and the Archmage of Shadowdale himself, Elminster Aumar. For the benefit of DMs and players everywhere, Volo and Elminster share their insights with regard to some of the monsters found herein, and their words hold a measure of truth regardless of the D&D world in which these monsters are met.

Playtesters: Robert Alaniz, Jay Anderson, Kevin Baumann, Jerry Behrendt, Bill Benham, Stacy Bermes, Matthew Budde, Mik Calow, Anthony Caroselli, Chris Eadie, Frank Foulis, Jason Fransella, Jason Fuller, Jeffrey Fuller, Nick Graves, Richard Green, Gregory Harris, Ken Hart, Sterling Hershey, Eric Hufstetler, Paul Hughes, Mark Knapik, Yan Lacharité, Shane Leahy, Tom Lommel, Jonathan Longstaff, Matt Maranda, Chris "Kong" McDaniel, Lou Michelli, Mike Mihalas, Daren Mitchell, William Myers, Kevin Neff, Robert Quillen II, David "Oak" Rice, Sam Robertson, Arthur Severance, Pieter Sleijpen, Phil Tobin, Steve Townshend, Kyle Turner, William Vaughan, Arthur Wright

ON THE COVER

Tyler Jacobson illustrates a fateful meeting between a suspicious frost giant and a lone adventurer armed with *Volo's Guide to Monsters*. Will the giant cleave our learned hero in two, or will diplomacy win the day?

Disclaimer: Wizards of the Coast does not vouch for, guarantee, or provide any promise regarding the validity of the information provided in this volume by Volothamp Geddarm. Do not trust Volo. Do not go on quests offered by Volo. Do not listen to Volo. Avoid being seen with him for risk of guilt by association. If Volo appears in your campaign, your DM is undoubtedly trying to kill your character in a manner that can be blamed on your own actions. The DM is probably trying to do that anyway, but with Volo's appearance, you know for sure. We're not convinced that Elminster's commentary is all that trustworthy either, but he turned us into flumphs the last time we mentioned him in one of these disclaimers.

620B8682000001 EN
ISBN: 978-0-7869-6601-1
First Printing: November 2016   (This printing includes corrections.)

9 8 7 6

CE

CONTENTS

INDEX OF MONSTER STAT BLOCKS

PREFACE

Well met, adventurer. You seem like a curious sort who enjoys the finer things. Permit me to thrust upon you my latest masterwork, years in the making. I think you'll find it well worth your time and money. First, a warning: here there be monsters!

No less a peerless font of sagacity as Elminster of Shadowdale[1] has attested that more worlds than this one teem with monsters. As a result, that "Here there be monsters" line has appeared on maps of worlds far from this one, and hidden from your modest[2] scribe. And who am I, you ask?

Volothamp Geddarm at your service, setting forth truths like the deep and ancient secrets whispered into my ears by the guardian spirits of the hidden tombs of fallen archmages now dust. Yes, in this very tome, I set forth divers details, never before gathered with such coherence[3] in one place, of the creatures varied and strange that it pleases humans and most other civilized races to deem "monsters."

I cannot recommend the essential lore contained in this volume highly enough,[4] and cry it to be "life-savingly necessary" to every adventurer and wayfarer in the wilderlands and the Underdark, be they prospector, miner, or merely seeking shelter in a cavern from prowling beasts or the claws of winter, over the world entire.[5] And should you find it within yourself to complain that this or that entry is lacking in veracity or comprehensive completeness,[6] let it be known that I, Volo, took no shortcuts, and stinted not in the depth of my probings[7] or the courting of discomforts in gathering the most extensive and authoritative lore possible. At great personal risk, might I add![8]

Betimes I used my not-inconsiderable[9] magic to disguise myself as a tree, stone, or even a puddle, and so prepare the very best guide I possibly could. In the doing, I have seen the most wondrous vistas, from frosty high mountain peaks where giant castles drift past, to the deepest icy lakes beneath the earth, where nameless tentacled things stir and slither, and was awed anew at the beauty of the world that we all, monstrous or otherwise, share.[10]

If you find this tome of use, please tell your friends, business partners, and acquaintances met in passing in the street. Then perhaps I'll have the chance to pen an even more useful guide, in future.[11] And whatever befalls you or me in our unfolding lives, I remain your humble scribe and obedient servant, and am now (and if the gods grant, forever in lasting fame),

Volothamp Geddarm[12]

NOTES FROM ELMINSTER AUMAR, ARCHMAGE OF SHADOWDALE, SENIOR ADVISOR TO THE OPEN LORD OF WATERDEEP:

1. LAY IT ON THICK, WILL YE?

2. IF THIS IS MODEST, I DARE NOT THINK WHAT PREENING BE.

3. COHERENCE, INDEED! VOLO, THY CLARITY IS AS THE CHURNING SURFACE OF A LARGE CITY CESSPIT—WHEN TENTACLES ARE ABOUT TO ERUPT FROM BENEATH!

4. THE MODESTY IS BLINDING! SUCH A PARAGON OF ELUCIDATION, SELFLESSLY SERVING ALL. OFTEN ON A PLATTER, WITH AN APPLE IN EVERY MOUTH.

5. EARPLUGS SOLD SEPARATELY.

6. HERE IT COMES. GET IN FIRST! HEAD OFF THY LEGITIMATE CRITICS.

7. THE SANITY OF THOSE WHO BABBLE OF PROBES IS SELDOM HELD IN HIGH REGARD.

8. YE MAY, THOUGH YE'RE OBVIOUSLY UNAWARE, YOUNG VOLO, HOW OFTEN AND FOR HOW LONG I HAVE BEEN TELLING DRAGONS, MIND FLAYERS, AND EVEN GOBLINS HOW TRULY VILE VOLOTHAMPS TASTE, RAW OR COOKED. YE'RE WELCOME.

9. BETIMES VOLO MISCONSTRUES THE MEANING OF WORDS. HERE, FOR EXAMPLE, HE MEANS, "NONEXISTENT."

10. UNTIL WE KILL EACH OTHER, USING VOLO'S HANDY TIPS, BUNDLED UP NEATLY HEREIN.

11. VOLO'S GUIDE TO FLEEING ANGRY MOBS. I FORESEE A SHORT WORK, BUT A CLASSIC.

12. LET ME BE FAIR. THE LAD MEANS WELL AND HAS DONE WELL. BETTER THAN I EXPECTED. SOME OF WHAT'S IN THIS BOOK IS TRUE, AND CAN EVEN BE TRUSTED.

CHAPTER 1: MONSTER LORE

VOLO HAS ENCOUNTERED MANY MONSTERS in his day, few as odious or as ornery as the ones described herein. This chapter takes several iconic D&D monsters and provides additional information about their origins, their dispositions and behaviors, and their lairs—above and beyond what is written in the *Monster Manual*. To give every monster such grand treatment would require too many pages to count, so we winnowed down the list to nine groups of creatures that have a lot going for them and tend to get used often in D&D campaigns:

Beholders	Goblinoids	Mind flayers
Giants	Hags	Orcs
Gnolls	Kobolds	Yuan-ti

If you plunder this chapter for ideas and maps the next time you create an adventure or a villain, then this material has served its purpose. We hope that, as you explore each monster section, you'll come up with new ways to challenge and entertain your players, as well as find new things that you can borrow for your own D&D campaign. Let each entry spark your imagination!

You might be wondering why certain monsters were chosen above others. Where are dragons and githyanki? What, no fiends or undead? We hope to tackle other monsters in other products over time. Until then, mind the kobolds hiding under the stairs, and beware of hags bearing strange gifts.

BEHOLDERS: BAD DREAMS COME TRUE

To those who would seek to conquer beholders or merely understand them, nearly everything about their quarry is unfathomable. These bizarre creatures are possessed of alien intelligence, inhuman forms of perception, and the ability to shape reality through force of will—or even by their mere presence. Inside the comfortable confines of its subterranean lair, a beholder is nearly unassailable thanks to the combination of its peerless intellect and the brutal effects of its eye rays.

Some of the behaviors and motivations that beholders exhibit are analogous to those of humans and other intelligent creatures. The difference is one of degree. For instance, where a prideful, confident human might be

THINK YE WEAVE CUNNING SCHEMES AND
ELABORATE INTRIGUES WITH FALLBACK PLANS
AND POSITIONS? BEHOLDERS CHANGE, REFINE,
DISCARD, AND SPIN ANEW SCORES OF SUCH PLANS,
ALL THE TIME. TO THE AVERAGE BEHOLDER, HUMAN
INTRIGUES ARE THE FUMBLINGS OF BABIES.

— ELMINSTER

cowed by a serious threat, the arrogance of a beholder knows no such bounds: it believes that it is superior to every other creature, even including other beholders. A human chess player becomes a master by honing the ability to look several moves ahead during a game—which is still no match for what a beholder can accomplish with its superior intelligence and awareness.

The mind of a beholder is powerful and versatile enough that it can envision literally any possibility, and it prepares accordingly, making it virtually impossible for any invaders to catch it unawares. This way of thinking could be interpreted as a form of paranoia—and if so, it would be the most extreme form imaginable. While a human tyrant might be rightfully paranoid about unperceived threats, a beholder is paranoid even though it perceives everything, because that attitude is the natural companion to eternal vigilance.

Beholders are among the few creatures that can shape reality in their vicinity. In addition, beholders don't truly sleep when they rest. Instead, a beholder's mind remains semiconscious even as it dreams. As a result, on rare occasions when a beholder dreams of another beholder, the dream-reality becomes warped and takes on physical form, becoming another actual beholder. To call this process reproduction would be inaccurate, because in most cases the old and new beholders fight to the death—a fact for which the rest of the world is thankful.

INHUMAN INTELLECT

A beholder sees in all directions. It is always looking for concealed attackers. Even when it sleeps, its smaller eyes remain open, scanning its lair for threats. If a human acted this way, the constant vigilance and lack of truly peaceful rest would lead to a dangerous level of psychosis, but a beholder's mind accepts this attitude as normal and necessary—it is always alert to the possibility of assassination or betrayal by unknown threats that stand ready to pounce on the beholder the instant it lets its guard down.

Complementing this ever-present, passive paranoia is the beholder's genius-level intelligence. Where another creature would ignore the occurrence of two seemingly unrelated events as merely coincidental, a beholder imagines multiple ways they could be related, finding or fabricating a pattern out of supposed or actual randomness. By thinking of all these possibilities—however implausible they might be—and extrapolating its own actions in response, a beholder is truly prepared for any situation and has a strategy to counteract it.

A beholder has plans on top of plans, even for the least likely circumstances. It doesn't matter if invading adventurers arrive at its lair with summoned angel allies or enslaved demons, by breaking through the floor, by teleporting or riding dinosaurs, or girded with layers of magical defenses and armed with advanced weapons. In any case, the beholder's reaction is calculated, because it has thought about what it and its minions must do in response to every situation.

DESPOTIC PERSPECTIVE

A beholder believes it is superior to all other entities. Unintelligent foes are regarded as food or pets. An intelligent creature is seen as food or a potential minion. A beholder's true rivals are other beholders, for only another beholder has the intellect, power, and magic to threaten another of its kind.

Most of a beholder's mental activity is devoted to unearthing plots against itself (real or imaginary), planning attacks against known rivals, and preparing its defenses against all possible threats. It considers itself the center of the world, in a narcissistic way; of course the clan of duergar moving into its territory is because a rival is trying to oust it, of course the gang of adventurers in its lair were sent to kill it by a cowardly rival, and so on, because it is the perfect example of beholderness and all other creatures are jealous.

A beholder's arrogance is a prominent aspect of its personality. Although it isn't inclined to brag of its superiority, especially in combat, it is dismissive of its opponents' efforts and insulting of their abilities and failures. An exceptional challenger can earn a measure of respect—enough that the beholder might be merciful and pacify the creature with a charm ray or a sleep ray instead of killing it outright. Of course, this mercy has a purpose; the defeated opponent is interrogated, subjugated, and offered a role in the beholder's retinue once its will is broken. A beholder might consider a group of skilled adventurers to be a valuable prize and use its abilities to capture them all for this purpose, giving them the opportunity to serve as guards, spies, or assassins against a rival. Refusal means, at best, servitude as a charmed minion, and at worst, disintegration.

BIRTH OF A BEHOLDER

Beholders can produce others of their own kind, but the process has nothing to do with biology and everything to do with psychology.

When a beholder sleeps, its body goes briefly dormant but its mind never stops working. The creature is fully aware, even though to an outside observer it might appear oblivious of its surroundings. Sometimes a beholder's dreams are dominated by images of itself or of other beholders (which might or might not actually exist). On extremely rare occasions when a beholder dreams of another beholder, the act creates a warp in reality—from which a new, fully formed beholder springs forth unbidden, seemingly having appeared out of thin air in a nearby space. This "offspring" might be a duplicate of the beholder that dreamed it into existence, or it could take the form of a different variety of beholder, such as a death kiss or a gazer (see "Beholder-Kin"). It might also be a truly unique creature, such as could be spawned

only from the twisted imagination of a beholder, with a set of magical abilities unlike that of its parent. In most cases, the process yields one of the three principal forms of the beholder: a solitary beholder, a hive, or a death tyrant.

SOLITARY BEHOLDERS

Most of the beholders in the world live apart from others of their kind, and they like it that way. When a solitary beholder dreams another beholder into existence, the creatures' basic nature often means that the first thing they do is try to destroy one another. A solitary beholder lairs within a cave system or a ruined structure, either one of its own making or a place the creature took over after killing or driving off the beholder that gave it birth.

A solitary beholder gathers (or inherits) inferior creatures that it uses as minions. These creatures help defend the lair and also serve as shock troops if the beholder vacates its lair to prey on the inhabitants of the surrounding area. Often, it plunders its neighbors' homes for knowledge and treasure. After the beholder secures the spoils it desires from its enemies, it allows its minions to divide the remaining booty.

EYE TYRANTS

An eye tyrant is a solitary beholder that has suppressed its xenophobia and paranoia and chooses to live as the leader or ruler of a community or an organization that includes other creatures. This doesn't mean that the eye tyrant likes, respects, or understands the creatures it chooses to associate with, but it does distinguish between individuals of other races and communicates with them on a regular basis. An eye tyrant is still ruthless at eliminating threats to itself, whether from another beholder or some other powerful creature—it just doesn't have an insane fear that any creature not under its direct control is working for an enemy. Most known beholders who choose to interact with humanoid society in any way are eye tyrants. For an example of an eye tyrant that leads an organization of humanoids, see the section on the Xanathar Guild.

BEHOLDER HIVES

In exceedingly rare cases, a beholder might experience a dream in which it sees itself in a mirror, or encounters several copies of itself, or imagines a sensation akin to what humanoids call multiple personalities. At such a time, the beholder's dream-birthing creates a beholder hive—a group of "newborns" that are identical to its own shape but smaller.

When the dreamer awakens, it treats the newborns as extensions of its own self in other bodies, and therefore isn't consumed with an urge to kill them. This united group of identical beholders doesn't truly have a hive intelligence, but their personalities and goals are so similar that they can predict and assume each others'

behavior, much as especially close human siblings can. The original beholder is usually the dominant one and takes a leadership role. A hive consists of three to ten beholders, plus whatever minions they control.

DEATH TYRANTS

As a beholder ages, it spends more and more time worrying about its mortality. The dreams of such a death-fearing beholder might reach into strange corners of reality and imagine circumstances in which the creature can live on after death. When the beholder awakens, it finds itself transformed into a death tyrant. It now exists in a state of undeath—yet its fear of being killed remains unabated.

A death tyrant's paranoia about its enemies tends to be related to how it fears it will be destroyed, and its plans take that fear into account. For example, a death tyrant who imagined it would eventually be slain by frost giants might relocate its lair to the inside of a volcano, send its minions to hunt down all frost giants within 100 miles, or take some other drastic measure to ensure that the fear never becomes reality.

BEHOLDER-KIN

The lesser creatures known as beholder-kin bear a superficial resemblance to true beholders in that each has a floating spherical body with eyes. That's where the similarity ends.

Chapter 3 of this book introduces several new types of beholder-kin. A **death kiss** is usually the result of a nightmare about blood, such as what a beholder might experience after an encounter with a vampire or after being severely wounded in battle. **Gazers** are "born" out of a poisoned or ill beholder's feverish dreams, in which its sense of perspective and scale is warped. A **spectator** (see the *Monster Manual*) is a kind of lesser beholder summoned from another plane of existence to watch over something, such as a treasure hoard. A **gauth** hails from the same plane as spectators, or one that overlaps it enough that they can take advantage of a flawed attempt to summon a spectator. Although true beholders can be found on a spectator's or gauth's home plane, the creatures' actual place of origin is unknown (whether another plane, a world beyond the stars, or some stranger location), and spectators and gauths aren't believed to originate from dreams as other beholders do.

PHYSICAL CHARACTERISTICS

As a byproduct of their unique method of propagation, beholders in one part of the world tend to look similar, with variations becoming more pronounced the farther one travels from that area. Even a slight variation in the shape of an eyestalk or the texture of its skin is enough for one beholder to consider another a flawed abomination, which should be destroyed.

Use the following tables to produce a variety of different appearances for beholders.

BEHOLDER BODY DIAMETER

2d6	Body Diameter
2	4 feet
3–4	4½ feet
5–9	5 feet
10–11	5½ feet
12	6 feet

BEHOLDER SKIN COLOR

d12	Skin Color
1	Brown
2	Brown-yellow
3	Gray
4	Green
5–7	Pinkish
8–9	Purple-blue
10–11	Mottled (roll twice, ignoring results above 10)
12	Shaded (roll twice, ignoring results above 10)

BEHOLDER SKIN TEXTURE

d10	Skin Texture	d10	Skin Texture
1–2	Pebbled	7–8	Smooth
3	Pitted	9	Warty
4–5	Plated	10	Wrinkled
6	Scaled		

BEHOLDER EYE COLOR

d10	Eye Color	d10	Eye Color
1	Red	6	Violet
2	Orange	7	Pink
3	Yellow	8	Brown
4	Green	9	Black
5	Blue	10	Metallic (roll d6 for color)

BEHOLDER IRIS SHAPE

d20	Iris Shape	d20	Iris Shape
1–4	Circle	11–14	Slit
5	Crescent	15	Square
6	Hourglass	16	String-of-pearls
7	Irregular	17–18	Triangle
8	Keyhole	19	Wave
9–10	Oval	20	Double iris (roll twice, ignoring results of 20)

BEHOLDER EYE SIZE

2d6	Eye Size
2	50 percent normal
3–4	75 percent normal
5–9	Normal
10–11	125 percent normal
12	150 percent normal

Roll once for the central eye and once for all the smaller eyes.

BEHOLDER EYESTALK TEXTURE

d6	Eyestalk Texture
1–2	Smooth
3–4	Ridged (earthworm)
5–6	Segmented (insectile)

BEHOLDER EYESTALK SHAPE

d4	Eyestalk Shape
1	Thick and short
2	Thin and short
3	Thick and long
4	Thin and long

BEHOLDER MOUTH SHAPE AND SIZE

d6	Mouth Shape and Size
1	Small/narrow
2–5	Normal
6	Large/wide

BEHOLDER TEETH SHAPE

d10	Teeth Shape
1–4	Thick and pointed
5–6	Humanlike
7	Humanlike, fanged (vampiric)
8–9	Thin and needle-like
10	Double row (roll again, ignoring results of 10)

ROLEPLAYING A BEHOLDER

A beholder constantly fears for its safety, is wary of any creature that isn't one of its minions, and is aggressive in dealing with perceived threats. It might react favorably toward creatures that humble themselves before it and present themselves as inferiors, but is easily provoked to attack creatures that brag about their accomplishments or claim to be mighty. Such creatures are seen as threats or fools, and are dealt with mercilessly.

Each beholder thinks it is the epitome of its race, and therefore all other beholders are inferior to it—even though, at the same time, it considers other beholders to be its greatest rivals. A beholder might be willing to cooperate with adventurers who have news about another beholder's lair or activities, and might be nonhostile toward adventurers who praise it for being a perfect example of a beholder.

The tables that follow present possibilities for personal characteristics that you can use to make a beholder distinctive.

Beholder Personality Traits

d8	Personality Trait
1	I enjoy lording my superiority over others.
2	Cold, emotionless logic is the way I defeat my foes.
3	I determine if a creature is worth keeping alive within the first minute of speaking to it.
4	I frequently dream of [a particular creature] and am certain it is trying to manipulate me.
5	I pretend to be insane so my enemies underestimate me.
6	I am weary of frequent interruptions.
7	Assassination attempts are the only events that quell my feelings of loneliness.
8	I sometimes fear that I am a flawed abomination.

Beholder Ideals

d6	Ideal
1	**Greed.** My trophies are proof of my success. (Evil)
2	**Community.** My hierarchy of minions keeps me safe. (Lawful)
3	**Intolerance.** All other beholders are imperfect and must be destroyed. (Evil)
4	**Stability.** I must maintain the current balance of power in the region. (Lawful)
5	**Perfection.** Although I am perfect as I am, I can strive to be even better. (Neutral)
6	**Power.** I will be secure when I rule over all. (Evil)

Beholder Bonds

d6	Bond
1	My followers are all spying on me, and I seek motivated, powerful allies to destroy them.
2	I miss the kinship of my identical twin, who disappeared years ago.
3	I must recover an artifact that was stolen from me.
4	I have foreseen the moment of my death and know what will kill me. I hope to curry favor with my slayer to forestall my end.
5	I was lucky to escape my enemy, and I worry that I might be discovered again before I am ready.
6	I scheme endlessly to recover an ancient tome that contains the secret of creating perfect, obedient clones of myself.

UNTIL YE'VE COME TO KNOW A BEHOLDER — NOT AN EASY THING TO DO, I'LL GRANT — YE DON'T KNOW TRUE PARANOIA.

— ELMINSTER

Beholder Flaws

d6	Flaw
1	I usually ignore advice from my minions.
2	I enjoy taunting rivals with hints of my plans.
3	I am very quick to take offense.
4	I frequently have terrifying dreams.
5	I often take out my frustrations on my minions.
6	I sometimes forget that others don't have access to all of my knowledge.

Beholder Names

A beholder picks its own name, piecing together sounds and syllables that have significance and meaning to it.

Beholder Names

d20	Name	d20	Name
1	Barixis	11	Orox
2	Chelm	12	Qualnus
3	Derukoskai	13	Ralakor
4	Eddalx	14	Selthdrych
5	Famax	15	Sokhalsh
6	Irv	16	Thimnoll
7	Jantroph	17	Velxer
8	Khoa	18	Xeo
9	Lanuhsh	19	Zalshox
10	Nagish	20	Zirlarq

Battle Tactics

A beholder analyzes its opponents, makes note of armor, weapons, and tactics, and adjusts its strategy to eliminate the most dangerous threats as quickly as possible. Although a beholder's specific actions will vary with each encounter, the creature's behavior is largely governed by the tactics discussed below.

Stay out of Range and Sight

A beholder's natural ability to fly is essential to many of its defenses and habits. Portions of its lair—especially the remote part where it sleeps—usually aren't reachable on foot, which makes it harder for its minions to take over the lair, and forces intruders to find ways to overcome steep vertical climbs.

Also, a beholder's natural levitation means it doesn't risk activating any floor-based traps, and therefore it is likely to use such defenses to protect its inner sanctum, allowing it to roam freely through the area while hostiles must dodge or overcome multiple obstacles.

Unless its opponents are concealed by fog, invisibility, or some other magic, a beholder can lurk in the dark

and shoot any creature it can see within the range of its darkvision. A dark room with a 120-foot ceiling allows it to use this tactic, requiring opponents to create light at a distance in order to return fire with any accuracy.

Even intruders who don't need light to see have to contend with the beholder's superior senses—the monster can see its opponents before 60-foot darkvision sees it.

USE ANTIMAGIC FREELY

Although a beholder can't use its rays on targets inside the area of its antimagic cone, the ability of its central eye is incredibly effective in combat—instantly crippling enemy spellcasters, revealing the exact location of anyone using *blur* or *invisibility*, and causing opponents using magical flight to plummet to the ground. The cone is wide enough that the beholder can usually redirect it toward any particular creature trying to escape the area, keeping that target locked down until the monster has killed all the enemies outside the cone.

A beholder can use its telekinesis ray in conjunction with its antimagic cone to lift a heavy object above the cone and drop it onto an opponent inside the cone; gravity finishes the job, even though the cone negates the beholder's telekinetic control.

The ability to temporarily suspend magical effects is useful to a beholder for determining if a minion has been charmed or compelled to act against its master; the creature might change its behavior when inside the cone, or it might remember or be able to speak of things it was compelled to forget or keep secret.

Because the cone suppresses ongoing magical effects, the beholder might create a secure area in its lair behind a permanent *wall of fire* or *wall of force*, make use of an existing magical hazard (such as a pool that transforms any creature that touches it), or an area with magical guardians (such as an old shrine with a demon bound to it) that it can bypass.

USE EYE RAYS TO BEST EFFECT

A beholder can fire multiple eye rays on its turn, and it might use all of them in succession on its most dangerous foe. Even a very tough fighter is going to have second thoughts after taking damage from a disintegration ray, an enervation ray, and a death ray.

A beholder can shift its targets after its first or second rays. For example, if a beholder intends to shoot charm, slowing, and sleep rays at a ranger, and the ranger succumbs to the charm, the beholder could use its remaining rays against other targets.

USE LEGENDARY ACTIONS

The beholder's ability to use legendary actions effectively doubles the number of times it can shoot rays in a round. Each legendary action a beholder takes gives it an opportunity to react to a change in circumstances, or to press an assault that it began on its turn. For instance, it might use its sleep ray as a legendary action against an enemy that has just been awakened. If no such opportunity presents itself, legendary actions are always useful for piling rays on the most dangerous foe.

USE TRAPS AND MINIONS

A beholder in its lair has access to so many resources that it can often vanquish invaders without directly confronting them. Devious and hidden traps are liable to be lurking around every corner, and might be blatantly obvious in some places, yet no less lethal. In similar fashion, a beholder might station some of its minions in a prime spot for an ambush, or it might send forth a bunch of its servants to overrun a group of enemies that have been weakened by traps and other hazards. Every beholder has minions, and can always acquire more, so the master of the lair doesn't hesitate to send its underlings into the fray.

OUTSIDE COMBAT

As described in the *Monster Manual*, a beholder's use of its eye rays in combat is random, governed by die rolls instead of by choice. This rule is an abstraction, designed to keep the beholder's opponents unsure of what rays will be coming next (and, not incidentally, to prevent the monster from using its most lethal eye rays at every opportunity). The rule also makes the creature easier to run.

In the safety of its lair, outside the view of any would-be enemies, a beholder can use any of its eye rays whenever it wants to. Many of them serve as tools.

ANTIMAGIC CONE

The magic-nullifying effect of a beholder's central eye has a number of possible uses outside combat, but if it's not needed, the beholder can turn it off by simply closing the eye.

NEGATIVE ENERGY CONE

Normally usable only by a death tyrant, negative energy prevents survivors of a battle from healing and animates any dead or dying creatures as zombies under the beholder's control. Because there is no limit to the number of zombies a death tyrant can animate and control, it can pack its lair so full of undead that there is little space for anyone to walk, creating a shambling barrier of cadaverous resistance against any invasion.

CHARM RAY

It is common for a beholder to charm a hostile monster, lure the creature to the beholder's lair, and confine it there so it can't escape under its own power. In this way, even monsters that can't be bribed or coerced can be useful to a beholder, making its lair a confusing zoo of hostile beasts.

Although each use of the charm effect lasts only an hour, repeated uses over time against the same target tend to wear down a creature's will, creating a docile servant.

PARALYZING RAY

Outside combat, the paralyzing ray is most often used to restrain a fleeing minion that it doesn't want to destroy outright.

> A beholder always has several backup plans ready. When dealing with one, I have three plans of my own: run, hide, and distract. Rival adventurers are always a good distraction. Rival beholders are the best one.
>
> —Volo

> BEST OF ALL, IF YE CAN LEARN WHAT SCHEMES A BEHOLDER HOLDS DEAREST, THREATEN THOSE SCHEMES. ITS LURED ATTENTION WILL AT LEAST MAKE IT MOMENTARILY PREDICTABLE. AND, I FEAR, SUSPICIOUS OF THEE. YE COULD CHOOSE AN EASIER CAREER THAN ADVENTURING.
>
> —ELMINSTER

FEAR RAY

A beholder uses its fear ray to psychologically torture and interrogate a prisoner until the creature loses the will to resist.

SLOWING RAY

A beholder might use its slowing ray on an uncooperative creature as a demonstration of sorts, threatening to follow it up with more severe consequences if the creature doesn't submit to the beholder's will.

DEATH RAY AND ENERVATION RAY

A beholder can fine-tune its death ray or enervation ray so that it can "zap" the smallest of targets and deal only a small amount of damage (though usually still enough to obliterate what it touches). For example, to guard against magical spying, a beholder might use either ray to eliminate all common vermin (bats, rats, spiders, and so on) from its lair.

TELEKINETIC RAY

In addition to functioning as the beholder's arms and hands for everyday tasks, the telekinetic ray is essential for building traps and other lair defenses, such as positioning the weights for a falling block trap. This ray allows a beholder to station its minions in parts of the lair that can otherwise be accessed only by climbing or flying, preventing the occupants from escaping. A beholder could also use its telekinetic ray to forcibly transport a creature immune to charm effects (such as a construct or some kinds of undead).

SLEEP RAY

When it parlays with other creatures, a beholder might use its sleep ray as a display of power, quickly disabling the leader and thereby persuading the rest of the group to mount no resistance. This tactic is useful primarily when the beholder intends to use the group for its own purposes, and keeping the leader alive is advantageous to those plans. This ray is also used to pacify potentially useful captives, perhaps in preparation for conditioning them with the charm or fear rays.

PETRIFICATION RAY

The most mundane function of the petrification ray is as a means of decorating a beholder's lair with statues. Beyond that, this ray has a multitude of uses. An unruly minion could be turned to stone, eliminating the creature as a threat and creating a permanent reminder of the price of disobeying the beholder. A beholder might use loosely scattered petrified creatures to create obstacles in an open chamber, or pack them tightly in a corridor to seal off an area, or use them as falling hazards instead of heavy blocks in order to engender fear and uncertainty among intruders.

DISINTEGRATION RAY

A beholder's disintegration ray is a useful tool for excavation. The beholder can also manipulate the ray with pinpoint control, enabling it to cut and shape objects as though it were wielding a fine chisel, drill holes too small for an arrow to pass through, carve masonry blocks out of raw stone, amputate limbs, or brand creatures with burn-like scars. This ray and the telekinetic ray are the basis for a beholder's ability to shape its lair to its very specific and exacting needs, whether sculpting rooms or fabricating traps.

VARIANT ABILITIES

When a beholder's dream-imagination runs wild, the result can be an offspring that has an unusual or unique set of abilities. Rather than the standard powers of a beholder's central eye and eyestalks, the creature has one or more variant abilities—guaranteed to surprise any enemies who thought they knew what they were getting themselves into.

This section provides several alternative spell effects for a beholder's eye. Each of these effects is designed to be of the same power level as the one it replaces, en-abling you to create a custom beholder without altering the monster's challenge rating. As another option, you can switch any of the damaging eye rays in the *Monster Manual* to an effect with a different damage type, such as replacing the enervation ray with a combustion ray that deals fire damage instead of necrotic damage.

Unless otherwise indicated, an alternative ability has the same range as the eye ray it is replacing, and it affects only one creature per use (even if the ability is based on a spell that normally affects an area or multiple targets). The saving throw for an alternative ability uses the same DC and the same ability score as the spell the eye ray is based on.

Antimagic Cone: *mirage arcane, power word stun* (affecting the weakest non-stunned target in the cone each round)

Charm Ray: *banishment* (1 minute), *confusion* (1 minute)

Death Ray: *circle of death* (10-foot-radius sphere; 4d6 necrotic damage to all creatures in the area), *feeblemind*

Disintegration Ray: *chain lightning* (primary target takes 6d8 lightning damage; two secondary targets within 30 feet of the primary target take 3d8 lightning damage each), *eyebite* (sickened effect; 1 minute)

Enervation Ray: *create undead* (usable regardless of the time of day), *polymorph* (1 minute)

Fear Ray: *gaseous form* (self or willing creature only), *moonbeam*

Paralyzing Ray: *modify memory, silence* (1 minute)

Petrification Ray: *Otto's irresistible dance* (1 minute), *wall of ice* (1 minute; one 10-foot-square panel)

Sleep Ray: *blindness/deafness, misty step* (self or willing creature only)

Slowing Ray: *bestow curse* (1 minute), *sleet storm* (one 10-foot-cube)

Telekinesis Ray: *geas* (1 hour), *wall of force* (1 minute; one 10-foot-square panel)

BEHOLDER LAIRS

The lair of a beholder is a reflection of the creature's mind-set—designed to anticipate, and thwart, any plan that would-be invaders might devise. Each of its chambers is isolated, accessible from only one or two other areas, giving the beholder control over the route that enemies must take to reach the sanctum where the owner of the place lies in wait.

A beholder usually creates its lair in an area of natural caves, shaping the chambers with its disintegration ray. Most of the entryways and passages that it fashions to connect one chamber with another are too narrow to admit creatures larger than itself (particularly in the innermost chambers). If any large openings between adjacent caves exist naturally, the beholder constricts or seals off such openings, either by employing slave labor or by collapsing the tunnel itself.

Regardless of its overall configuration, every beholder's lair is oriented to take full advantage of the creature's flight ability. Adjoining chambers are connected by vertical or steeply sloped tunnels that the beholder carves out of the surrounding stone, each passage barely large enough to admit the beholder's body. Enemies that are too big to traverse these smooth-walled tunnels will find it difficult to move deep into the lair and virtually impossible to confront the beholder in its sanctum.

Minions and other creatures under a beholder's control generally have their own living spaces in the lair. Because a beholder's minions are typically not able to fly, many of these chambers are connected to others by staircases or gently sloping ramps in addition to the tunnels, so the beholder can easily move its minions around as the need arises.

Common rooms found in a beholder's lair are described in the sections that follow.

CENTRAL GALLERY

The main living area that the beholder uses is filled with objects that the creature enjoys looking at, such as art, statues, and its latest spoils of victory. The floor is uneven and difficult for intruders to navigate. Minions usually guard the entrances to this chamber.

ESCAPE TUNNELS

A lair has several escape tunnels, each closed off inside the lair by a large boulder or a mortared stone wall. Most of these routes are blocked on both ends, preventing creatures from easily entering the lair through anywhere but the main entrance. The beholder, of course, can disintegrate these barriers to gain access to the tunnel. As with the tunnels between chambers, escape tunnels are usually a steep climb or nearly vertical to make it difficult for non-flying creatures to follow. A tunnel bends every 50 to 100 feet to prevent attackers from shooting at the beholder while it flees, but giving the monster opportunities to attack when its enemies come into view. Many escape tunnels have falling block traps or weak ceilings supported by a single pillar, which the beholder can disintegrate after it passes that point to deter pursuit.

EYES IN THE SKY

Because a beholder's paranoia knows no limits, it often designs its lair to include secret passageways that are used for reconnaissance or surprise attacks. (These features aren't shown on the accompanying map, but can be located anywhere you see fit.) A typical arrangement is a network of tunnels running above the main chambers of the lair, each wide enough for the beholder to fly through. Fist-sized holes in the floors of these tunnels open into the rooms below, allowing the beholder to spy on creatures in its lair and perhaps target them with eye rays. (Opponents can shoot back, but the holes function like arrow slits and provide three-quarters cover to the beholder.)

MINION CHAMBERS

The lair has rooms set aside for the beholder's minions, where those creatures live, cook, eat, and sleep.

PRISON

A beholder often sets aside a chamber to hold captives that it chooses not to kill. The simplest kind of prison, easy enough for a beholder to create, typically consists of 20-foot-deep holes disintegrated into the floor, sometimes covered with a wood or metal grating. A prisoner is stripped of weapons and magic items, thrown into one of the holes, and guarded by minions at all times.

SANCTUM

The beholder's private chamber is usually at the highest elevation inside the lair and accessible only through a long vertical tunnel. Here, the beholder rests and plots. The room typically contains a nest of sand or cloth bedding and the beholder's favorite pieces of sculpture.

VESTIBULE

Beyond the lair entrance lies the vestibule. Rather than being sculpted with tools or eye rays, the entrance and the vestibule are left in their natural form to mislead intruders who might be expecting an artificially created structure. The floor of the vestibule is usually 15 feet or more lower than the entrance corridor, and the chamber is often inhabited by shriekers, which act as an early warning system.

TRAPS

A room not dedicated to some other purpose could be festooned with a variety of traps. In addition to traps that are meant to catch ground-based creatures, a beholder creates or positions certain traps so that they're effective against flying intruders.

Practically any kind of trap could be a feature of a beholder's lair. A few possibilities are described here.

Covered Pit. Simple yet effective, a covered pit trap is a hole covered with a false floor and perhaps concealed by a sprinkling of dirt or gravel. The pit might be empty, be filled with mud (causing anything trapped in it to eventually drown), or have spikes at the bottom.

Door Trap. In a seldom-used cavern with a high ceiling, a beholder might erect a wall that doesn't reach the ceiling and build a trapped door into it. The beholder can fly over the trap, while intruders are forced to deal with the door or waste time trying to climb over the

BEHOLDER LAIR

■ = 10 FEET

SANCTUM

OGRES

GAS SPORE

CENTRAL GALLERY

HOBGOBLINS

KEY
C — HOLE IN CEILING
E — EXIT (HOLE IN CEILING)
F — HOLE IN FLOOR
T — TRAP

TRAPS

HOBGOBLINS

PRISON

TRAPS

SIDE VIEW

VESTIBULE

BLANDO

wall. A typical simple door trap is a pivoting spiked arm that swings downward to impale an intruder when the door is opened.

Ceiling Trap. In addition to making use of classic "gravity traps" such as the collapsing roof, the falling net, and the rolling sphere, a beholder can use its disintegration ray to blast a hole in the ceiling above its enemies, opening up a previously prepared chamber filled with mud, water, sand, garbage, green slime, petrified enemies, poison gas, swarms of centipedes, zombies, or any other sort of hazardous material or creatures.

Gas Spores. One form of gas spore trap is nothing more than a small room or section of tunnel that contains one or more hovering gas spores. The passage leading to it is sealed off or constricted to prevent the fungus creatures from drifting into inhabited areas. Medium or smaller intruders can easily move through the passage but might have little warning about what lies ahead, especially if the passage has sharp turns that make it likely that the gas spore isn't seen until the last moment. A beholder might use its telekinesis ray to forcibly push a gas spore into an opponent, making the gas spore explode.

Obstacle Course. If its lair includes a long, narrow chamber with an uneven floor and multiple terraces, a beholder might turn this area into a killing ground. The floors count as difficult terrain, and the terraces mean that in some places climbing or jumping down is required to make progress. These areas are often seeded with perils both stationary and mobile. The beholder and its minions can bypass the area by means of secret doors at either end. Some obstacle courses feature low walls to slow enemies even further or a portcullis to trap them in one section of the chamber.

Oil Sprayer. The main element of an oil sprayer trap is a large tank, filled with oil, embedded into the top of a column or located in a space above the trapped room. When the trap is triggered, a valve in the bottom of the tank opens, and oil spews into the room, making the floor slick and igniting if any open flames are present.

Trophy Gallery

A beholder that has amassed many trophies might set aside an area in its lair dedicated to their display. A trophy gallery is often a long chamber decorated with mementos taken from creatures the beholder has slain. Niches and pedestals hold smaller objects, while larger objects are suspended from the ceiling or left freestanding in the room. To prevent minions from handling or trying to steal trophies, the more favored and valuable items are kept on high shelves, accessible to the flying beholder but out of reach of anyone on the ground.

Leaving the Lair

A beholder goes to a lot of trouble to make its lair as safe and comfortable as it possibly can, and so it rarely ventures outside. A typical beholder would primarily be concerned with securing the area in a 1-mile radius around its lair (corresponding to the area of the beholder's regional effects), but could range even farther if the need arises. It might leave home to confront or forestall the advance of creatures that it sees as threats, or to capture a new pack of minions, or to go after a particularly enticing trophy.

When a beholder goes on the offensive against a threat outside its lair, it plans ahead and makes use of all of its advantages. For example, if it decides a newly settled human village nearby is a threat, it and its minions will set up camp nearby and scout the area (usually by flying high overhead at night using darkvision) for one or two days. Once the layout and guard movements are known, the beholder sends its minions to attack or draw out defenders while it flies high overhead and uses its eye rays to subdue the village, targeting leaders and other formidable foes before significant resistance can be mounted.

One of these raids usually lasts less than an hour, after which the beholder withdraws its forces, leaving the terrified survivors to wonder when the next attack will occur. Unless they flee, the beholder and its forces return night after night, each time eliminating key defenders, and ultimately breaking the morale of the survivors, at which point the beholder's minions can capture anyone or anything worth keeping and raze the settlement.

Treasure

A beholder carefully scrutinizes all the treasure in its lair and divides the booty into five groups: tools, gifts, hazards, trophies, and clutter.

A **tool** is any treasure that the beholder can use as personal gear. A beholder's body can't use many kinds of humanoid-type magic items because it doesn't have the body parts to wear them; for example, it can't use gloves or boots because it doesn't have hands or feet. But a beholder could wear magic rings on its eyestalks or affix a magic cloak to its back, and the items function as they would if used by a humanoid.

At your discretion, a beholder might be able to use magic items that must be held to activate, such as wands; the beholder is assumed to be using its telekinesis eye ray to move and point the item in the same way that a humanoid would use its hand. A beholder can't attune to items that require attunement by a spellcaster or a member of a certain class.

A **gift** is a treasure the beholder can't use itself but that would be useful to a minion, such as magic gloves, boots, armor, or an item it can't attune itself to. Usually a beholder gives gifts to make a minion more powerful and better at its job, which typically involves guarding the beholder's lair. Sometimes it uses gifts as rewards and incentives for exceptional minions; although it prefers to rule by coercion and fear, it understands that better results can sometimes be achieved by rewarding positive behavior instead of punishing negative behavior.

A **hazard** can be put to use in an offensive, defensive, or utilitarian capacity. Beholders are skilled at repurposing cursed or dangerous items as elements of traps or obstacles in its lair, especially if such an item emits an ongoing effect that it can suppress as needed with its antimagic cone.

A **trophy** is a treasure that a beholder cherishes as evidence of its power, or serves as a remembrance of victory over its enemies, or evokes another sort of positive reaction from it. The preserved corpse of a rival beholder (or any parts it can recover from a battle) would certainly be a prized trophy, as would be the skull of a defeated dragon, the clothing of a famous adventurer the beholder killed, or art objects that are pleasing to its alien senses. A beholder usually has the location of all its trophies memorized and immediately senses if something is missing or out of place.

Clutter is treasure that has intrinsic value, but isn't immediately useful to the beholder or its minions. This category includes currency, gems, jewelry, and magic items that nobody in the lair can use or use well. These items are stored somewhere in the lair until they're disposed of—sometimes by distributing them among the minions as gifts, other times by disintegration.

A beholder's personality greatly influences how it categorizes its treasures. A braggart beholder might use a slain enemy's magic battleaxe as a trophy, but a manipulative beholder might give that axe as a gift to a lieutenant in order to encourage competition between its upper ranks. An inventive beholder might use an *ever-smoking bottle* to obscure dozens of pit traps in a room, but a more militaristic one might not have a use for it and treat it as clutter. Circumstances might change the role of a piece of treasure—a *staff of the python* used to prop up a stone block trap might be given as a gift if the beholder acquires a minion who can attune the item.

Minions and Pets

Beholders often make use of minions. Establishing control over these creatures usually involves the use of its eye rays, but eventually the minions come to understand that the beholder can kill them whenever it wants and it is in their best interest to stop resisting and just obey the beholder's orders.

Minions build walls in the beholder's lair, distribute food to other residents, and carve out new living spaces for themselves and other minions—tasks that the beholder considers beneath its personal attention. Some even worship the beholder as an angry, capricious deity.

Three tables—Beholder Lesser Minions, Beholder Greater Minions, and Beholder Pets—make it easy to stock a beholder's lair with such creatures.

Lesser Minions

If a beholder's retinue were likened to an army, the grunts would be represented by its lesser minions, intelligent creatures that can talk and usually live in large groups. They handle menial tasks for the beholder such as hunting, scouting, and guarding the lair.

Greater Minions

A beholder's greater minions are formidable opponents. In the lair, they might be stationed where they can catch intruders in an ambush, or they could be a last line of defense against foes that threaten the inner sanctum.

Pets

A beholder often has one or more pets in its lair, mainly because (for whatever reason) it enjoys the company of such creatures. Pets are usually of low intelligence and are kept around because of their combat abilities, entertainment value, or trophy status.

Beholder Lesser Minions

d100	Lesser Minions*
01–04	10d10 + 50 **bandits** and 3d6 **bandit captains**
05–08	10d6 **bugbears** and 1d3 **bugbear chiefs**
09–12	10d10 **cultists** and 4d6 **cult fanatics**
13–14	10d6 **duergar**
15–22	10d10 + 50 **goblins** and 3d4 **goblin bosses**
23–25	10d10 + 50 **grimlocks**
26–35	10d10 **hobgoblins** and 2d4 **hobgoblin captains**
36–43	10d10 + 50 **kobolds**, 2d4 **kobold inventors**,** and 2d6 **kobold scale sorcerers****
44–48	10d10 + 50 **lizardfolk**
49–56	10d10 **orcs** and 1d6 **orc war chiefs**
57–59	6d6 **quaggoths**
60–65	10d10 + 50 **troglodytes**
66–00	Roll twice, ignoring results above 65

* For death tyrant lairs, use this table, but replace approximately half of its humanoid minions with zombies.

** See chapter 3 of this book for statistics.

Beholder Greater Minions

d100	Greater Minions*
01–03	2d4 **barlguras**
04–10	1d12 **ettins**
11–20	1d2 **fire giants**, 1d3 **frost giants**, 2d4 **hill giants**, or 1d6 **stone giants** (as appropriate to the terrain)
21–25	3d6 **hook horrors**
26–32	3d6 **manticores**
33–40	3d6 **minotaurs**
41–55	6d6 **ogres**
56–70	2d4 **trolls**
71–75	3d6 **wights**
76–00	Roll twice, ignoring results above 75

* For death tyrant lairs, use this table, but replace approximately half of its living minions with ogre zombies.

Beholder Pets

d100	Pets
01–10	1d3 **basilisks**
11–13	1d3 **beholder zombies**
14–22	1d4 **chimeras**
23–26	1d4 **flesh golems**
27–29	3d6 **gazers***
30–37	3d6 **hell hounds**
38–41	2d6 **nothics**
42–53	2d4 **otyughs**
54–66	2d4 **ropers**
67–75	1d6 **wyverns**
76–00	Roll twice, ignoring results above 75

* See chapter 3 of this book for statistics.

The Xanathar Guild

The Xanathar Guild is a thieves' and slavers' guild operating underneath the city of Waterdeep in the Forgotten Realms setting. The guildmaster is a beholder—the latest in a series of such creatures. Like its predecessors, the beholder uses "the Xanathar" as a title rather than its personal name (which is Zushaxx). The guild has been in operation for nearly two hundred years, with a different beholder taking over every few decades.

Paranoid Megalomania

The Xanathar, like its forerunners, is an eye tyrant—a type of beholder that chooses to live among other creatures in a position of superiority over them. Its paranoia is kept under control most of the time, and it turns its strange mind to the pursuit of organized crime in Undermountain and Waterdeep. The Xanathar believes its intelligence and magic make it uniquely suited for this—even more so than its slain predecessor—and it uses its abilities to ruthlessly enforce its will on as much political and criminal territory as possible.

The Xanathar's bond is its lair, an elaborate cavern complex created by its predecessors, carved out between the twisting sewers of Waterdeep. It almost never leaves its home, for at the center of this world it is the master of all it sees and safe from outside threats. The expansive lair is well stocked with the exotic pleasures it craves, such as scented oils for bathing, fragrant incense, and fine foods prepared by skilled chefs. It surrounds itself with evidence of its wealth and success, eating off gold plates, drinking from diamond-encrusted chalices, decorating its sleeping area with marvelous tapestries, and adorning itself and its sanctum with powerful magic items.

Its fear of conspiracies is merely dormant, though, not absent. From time to time it is gripped by overwhelming concerns about assassination plots, revenge-seekers, and other schemes against it. When these thoughts bubble to the surface, the Xanathar might crack down on its lieutenants, interpreting their mistakes as disobedience, their failures as deliberate attempts to undermine its power, and their successes as challenges to its superiority. The beholder's ire might manifest as abruptly as a disintegration ray or as slowly as an angry glare and increasing scrutiny over the next few weeks.

The Xanathar is ambitious and wants to expand its power by making alliances, but it is constantly wary of betrayal. The only allies it considers relatively safe are individuals that it (or its predecessor) has worked with for years, and most of these are creatures it has no reason to fear because they aren't a physical threat to it or the guild. It is hesitant to form alliances with other powerful groups, and is likely to break off ties with a new ally if it senses even a hint of betrayal or difficulty. If an organization is useful but significantly weaker than the guild, the Xanathar is likely to absorb its members and resources into its guild (either immediately or gradually) so it can keep an eye on threats from within that group.

Like all beholders, the Xanathar craves information. It is aware of the great library at Candlekeep and the lore stored there, and one of its main objectives is to get an agent into the place that can start sending copies of that information back to the Xanathar for review. The Xanathar's ultimate goal is to control the entire region under Waterdeep (both Undermountain and Skullport), giving it as much political clout as all the Lords of Waterdeep combined.

BEHOLDERS RULE TERRITORIES AND TRY TO MANIPULATE THE WIDER WORLD FROM THEM. FOR ADVENTURERS, THE TRICK IS LEARNING WHERE A GIVEN BEHOLDER BELIEVES ITS TERRITORY'S BOUNDARIES ARE.

—Elminster

It's easy. You just have to think like a beholder. According to Elminster, they all think of themselves as the center of the world. Well, I know I am.

—Volo

Division of Labor

Thanks to its superior intelligence and its unique way of thinking, the Xanathar is able to efficiently supervise and direct the efforts of many creatures at the same time. It holds sway over a dozen specialized lieutenants. Each lieutenant is responsible for operating one of the aspects of guild business, including assassination, blackmail, extortion, mercenaries, slavery, smuggling, spying, and thievery (of these operations, slavery and thievery are the largest). When one needs to be replaced, the best candidates are those who appreciate the benefits of strict organization (and thus are lawful evil or at worst neutral evil) and who have a high tolerance for their boss's sometimes erratic behavior.

Each lieutenant is allowed to manage its part of the guild operation as desired. Some use a direct, hands-on approach, and some establish a chain of command that establishes a clear hierarchy from the top to the lowest underling. As long as a lieutenant's operation runs smoothly, the Xanathar doesn't object to methods or micromanage day-to-day activity.

When a human megalomaniac rises to power in an evil organization, that individual is always at risk of being killed or replaced by a power-hungry rival. When such a group is led by a beholder rather than a human, the tyrant has incredible staying power against challengers. Not only are its opponents unsure of the best way to kill it, but it can quickly retaliate with lethal force against multiple enemies at the same time, and it literally sleeps with its eyes open. The only real threat to the Xanathar's rule is another beholder, which speaks to the reason why the Xanathar Guild has been led by a succession of beholders instead of by various humanoid or inhuman creatures. Lieutenants who have their own ambitions, who might come to oppose the tyrant or fear for their safety, are much more likely to flee (or "retire") than to confront the beholder. The petrified heads of several traitorous lieutenants decorate the Xanathar's lair as testimony to how it deals with challengers.

In addition to its lieutenants, the Xanathar has many minions with specific jobs. These underlings don't have as much clout as the lieutenants do, but they do hold key roles in its guild and have some degree of influence in the organization. Among these are the beholder's accountant, chamberlain, chief messenger, doctor, fish-keeper, fortune-teller, lawyer, master entertainer, monster trainer, trap-setter, and warden for its private prison. The individuals in these roles generally serve the Xanathar for months or years, because replacements that have the same specialized skills can be hard to come by.

What Others Know

The organization's grunt-level employees—thieves, slavers, and ordinary thugs—work for the Xanathar Guild because it pays well. They don't necessarily know their leader is a beholder; they just know the boss is powerful, dangerous, and doesn't tolerate mistakes. Although previous Xanathars carefully guarded the facts of their true nature and allowed only a handful of their lieutenants to know the truth, the current Xanathar treats the matter more like an open secret. All of its lieutenants, as well as many mid-level members of the guild that the Xanathar trusts, know that the guild is run by a beholder.

Most of the guild's low-ranking members have an idea that the boss isn't human, especially given how long the Xanathar has been in power (they aren't aware that several beholders have held the job). Most believe their leader is a member of a long-lived race, perhaps a dwarf or an elf. Some think the truth is more monstrous, and that the Xanathar is a drow or perhaps a dragon in humanoid form.

The people of Waterdeep are generally aware that there are one or more guilds controlling criminal activity in the city. Rumors occasionally surface about a monstrous crime lord, such as a demon or a dragon, that guides its organization from the shadows. Most common folk dismiss these rumors and the fools who circulate them, asserting that the Lords of Waterdeep would never allow such creatures to roam the city.

Giants: World Shakers

The saga of giantkind began in the dawn of the world. Elves had yet to set dainty foot out of the fey realm when the thunder of the giants' steps shook the world to its bones, and even the dragons were yet unaware of the power and glory they would attain. The record of that early age had already vanished into the mists of legend by the time humankind came onto the scene. Now, not even the giants know the full truth of their beginnings.

All that the giants and their kin know for certain is that they are sibling races. Humanoids such as elves, humans, and dwarves are more similar in size and shape than the disparate giant types are to one another, but those races have no shared heritage. In contrast, every true giant, regardless of type, can trace its ancestry directly to Annam the All-Father. Most giants believe that Annam took a number of consorts in addition to his mate Othea, accounting for the variety in appearance and abilities among the types of giantkind.

Giants and giant kin rank among the world's most fearsome creatures, literally towering over the other, younger beings that crowd the world. Yet nowadays most giants live in isolation or in obscure locations, exhibiting none of the collective grandeur and power of their forebears.

First Impressions

Encountering a giant can be an awe-inspiring and disorienting experience. First comes a rhythmic booming, felt more than heard, that resolves slowly into the sound of footsteps: a giant is near! Loose stones vibrate and tumble down the hillside. Trees sway, then bend aside as the colossus emerges. How can anything be that big? Is it a trick of perspective?

When giants first appear before a band of adventurers, they demonstrate the qualities that make them spectacular to behold:

Giants Are Huge. Most giants can easily peer in a second-floor window. The larger ones would have to stoop to get down to that level! A giant's metal hammer could serve as an anvil for a human smith, and a giant's shield is bigger and heavier than a feasting table.

Giants Are Heavy. If a giant sits on a wagon, its wheels and axles are liable to snap like twigs. A giant can crush a house or capsize a ship simply by carelessly shifting its weight. An ox that strays too close to a sleeping giant could wind up pinned or crushed if the giant rolls over suddenly.

Giants Are Loud. The footsteps of giants in the distance are often initially mistaken for thunder, even on a clear day. The sounds of a giant beating a weapon against its shield and bellowing a challenge to foes are strident enough to knock dishes from shelves and rattle doors in their frames.

Giants Are Strong. A charging warhorse at full gallop, capable of bowling over a line of human warriors, merely crumples against the bulk of a giant. A giant could kick a cart with enough force to send it smashing through a house, and a giant's club—the size of, if not actually, an entire tree—could level the same house with a single blow.

Children of the All-Father

In an age before human and elf, when all dragons were young, Annam the All-Father put the first giants upon the world. These giants were reflections of his divine offspring and also children of the world, birthed from the marrow of mountains, the hot blood of volcanoes, and the breath of hurricanes.

Annam conceived the giants to be masters of the world. He gave them great height so they would look down on all they ruled. He created a hierarchy for his children—the ordning—so that all would know their status with respect to one another, and would know who among them stood nearest the knee of the All-Father.

United in purpose, Annam's children built Ostoria, the fabled empire of the giants, where they lived according to the ordning. Storm giants ruled all from both below and above. They held sway over the oceans from under-sea fortresses and lorded over the land from castles in the sky. Cloud giants built immense floating cities and served the storm giants as their strong right hands. Stone giants and fire giants settled on the mountaintops and in the sprawling caverns beneath them, where they carved and forged the greatest works of giant art and craft. Frost giants defended Ostoria with the might of their arms, not just on the chilly peaks and glaciers but on every frontier. Hill giants sprawled over all other lands, subjugating lesser creatures through brute force.

BEGINNING OF THE END

All told, the empire of Ostoria dominated the world for four millennia before its decline began in a genocidal struggle against the dragons that came to be known as the Thousand-Year War.

Dragons had lived in and around Ostoria in relative peace since the empire's foundation. Conflicts between dragons and giants in those days were personal, not tribal or regional, and usually involved bragging rights or hunting territory. Differences were settled by indi-vidual contests of might, wits, or skill. That situation persisted for generations, until the red dragon Garyx inflamed the greed and envy in its followers by rail-ing against the giants' prosperity, and they rose up in response.

At least, that's what most giants believed to have happened. No one really knows any longer what set off the war. But once battle began, the long-standing peace between giants and dragons crumbled everywhere. Foes tore at each others' throats in all parts of Ostoria. There were no front lines or safe havens, only endless ambushes, sieges, and atrocities committed against gi-ants and dragons alike. Eventually, none were left alive on either side who had seen the war's beginning. Age and brutality had claimed them all, and the few giants and dragons then alive had spent their entire existence at war. The Thousand-Year War didn't truly end so much as it wasted away through attrition and exhaustion.

The realm that could still be called Ostoria survived only far in the north. A few outposts and fragment king-doms, such as the fire giants' Helligheim and the stone giants' Nedeheim, clung to life in deep caverns and hid-den valleys. In the millennia that followed, even these places fell, and what remained of Ostorian territory became barren, shrouded in ice as thick as mountains. Since that time, many lesser races have attained great-ness and themselves fallen into obscurity. Few hints of the giants' once-great empire have survived the relent-less accumulation of years.

OSTORIA AND OTHER WORLDS

The tale of Ostoria is drawn from the Forgotten Realms. Think of it as a good example of how giants developed on many worlds, as it captures their rise and fall from prom-inence in a manner that is iconic to many D&D settings. In your own world, you can replace Ostoria with another giant empire or adapt it to create your own origin story.

VONINHEIM, THE LOST CAPITAL

Voninheim ("Titan Home" in the Giant language) stood as the capital of Ostoria for millennia. It was an awe-inspiring structure of iron and stone, raised by magic as much as by mortal hands. Some attributed its construction directly to one or more of Annam's sons, arguing that even giants couldn't have erected such a monumental edifice. The pal-ace stood firm and unshaken as glaciers that could flatten mountains assailed it and flowed around it, until only its iron spires jutted above the ice like great, gray fangs. Even-tually the relentless ice buried it utterly, and Voninheim was abandoned. Many giants seek to rediscover its loca-tion: some hope to recapture the lost glory of Ostoria, but others want only to claim the mighty weapons of legend said to be entombed in its frozen halls.

But the giants remember. Their empire and their unified purpose are long gone, but a yearning for a re-turn to the greatness that was once theirs burns in all their memories.

ANNAM'S OFFSPRING: THE GIANT PANTHEON

When Ostoria fell, Annam disowned his children, swearing never to regard the giants again until they returned Ostoria to its past prominence and reclaimed their rightful positions as rulers of the world. Giants, therefore, don't pray to Annam, who refuses to hear them. Instead, they revere his divine children, as well as a host of other hero-deities and godly villains that are minor members of the pantheon.

Chief among the giant gods are the six sons of Annam. The brothers are Stronmaus (champion and favorite of storm giants), Memnor (cloud giants), Surtur (fire gi-ants), Thrym (frost giants), Skoraeus Stonebones (stone giants), and Grolantor (hill giants).

Although each of Annam's sons is typically worshiped by giants of a particular type, they, like Annam himself, aren't racially distinct. Stronmaus, for example, doesn't look like a storm giant, though he is often depicted as one in carvings and other art. Like Annam and each of his brothers, Stronmaus is a unique godly being with no mortal equivalent. His temperament and interests are similar to those of the storm giants, so most of his fol-lowers are of that type.

Similar statements can be made about the other five brothers. Most cloud giants revere Memnor, for exam-ple, but many reject him because of his deceitfulness and venerate Stronmaus instead. A storm giant living amid blizzards and icebergs in the far northern sea might pay homage to Thrym rather than to Stronmaus. Giants that have given up hope of rising in the ordning sometimes worship Vaprak the Destroyer, who is recog-nized by giants as the father of trolls and ogres.

Giants don't worship male deities exclusively, either. Annam's mate Othea, Hiatea the huntress and home warden, Iallanis the goddess of love and peace, and Diancastra, an impetuous and arrogant trickster, have substantial followings. Like humans, some giants even fall prey to demon cults, in which they pay homage to a demon lord such as Baphomet or Kostchtchie. Worship-ing such entities, or any non-giant deity, is considered a great sin against the ordning. Being discovered means being cast out from family and clan.

THE GIANT TONGUE

The language that giants share is one of the few remnants from their once-grand empire. Over time it has fragmented into many dialects, and each type has its own distinctive accent, but giants of different types can generally understand one another.

Any non-giant who learns the Giant language can converse with all types of giants, but giants sometimes have a hard time hearing the tiny voices of human-sized creatures, and some vowel sounds emitted by giants are nearly impossible to reproduce for any creature that doesn't have lungs as large as beer barrels.

MAAT AND MAUG

Two words have special significance in the Giant language and the giants' worldview. Neither one of them translates directly into Common or any other language, because their definitions encompass several related concepts. **Maat** (pronounced *mott*) is the term giants use to describe ideas, behaviors, creatures, and objects that they consider good, holy, honorable, or desirable. **Maug** (pronounced *mog*) is the counterpart term, embodying what other languages call evil, unholy, dishonorable, or undesirable.

Individual giants aren't necessarily thought of as maat or maug by their kin. What matters isn't a giant's personal philosophy but its standing within the ordning, which is influenced by behavior and attitude but also by a host of other factors. Every individual commits both maat and maug acts, and rises or falls in the ordning as a consequence. A giant isn't judged by other giants on the basis of whether what it did was inherently good or evil, but on whether its actions enhanced or diminished the qualities giants admire—the "giantness," if you will—in themselves and their clans.

A storm giant, for example, might see the raiding practices of hill giants as distasteful but not maug, because brutal raiding is an inborn trait of the hill giants. If those same hill giants worshiped Yeenoghu, however, that act would represent a flagrant turning away from the traditions of the ordning. Hill giants who choose that path make themselves maug.

Non-giants are considered maug out of hand and must usually prove themselves maat to gain a giant's respect.

RUNES AND TALE CARVINGS

For much of their written communication, giants use a modified version of the runic letterforms claimed by the dwarves as their own. This alphabet is used widely today, including by many traditional enemies of the dwarves such as orcs, giants, and goblinoids. That giants were first in the world and thus the creators of the script is a fact that giants take for granted but which dwarves hotly dispute.

Many giants are illiterate or nearly so—particularly hill, frost, and fire giants, which place little value on learning. Instead of writing stories with words, they typically tell their tales with pictograms etched in wood, ice, stone, or even earth, in the case of hill giants. These "tale carvings" relate legends or the stories of important events or meetings in the manner of highly sophisticated cave paintings. Often they employ aspects of legends

about the giant pantheon. For example, Memnor's face or head floating above the shoulders of another giant indicates that the giant was a liar or a deceiver; a depiction of Iallanis being stabbed in the back represents the betrayal of love. Such symbols and visual allegories are well understood by giants, but they can be indecipherable to viewers who aren't steeped in the giants' mythology. Most non-giants find a tale carving as unintelligible as giants would find poetry written in Elvish.

A GLOSSARY OF GIANT WORDS

armor—*harbunad*	home—*heim*
arrow—*pil*	honor—*rang*
battle—*slag*	intruder—*ubuden*
black—*sort*	journey—*ferd*
bravery—*prakt*	human—*van*
cloud giant—*skyejotun*	king—*kong*
cow—*kue*	light—*stig*
chieftain—*forer*	meat—*kjott*
danger—*fare*	mother—*hild*
death—*dod*	red—*rod*
dwarf—*dverg*	shield—*skold*
enemy—*uven*	silver—*solv*
elf—*alv*	stone giant—*steinjotun*
evil/unholy/dishonorable—*maug*	storm giant—*uvarjotun*
fire giant—*ildjotun*	teeth—*tenner*
fortress—*festing*	temple—*bapart*
frost giant—*isejotun*	tribe—*stomm*
gold—*gil*	up—*opp*
good/holy/honorable—*maat*	warrior—*krigga*
greetings—*helsingen (hels)*	white—*kvit*
hill giant—*haugjotun*	wind—*vind*

GIANTS AND MAGIC

Giants have a paradoxical relationship with magic. The most outwardly magical are the cloud giants, followed closely by storm giants. Both types have an innate ability to use some forms of magic related to air, weather, and gravity. Very few giants, however, study magic in the way that humans, dwarves, and elves do. Arcane scholarship by itself isn't acknowledged by the ordning; it isn't maug, but it isn't maat, either. Mastering the secrets of magic, though, demands a degree of devotion that would take giants away from pursuits that are valued by the ordning. As a consequence, it's a path rarely taken.

The exception is rune magic. Giants are drawn to the solidity and permanence of magical runes. Stone giants are great practitioners of rune carving, both because of the artistry it demands and because their environment is perfect for its use. At least a few *skiltgravr* ("rune cutters") can be found among any type of giants, even the slow-witted hill giants who stomp enormous marks into hillsides or gouge them into their own flesh.

Crafting this form of magic is painstakingly slow. Imagine a wizard who crafts a scroll and who eschews the convenience of parchment and ink in favor of stone and chisel, glacier and axe, or iron and forge.

Carving a magical rune into an item imbues it with power. Like any other magic item, it can be used to activate one or more magical effects. A magical rune can also be inscribed upon a surface to create effects similar to those of a *glyph of warding* or *symbol* spell. The rune itself determines what sort of magic the item or surface holds. For example, a storm rune carved into a stone might allow the stone's possessor to control the weather. The same rune carved into door or chest might deal thunder damage to anyone who opens it.

A Giant's Bag

A giant on the move always has a sack slung over its shoulder. The primary purpose of a giant's bag is to carry food. With such an enormous belly to feed (particularly in the case of hill giants), it's unwise for a giant to travel without a supply of nourishment.

Giants also carry rocks in their bags: a few for battle, a few others for hunting, and one or two special ones for games. Beyond that, a bag might contain anything: tools, mementos, items for trade, or merely curios the giant wanted to bring along. Some possible contents are:

- A live pig
- Three bear skins
- Longsword wrapped in a blood-caked cloak (used as a knife)
- Keg of ale
- Caged halfling (for amusement)
- Chest full of broken window glass
- Human's backpack filled with coins
- Skull of an owlbear
- Large bundle of dry wood tied up with vines
- A once-fine tapestry that's now tattered from being used as a towel
- Four mostly intact wagon wheels
- A tombstone (for skipping across water)

Champions of Rock Throwing

Giants have a well-deserved reputation as living siege engines—all of them can hurl boulders with accuracy across great distances. Rock throwing—for battle, hunting, and sport—is a tradition that goes back to the ancient times of the giants. Other races developed the sling, the spear-thrower, or the bow to artificially improve the strength and accuracy of their ranged attacks, but giants never perceived a need for mechanical assistance. Even in places where giants have adapted bows or javelins for use in combat, they've never neglected the straightforward strategy of picking up a rock and letting it fly. Few activities, in fact, seem to give them as much satisfaction as the simple act of tossing boulders.

Most of the games that giants play involve throwing rocks in ways that hone their skills for hunting and war. One of the most popular contests, especially among fire giants, involves nothing more than taking turns trying to knock each other down with boulders. Frost giants build targets out of snow and ice and compete to see who can knock down the most with a single toss. A popular one-on-one game begins with the challenger throwing a stone as far as it can. The giant who was challenged then goes to where the stone landed and hurls it back at the challenger. A challenger who is stronger wins, because the return throw will fall short, but a giant who took on a better thrower will stumble away, nursing its injuries, as a lesson that arrogance has a price.

In battle against puny creatures, giants use boulders that fit in one hand. When giants fight enormous foes (such as dragons) or enormous targets (such as castles), they prefer to hurl stones so large that even a giant must use both arms to lift and throw one. Giants throw just as accurately with both arms as with one, a feat most humans would find impossible. These attacks are effective only at shorter ranges, however, for obvious reasons.

When they hunt by rock throwing, giants use smaller stones, about the size of a human head, that can kill an elk or a bear without smashing it into pulp.

How to Lay a Giant Low

A force allied with giants—or worse, a force made up of giants—is one of the most fearsome opponents on the battlefield. The giants can rain boulders onto an enemy from a distance where only skilled archers, heavy siege weapons, or spellcasters can strike back at them.

At first blush, it might seem that a potent wizard would make the best giant-killer, but few spellcasters can stand up to a giant in direct confrontation. One might do harm to a giant, but odds are it will survive the one or two spells that can be thrown at it before a well-placed boulder or the swing of an enormous club quashes the threat.

Among those with experience fighting giants, dwarves have developed the most effective tactics. To defeat a giant, dwarves rely on prolonged, accurate, massed archery (favoring heavy crossbows for such work), fast-moving cavalry that can force the giant into a disadvantageous position, or fanatical troops armed with pole arms, ropes, and grappling hooks. If a giant can be tripped or pulled down—preferably onto its belly so it's less able to defend itself—then it can be entangled in nets and cables and disabled by concentrated attacks on its head and neck.

On the other side of the field, giants understand that smaller foes will try to target their legs and lower bodies. Thus, when they head into a fight against human-sized opponents, they don thick boots, greaves, armored codpieces, and wide, heavy hide or metal belts to protect their bellies. Even savage hill giants peel thick bark from trees and strap it around their legs and dangle logs or stones from their belts to make the going more perilous for an enemy that tries to get underfoot.

Living the Giant Life

Giants are exceptionally long-lived compared to humans, but none are immortal. A peaceful death from old age is a common occurrence among cloud giants and storm giants and isn't unusual among stone giants and fire giants. It's the exception among hill giants and frost giants, most of which die violently in battle against humans, dragons, other monsters, or their own kind.

Giants live at a slower pace than humans do. In the space of four heartbeats for a man, a stone giant's great heart beats just once. Giant mothers stay with their child for longer than human mothers do, and giant children grow to adulthood more slowly. Giants' families are small, because a couple seldom has more than a few children, and many have none at all.

The life spans of the various types of giants are generally in keeping with their place in the ordning; the lowliest giants have the shortest life spans, and the noblest giants are the longest-lived. Stone giants are the exception. Because of their long life spans, despite their low position in the ordning, other giants consider stone giants to be the wisest of all giant types, just as Skoraeus Stonebones is often seen as the wisest of all the giant gods.

Giant Life Spans

Giant Type	Life Span
Hill	200 years
Frost	250 years
Fire	350 years
Cloud	400 years
Storm	600 years
Stone	800 years

ROLEPLAYING A GIANT

Giving a giant a personality trait, an ideal, a bond, and a flaw helps to create a more vibrant NPC. You can also give a character background to a giant. The noble background, for example, could apply to a cloud giant.

GIANT PERSONALITY TRAITS

d8	Personality Trait
1	The brutality of my peers is a relic of a bygone era that should be stamped out. I seek a more enlightened path.
2	As the most powerful beings in creation, we have a duty to use our strength for the benefit of all.
3	I take what I want. I don't care who gets hurt.
4	A giant lives for a few centuries, but giantkind is eternal. Everything I do is to glorify my ancestors and make my descendants proud.
5	Dragons are my mortal enemies. Everything I do is to ensure their destruction.
6	I measure a creature's worth by its size. The small folk are beneath my concern.
7	The small folk are vermin. I enjoy torturing and killing them.
8	Good or bad, Annam's sons represent the ideals that we, as giants, must strive to uphold.

GIANT IDEALS

d6	Ideal
1	**The Ordning.** Annam created the ordning for the good of all giants, and it's our duty to uphold his vision. (Lawful)
2	**Skill.** What sets my clan apart is its mastery of our traditional crafts. (Good)
3	**Strength.** No other race can match the strength of giants, and none should dare to try. (Evil)
4	**Lordship.** Giants are the rightful rulers of the world. All will be well when our empire is restored. (Neutral)
5	**Tribute.** The lesser races owe giants not just respect but payment of tribute, and what they don't pay willingly, we will take by force. (Chaotic)
6	**Religion.** Of Annam's many sons, none is greater than my patron deity. (Any)

GIANT BONDS

d6	Bond
1	My clan is the most important influence on my life; our collective place in the ordning depends on our devotion to one another.
2	My clan mates who serve in our deity's temples are the closest companions I'll ever know.
3	My place in the ordning is ordained by our patron deity, and it would be blasphemous to aspire to anything higher or lower.
4	Though I can never rise above my clan's position in the ordning, I can be a leader among my clan.
5	My own kind have turned their backs on me, so I make my way among the lesser creatures of the world.
6	Humans have proven their worth in the world and earned a measure of respect from giantkind.

GIANT FLAWS

d6	Flaw
1	The ordning is too restrictive for the likes of me.
2	The lesser creatures of the world have no souls; they exist only to be fodder for the ambitions and appetites of giants.
3	Unity among giants is a myth; anyone not of my clan is a fair target for my weapons.
4	I care nothing for what others expect, to the point where I cannot help but contradict what others ask of me.
5	I am terrified of arcane magic and can be cowed by overt displays of it.
6	Ancient dragons fill me with dread. My knees grow weak in their presence.

CLOUD GIANTS

Cloud giants are aptly named, or at least were at one time. Few of them live literally on clouds anymore, but most do reside atop high mountains, inside or even above a near-perpetual cloud layer. A select few—those at the apex of the clan's ordning—claim the last of the ancient cloud castles that still drift across the sky.

No one can build those majestic structures any longer. The methods of their construction were lost (along with much other knowledge) when Ostoria fell. Some cloud giants believe the information might yet be buried in some long-forgotten, ruined library. Rumors of its existence crop up from time to time, stirring debate and dreams of resurgent glory among the cloud giants, but definite information has proven impossible to obtain. Many cloud giants think that someday, a hero will unearth this ancient secret. Until then, they must be satisfied with watching clouds drift past their mountaintop homes instead of living atop those clouds as in days of yore.

FAMILY FIRST

Most types of giants live communally in large groups of clan mates, but the central unit of cloud giant life is the family—a mated pair, their offspring (if any), and

perhaps a couple of close relatives. Cloud giants prefer not to congregate in great numbers in any one place, to avoid drawing too much attention. It's not that they fear attack from humanoids or monsters, because few creatures other than dragons can challenge them. But if more than a few lived in the same place, the size of their combined treasure hoard would attract an incessant stream of adventurers and other would-be thieves—a nuisance on the order of rats in the larder.

Despite the distances that separate the homes of families, cloud giants aren't isolated. Every family or individual knows where its nearest neighbors are, even if the location is hundreds of miles away, and those neighbors know where their nearest neighbors are, and so on across the world. In a crisis, word is spread from family to family, so that a mighty squad of cloud giants could be assembled, in time, if need arises.

Most cloud giant homes include one or more pets. Wyverns, griffons, giant eagles and owls, and other beasts of the sky are popular choices. Pets aren't limited to flying creatures, though. Any sort of creature might be found in a cloud giant menagerie, with rare specimens treated more as status symbol than as companions.

BENEVOLENT OVERLORDS

Cloud giants are famous (or infamous) for demanding tribute from the humanoids that live beneath them. Such tribute is only proper from their perspective, for two reasons. First, their presence in an area benefits everyone by driving away many evils, especially flying predators such as manticores and wyverns. Second, the giants believe they deserve to be rewarded for their

forbearance; no one could stop them from simply taking what they want, but instead of doing that they allow their tribute to be freely given. (The logic of that position is clearer to the giants than it is to those on the other end of the arrangement.)

Much of the tribute that cloud giants accept is in the form of livestock and crops, but this isn't their only source of food. Cloud giants are avid gardeners. Almost all cloud giant strongholds devote space to a garden that produces enormous yields: beans as big as turnips, turnips as big as pumpkins, and pumpkins as big as carriages.

The garden of a cloud giant family is seldom affected by drought, frost, or locusts. When such a calamity strikes nearby farms, families have been known to share their bounty to ease the humanoids' food shortage. Such events are at the root of tales about magic beans and others about a human family living in a cottage carved from a single, enormous gourd. Beyond that, the cloud giants' generosity in times of want helps to cement their reputation as friends of humankind—a reputation that serves them well, even though it's not entirely deserved.

ORDNING OF EXTRAVAGANCE

A cloud giant's position within the ordning doesn't depend on talent or skill. It depends on wealth. The more treasure a cloud giant possesses, the higher its standing. It's as simple as that. Almost.

Ownership is one thing, but wealth that's kept locked away means little. To fully contribute to one's status, wealth must be displayed, and the more ostentatious the display, the better. In a cloud giant family's home, extravagance is omnipresent. One might boast windows framed in gold leaf, rare perfume stored in vials of crystal with silver lids, or a scene in the sky depicted in a tapestry composed entirely of pearls.

Another way for a family to demonstrate its wealth is by bestowing lavish gifts on other families. (A gift from one family member to another doesn't prove anything about the family's largesse.) No cloud giant truly believes that it's better to give than to receive; a family does so only with an eye toward how the giving can elevate its status. Memnor and his trickery play a role in this "game." The very best gift (from the giver's perspective) is one that everyone believes to be far more valuable than it truly is. Only the giver and the receiver will ever know a gift's true value, and neither of them would ever reveal that a gift is worth less than it appears to be, because to do so would reduce the status of both.

Wealth also changes hands between cloud giants when they indulge their obsession for gambling and wagering. Cloud giants don't engage in betting for enjoyment; it is less a form of entertainment than a type of bloodless feud. No cloud giant is a good loser, and one would be aghast to hear someone else say, "I lost 40 pounds of gold, but I had a good time." Betting wars between families can go on for generations, with fortunes and estates (and the position in the ordning that goes with them) passing back and forth repeatedly. What a parent loses, a child hopes someday to win back, plus more; what the child wins back, a grandchild probably will eventually lose again. The tales that cloud giants tell of their ancestors are seldom about wars or magic or battles against dragons—they're about brilliant wagers won through boldness or deceit, and rival families brought to disgrace and ruin by the same.

Masks of Nobility

Ancient depictions of Memnor often showed him wearing a two-faced mask. Because of this, cloud giant nobles seldom show their faces, but instead wear exquisite masks made of precious materials adorned with gemstones. Each noble has a collection of these masks that it wears to conceal its face but still reflect its current mood; an individual might change masks many times during the day as its emotions shift.

A mask is prized both for its material value and for its accuracy in expressing the mood it represents. Only the

TWO FACES OF MEMNOR

The chief deity of cloud giants is Memnor, the cleverest of Annam's offspring. But Memnor isn't only clever, he's sly and deceitful. Tales of his exploits emphasize his charisma, his smooth manner, and his ability to manipulate and mislead his siblings and other legendary figures into doing exactly what he wants, usually to their great detriment.

Thus, cloud giants have two distinct aspects of Memnor to admire and emulate. Those of a benign disposition revere him for his charm, intelligence, and persuasiveness, while those of a more malign bent take Memnor's self-interest to heart and imitate his trickery. Cloud giants that take a particular interest in trickery, known as "smiling ones," wear two-faced masks as they practice their deceptions and prey on those who are susceptible to their charms. Statistics for cloud giant smiling ones appear in chapter 3 of this book.

> Every thief has a story about the treasure that was too rich to haul away. You think you've seen magnificence? The halls of the pashas in Calimshan, maybe, or some patriar's estate in Baldur's Gate? Let me tell you, you've seen nothing. Those places are hovels compared to the palaces of the skyejotuns.
>
> —Volo

richest of cloud giants can afford the dozens of masks necessary to show all the subtle differences in emotion possible among their kind. Artisans who can sculpt and craft masks that meet the cloud giants' exacting standards in such matters are richly rewarded for their skill.

FIRE GIANTS

The fire giants were the officers, engineers, and crafters of ancient Ostoria. Their position and unparalleled skill, along with their domineering outlook, make them haughty and arrogant.

Ordning of Craftwork

Fire giants are the greatest smiths, architects, and technicians among giantkind. The iron-lined halls of a fire giant stronghold, deep inside a mountain or a volcano, support the unimaginable weight of the stone above them and enable the giants to harness the heat of rivers of magma to power their forges.

A fire giant's prowess in the occupations of crafting determines its place in the ordning. Although fire giants put stock in combat skill, they recognize that success in battle or on the hunt derives mainly from the quality of one's weapons and armor, and those that can fashion the finest gear enjoy the highest status in the clan. Master artisans, architects, and engineers select the best disciples to pass their knowledge on to, along with their standing. Often pupils are children or siblings of their teachers, but that's not always so. Leaders are chosen by general recognition from among the best crafters in the clan.

One group of fire giants, known as the dreadnoughts, owe their place in the ordning not to their crafting ability but to their extraordinary physical prowess. They take on a lot of the work of guarding the forges and keeping them stoked—effort without which the crafters couldn't succeed. (See chapter 3 of this book for more information on fire giant dreadnoughts.)

Fire giants don't spend a lot of time crafting works of art, although they would maintain that all of their feats of metalworking and engineering are themselves forms of artistic expression. Beyond such accomplishments, true artwork is scarce among fire giants, and most of what exists is jewelry, made from gems and ore that they mine and then refine. A unique form of art that some fire giants produce involves manipulating magma as it cools, forming it into fantastical, one-of-a-kind shapes. The most striking of these works are collected and displayed inside the stronghold, not unlike how other cultures create topiary gardens.

MIGHTY FIGHTERS, POOR PLANNERS

When fire giants aren't honing their crafting skills,
they're drilling with weapons or exercising to keep
themselves fit for battle. The typical fire giant has a mastery of combat tactics that few other warriors can match,
but the giants' understanding of strategy is rudimentary.

This deficiency isn't born from a lack of ability, but
has its roots in tradition. In ages past, when the giants
worked together to dominate the world, strategy was
determined by the cloud giants and the storm giants.
Ever since the clans went their separate ways after Ostoria's wars against the dragons, the fire giants have not
mounted a grand, strategic effort to extend their sway,
but they have fought countless skirmishes and other tactical engagements, mainly to solidify their hold on territory they have already claimed. If an ambitious fire giant
ever became a master of strategic planning (or captured
and enslaved a cooperative general), little could stop a
tribe of fire giants that enjoyed this additional advantage
over their neighbors.

Fire giants raise and train hell hounds as war dogs,
and they sometimes persuade human wizards (free or
enslaved) to harness fire elementals as guardians for
their strongholds. Some allow trolls to roam free in
rarely used parts of their fortresses, serving as perimeter guards of a sort. Trolls require little maintenance,
able to survive on the fire giants' scraps and on dead or
diseased slaves; they're tough enough to deter most intruders; and their susceptibility to fire makes them little
threat to a fire giant.

SLAVES: LABOR-SAVING DEVICES

It takes a lot of work to build and maintain a fire giant
stronghold. Most of that effort comes not from the giants
themselves, but from the slaves that they keep. Fire
giants enslave other creatures to accomplish unskilled
labor, so the giants can concentrate on the more vital
aspects of foundry operation and crafting that only they
are capable of. They aren't overly cruel masters, but neither are they particularly kind—they are uncaring about
their slaves, because slaves aren't giants, and there are
always more to be had if the supply runs low.

Most creatures that fire giants capture are put to work
in the giants' mines or on surface farms the giants claim
as part of their domain. Even master crafters of other
races are consigned to unskilled labor, because so few
of them have talents the fire giants consider "skilled."
Only creatures that have skills the fire giants need but
don't practice (because they aren't valued in the ordning), such as accounting, brewing, and medicine, are
allowed to continue plying their trades.

Skilled slaves receive better treatment, at least in
the sense that an owner uses less force with a delicate
tool, but as a rule fire giants view humans in much the
same way that humans view horses: they have utility if
properly directed, and some might be prized for rare
qualities, but even the smartest, best trained horse isn't
a person. That said, it's not unheard of for a fire giant to
"consult with" a slave physician when it falls ill, or with
a slave engineer right before beginning a difficult stage
of tunnel excavation. (Such a consultation would only be
to ensure that the right tools and materials are on hand
for the excavation, not to solicit a second opinion on the
giant's personal assessment of the structure's integrity.)

Giants that stand low in the ordning are assigned to
manage slaves and mining operations. Excavating mine
shafts and digging out ore is important work, but smelting and metalwork are valued more highly than effort
spent keeping a tunnel from collapsing on slaves.

PAYING THE PRICE

Fire giants on many occasions have ransomed captives
back to their families or communities, once the giants
determined that a slave had no particular talent they
needed and others were willing to pay for its return. Af-
fluent prisoners such as merchants and aristocrats are
the most likely to win this sort of reprieve, for obvious
reasons. The ransom demanded rarely involves baubles
such as gold or gems: fire giants prefer payment in mi-
thral, adamantine, or different slaves (ones with more
useful talents or stronger backs).

FROST GIANTS

Frost giants dwell in the remote, frozen places of the
world. Anything warmer than the flesh of a recently
killed elk is as flame to them. As a sailor fears the howl
of the wind heralding a storm, the denizens of ice-
capped mountains and northern steppes shudder at
the war horns that presage the arrival of Thrym's blue-
skinned, icy children.

SURTUR'S CLEANSING FIRE

Surtur, the chief deity of fire giants, is believed to have
been born alongside Thrym. Each twin then tried to be the
first to cry out, the first to walk, and the first to talk, and
they have competed with one another ever since. Often
in legends these contests are bloody battles, but some
tales have the brothers acting side by side on grand adventures. Surtur is seen as the more clever of the two, and
fire giants emulate his unsurpassed skill at creating and
building things.

In the fire giants' world, fire is strength. It burns away
impurities and leaves behind only what is strong enough
to withstand the heat, such as the best steel from the
forge. When fire is controlled, it is the giants' most powerful tool; when it rages unchecked, it can bring down forests
and lay waste to cities.

Because of the destructive power of fire, the worship of
Surtur is tinged with an apocalyptic air. Some observers
suspect that priests of Surtur maintain clandestine work-
shops and armories where they manufacture and stockpile
battle gear in preparation for a final, all-encompassing battle that will decide the fate of the world. If the suspicions
are true, these sites are expertly hidden and kept secret
even from most fire giants.

Ordning of Might

Position within the frost giant ordning is determined by sheer, brute strength. Frost giants know that those that use cunning, agility, and magic are dangerous foes and can sometimes overcome pure strength, but never in a straightforward, fair manner; enemies that act that way are maug, and strength alone is maat.

Doubt or disagreement between frost giants over which is strongest is settled by a trial of strength. Such a contest typically involves wrestling but can also be a rock-throwing competition, a hunt, or one-on-one combat.

To show proof of their superiority, frost giants keep and display trophies of their victims. Mammoth tusks, griffon beaks, and manticore tails adorn the walls of frost giant lairs. Formidable humanoid enemies are memorialized in trophies, too, but only rarely do giants put the heads or bodies on display. A human hero's greatsword or a wizard's staff is a more appropriate trophy in such cases.

A frost giant's armor and weapons are as much a record of its battle honors as its trophy collection is, for those who know how to read the signs. Notches carved into the haft of a weapon show the number and type of foes it has brought down. Horns, feathers, claws, and tusks affixed to helmets and armor serve as decorations commemorating the giant's greatest feats of strength.

The ordning is determined by strength and strength alone, and there is no difference in physical prowess between the genders of frost giants. (Most child-rearing duties are handled by the elderly of both sexes, not solely by females.) It is considered highly maug to attack or challenge a pregnant female, even to improve one's standing, just as it would be to attack a frost giant as it slept.

A frost giant that is innately weaker than its kin has a low rank in the ordning and practically no chance of rising any higher. At times, when a giant becomes intensely frustrated with that situation, it turns to clandestine worship of Vaprak, the deity of trolls and ogres. An individual touched by Vaprak's favor is transformed into an everlasting one—a giant with enough strength to rival the leaders of the clan, but destined to be cast out or destroyed if its secret allegiance becomes known.

Because strength is their only standard of measurement, frost giants are more likely than other giants to welcome a non-giant into their group. The might of a human who hunts polar bears bare-handed as frost giants do, or who wrestles a frost giant into submission, can't be denied. Such a human could never become the chieftain of a tribe but could earn a place of honor as one blessed by Thrym.

Ruthless Raiders

Frost giant society has no industry to speak of. It takes what it needs from others, and if it can't take something, it has no need for it. Frost giants do make leather, clothes, and bone tools and adornments from the animals they hunt, but those activities account for almost all of their craftwork.

When frost giants plan a raid on a nearby settlement or outpost, they time it to take place under the cover of a blizzard, believing the storm to be a sign from Thrym that the weak-boned humanoids are ready to be plundered, in the same way that a farmer might look at a rainstorm as a blessing from the harvest god.

Frost giants recognize two kinds of loot: *rod* and *kvit*. Rod ("red") plunder consists of living creatures, either livestock or slaves. Kvit refers to material goods, the most prized being objects of steel, alcohol, and large gems. Frost giants like to grab gems for adorning their clothing, but ordinary currency is usually left behind after a raid. Tiny, round coins simply have no worth to a frost giant.

Because frost giants can't stand the heat of a forge, they don't mine their own metal or craft their own weapons and armor. The fire-forged items of steel and iron that they wield and wear are prized as though they were made of gold. The giants are always on the lookout for such booty on their raids, but they don't often come across gear that is large enough for them to wear. Many of the giants in a tribe boast arms and armor handed down from their ancestors; others make do with items cobbled together from smaller parts. Shields sized for a human, for example, can be lashed together into a crude suit of scale armor; an anvil riveted onto a log serves as a warhammer.

MASTERS OF BEASTS

Frost giants dominate wild creatures both as evidence of their strength and to use them as hunting companions. They don't, however, have much grasp of animal husbandry, so their "pets" are bullied and beaten into submission more than they're trained. When a frost giant commands a beast to attack, it's less a command than an acknowledgment to the creature that the giant won't beat it for satisfying its hunger. A creature that proves willful or that resists "training" is fated to end up on the giant's dinner table.

The roster of creatures in a frost giant lair can include polar bears, winter wolves, and mammoths, but the giants' most prized living possessions are remorhazes. Adult remorhazes are untrainable by anything short of powerful magical compulsion, but one taken as an egg can be trained as it is raised. In fact, remorhaz hatchlings are surprisingly pliant to the frost giants' manner of teaching by bullying.

THRYM'S FRIGID MIGHT

Thrym has long rivaled his twin brother Surtur for Annam's affection and pride. Frost giants pride themselves on Thrym's victories over Surtur and other legendary threats when he proved to have more strength or a steadier heart. Yet, Annam was swayed more by Surtur's well-crafted gifts than by the trophy heads Thrym laid at his feet. For this reason, frost giants bear more ill will toward Annam than most other giants do.

Unlike his brothers, Thrym is seldom depicted alone. He is usually accompanied by up to ten shield-brothers and shield-sisters, heroic frost giants that won such great glory during the war between giants and dragons that Thrym granted them the honor of fighting forever at his side.

HILL GIANTS

Hill giants live to eat. Anyone who understands this one fact about them knows everything there is to know.

ORDNING OF GLUTTONY

Hill giants are the weakest of the true giants. They have the shortest stature, the smallest brains, and the least ambition. The only area in which they excel is girth.

Since eating is the only thing hill giants care about, a tribe is always led by its fattest, heaviest member—the most successful and thus the most admired one in the group. The qualities that other creatures expect or demand of their leaders—such as intellect, decision-making ability, and personal magnetism—have no importance to hill giants. They are neither recognized nor rewarded, except to the extent that a hill giant with slightly above average smarts might use trickery or intimidation to grab more food than its neighbors.

DENS OF SQUALOR AND STENCH

Hill giants stuff the most repulsive, rotting things into their mouths without hesitation, suggesting that either they have no sense of taste or their hunger is so all-consuming that flavor isn't a consideration. Whatever the reason, the upshot is that hill giant dens are filthy, reeking places. Decaying carcasses and cracked bones are strewn about. The ground is saturated with blood and with the giants' own filth.

Not every hill giant's digestive system is so indiscriminate; from time to time a giant does get sick, but most of them recover and don't learn anything from the experience. The rare exceptions are called mouths of Grolantor—giants that are confined and starved to the point of emaciation before being unleashed during a battle or a raid.

The stench that exudes from a hill giant den might attract monstrous scavengers such as oozes, ropers, carrion crawlers, or otyughs. Hill giants don't domesticate or tend these creatures but do tolerate their presence. A visit from a gelatinous cube or a carrion crawler probably is the only "housekeeping" a hill giant's den ever sees.

Ghouls are known to lurk around the edges of hill giant encampments, but they're less welcome than other kinds of scavengers. With their greater craftiness—especially if they're led by a ghast—ghouls can use simple trickery to steal the giants' meals. A hill giant wouldn't mind if a roper dragged away a few scraps, but it would be angry if a trio of ghouls stole an entire carcass.

STUFF-STUFF

Hill giants sometimes amuse themselves with inane games that typically involve food or eating. One such game is called stuff-stuff, in which hill giants see how many halflings, gnomes, or goblins they can fit into their mouths at once without swallowing.

STONE GIANTS

Stone giants—reclusive, reflective, and inscrutable—take pains to remain apart from the world of sunlight and sky. Only when they're surrounded by stone do they con-

GROLANTOR: ALWAYS HUNGRY, NEVER FULL

The deity most revered by hill giants is Grolantor, the least of Annam's six sons, the black sheep of the family who was scorned by his siblings and his parents. Most of Grolantor's problems, however, were of his own doing.

Proud of his great strength (his only redeeming quality), Grolantor refused to recognize the superiority of his older, smarter, stronger siblings, and insisted on being treated as their equal. He complained constantly of his endless hunger, but rather than hunt for himself, he snatched food from the plates of his siblings and his parents.

This behavior caused many fights between Grolantor and his siblings, most of which Grolantor lost. Tales about Grolantor invariably end with his gaining yet another scar on his back, received as he escaped the wrath of a family member who had been pushed too far by Grolantor's insulting boasts and selfishness.

sider themselves to be in reality. A world of all-encompassing stone is a realm of permanence and solidity, one where a lifetime of laborious carving can last through countless eons. The surface world, with its shifting light, endless sky, changing climate, and eroding wind, represents a dream state, an unreality where nothing lasts and therefore nothing has significance.

ORDNING OF ARTISTRY

Among stone giants, mastery of an art ranks as the greatest virtue, and among all the arts, stone carving is held in highest regard. Most stone giants spend their lives in unending pursuit of the perfect artistic creation. Young stone giants practice tirelessly, hoping to prove themselves worthy of assisting the tribe's best carvers. A stone giant master carver might devote years to finding the best stone before beginning a great work. The best carvers are honored as the leaders and shamans of the tribe, and their hands are seen as holy—literally becoming the hands of Skoraeus Stonebones as they work.

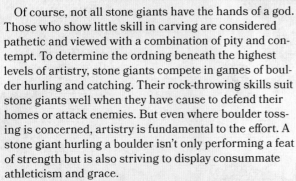
We all know of dwarves who fell so deep in love with their craft, or the seeking of treasure or ale, that they forgot how to live in any other way but in pursuit of it. That's what stone giants do.

— Elminster

Of course, not all stone giants have the hands of a god. Those who show little skill in carving are considered pathetic and viewed with a combination of pity and contempt. To determine the ordning beneath the highest levels of artistry, stone giants compete in games of boulder hurling and catching. Their rock-throwing skills suit stone giants well when they have cause to defend their homes or attack enemies. But even where boulder tossing is concerned, artistry is fundamental to the effort. A stone giant hurling a boulder isn't only performing a feat of strength but is also striving to display consummate athleticism and grace.

Those who can't infuse artistry into every aspect of their lives fall to the lowest rungs of the ordning and are often pushed literally to the perimeter of stone giant society, to serve as guards on the tribe's most distant borders or as hunters that wander beyond those borders. As such, the stone giants that are first encountered by outsiders are almost always the least successful members of stone giant society and the poorest examples of the ideals stone giants aspire to. They are the brutes and boors cast out by a society of artists and philosophers.

Skoraeus Stonebones, the Great Creator

Stone giants worship Skoraeus Stonebones as the Great Creator, second in skill to Annam, but master of the other deities in his father's absence. He appears in stone giant art in two ways: as a pair of hands, one holding a chisel and the other a hammer, and as the largest statue or relief carving of a stone giant in a tribe's caves. Typically, Skoraeus is depicted twice as tall as any other stone giant.

In the legends of the giants, Skoraeus often sits on the sidelines during the schemes and battles of his siblings. He acts as an observer, a confidant to the other gods, and a keeper of secrets that he must be forced or tricked into divulging.

In a classic tale, Memnor came to Skoraeus and whispered something in his ear. When Surtur demanded to know what Memnor had said, Skoraeus told his brother exactly what he had heard. Surtur brooded on that message, which was misleading when taken out of context, and eventually reacted rashly, but the consequences of his acts were seen as no fault of Skoraeus. If Surtur had instead asked Skoraeus for advice about Memnor's words, the legend would have ended differently.

Skoraeus is considered the most knowledgeable of the giant gods about magic, wards, banes, hidden treasures, and the secrets of the earth. Skoraeus gave the secret of smelting to Surtur. Skoraeus showed Thrym how to carve runes on his old weapons to imbue them with magic when Surtur refused to forge new ones for him. Skoraeus crafted spears for Hiatea so she could complete her ten tasks of valor. Skoraeus tapped with his hammer on the stone under the sea, so that Stronmaus could find the chain-tunnels that allowed him to pull the tarrasque down to the bed of the ocean where at last it would drown.

For a people that spend their lives mostly in darkness, stone giants have a nuanced appreciation of the effects of shadow and light. They design carvings to produce shadows in specific ways when a light source is placed in the proper location. Without both the light and the shadow, the carving is incomplete and can't be viewed in its true form. For example, a tale carving made with these special techniques tells one story when it's viewed in flat, dim light, but it reveals a second, much deeper tale with the addition of proper illumination.

Speaking Stones

Although they are unsurpassed masters of tale carving, stone giants also employ mundane writing in their stone tableaux. Names, dates, and descriptions appear in their tales, often as part of an image (a character's arms or armor might incorporate runic letterforms, for example).

Stone giants also make extensive use of the carved word through "speaking stones." A speaking stone is an upright stone cylinder into which writing is carved in a descending spiral. When the cylinder is turned in one's hands (a feat impossible for any creature of human size and strength) or when it's rotated with its base placed in a cradle designed to balance it upright, the writing can be read as the cylinder goes around. The message wraps around the pillar like the threads of a screw, but in two alternating spirals. The first is read from top to bottom as the cylinder rotates; then the cylinder must be flipped over to reveal the second line of script, also read from top to bottom.

Speaking stones are sized to match the length of the message they carry, so there is no blank space on a stone. A cylinder that turns out to be too long or too thick, so that the message ends before the entire surface of the stone is used, is considered poor artistry. Tradition and honor demand that it be crushed into gravel and a new speaking stone begun.

Gentle Giants?

Newcomers who know only about the stone giants' focus on artistry might think them to be a peaceful and reasonable people. Among their own kind, they tend to be so. But outsiders, particularly non-giants of any sort, are unwelcome in the stone giants' caverns, and trespassers aren't treated politely.

A creature's first sign that it has intruded into stone giant territory might be a boulder, thrown seemingly from nowhere and exploding into shards against a nearby rock. Those who know anything about stone giants understand that this wasn't a miss; it was a measured warning, and the next stone won't land so harmlessly.

It's possible for travelers to negotiate with stone giants for safe passage through their territory, if someone in the group speaks Giant and the giants are offered a tribute. Beautiful and large furs, exotic food, or art objects are suitable tributes; money is a weak inducement for all but the lowest of stone giants. If offered such enticements, one or two giants might come forward to negotiate while others remain at rock-throwing range.

To unfamiliar eyes, stone giants encountered on the fringes of their territory look and behave like primitives. First, personal adornment has little value in the ordning of stone giants, so their clothing tends to be simple and practical. Second, these giants are the least accomplished members of the clan. They are good at ambushing and throwing rocks, but they aren't leaders or even typical examples of their kind.

Even if the giants accept the offered tribute as permission to enter their territory, they might demand a higher price to pass through it. Usually this "gift" is a service of some kind—a task the giants would rather not do or that they're unable to perform, such as chasing kobolds out of a narrow cave or retrieving something from deep within a lake. (Stone giants are poor swimmers; they dislike entering water at all unless they can easily walk across the bottom.)

Stone giants rarely keep pets. They sometimes cultivate colonies of giant bats at the edges of their territory, both for a food source and as a warning system against intruders. They also don't mind sharing their caves or warrens with cave bears, fire beetles, and other beasts that mean them no harm. They keep their other subterranean neighbors at arm's length. Purple worms are their greatest bane, because a hungry worm chews through everything it encounters, including the giants' finest carvings and sculptures. Xorns are among the few creatures that are appreciated by stone giants; their passage through the earth causes no damage, and their alien modes of thought make them interesting to talk with.

Life in the Dark

Stone giants see well in darkness, and the caves and grottoes where they live are kept dark most of the time. They don't prefer to use illumination for any purpose that's not related to creating or displaying art.

Most of a giant's waking hours are taken up with meeting its responsibilities, whether that is a low-ranking pursuit or an artistic one. A tribe's chieftain or another leader such as a shaman determines when the tribe's guards and hunters are on or off duty. Other giants align their sleeping and waking schedules with stone giants higher in the ordning from whom they seek to learn.

Masters of the arts can ask much of lower-ranking students, including waking early to be sure the master has food upon rising, or staying awake while the master sleeps to create something the master will need (or will judge) upon waking. For one reason or another, about three quarters of a tribe's members are awake at any given time.

When outside their settlements, stone giants travel almost exclusively in darkness or—when they dare to visit the surface world—at night, the better to avoid the glaring dreams and visions that would assail them during daylight. A stone giant that visits the surface for too long or is forced out from underground risks becoming lost in the realm of dreams, living ever after as a twisted version of its former self that the giants call a dreamwalker (see chapter 3 for more information on this creature).

The Linjenstein

When a stone giant reaches the end of its tremendously long life, it joins the *Linjenstein* ("ancestors of stone").

The term refers both to the giants' forebears and to the chamber inside each stone giant settlement where they "reside."

A dead (or sometimes merely dying) stone giant is carried into the ancestors' chamber and leaned upright against the end of one of the rows of dead already there. The body gradually calcifies over many decades, until it becomes indistinguishable from an enormous stalagmite.

Family members visit this tomb-chamber often to pay respects to their ancestors. Some of these visits, especially by elderly giants who know they will soon take their place there, last for weeks or even months.

Storm Giants

Storm giants, the most powerful and majestic of giant-kind, are also the most aloof and the least understood. *Uvarjotens* aren't just forces of nature; they are bound to nature, and are extensions of it, in mystical ways that humans find hard to comprehend.

Ordning of Omens

Each storm giant knows its status in the ordning by the signals the universe sends them. Omens might be seen in the wheeling flight of a flock of birds, the patterns in sand left by a receding tide, the shapes of clouds, or any number of other natural phenomena. Storm giants that receive the greatest number of such messages generally rank highest, but the significance of individual signs can also affect one's status. On the rare occasions when storm giants meet, omens and signs accompany each individual, making it plain to all present who ranks where. Arguments about ranking within the ordning are rare, but all the giants in the group studiously examine every sign for evidence that one among them might be the greatest yet, since the revelation of that fact would herald Annam's return.

Ever since Ostoria fell and Annam abandoned his children, no sole king or emperor has ruled over giant-kind. According to legend, the arrival of such a leader will be presaged by signs and omens in all the elements of the world: the sky (air), the sea (water), the continents (earth), and the underworld (fire). All of these are

---

MOODS OF STRONMAUS

Storm giants pay homage to Stronmaus, the eldest of Annam's children, who is also the most joyful and the most prone to laughter and enjoying fellowship with his siblings. That image of Stronmaus is in sharp contrast to how storm giants are perceived in the world: aloof and dour. Nonetheless, it is an accurate one.

In the giants' legends, Stronmaus is subject to gray moods and deep brooding that are just as intense as his moments of good humor. It is also true that storm giants aren't as humorless as popular notions paint them to be. They're quiet and reserved when they're by themselves, which is how they spend most of their time. But when they get together with others of their kind, they enjoy mirth, song, and drink as much as Stronmaus does. For the sake of their privacy and for the safety of smaller beings in the vicinity, these rare gatherings occur far from the presence of other creatures, thus perpetuating the giants' reputation for always being gloomy and grim.

realms of the storm giants, which maintain a constant watch for the all-important signs. In ages past, when giant dynasties reigned, the signs that accompanied the leader of them all were clear and unmistakable. In the crawl of centuries since the empire's collapse, the few signs manifested have been muddied, conflicting, and contentious.

For an obvious reason, every storm giant has a strong personal interest in how soon Annam's return comes to pass—they all want to live to see it. Some individuals gain a measure of immortality for themselves by merging with elemental forces. These storm giant quintessents are the most reclusive of their kind, lairing in remote and inhospitable sites surrounded by brutal winds and murderous weather (see chapter 3 for more information on these creatures).

Without an emperor to serve as their political and spiritual head, the storm giants are adrift on an uncertain sea. Every possibility encapsulated in every sign is exhaustively examined. Debates over the meaning and validity of this or that omen are conducted across human kingdoms and spanning human lifetimes.

Explorers and adventurers can find opportunity in this situation, since the giants sometimes hire agents that they dispatch to investigate portents and to retrieve items the giants need for their oracles. It's dangerous work, for two reasons. The obvious one is that the task involves delving into Ostorian ruins that have been sealed for millennia. The less obvious one is that certain portents, if confirmed to be true, would indeed bring about the return of Annam, upending the giants' social order and initiating a new age. Some would welcome such a change; others would oppose it bitterly and do all they could to stop it, possibly resorting to all-out war.

OUT FOR THEMSELVES

In the absence of both Annam and a worldly emperor, storm giants recognize no higher authority. Human, elf, and dwarf kings, liches, grand sorcerers and wizards— all might amass what they consider great power, but they have no influence over the storm giants. Any who try extending their reach in that direction are guaranteed to come to grief.

But as long as the world leaves the storm giants alone, the giants will leave the world alone. They wish neither good nor ill on the realms of humanity; they simply don't give much thought to the matter, except on the rare occasions when humans crop up in a prophecy or are hinted at by an omen.

When storm giants do interact with non-giants, those on the receiving end of their attention might question the notion that storm giants are "good" creatures. They respect the principle of the sanctity of life, but even the calmest of storm giants has a tremendous temper. When one is roused to anger, principle gives way to fury, and an offense committed by one person against a giant can bring furious retribution down on an entire community.

A storm giant that destroys a town and kills innocents in a fit of rage is likely to regret it afterward and might offer payment to make amends, though a sack of gold is likely little comfort to those who lost loved ones, homes, and livelihoods. It's always wise to tread softly, speak deferentially, and act respectfully in the presence of a giant, but this is especially true of storm giants.

LIVING ON THE EDGE

Once they're old enough to fend for themselves, storm giants spend most of their lives in contemplative isolation. Storm giants are capable of living wherever they choose, whether that's atop a mountain, in a glacial cave, or at the bottom of the deepest oceanic trench. One kind of location that invariably draws their attention is an elemental crossing—where the Material Plane and the Elemental Planes intersect and interact. Elemental influence pervades the architecture of storm giants and lends a tempestuous, unearthly quality to their homes.

Storm giants use elemental crossings for their own transplanar wandering, especially into the Elemental Plane of Air and the Elemental Plane of Water. The frequent whirlpools, tornadoes, and lashing rainstorms that buffet the passages to those two planes help to safeguard the giants' homes and ensure their privacy.

Although a storm giant prefers to live outside the company of other giants, it isn't necessarily alone in its stronghold. Storm giants share their abodes with other creatures that are comfortable in the environment: a sea-dwelling storm giant, for example, might have a few merfolk, water weirds, or even a dragon turtle for companions, while a storm giant living on a mountain peak would extend a friendly hand to any pegasus that happened by, and might even welcome yetis into its home for a time if it believed they could be trusted. The giant's guests are expected to be respectful, to make themselves useful, and to provide interesting conversation or other entertainment when the giant feels like being sociable.

GNOLLS: THE INSATIABLE HUNGER

Gnolls remind the world of the horrors posed by the hordes of the Abyss, and the damage that even the briefest demonic incursion can inflict on the world.

Whenever the demon lord Yeenoghu enters the Material Plane and goes on a rampage, he leaves a great trail of corpses in his wake. As the Lord of Savagery despoils the land, packs of hyenas trail him and feast on the victims until the dead flesh of Yeenoghu's prey leave them bloated and unable to move. Then, in a shower of blood and gristle, the hyenas transform into gnolls, which take up Yeenoghu's awful mission to kill and destroy anything in their path.

YEENOGHU

Gnolls embody the dark urges of Yeenoghu, the demon lord of slaughter and senseless destruction. Although Yeenoghu has been defeated and cast back into the Abyss more than once, gnolls continue to pursue his horrid, apocalyptic vision of a world transformed into a barren, empty ruin, with only the decaying corpses of the last few surviving gnolls left to mark its passing.

As creatures that sprang up in the wake of a demon lord, gnolls are creatures of savage blood lust, incapable of understanding or acting on any other impulse. They are extensions of Yeenoghu's will. They pause only to devour what they have killed, and to fashion crude weapons and armor from their victims' corpses.

A gnoll war band exemplifies Yeenoghu's plans for the world. He wants to transform it into a vicious realm of endless fighting. When the last battle ends, Yeenoghu will enter the world, slay its last surviving champion, and preside over a wasteland of rotting corpses. To Yeenoghu, pure destruction is beauty.

THE GIFT OF YEENOGHU

Yeenoghu imparts to the minds of his followers an unquenchable, supernatural hunger, both for violence and for the flesh of intelligent creatures. A gnoll feels a constant, gnawing demand for blood and destruction that abates only when it kills and eats intelligent creatures. Other prey might provide temporary sustenance, but it does nothing to quell Yeenoghu's hunger.

INSIDE THE MIND OF A GNOLL

From a journal recovered from a slain cultist of Yeenoghu:

Day 2: The subject continues to growl and struggle, despite the removal of its arms and legs. I will let it starve for a few days to weaken its mental fortitude. If the gnoll does have some sort of tie to the Abyss, I must keep my focus on exploiting that link, even though the creature's mind might remain aware.

Day 6: No appreciable loss of vigor.

Day 11: Still no appreciable loss of vigor.

Day 13: Ritual must commence tomorrow despite subject's high level of mental activity.

Day 14: The ritual brought our minds together. I was assailed simultaneously by hunger and rage, as if some great force from beyond had reached out and commanded me only to kill and eat. Though it lasted only a short time, it was a terrifying feeling to my human mind, but in a way it was also comforting to feel myself a part of a much greater design. What I felt was not the hunger of one beast, but the hunger of all of them.

Day 15: Used the ritual to join our minds again. This time I realized where the hunger began. I was consumed by the infinite hunger and boundless rage of great Yeenoghu, and I knew it could never be sated. Yet I felt driven to feed my lord. I killed and devoured a goat while linked to the gnoll's mind. I had set aside a knife for the deed but killed it with my bare hands instead. The flesh was warm. I fed myself. I fed Yeenoghu.

Day 16: Third use of ritual. As my connection to my lord deepens, I leave my old concerns behind. His hunger is all that matters. It is greater than me; it is greater than us all. It is His mark. He made us. He drives us. He eats what we eat. He kills what we kill. He will come if we eat well. He will come if we kill well. He will come if we eat well. He will come if we kill well. We will kill and He will eat, and we shall be He and He shall be we, never alone, never afraid, never hungry.

Gnolls wander the land continually in search of new victims, rarely sleeping and never settling down. Only a large-scale assault, such as the massacre of an entire village, can satisfy their desire even temporarily. A sated gnoll rests, knowing that it has pleased Yeenoghu. Its relief is short, no more than a few days, before the gnoll once again becomes a slave to its desires.

Strength, hunger, and fear are the three concepts that every gnoll extols. Strength allows a gnoll to overwhelm, kill, and devour a foe. Hunger motivates a gnoll to go forth and slay in Yeenoghu's name. Fear is a weapon used against enemies to make them easy prey. In concert, all three play a role in advancing Yeenoghu's goals.

Omens from Beyond

Of all the demon lords, Yeenoghu is perhaps the most active on the Material Plane. He shows support to his followers by sending them omens in the form of visions, dreams, and signs. As such, gnolls instinctively look for such omens to guide their activities, and they find them in many places.

Among the signs that gnolls rely on are the blood trails and spatters left behind after making a meal of an intelligent humanoid. They attach significance to a number of other phenomena as well, including the sight of arrows in flight, the rush of the wind, and sounds of howling or cackling laughter that have no discernible source.

Non-gnoll Cultists

Few creatures aside from gnolls worship Yeenoghu, and those that do mimic gnolls in their actions and beliefs.

Yeenoghu's cultists are folk who lack all hope and have descended into nihilism. One might have suffered a tremendous personal loss, been banished from its home, or been the victim of a terrible betrayal. Whatever the reason, the would-be cultist is left isolated and abandoned, making it vulnerable to Yeenoghu's teachings.

The creature's thoughts and dreams are plagued by visions sent by Yeenoghu. The promise of ultimate power, fueled by acts of brutality, tempt and torment it. Most folk ascribe these feelings to a fleeting bout of depression or madness and are able to resist the call to violence, but a few cannot. For these rare individuals, the true lure of Yeenoghu's promises lies not in the power they offer, but in the deep sense of belonging they create.

Those that are swayed by this offer consider themselves gnolls in mind and deed, and soon set out to commit their first atrocities in Yeenoghu's name. Most of these cultists are almost as quickly killed by guards or other authorities. A few escape into the wilderness and continue to rampage on their own, perhaps eventually falling in league with a gnoll war band.

Gnoll Tactics

Gnolls might seem to throw themselves into battle mindlessly, driven only by fury and hunger, but they do possess a rudimentary form of cunning that is borne out by several tactics they use consistently.

Trying to talk to a gnoll is the quickest path to its stomach.
—Volo

BUTCHER THE WEAK

Gnolls seek only to kill, and as such prefer to deal with weak, easy targets. An enemy that can fight back is an enemy to save for later. Gnolls have no sense of honor, glory, or individual achievement. They care only for the raw number of creatures they can slay. In the face of a gnoll incursion, it is best for refugees to seek shelter in castles and other fortified positions. Gnolls avoid protracted battles if they can, much preferring to slaughter those that can't defend themselves.

OVERWHELM THE STRONG

Gnolls attack intelligent prey that is capable of resisting them only when the most powerful omens from Yeenoghu compel them to do so. They cooperate to gang up on each of the individuals in a group of explorers or adventurers, or if the prey is more numerous they rush forward in waves. The creatures will crawl over their own dead to climb a castle's walls and kill all within it. A commonly held belief is that a fortress besieged by gnolls needs ten arrows for each one to keep the creatures from scaling the walls.

SPREAD FAR AND WIDE

Gnolls never set up permanent camps, though they might linger for a few days at the site of a particularly great slaughter as they devour the corpses of both their victims and the gnolls killed in battle. During this time, the hyenas that follow a pack of gnolls feast until they become bloated, then burst open to spawn more gnolls. In this manner, gnolls replenish their ranks before wandering off in ragged bands to continue their rampage.

KILL FROM A DISTANCE

Almost every gnoll carries a bow scavenged from a past victim. Gnolls use ranged attacks mainly to prevent their prey from fleeing, rather than softening up their targets with an initial barrage of arrows before an assault. A target wounded by a bow shot becomes easy prey for any gnolls near it. Some particularly clever gnolls have been known to use burning arrows to spark fires, cutting off their prey's escape routes and driving victims into their jaws.

LEAVE NO SURVIVORS

A band of gnolls lives in a state of eternal war with everything it encounters, aside from fellow worshipers of Yeenoghu. To keep from being detected between major raids, the gnolls move through the wilderness with as much stealth as they can marshal. They never leave survivors in any group they set upon, and will pursue a fleeing enemy for days to prevent it from getting to a town or a city and raising an alarm.

If the area they hunt in becomes too well-defended, the gnolls relocate in search of easier prey. Large tracts along the fringe of civilization might be devastated before the wider world becomes aware of a gnoll threat.

TREASURE

A cautious and skilled gang can follow in the tracks of a gnoll war band, keeping hidden and waiting for the creatures to move on after ravaging a village or a town. The

ON DEFEATING GNOLLS

An excerpt from *One Hundred Years of War*, a famous manual of dwarven battle tactics:

Gnolls remain a threat across all seasons. Happily, our redoubts are too fortified for their tastes, but caravans, foraging expeditions, and patrols must deal with them.

Gnolls take care to move quietly when they are on the hunt for prey. The events that presage their presence are easy to misinterpret as the results of other threats. A scout might go missing, a caravan fail to arrive on time, or a village be left deserted. Several kinds of creatures, such as orcs and goblins, can cause such events, but the evidence that gnolls leave of their involvement is unmistakable. Their enemies aren't merely killed, they are dismembered and devoured. The loot that other marauders would scoop up is left where it falls, of no use to a creature that requires only flesh to feed its urges.

If you suspect that gnolls are encroaching on dwarven territory, send reliable spies to human settlements in the region, while pulling back as many of our folk as you can manage. Instruct the spies to pass along updates each day, preferably by messenger bird. Do not tell the spies of your suspicions. Invent a story, such as the search for an outlaw or some other deception.

If a spy fails to report, you must strike quickly. Send your fastest warriors and strongest spellcasters to the spy's location. If the gnolls have struck a settlement, they will rest for up to a week, bloated on their kills. In this state, they are their most vulnerable. Surround the place in silence, and advance as one to catch them in a vise. Let none survive. A single gnoll can, over time, create a new war band.

Some may argue for an approach that doesn't rely on the loss of human life to see it succeed. I would gladly suggest one if such existed. Your best strategy is to defend our halls and let the humans serve as bait. Moradin knows they multiply quickly enough that their losses will soon be recouped.

gnolls leave the town's gold and gems and other durable goods battered and gnawed, but still intact, though they invariably ruin delicate or flammable objects in their fits of destruction.

Gnolls do possess a basic understanding of the value of weapons and armor, so one might decide to hold onto an object seen as useful. In this way, a gnoll might come to possess a magic item, though it might not know exactly how to use it. Gnolls regard objects of "treasure" only in terms of their ability to cause harm or preserve a gnoll's life. Everything else is fit only for destruction.

LANGUAGE

The language of gnolls, such as it is, consists of whines, cackles, and howls mixed with gestures and expressions. Gnolls use it to communicate only basic concepts, such as an alert about approaching prey or a call to their allies to join the fray. When gnolls fight among themselves, they rarely bother with threats or words before leaping at each other's throats.

When gnoll leaders must share complex concepts with each other, they use a broken form of Abyssal gifted to them by Yeenoghu. The gnoll language lacks a script or written form, though elite gnolls can use their limited knowledge of Abyssal to leave messages. In most cases, though, a gnoll war band has little use for written notes or signs. Gnolls simply wander, attack, kill, and feed. Anything more sophisticated is beyond the band's concern.

ROLEPLAYING GNOLLS AND CULTISTS OF YEENOGHU

Gnolls have little variation in personality and outlook. They are collectively an elemental force, driven by a demon lord to spread death and destruction.

The only real opportunity for interaction with gnolls is provided by the cultists that sometimes accompany a war band. This humanoid rabble might have information the characters need or could even be former friends corrupted to the worship of Yeenoghu. To portray a gnoll that is more intelligent or social than the usual, you can give it characteristics similar to Yeenoghu cultists.

GNOLL/CULTIST PHYSICAL FEATURES

d12	Physical Feature
1	Missing an arm
2	Infested with maggots
3	Fur matted with dried blood
4	Missing an eye
5	Walks with a severe limp
6	Covered in burn wounds
7	Vestigial twin embedded on back
8	Loud, wheezing breaths
9	Drool is mildly acidic
10	Covered in weeping sores
11	Horrific smell of rot
12	Weapon still embedded in old wound

GNOLL/CULTIST PERSONALITY TRAIT

d6	Personality Trait
1	Once an enemy defies me, I dedicate everything to its destruction.
2	The best enemy to fight is one caught by surprise.
3	I hate the sun and travel only by night.
4	I have stopped using language and instead rely on growls and shrieks.
5	I have no fear of death and welcome it in battle.
6	My berserk fury makes a rabid dog look gentle.

GNOLL/CULTIST IDEALS

d6	Ideal
1	**Strength.** I must remain strong to survive. (Any)
2	**Slaughter.** If I destroy the weak, I please Yeenoghu. (Evil)
3	**Destruction.** Yeenoghu will return when only those worthy of his fury remain. (Evil)
4	**Paranoia.** Others are planning to kill and eat me. I must find a way to kill and eat them first. (Chaotic)
5	**Self-Sufficiency.** When the time comes, even my allies will die by my hand. (Evil)
6	**Leadership.** I am not part of the pack. I am above it. (Chaotic)

GNOLL/CULTIST BONDS

d6	Bond
1	I would die before betraying the Lord of Savagery.
2	I would follow the leader of our war band anywhere and gladly sacrifice myself to protect him or her.
3	I cull the weak from our war band, so that we remain strong.
4	Yeenoghu's omens guide my every choice.
5	If I die in battle, I was simply too weak to please Yeenoghu.
6	I devour the weak to purge them from the world, the strong to blunt their power.

GNOLL/CULTIST FLAWS

d6	Flaw
1	I lack tactical guile and rely on overwhelming attacks.
2	I flee from opponents that can match my strength.
3	My supposed allies are my first victims.
4	Deep down inside, I am terrified I will fail Yeenoghu.
5	My desire to torment my foes sometimes gives them the opportunity to outwit me.
6	My arrogance causes me to overlook opportunities.

GNOLL NAMES

As befits creatures with a language that is little more than whines, growls, and shrieks, most gnolls lack a name and would have little use for one. Powerful gnolls, usually fangs, pack lords, and flinds, receive names directly from Yeenoghu. The same applies to Yeenoghu's blessed followers among humans, orcs, and other races.

GNOLL NAMES

d12	Gnoll Name	d12	Gnoll Name
1	Aargab	7	Immor
2	Alark	8	Oduk
3	Andak	9	Orrom
4	Ethak	10	Otal
5	Eyeth	11	Ulthak
6	Ignar	12	Ustar

ANATOMY OF A WAR BAND

A gnoll war band is likely to contain a variety of gnolls and other creatures, and no two of these groups have the same composition.

The gnolls that make up the rank and file have different attributes and thus different roles in the war band's assaults. Augmenting the warriors that comprise the bulk of the force are the hunters, specialists in sneaking and attacking at range, and the flesh gnawers, which rely on natural savagery rather than weapons to tear apart their foes. A pack of hyenas is always part of the band, and sometimes these beasts are as numerous as the gnolls themselves. A war band that has been through hard times might contain a number of gnoll witherlings, while one that enjoys Yeenoghu's favor might be led by a flind—the scarcest and strongest of all gnolls. It's also possible, though quite rare, for a war band to include cultists—other humanoids that have dedicated themselves to Yeenoghu and attached themselves to the war band to prove their loyalty.

Each of these elements of a war band is further described below. Statistics for gnoll flesh gnawers, gnoll hunters, gnoll witherlings, and flinds appear in chapter 3 of this book.

GNOLL PACK LORD

Most war bands are led by pack lords. These champions of Yeenoghu curry their lord's favor with living sacrifices. They mark their hides with bloody runes, which sometimes grant supernatural power conferred by Yeenoghu himself. Pack lords favor big, heavy weapons, such as glaives and axes.

GNOLL FANGS OF YEENOGHU

Fangs of Yeenoghu are gifted with the power to spawn more gnolls. They anoint the remains of their foes using bizarre rituals. A hyena that feeds on such a corpse spawns a gnoll, while other humanoids who join in the feast become cultists of Yeenoghu. Fangs use their claws in battle, the better to imbue their victims with the magic needed to spawn more gnolls.

GNOLL WARRIORS

Common gnolls comprise the bulk of a war band. They fight mainly with spears fashioned from wood and bone. While they lack any particular blessing of Yeenoghu, their ferocity makes them formidable enemies.

GNOLL HUNTERS

When a war band is on the move, the hunters travel in a wide arc around the perimeter of the force. Hunters are more adept than other gnolls at sneaking and moving through an area undetected, which makes them useful for reconnaissance. Sometimes a team of hunters is used to silently pick off sentries on patrol before they can raise an alarm, which makes the upcoming onslaught by the rest of the war band even more lethal. Another function that hunters perform is to trail along behind a war band, making quick work of wounded gnolls and those who can't keep up the pace.

GNOLL FLESH GNAWERS

All gnolls are ruthless and brutal, but the flesh gnawers in a war band use their quickness and agility to augment their savagery. At the start of a raid, flesh gnawers lurk around the edges of the gnoll forces, hoping to jump on enemies that become isolated. When a flesh gnawer springs into action, its blades and teeth turn it into a whirling dealer of death, able to dash from one target to the next as though it had been shot from a bow.

GNOLL WITHERLINGS

A war band might go for weeks without coming across the sort of prey it craves. Gnolls can eat wild animals for sustenance, but only the flesh of intelligent humanoids can calm the endless hunger bestowed upon them by Yeenoghu.

When a war band grows desperate for food, its members turn on each other. Those who succumb to the violence are devoured, but their service to the war band doesn't end at that point. The survivors preserve the bones of their fallen comrades, so that a pack lord or a flind can perform a ritual to Yeenoghu to turn them into loyal, undead followers known as witherlings.

Even after death, gnoll witherlings serve the war band much as their comrades do. Although not as formidable in battle as warriors or hunters, they are just as relentless.

FLINDS

A flind is an exceptionally large and strong gnoll. No war band contains more than one flind, and such a creature is always the leader of its band. A flind wields a weapon that carries Yeenoghu's blessing: a magical flail that saps the body and the mind of any foe that feels its touch.

Because flinds are so rare, other gnolls see them as Yeenoghu's special messengers, gifted with a keen eye for omens and an ear for Yeenoghu's whispers. Each day, a flind consults the signs around it and determines the war band's direction.

During a battle, a gnoll that delivers the death blow to a flind claims its flail and, in a burst of abyssal energy, is touched by Yeenoghu and turns into a flind itself. The death or disappearance of a flind for any other reason causes a war band to descend into brutal infighting. Sometimes a new leader emerges from the pack after putting down its rivals; more often, the band fragments and the survivors go their separate ways.

CULTISTS

Rarely, a war band includes orcs, humans, or other humanoids that have sworn loyalty to Yeenoghu. The gnolls treat these cultists as they would other gnolls, refraining from killing them so long as they join in the slaughter when the band finds prey.

Almost all cultists are brutish individuals touched by insanity, one step above the hyenas that trail behind the war band's path. They aren't gnolls, and thus don't receive their inspiration directly from Yeenoghu. Yet exceptions do occur. If an individual of great intelligence and great ability heeds Yeenoghu's call, the Lord of Savagery might elevate it to the leadership of its band. Such champions are rare, and a band led by a cultist is capable of feats that are beyond a group of gnolls—accomplishments that combine the gnolls' savagery with a humanlike level of intelligence and planning.

GNOLLS ARE DRIVEN BY BLOODLUST. WHAT SWAYS THEM FROM THEIR SAVAGERY ARE SIGNS. THEY SEE SIGNS FROM YEENOGHU EVERYWHERE, EVEN IN BLOOD SPLATTER. A GNOLL ACTING ODDLY IS PROBABLY FOLLOWING ITS INTERPRETATION OF A SIGN.
— ELMINSTER

Gnoll Allies

Gnolls wage war against any creatures they meet, except for those that have dedicated themselves to Yeenoghu and those that act in accordance with his wishes. The Lord of Savagery stains the souls of his followers and kindred creatures in such a way that they and his gnolls recognize one another on sight and don't immediately leap into battle. Thus, a war band might include or be accompanied by other beings of evil.

Demons

A fang of Yeenoghu is sometimes gifted with the cosmic insight needed to summon forth mindless demons. When Yeenoghu deigns to allow it, a war band might find itself augmented by some of his favorite demons, such as barlguras, dretches, hezrous, or manes. The Lord of Savagery also has a special affinity for maw demons, which share his insatiable hunger.

Demonic hyenas known as shoosuvas are dispatched by Yeenoghu to aid his most exalted champions. Among the gnolls, the appearance of a shoosuva is a reward for recent triumphs and a harbinger of great victories and much feasting to come. A shoosuva protects the war band's most powerful members and serves as a companion to the strongest fang of Yeenoghu in the group.

For more information on maw demons and shoosuvas, see chapter 3 of this book.

Ghouls

Ghoul packs emerge from graveyards and dungeons to trail in the wake of a war band, feasting on the remains of its victims and sometimes eventually merging with the group. Although ghouls typically revere Orcus, their endless hunger can prompt them to turn to Yeenoghu.

Hyenas

Large packs of hyenas follow gnoll war bands. For their part, the gnolls largely ignore these animals. They tend to gather around fangs in battle, eager to partake of Yeenoghu's blessing and its horrid transformation.

Leucrottas

Brought forth during Yeenoghu's ancient incursions into the world, leucrottas are bigger, smarter, and faster than gnolls. When one joins a war band, it doesn't strive to lead the group (which would cause unneeded conflict) but rather to serve and protect its leader. A leucrotta's dedication to Yeenoghu is as fervent as that of any gnoll,

---

The Hunter's Chant

This simple declaration of Yeenoghu's power was devised by a small cult to the demon lord discovered deep in the forest. A group of woodcutters, facing starvation, turned to cannibalism to survive and ultimately fell under Yeenoghu's sway. Gnolls sing a similar chant in their language while they seek out prey.

The first gift is hunger.
It is His blessing.
It is our call to bring death.
The second gift is death.
Death proves our strength.
Death purges our fear.
The third gift is fear.
We fear that we will fail him.
We fear the onset of hunger.

and its main goal is always to advance the cause of the Lord of Savagery over its own.

For more information on leucrottas, see chapter 3 of this book.

TROLLS

Of all the creatures encountered by gnolls, trolls are the most likely to join them simply because the gnolls' way of life appeals to them. As ravenous creatures with incredible toughness, trolls fit well into the loose scheme of a gnoll war band.

CREATING A GNOLL WAR BAND

To include a gnoll war band in your campaign, or if you need to generate one quickly for use in an encounter, use the tables in this section. Roll on each one in turn to determine the war band's name, components, and unique traits.

The War Band Name table is set up to create two-word names. Some war bands become infamous enough to earn an epithet from their enemies, but only the most powerful flinds and pack lords bother to name the groups they lead.

The War Band Composition table determines how many gnolls and hyenas the band contains. The War Band Leadership table indicates the war band's commander (if it has one) and gives a modifier to apply to the composition results: for a band led by a flind, double all the results, and for a band that lacks a leader, halve them.

Roll once on the Special Creatures table to see which special creature is part of the war band and in what numbers. The Shared Physical Trait and Notable Behavior or Tactics tables add some distinctive flavor to the war band. Finally, the Demonic Influence table adds an abyssal tinge to the group: owing to the gnolls' supernatural link with the Abyss, their advance toward a community might be heralded by strange effects that afflict the area or the people in it a day or so before they strike the settlement.

GNOLL WAR BAND NAME

d6	Name Part 1	Name Part 2
1	Abyssal	Harbingers
2	Dire	Hunters
3	Howling	Mongrels
4	Rabid	Mutilators
5	Rotted	Ravagers
6	Screaming	Slayers

WAR BAND COMPOSITION

War Band Composition	Number Appearing
Gnoll fangs of Yeenoghu	1d4 + 1
Gnoll hunters	1d4 + 1
Gnoll flesh gnawers	2d4
Warriors (common gnolls)	6d6
Hyenas	4d6

WAR BAND LEADERSHIP

d6	Leader	Number Appearing Modifier
1	Flind	Double
2–4	Gnoll pack lord	None
5–6	None	Halve

SPECIAL CREATURES

d20	Special Creature(s)
1	1 barlgura
2–5	3d6 dretches
6–8	2d6 ghouls
9–10	2d6 gnoll witherlings*
11	1 hezrou
12–13	1d4 leucrottas*
14–16	2d6 manes
17–18	2d4 maw demons*
19	1 shoosuva*
20	1d3 trolls

* See chapter 3 of this book for statistics.

SHARED PHYSICAL TRAIT

d10	Shared Physical Trait
1	Rune branded on forehead
2	Bone piercings
3	Ritual scarring
4	Surrounded by clouds of flies
5	Constant, cackling laugh
6	Covered with strange mushroom growths
7	Horrid stench
8	Eyes glow like fire
9	Long, black fangs
10	Albinos

NOTABLE BEHAVIOR OR TACTICS

d8	Notable Behavior or Tactics
1	Use of flaming arrows and burning pitch
2	Use of drums and screeching horns to spread fear
3	Attempts to capture and use siege engines
4	Carry and spread disease
5	Prisoners kept in cages and tormented
6	Use of nets to take captives for feasting later
7	Leader has a powerful item, such as a *horn of blasting*
8	Actions magically controlled by a spellcaster

DEMONIC INFLUENCE

d12	Demonic Influence
1	Food and drink spoil
2	Animals become rabid, vicious
3	Terrible storms erupt
4	Minor earthquakes strike
5	Residents suffer bursts of short-term madness
6	Folk indulge in decadence, excessive drinking
7	Quarrels turn violent
8	Friends betray one another
9–12	None

GOBLINOIDS: THE CONQUERING HOST

Maglubiyet is truly the Conquering God. He stiffens the spines of cowardly goblins. He rouses bugbears from their lazy slumber. He sets the thunderous step of hobgoblin legions. Maglubiyet takes three races and turns them into one people.

In bygone times the goblinoids were distinct from one another, with separate faiths and different customs. Then Maglubiyet came and conquered all who stood before him, mortals and deities alike. Gods and heroes who wouldn't bend to his will were broken and discarded. He put his foot on the neck of mighty Khurgorbaeyag, bound the will of intractable Hruggek, and forced sadistic Nomog-Geaya to fall in line. What the goblins, the bugbears, and the hobgoblins were before their gods bowed to Maglubiyet no longer matters. Now they are, first of all, followers of Maglubiyet.

On the surface, goblins, bugbears, and hobgoblins are as different as halflings, dwarves, and elves. Each race has its own tendencies, outlook, culture, and gods. But Maglubiyet's hand joins them together, just as he made all their other gods parts within a greater whole. When one kind of goblinoid encounters another kind, the two groups don't see one another as strangers or foes. Instead they know that by the fact of their meeting alone, Maglubiyet has commanded them to come together. They know the time has come to form a host.

GOBLINS

Goblins occupy an uneasy place in a dangerous world, and they react by lashing out at any creatures they believe they can bully. Cunning in battle and cruel in victory, goblins are fawning and servile in defeat, just as in

---

Ahh, the Sly Fox. Soft beds, warm turnip pie—such pleasant memories. Alas, the tavern's no more. Goblinoids plundered her stores and burnt her to the ground. Those heathens have no appreciation for the finer things!

—Volo

their own society lower castes must scrape before those of greater status and as goblin tribes bow before other goblinoids.

BEAST MASTERS AND SLAVE DRIVERS

Goblins know they are a weak, unsophisticated race that can be easily dominated by bigger, smarter, more organized, more ferocious, or more magical creatures. Their god was conquered by Maglubiyet, after all, and now when the Mighty One calls for it, even their souls are forfeit. It is this realization that drives them to dominate other creatures whenever they can—for goblins, life is short.

Goblins seek to trap and enslave any creatures they encounter, but they flee from opposition that seems too daunting. For miles around their lair, they employ pit traps, snares, and nets to catch the unwary, and when their hunting patrols encounter other beings, they always look for ways to capture their foes instead of killing them. Goblins that run up against the fringes of a society first test its defenses by stealing objects, and if these crimes go unpunished, they begin stealing people.

Enslaved creatures receive the worst treatment the goblins can dish out while still getting decent performance out of the slaves. But humanoids and monsters that are especially capable or that provide unusual services find themselves treated like favored (though occasionally abused) pets.

KHURGORBAEYAG: THE OVERSEER OF ALL

Goblins once had many gods, but the only one who survived Maglubiyet's ascendancy is cruel Khurgorbaeyag, known as the Overseer. Khurgorbaeyag drives his worshipers to be the masters of others. Only by wielding the whip can they hope to escape its lash. Khurgorbaeyag sometimes makes his presence or his desires known through wrathful signs and magical blessings: the crack of a whip without a visible source, chains or ropes that move of their own accord, or a glowing cage that appears to trap foes or those who displease him. Worshipers of Khurgorbaeyag are sometimes overtaken by sudden onsets of depression, which they take as a sign that they have somehow displeased their god. When they rouse themselves from this despondency, they take up the master's whip with renewed zeal and seek out more creatures upon which they can wield it.

Khurgorbaeyag's holy symbol is a yellow-and-red striped whip made of leather. This mark of his authority is used by its wielder against goblins of a lower caste as well as on slaves and enemies. The knowledge of how to make such a whip is enough to elevate a goblin to the master caste of lashers. Often the secret is guarded by one family in a tribe, which enjoys prestige and influence because it controls the supply of whips.

Virtually any kind of creature that can be browbeaten into service might be found with a goblin tribe, but rats and wolves are nearly always present. Both have lived in concert with goblins for at least as long as humans have worked with dogs and horses, and in goblin society those two animals serve similar purposes.

FAMILY MATTERS

A goblin tribe is organized in a four-tiered caste system made up of lashers, hunters, gatherers, and pariahs. The status of every family in the tribe is based on its importance to the tribe's survival. Families that belong to the higher-ranking castes keep their status by not sharing their knowledge and skills with other families, while those in the lower castes have little hope of escaping their plight.

Outsiders who don't understand the goblins' social system are sometimes surprised by how different castes interact with them. A single human warrior might frighten away a dozen gatherers, only to be shocked when two hunters viciously attack. A captured group of invaders might hang in a net while dozens of goblins pass by and pay them no heed until a group of gatherers shows up.

Lashers. The closest thing a goblin tribe has to nobility is the caste of lashers—families of goblins trained in the ways of battle, and also possessed of key skills such as strategy, trap-building, beast taming, mining, smelting, forging, and religion. If the tribe has any spellcasters, this caste includes them. Lashers follow the lead of the tribe's boss, and enforce their will on other goblins with whips.

Hunters. The families of goblins that are skilled in the use of weapons but not privy to any other special knowledge have the second highest status in the tribe. Hunters are often the best wolf riders and know the most about the territory farthest from the tribe's lair. These individuals hunt game in peaceful times, and in combat they serve as scouts, foot soldiers, and cavalry.

Gatherers. Families in the second lowest caste are responsible for getting food from the surrounding area, taking what's naturally available or stealing whatever they can. Gatherers also do the little amount of farming of which goblins are capable and are charged with checking traps for captured people or beasts. Gatherers aren't usually armed with weapons more deadly than a sling or a knife, but they frequently carry nets, caltrops, lassos, and nooses on poles for controlling captured creatures. These goblins cook for the tribe, and in times of war they are also responsible for making poison.

Gatherers, and the pariahs beneath them, greatly fear for their lives in battle, believing that the lashers and the hunters have special knowledge of how to survive. It is the members of the lower castes that give goblins their reputation for cowardice.

Pariahs. Some goblin families are the lowest of the low, composed of the most dimwitted, least educated, and weakest goblins. They get the worst jobs: mucking out animal pens, cleaning up after other goblins, and doing any hard labor such as digging mines. If the goblin tribe has slaves to do some of this work, the pariah families enjoy the opportunity to supervise and dominate such creatures, which have no status at all.

Status Symbols

Goblins love symbols of authority, and thus the tribe's boss often has such trappings wherever he or she goes. Such a symbol can take a typical form, perhaps a crown or a throne, but also can be a more distinctive objects like a high-backed wolf saddle or colorful boots. The castes in a tribe also adopt symbols to indicate membership or kinship, but the symbols used are rarely the same between different tribes and often make little sense to other creatures. Some possible status symbols are given in the Status Symbols table. A caste or a boss might display more than one of these items.

Booyahgs

Spellcasters of any sort among the goblins are rare. Goblins typically lack the intelligence and patience needed to learn and practice wizardry, and they fare poorly even when given access to the necessary training and knowledge. Sorcerers are less prevalent among them than in many other races, and Khurgorbaeyag seems to dislike sharing his divine power with his followers. And although many goblins would readily offer anything to have the abilities of a warlock, the patrons

WHO'S THE BOSS?

Goblins pattern the rule of their tribes after the whip-cracking rule of their god, Khurgorbaeyag, and thus each group has one leader that exerts autocratic control. But as with many tyrannies, the passing of a leader often results in a chaotic transition to the next. Sometimes a goblin boss has the foresight to declare a successor, often a child or other family member the boss has been able to trust. But such a declaration doesn't always prevent a mad scramble for influence and allies, or secret backstabbing and outright fights over the title. Most often, the victor in such a struggle comes from another family of the lasher caste, and any allies of the previous boss count themselves lucky if their only punishment is demotion to the pariah caste.

Sometimes another creature assumes control of a goblin tribe, by killing or subjugating the current boss and cowing most of the rest of the tribe. If the creature is dimwitted, like a troll or ogre, the lower-class goblins give it obeisance, but before long the upper-class goblins begin to think that whoever can bend the ear of the new leader can act as the real boss. If the creature brushes aside such manipulation, the tribe falls into line behind the new tyrant—better to abide the new rule than conspire against it and be called out as a traitor.

Status Symbols

d20	Status Symbol
1	Earrings and notches in an ear
2	Rib bones tied into hair
3	A belt made from raccoon pelts
4	A gnome's boot used as a hat
5	A pouch of toenail clippings from an allied ogre
6	A frog kept in a jar
7	Fragile helmets made from axe beak eggs
8	Nose rings
9	Painted or stained hands
10	Bugs kept in a bag for snacking
11	War cry tattooed on chest
12	Shields made from ankheg chitin
13	Bracelet made of pieces of goblins turned to stone
14	Special breed of rat kept as pet
15	Teeth pulled out in certain places
16	Owlbear-feather cloaks
17	Scars from lashings
18	Orc-tusk lip piercings
19	Umbrellas made from dead darkmantles
20	Cloaks made of scraps from an elven tapestry

that grant such power know a goblin is unlikely to be able to uphold its end of any bargain.

Even when a goblin is born with the ability to become a spellcaster, the knowledge and talent necessary to carry on the tradition rarely persists for more than a couple of generations. Because they have so little experience with magic, goblins make no distinction between its forms. To them all magic is "booyahg," and the word is part of the name they give to any of its practitioners. A goblin with access to booyahg becomes a member of the lashers and can often rise to the role of boss.

Booyahg Caster. This goblin served under a hobgoblin wizard, stole a look at its master's spellbook, and learned a little wizardry by aping the gestures and words it remembered. The goblin can cast a randomly determined 1st-level wizard spell once per day. Intelligence is its spellcasting ability.

Booyahg Wielder. This goblin found a magic item (a *necklace of fireballs*, a *circlet of blasting*, or the like) and learned how to use it.

Booyahg Whip. Khurgorbaeyag saw fit to gift this goblin with powers that enable it to dominate others. The goblin has 1d3 other goblins that slavishly obey its orders.

Booyahg Slave. This goblin warlock serves a patron who can extract payment in flesh if the goblin doesn't do as promised. Often this patron is a coven of hags serving as the tribe's boss, a fiend that has made its way into the world, or an undying lord such as a lich or a vampire. (For more information on undying lord patrons, see the *Sword Coast Adventurer's Guide*.) Use one of the warlock stat blocks in appendix B to represent this goblin, adding darkvision and the Nimble Escape traits common to all goblins.

Booyahg Booyahg Booyahg. This goblin is a sorcerer with the wild magic origin whose every casting, including cantrips, is accompanied by a wild magic surge. Use the **mage** stat block in the *Monster Manual* to represent this goblin, adding darkvision and the Nimble Escape traits common to all goblins. Each time the goblin casts a spell, there is an accompanying surge of wild magic; roll on the Wild Magic Surge table in the *Player's Handbook* to determine the wild magic effect.

GOBLIN LAIRS

Tribes of goblins take up residence in shrouded valleys, shadowy forests, and caves and tunnels beneath the surface of the world. Capable miners and crafters, they seek to settle in places where they can get the raw materials to make weapons and armor. Their need for iron and other metals sometimes puts them in conflict with other races, but just as often, goblins get what they need by claiming mines abandoned by other races and scratching away at veins thought to be played out.

When goblins expand a mine, the tunnels they dig are narrow and warren-like. Goblins live both within these tunnels and on the surface around the outside of the area. They guard the territory around the mine for miles, sending out patrols of hunters equipped with war horns and using wolves as watchdogs to alert them to intruders.

Outskirts. The territory around a goblin lair has several hallmarks, most of which aren't readily apparent. Packs of wolves allied with the goblins serve as effective perimeter guards, without giving away the fact that a tribe of goblins lives nearby. Hunters take up guard posts in tall trees and atop high rocky outcrops from where they can view the terrain while staying unseen. Any obvious path through the territory (a valley, a clear trail, or a river) might be turned into an ambush point where a force of goblins can capture intruders. Such places might also be set with net traps, snare traps, or hidden pit traps that gatherers regularly check for new slaves. The area also includes burial grounds for each caste, always placed far from the lair.

Lair Exterior. Anyone who is skilled or fortunate enough to pass through the territory of a goblin tribe without being detected is likely to come upon some telltale signs of habitation—complete with goblins at work and other goblins standing guard over them.

If the lair was built around a mine, the tribe's smelting furnace and forge will be in the vicinity. A lair inside a forest likely has piles of cut timber (and suitable tools) nearby. In appropriate terrain, the goblins might set aside some land for simple farming (raising mushrooms and gourds). If the lair doesn't have enough space underground for everyone, gatherers and pariahs are housed in huts on the surface, near the areas where they work.

Lair Interior. The ideal place for a goblin lair is an abandoned mine that features two or three large chambers and a few smaller ones, with tunnels connecting them. In such a place, the tribe can protect its most valuable assets while providing for a modicum of comfort. Most lairs have only a single entrance, but the goblins might build a number of escape tunnels that emerge far from that location.

Close inside the entrance, if a suitable area exists, the goblins set up a den for their wolves. The animals come and go as they please, unless the goblins have use for them. Any tunnel in the lair, whether dug by goblins or not, is likely to be trapped, typically in a way that not only injures the enemy but also collapses the passage.

Open spaces inside a lair are useful for a number of reasons, and the goblins will hollow out chambers for their use if need be. Slaves and tamed monsters are best kept in large areas with limited access, making them easier to guard. The tribe's boss lays claim to a space that's treated as a throne room of sorts. The lashers and hunters of a tribe occupy other caverns and chambers, enjoying the comfort and safety of underground living as a reward for their status and their value to the group.

BUGBEARS

Bugbears feature in the nightmare tales of many races—great, hairy beasts that creep through the shadows as quiet as cats. If you walk alone in the woods, a bugbear will reach out of the bushes and strangle you. If you stray too far from the house at night, bugbears will scoop you up to devour you in their den. If a bugbear cuts off your head, your soul stays trapped inside, and the bugbears use your head to magically command all whom you once knew.

Lurid tales such as these have flowered from the seeds of truth. Bugbears do rely on stealth and strength to attack, preferring to operate at night. They do take the heads of enemy leaders, but they are no more likely to eat people indiscriminately than humans are. Bugbears aren't likely to attack lone travelers or wandering children unless they clearly have something to gain by doing so. From the viewpoint of the rest of the world, their aggression and savagery are thankfully offset by their rarity and lethargy.

SHIFTLESS, SAVAGE LAYABOUTS

When they're not in battle, bugbears spend much of their time resting or dozing. They don't engage in crafting or agriculture to any great extent, or otherwise produce anything of value. They bully weaker creatures into doing their bidding, so they can take it easy. When a superior force tries to intimidate bugbears into service, they will try to escape rather than perform the work or confront the foe. Even when subsumed into a goblinoid host and drawn into war, bugbears must often be roused from naps and bribed to get them to do their duties.

This indolence offers no clue to how vicious the creatures are. Bugbears are capable of bouts of incredible ferocity, using their muscular bodies to exact swift and ruthless violence. At their core, bugbears are ambush predators accustomed to long periods of inactivity broken by short bursts of murderous energy. Ferocious though they may be, bugbears aren't built for extended periods of exertion.

GANG MENTALITY

Since bugbears aren't a particularly fecund race, their overall population is small and spread over a wide area. Bugbears live in family groups that operate much like gangs. The individuals in a group typically number fewer than a dozen, consisting of siblings and their mates as well as a handful of offspring and an elder or two. A gang lives in and around a small enclosure, often a natural cave or an old bear den, and it might have supplementary dens elsewhere in its territory that it uses temporarily when it goes on long forays for food.

In good times, a bugbear gang is tight-knit, and its members cooperate well when hunting or bullying other creatures. But when the fortunes of a gang turn sour, the individuals become selfish, and might sabotage one another to remove opposition or exile weaker or unpopular members to keep the rest of the gang strong. Fortunately for the race as a whole, even young and elderly bugbears have the ability to survive alone in the wild, and the cast-off members of a gang might eventually catch on with a different group.

Left to their own devices, bugbears have little more impact on the world than wolf packs. They subsist by crafting simple tools and hunting and gathering food, and gangs sometimes come together peacefully to exchange members and goods between them.

MALEVOLENT WORSHIP OF MALIGN GODS

Bugbears worship two deities who are brothers, Hruggek and Grankhul. Hruggek is the fearsome elder sibling, possessed of legendary might and prowess in battle. Bugbears believe their strength and bravery come from him. Cunning Grankhul is the younger one, and in the stories bugbears tell, he gifted them with stealth but in return he sapped their vigor, so that bugbears sleep in his stead while he remains eternally alert and awake.

According to bugbear legends, Hruggek and Grankhul often fight alongside each other, preying upon all they encounter as is their right as superior warriors. Hruggek takes the heads of those he kills and puts them on spikes in his den, where they utter pleas for mercy and sing paeans to his might. Grankhul watches over Hruggek when he sleeps, but if he must be elsewhere, he whispers commands to the severed heads to wake Hruggek if any danger threatens him.

Bugbears admire the qualities of both brothers. Because of Hruggek, they consider bravery and physical superiority to be their natural state. Thanks to Grankhul, they can use their size and strength to work as stealthy assassins rather than blundering around like ogres.

Bullying, murder, and engaging in battle are all holy acts for bugbears. Garroting an unsuspecting creature and defeating foes in open battle are seen as acts of worship, in the same way that dwarves consider metalsmithing to be sacred to Moradin.

The bugbears recognize two other gods, both of which they disdain and fear: Maglubiyet and Skiggaret.

Maglubiyet, the leader of the goblinoid pantheon, forced both brothers to submit to his rule, but instead of killing them, he showed mercy and even honored them in a way by setting them free—under his control—so that bugbears could continue to employ their talents against his enemies. Bugbears understand that by venerating Hruggek and Grankhul, they also give tribute to Maglubiyet, even though they don't openly pay homage to their overlord. When bugbears are called to join a host, bugbears believe Maglubiyet has again corralled the brothers into a divine battle, and they honor their gods by following suit.

Skiggaret is the bugbear version of the bogeyman, as hateful and terrifying to them as bugbears are in the eyes of many other races. His name is rarely spoken, and never above a whisper. Skiggaret's influence manifests at times when bugbears are forced to act in a cowardly fashion; a bugbear that knows or feels itself to be in mortal danger is affected by a form of madness and will do anything, including trying to flee, in order to stay alive. Bugbears believe that this feeling of fear comes from being possessed by Skiggaret, and they don't relish experiencing it. After the madness has passed, bugbears don't dwell on things that were done in the presence of Skiggaret. Talking about such acts might call him back.

BLESSINGS OF THE BUGBEAR GODS

Bugbears have no use for priests or shamans. No one needs to tell them what their gods want. If the brother gods are angry with them, they let the bugbears know with bolts of lightning (Hruggek) or by striking them blind or dead (Grankhul). Bugbears worship their gods simply by preying on other creatures, using no other sort of ceremony to show obeisance—with one exception.

In an act of worship that also sometimes attracts favorable attention from their gods, bugbears sever the heads of defeated foes, cut away or stitch open the eyelids, and leave the mouths hanging open. The heads are then placed on spikes or hung from cords around a bugbear den. The heads themselves are trophies that honor Hruggek, and their ever-staring eyes are an homage to sleepless Grankhul.

The heads of leaders and mighty opponents are particularly sacred, and offering up such a trophy can provide a bugbear gang with a special boon. A gang that gains the favor of Hruggek and Grankhul in this way might find that the head will emit a shout when an enemy gets too close (in the fashion of an *alarm* spell). Sometimes the heads of people who have information the bugbears need speak their secrets amid blubbered pleas for mercy (as with the *speak with dead* spell).

> ONE USEFUL TRICK: IF YE FACE BUGBEARS WHO HAVE SEVERED HEADS ON SPIKES AS TROPHIES, CAST A SPELL TO MAKE THE HEADS SPEAK. AFTER THAT, YE CAN COZEN THE BUGBEARS INTO DOING ALMOST ANYTHING.
>
> — ELMINSTER

HOBGOBLINS

War is the lifeblood of hobgoblins. Its glories are the dreams that inspire them. Its horrors don't feature in their nightmares. Cowardice is more terrible to hobgoblins than dying, for they carry their living acts into the afterlife. A hero in death becomes a hero eternal.

Young hobgoblins start soldiering when they can walk and heed the mustering call as soon as they can wield their weapons capably. Every legion in the hobgoblins' entire society forever stands prepared for war.

BRUTAL CIVILITY

Hobgoblins hold themselves to high standards of military honor. The race has a long history of shared traditions, recorded and retold to keep the knowledge fresh for new generations. When hobgoblins aren't waging war, they farm, they build, and they practice both martial and arcane arts.

These trappings of civil society do little to conceal an underlying brutality that hobgoblins practice on each other and perfect upon other races. Punishment for infractions of hobgoblin law are swift and merciless. Beauty is something hobgoblins associate only with images of conflict and warfare.

The iron grip their philosophy holds on their hearts blinds hobgoblins to the accomplishments of other peoples. Hobgoblins have little appreciation or patience for

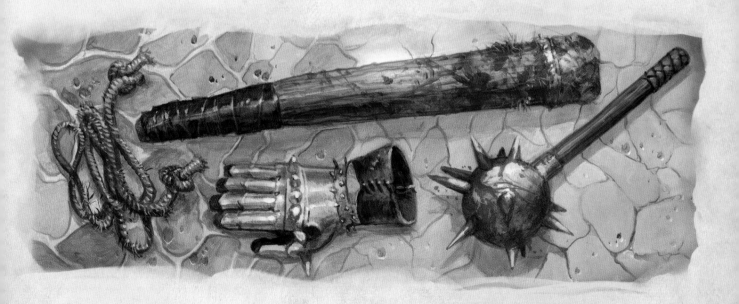

art. They leave little space for joy or leisure in their lives, and thus have no reserves of faith to call upon when in dire straits.

IMPLACABLE GODS

Hobgoblins revere two gods unique to their race, the only survivors of a pantheon that was decimated by Maglubiyet so long ago that hobgoblins don't remember the names of the fallen. Nomog-Geaya is the greater of the two and the more frequently honored. He is seen as a stoic, cold-blooded, and tyrannical leader, and hobgoblins believe he expects the same behavior from them. Bargrivyek is a god of duty, unity, and discipline, and he is thought to be pleased by displays of those principles.

In the stories that hobgoblins tell one another, Bargrivyek serves as Nomog-Geaya's second in command. Nomog-Geaya would prefer the position were filled by someone more like himself, but Bargrivyek was all he was left with after Maglubiyet's conquest. Although both deities are ultimately beholden to Maglubiyet, the greater god allows them to retain a measure of their influence over the hobgoblins because their philosophies are in line with his own.

Hobgoblins don't build temples to their gods, lest they displease Maglubiyet, but the few priests among them do tend small shrines and interpret the body of legends about their gods. Nomog-Geaya's priests always wield his favored weapons, a longsword and a handaxe. They are responsible for martial training as well as instruction in strategy and battlefield tactics. Bargrivyek's priests wield his symbol, a flail with a head dipped in white paint. They work as a police force in hobgoblin society, making judgments about honor, mediating disputes, and otherwise enforcing discipline.

RANK, STATUS, AND TITLE

As in any strict military hierarchy, every hobgoblin in a legion has a rank, from the warlord down through a cadre of officers to the soldiers that make up most of its number. These ranks, using the titles most often applied to them, are as follows:

1st rank: Warlord	5th rank: Spear
2nd rank: General	6th rank: Fist
3rd rank: Captain	7th rank: Soldier
4th rank: Fatal Axe	

A legion is organized into units called banners, each one made up of a group of interrelated families. Members of a banner live, work, and fight together, and each banner has a separate status within the legion that is reflected in the power of its officers. For instance, the captains of the highest-ranking banners can expect their orders to be followed by the captains of any banners of lower rank.

Rank and responsibility aren't necessarily commensurate from one legion to another or even between banners in the same legion. A phalanx of foot soldiers led by a captain in one legion might be two hundred strong, while in another such a force numbers just twenty. One banner might have four warriors mounted on worgs led by a fist, while a fist in another banner of the same legion might lead ten mounted warriors. If any rank

doesn't serve a purpose in the legion, the warlord eliminates it from the hierarchy to maximize efficiency.

HONOR BOUND, BY GLORY CROWNED

Advancement in rank comes as a result of attaining glory, but for the achievement to mean anything, a hobgoblin must abide by the race's code of honor in doing so.

Glory can be earned by discovery of great resources (such as finding a new vein of iron or a powerful magic item), by fine performances (writing and performing a great ballad about the legion), by designing and constructing a great defense or monument, and through other means. But the greatest respect is reserved for those who earn their glory in battle. In theory, the fortunes of war can elevate the lowest-ranking banner in a legion to the highest status. In practice, warlords are careful to position themselves and their banners to claim the greatest victories in any conflict, and they portion out opportunities and responsibilities to other banners as politics dictate.

Each hobgoblin legion has a distinct code of honor and law, but all follow a few general precepts that are at the heart of the hobgoblin honor system.

Follow Orders. Carrying out orders without question is critical on the battlefield, and hobgoblins follow this dictum in peaceful times as well in order to maintain stability in their society. Hobgoblins don't shrink from following orders that they know will result in death if the act will bring glory to the banner or the legion.

Honor the Gods. Hobgoblins give regular recognition to the deities left to them after Maglubiyet's conquest. Idols of Nomog-Geaya, as well as standards and flags with his image or symbol, receive a bow or salute at all times except emergencies. Bargrivyek's peacemakers receive due deference regardless of rank or banner status. Of course, Maglubiyet's call to conquest is always answered.

Suffer nor Give Insult. As befits their warlike nature, hobgoblins believe that any insult demands a response. Suitably (and somewhat ironically), the outward politeness and civility that they demonstrate among each other enables them to avoid conflicts in daily life. This same form of "courtesy" is often extended to other races the hobgoblins have dealings with, much to the outsiders' surprise. When such respect isn't reciprocated, though, relations can swiftly deteriorate.

Reward Glorious Action. Hobgoblins never deny advancement in status to a banner that has earned it, nor do they withhold higher rank from a deserving individual. If a banner attains great glory in battle but is nearly destroyed, the handful of members who remain are welcomed into another banner, taking their banner's name and colors along with them, and assuming places of leadership in the group.

Uphold the Legion. Hobgoblins care more for the survival of their legion than they do for others of their own kind. Two legions might battle over territory, resources, or power, or out of simple pride. Such a feud can continue over generations in an ongoing cycle of retribution. Each legion has a list of grievances against any others it knows about, and any legions meeting for the first time view each other with immediate hostility. Only a truly great warlord can force legions to work together as an army if Maglubiyet has not called forth a host.

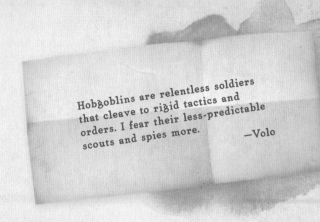

Hobgoblins are relentless soldiers that cleave to rigid tactics and orders. I fear their less-predictable scouts and spies more.

—Volo

IRON SHADOWS

A few hobgoblins have mastered a system of unarmed combat called the Path of the Iron Shadow. Its practitioners are known as Iron Shadows. They serve as a secret police force and a spy network in hobgoblin society. Statistics for a typical hobgoblin Iron Shadow can be found in chapter 3.

The Iron Shadows recruit from all ranks of hobgoblin society. They answer only to the priests of Maglubiyet, and use their talents for stealth, disguise, and unarmed combat to squash potential insurrections and treachery before an uprising can flourish.

These hobgoblins have the ability to command shadow magic to conceal their true nature, create distracting illusions, and walk from one shadow to the next.

When they operate in the open, they wear masks that resemble the leering faces of devils. As befits their role in society, they receive proper deference from all other hobgoblins that cross their path.

ACADEMY OF DEVASTATION

Hobgoblins know the value of arcane magic in warfare. Where other cultures treat magic as an individual pursuit, a calling that only a select few can even attempt, hobgoblins practice mass indoctrination and testing to identify every potential caster in their ranks.

The Academy of Devastation is a hobgoblin institution made up of spellcasters. Members are sent abroad to test young hobgoblins. Those who show an aptitude for magic are enrolled in the academy, brought to a hidden school, and subjected to a rigorous regimen of drills, exercises, and study. In the academy's view, every young student is a potential new devastator, destined to be forged into a weapon of war.

Hobgoblin devastators have little knowledge of or use for spells that have no use on the battlefield. They are taught potent, destructive spells and also learn the fundamentals of evocation magic. The death and destruction they bring about is worthy of as many accolades as the ruin wrought by traditional warriors. Luckily for their enemies, devastators seldom employ sophisticated tactics, functioning essentially as a mobile artillery battery. They can bring tremendous force to bear, but rarely display the versatility and inventiveness of spellcasting elves and humans. A few do become accomplished tacticians in their own right, and it isn't uncommon for such an individual to serve as the warlord of a legion.

Statistics for a typical hobgoblin devastator can be found in chapter 3.

HOBGOBLIN LAIRS

When hobgoblins aren't on the move, they have a stable lifestyle and society wherein they can raise new generations, train them, and prepare for future battles. If few enemies exist nearby and the hobgoblins in a legion have room to spread out, the members of each banner might live in a separate location, effectively its own settlement, with worg riders and messenger ravens passing communications between the sites.

In lands dominated by other humanoids, hobgoblins will settle for taking up residence in an old dungeon or ruin where they can hide their numbers and keep their presence secret. Such an arrangement isn't desirable, because space is usually at a premium.

Permanent Visitors. If a hobgoblin legion is looking for a place to set down roots, its first choice is an out-of-the-way area that has adequate resources or can be improved to suit the hobgoblins' needs. Land for farming or grazing is desirable, as is access to lumber, stone, or metal ore. If the hobgoblins find a place that fits the bill, they build non-portable facilities such as forges and sawmills, marking their intention to stay either until all the resources have been harvested or until Maglubiyet calls them off to war. If the hobgoblins are interested in doing business with the outside world, they might erect a trading post on the fringe of their territory where other people can come to exchange goods and coin.

Who Goes There? A hobgoblin lair resembles nothing so much as a military base. It is always well guarded, whether by lone sentries perched in trees or a stone tower with a full garrison of troops. As space permits, large areas are dedicated for use as training grounds, marshaling fields, target ranges, combat arenas, and similar facilities for the practice of warfare. Monuments, typically statues and pillars, are erected around these areas to remind the legion of past glories.

Every legion's headquarters includes a command center where the warlord meets with banner leaders and others of high rank. Inside the complex or somewhere near it is the Way to Glory—a road, river, tunnel, or valley on either side of which the honored dead are interred, each burial site complete with a description of the banner, rank, and glories of its occupant.

The quarters for troops are austere but sufficient, as are the necessary stables and dens to hold the legion's animals and beasts. Legions that have need of such amenities also set aside space for a library, which can

double as a school and training facility for spellcasters. If a hobgoblin lair has a prison, it's usually a small one—miscreants are incarcerated for only a short time before facing the hobgoblins' harsh justice.

MAGLUBIYET'S WILL BE DONE

When Maglubiyet conquered the goblins' gods, he taught the goblins to fear his cruelty. They bowed in sniveling obeisance to him and then turned their impotent wrath upon others, becoming petty tyrants. When Maglubiyet conquered the bugbears' gods, he taught the bugbears the practicality of cold brutality. When Maglubiyet conquered the hobgoblins' gods, he knew he had to take the hobgoblins firmly in hand. From him they learned discipline, and thus they became the natural leaders among all the goblinoids.

The goblinoids are bound together by Maglubiyet's subjugation of their individual deities. All types rightly fear Maglubiyet's wrath, but each carries out the Mighty One's divine will differently. Goblins typically flee from obvious threats, and hobgoblins often have to round up and threaten them before they can make use of them. Bugbears accept hobgoblin demands for assistance only grudgingly, and often they must be bribed with loot, spirits, battle gear, or the severed heads of enemy leaders—a particularly holy gift. Hobgoblins operating on their own will remain in their forts, content to deal with internal politics of rank and matters of defense, but when they encounter other types of goblinoids (or seek them out), it is viewed by all as a divine sign—Maglubiyet has called them together to do his bidding on a grand scale.

CALL TO WAR: FORMATION OF THE HOST

When the three types of goblinoids coalesce into a host, this new societal and military arrangement fundamentally changes how virtually every individual behaves.

Leaders in Word and Deed. Hobgoblins form the backbone of the new culture, taking up most leadership roles and acting as the strong center in any military action. Hobgoblins that are called to lead a host become fired with purpose, overtaken by a fanaticism that lends new urgency to their every action.

When multiple legions gather into a host, each of those legions has a separate status, just as each banner in a legion does. The legion of the host's warlord has the

---

NO OTHER GOD SHALL STAND

Goblinoids are indoctrinated from a young age to consider all gods but their own as lesser, false entities. Maglubiyet is the only true deity, they learn, and the world will be wracked by chaos and despair until he one day conquers all pantheons. Goblinoids harbor a special hatred for clerics of enemy deities, focusing on them in battle and desecrating their temples whenever they have the chance. Whether a deity is good, evil, or neutral is immaterial. All gods other than Maglubiyet and his servants are false and must be destroyed.

highest status, and warlords of lower status are demoted to the title of general. A member of the lowest-ranked banner in the warlord's legion has a higher status than those of other legions who share the same rank, but a general at the head of another legion still outranks everyone in the warlord's legion except for the warlord.

Hobgoblins in a legion set aside their animosity for other legions when a host forms. The warlords of rival legions don't seek to depose the leader of the host unless the fortunes of war create the opportunity. Each legion records all the insults directed toward it while a member of a host, and when the host disbands, those grudges again come to the forefront.

Stealthy Shock Troops. Bugbears that are subsumed into a host function as a special cadre of spies, assassins, and bodyguards, answering to the senior leadership of the host rather than to others of their own kind.

On occasion, their hobgoblin leaders will see fit to equip the bugbear force with improved equipment, such as metal-tipped javelins in place of stone-tipped ones, or chain shirts instead of the usual hide armor. Bugbears are never outfitted with ranged weapons (which they refuse to use) or with heavy armor (which compromises their stealthiness).

If some bugbears demonstrate a particular talent for some facet of combat or subterfuge, the hobgoblins might separate them into squads that employ those skills to best effect (see the "Bugbear Special Forces" sidebar).

Reluctant Little Tyrants. One of the first steps hobgoblins take when a tribe of goblins joins the host is to train the gatherers and the pariahs as soldiers, effectively elevating those goblins' status to that of hunters and reducing the number of castes in the host to two. Leaders and religious figures of the tribe still maintain some of their authority, but the lowliest hobgoblin or bugbear can give an order to a goblin chief, and that chief must leap to obey or, as is often the case, immediately yell orders for other goblins to do it.

Goblins that are conscripted into a host resign themselves to their fate—which could well be to have their souls claimed by Maglubiyet for eternal war in Acheron. Thus reconciled, they become humorless and show no pity toward whatever meager victims fall under their dominion, usually enslaved laborers or monsters that are pressed into service as battle beasts. When the need arises, they also work as scouts, sappers during sieges, and skirmishers on the battlefront.

Auxiliary Units. A host rarely consists of nothing but goblinoids, especially if it has been on the move for a while. In addition to wolf and worg mounts and flocks of squawking ravens, a host might attract or press into service many kinds of creatures. Some possibilities:

- A low, two-wheeled pushcart loaded with small wooden cages containing cockatrices.
- A hydra with goblins riding on each head that direct the beast by controlling the view of its blinkered eyes.
- Former slaves, often soldiers who once fought against the host, who now fight alongside the host to gain better treatment and protect loved ones held captive.

- A carrion crawler ridden by several goblins in a row and directed by a lead goblin using a long pole to suspend a lantern just out of reach of its tentacles.

THE HOST ON THE MARCH

A goblinoid host that is prepared for war doesn't wait for the enemy to approach its doorstep. In pursuit of ever greater glory for Maglubiyet, the host's leaders keep the army on the move, occasionally breaking off small garrisons (often of one type of goblinoid) to guard territory that needs to be held.

A host usually marches at night, with outriders, who carry messenger ravens, traveling ahead, behind, and on both sides of the main group. The ravens can distinguish between individuals from a great height and navigate over long distances. Thus, a raven can fly back to the main body when it is released by someone remote from the group, and it can be sent out again to look for the individual that released it in order to deliver a response.

Most of the army travels on foot, and wolf-riding goblins and worg-riding hobgoblins also make up a significant portion of the force. Hobgoblins might ride horses or other mounts they could obtain, such as hippogriffs, axe beaks, or giant vultures. Bugbears don't ride mounts, but they aren't above hitching a ride in the howdah of an enormous battle beast such as an elephant or a hydra.

BUGBEAR SPECIAL FORCES

Under any circumstances, bugbears are valued members of a goblinoid host. If some of them are specialized (or can be trained) in different aspects of warfare, their value increases, especially when they work in concert.

Thugs. Bugbears that serve as thugs have more of Hruggek than Grankhul in them. They leap in among massed foes and make wide, whirling swings with their weapons to create openings in enemy formations.

Bulwarks. The wild attack of a group of thugs is often followed by the charge of one or more bulwarks. A bugbear bulwark carries a spiked shield into battle that it uses like a plow, bashing aside whatever it encounters.

Murderers. Bugbears that are gifted in stealth are sent out to kill enemy sentries and thus clear the way for others to penetrate the foe's defenses. Murderers carry many javelins with them, which they throw from hiding and wield in melee, and they also carry garrotes to cut off sounds of screaming.

While a host pursues conquest, it is taboo for its members to copulate. Such proclivities must be suppressed so that all effort is focused on the task at hand. Breach of the taboo can bring summary execution, so it is rare for offspring to be born among the host even when it successfully campaigns for years.

The taboo doesn't extend to female goblinoids that come into the host already pregnant and give birth while on campaign. Such offspring are called Warborn, a title they keep for life. The Warborn are thought to be blessed by Maglubiyet, and as a result these young goblinoids are carried into battle like a standard and used to rally troops.

If the host has slaves, they pull wagons or sledges in the center of the army, dragging along the equipment of war while surrounded by its users. If slaves have yet to be acquired, goblins and beasts of burden perform this function.

CONQUEST AND OCCUPATION

Warfare in the name of Maglubiyet isn't conducted like the raiding of orcs or the wanton slaughter of gnolls. It is instead a practice of claiming territory and subjugating people. Those who surrender to the host with little or no resistance get fair and honest treatment. If they offer proper tribute, they can even look forward to avoiding goblin whips and chains. Warriors among the conquered people might be accepted as auxiliary units in the host, if they prove to be capable and trustworthy.

Typically, a goblinoid host seeks to retain enough of the population in a conquered settlement for the community to continue to produce goods and services. The labor force likely includes more youngsters and elderly than before the goblinoids' conquest, with a corresponding drop-off in production. In any case, a group of conquered people serves the host best when it continues to produce resources that the goblinoids can use. Only when a settlement offers stiff resistance or has no lasting value to the host do the goblinoids resort to slaughter and slavery to empty it of enemies.

A host that gains many victories might end up claiming vast amounts of territory and eventually become a true nation. Such an empire might last for generations if the military can continue achieving new conquests or at least claim victories when the goblinoids defend territory they previously took over. If triumphs of some sort don't keep coming, the bonds of allegiance among the goblinoids eventually fray. Legions of hobgoblins begin infighting, and goblins shirk their duties while the hobgoblins are distracted. Then, seeing the disarray of the host as a sign that Maglubiyet is no longer looking, the bugbears turn on their hobgoblin leaders, take a few of their heads as fresh trophies, and leave.

LIFE IN A SLAVE STATE

When a host conquers a settlement or a community, the surviving victims quickly learn to adapt to life under goblinoid rule. The hobgoblins bring their own legal code down upon the vassals, and it is liable to be harsher than that to which the inhabitants were accustomed. Yet the host will also respect traditions of law and custom among those they conquer, as an aid to maintaining or-

The war horns of the host signal that every goblinoid has the chance to prove his or her worth to Maglubiyet and join his Army of Immortals in Acheron, the plane of eternal battle. There Maglubiyet marshals his host against slavering orc hordes in a bid to bring Gruumsh and the other orc gods to heel, a mythic contest that has pitted the goblinoids and orcs of the world against one another since time immemorial.

der by pacifying the population. Some surviving civilian leaders are allowed to retain their positions, often gaining more privilege and power than they previously possessed by serving as agents of the goblinoids, helping to identify any who are disloyal to the host.

In matters of religion, there is little or no flexibility. The host eliminates any spiritual leaders or temple servants who offer any resistance. Clergy of gods that are deemed harmless, such as a deity of the harvest, can escape this fate. When the host encounters priests of deities of battle or conquest, they offer them a simple choice: Turn to the worship of Maglubiyet, or prove the superiority of your god in combat. Any such priest who remains faithful to some other god rarely lasts long, because the priest will face a succession of foes—as many as it takes for the priest to succumb and for others to see that resistance is pointless. Maglubiyet ultimately offers only two options: submit or die.

If the settlement has holy sites dedicated to conquered gods, these are converted into shrines to the Mighty One. All representations of the defeated gods are thrown down, ruined, or marred. Mosaics are broken apart. Stained glass is shattered. Flags and pennants are soaked in blood. Statues are put in chains. Altars become chopping blocks where Maglubiyet's bloody axe is used to decapitate all who refuse to bow to him.

GOBLINOID WAR CAMP

A goblinoid army doesn't stay on the move forever, but when they make camp, it isn't for rest and recreation. A goblinoid war camp is a place that is constantly ready for war, and the hobgoblins run it accordingly.

A war camp might be a permanent settlement that a hobgoblin legion uses as a garrison. The accompanying map depicts one such place, and it can also be used to represent a location constructed to serve as a staging area by a host that is actively campaigning.

The basic layout of a war camp is circular. To prepare the site, slaves, goblins, and any beasts fit for the purpose dig a ditch around the desired location, interrupted in places where wide paths provide access to the center of the enclosed area. Inside this ring of excavation are sections of a wooden palisade, each part capped with a gate and a tower on either end. These outer walls and gates aren't regularly manned or patrolled, because the occupants aren't concerned about being taken by surprise. If an enemy force does approach, though, these barriers do a good job of delaying any incursion until the goblinoids can rally their defenses.

Inside the surrounding bulwark, the goblinoids all have their separate quarters, organized according to their wonts. Typical of any camp are the wide paths that

GOBLINOID WAR·CAMP

KEY
- BUGBEAR DEN
- GATE TOWER
- GOBLIN HOVEL
- HOBGOBLIN BARRACKS
- SUPPLY WAGON

☐ = 5 FEET

DITCH

PIT

COMMAND CENTER

ANIMAL PEN

BLANDO

N

crisscross it, running from each gate through the center of the camp and out the other side. This configuration enables all the goblinoids to swiftly rally and exit the camp en masse to meet an approaching threat.

COMMAND CENTER

The camp's warlord resides in the command center, which is a large wooden building in the middle of camp. Here the warlord meets with advisors and makes plans for future conquest. Most of the time, a command center also holds elite bugbear bodyguards that protect the warlord and a goblin jester that serves as insurance against the appearance of a nilbog (see the "Nilbogs: Pranksters with Power" sidebar).

In a camp that doesn't have separate facilities for a library and a rookery, the command center subsumes those functions. Library records are stored in a chamber adjacent to where the war council meets, and posts for ravens are set all around the exterior of the building.

GOBLINOID QUARTERS

Each type of goblinoid has its own accommodations within the war camp.

Bugbear Dens. After the hobgoblins stake out their territory, bugbear gangs dig their dens wherever else they wish, sometimes building them in the shadow of the outer wall but most often scattering them about, seemingly at random. A den typically consists of a hole and a crawlspace big enough for a few bugbears.

Goblin Hovels. The camp's goblins settle wherever their hobgoblin commanders tell them to. Their quarters usually surround the areas where slaves and beasts. The typical goblin hovel is a round tent where related goblins sleep. In a permanent camp, these hovels often take the form of wattle-and-daub huts.

Hobgoblin Barracks. Not surprisingly, hobgoblins have the most spacious and well-appointed quarters in a war camp. Each of the banners in a legion has its own group of lodges in one of the quadrants of the interior, each one facing the pathway that runs past its front door.

LIBRARY

Hobgoblins know the value of improving one's base of knowledge, and so they value any documentation about the world around them—maps, accounting records, battle reports, and other important facts. This knowledge is sorted by a legion's librarian and stored in the camp's library. The library serves as a hub for communication and strategy, and it is never located far from the group's leaders. In the field, the army's library is carried in a fortified and fire-protected wagon, surrounded by battle-hardened caretakers (often devastators or Iron Shadows) willing to give their lives to protect it.

PENS AND PITS

Goblins are responsible for tending to the camp's slaves, battle beasts, and beasts of burden. These are hobbled, chained to posts, or placed in pens, cages, or pits as needed. Most of these containment sites are surrounded by goblin hovels, and those that aren't are nearby, so that the goblins can keep track of their charges.

The hags put a spell on me, three times three, and made me their slave for a thousand days. I was a young fool, 'tis true, but those were dark days.

— Elminster

Rookery

Hobgoblins keep flocks of ravens that serve them as messengers and spies. A huge, tree-like conglomeration of metal and wood serves the ravens as a roosting and nesting place. If a camp doesn't use one of these freestanding structures, its ravens are accommodated by perches and outcrops built on the outside of the command center. In the field, a wagon serves as a makeshift rookery.

Supply Wagons

Members of the army are expected to maintain their own battle gear, but ammunition and replacement gear are kept on hand, as well as other nonperishable supplies. Rather than being contained in a building, these items are on wagons distributed throughout the camp in such a way that all the vehicles are accessible and ready to be moved if the rallying horn is blown.

Every wagon is under watch by at least two guards, which are responsible for recording "withdrawals" and reporting on inventory to the camp's leaders.

The Block

Maglubiyet's holy symbol is a headsman's axe, and the block is where it is blessed by feeding it the lifeblood of conquered foes and goblinoids that neglect their duties. In a temporary camp, the block might be a simple slab of wood or stone laid on a hastily heaped-up pile of dirt. In a permanent garrison, the block is often attached to the command center and placed on a consecrated platform.

Near the block stands a post or a rack with various weapons that represent the symbols of the goblinoid gods, each placed in accordance with the god's rank. Maglubiyet's headsman's axe is always highest. Then comes Nomog-Geaya's sword and handaxe, Bargrivyek's white-tipped flail, and at the bottom, often touching the ground, the red-and-yellow whip of Khurgorbaeyag. Notably absent from this grouping are the symbols of the bugbear gods. Instead, severed heads hang in bunches around the block or are impaled upon spikes, their eyelids removed and mouths open. These honor the bugbears' deities, Hruggek and Grankhul, and their separate but subordinate positions in Maglubiyet's rule.

Hags: Dark Sisterhood

Hags are crones who represent corruption of ideals and goals, and they delight in seeing the innocent and good brought low. They are inhuman monsters, their forms twisted by evil. Shapechangers and blasphemers, they ally with other hags to form magical covens with extra powers. They collect and remember secret knowledge that is better lost and forgotten. Desperate mortals come to them looking for advice, only to have their requests fulfilled in ways that bring great suffering to themselves and their loved ones.

Ugly, Unpredictable, and Old

Hags are mysterious, unfathomable, and dangerous, especially from the viewpoint of mortals. One day a hag might be stealing and eating children that wander into the woods, on another day she might be making lewd jokes to adventurers asking her for advice, and the next she might be uprooting saplings to make a fence around her home for impaling intruders. It is nearly impossible to predict how a hag will act from day to day, sometimes moment to moment, which is why folk with any wisdom at all give hags a wide berth.

Hags perceive ugliness as beauty, and vice versa. They revel in having a hideous appearance and sometimes go out of their way "improve" upon it by picking at sores, wearing skins and bones as decoration, and rubbing refuse and dirt into their hair and clothing.

Because both the Seelie Court and the Unseelie Court appreciate and revere true beauty among the fey, hags are almost never found in either place. The Summer Queen and the Queen of Air and Darkness recognize that hags have valuable knowledge and impressive magic, but they can't abide the stain on the beauty of their surroundings, so most hags are excluded from both courts. The rare few accepted as courtiers are either so influential that their entry can't be refused, or young and humble enough to be willing to use magic to put on a prettier appearance. Other hags aren't upset by their exclusion; they like to be left alone to their own schemes, not constrained by a fey queen's whims, and to be able to talk out of both sides of their mouths.

Hags are virtually immortal, with a life span greater than that of even dragons and elves. The oldest, wisest, and most powerful hags are called "grandmothers" by other hags. Some grandmothers are nearly as powerful as some of the archfey.

Hags of lower but still respectable status are called "aunties." An auntie gains her status from being very old, a member of a powerful coven, directly serving a grandmother, or having many offspring (whether adopted or birthed).

Master Manipulators

Hags delight in corrupting others. They do so not by imposing their will or being outwardly violent, but by making sinister bargains with those who seek their aid. This desire to orchestrate the downfall of others is why so many hags make their homes near humanoid settlements, which gives them a ready supply of creatures to tantalize and torment.

Folk with nowhere else to turn are some of a hag's best customers. A farmer with a philandering spouse might seek out the local hag for a potion to make the spouse faithful again. The mayor with a demented father might ask the hag for something that makes him lucid again. A merchant whose child is deathly ill might go to the hag for a cure. The common element in these situations is that the mortals approach the hag for help; despite knowing that she is evil and dangerous, they are desperate enough to risk making a bargain with her, or foolish enough to think they can persuade her to be helpful without getting something in return.

Hags make bargains differently from how devils operate. A devil might approach a mortal to make a deal because it wants the individual to become tainted with evil, so that when the victim dies its soul goes to the Nine Hells. Hags are usually content to wait and conduct their own business, allowing mortals to come to them when the perceived need is great enough. Instead of being interested in a mortal's soul, a hag wants to bring the mortal low during its life as compensation for fulfilling her end of the bargain. Devils barter with the soul as the commodity; hags barter because they enjoy making people miserable. Night hags, as fey turned fiends, use aspects of both methods—corrupting a mortal's dreams until the creature commits enough evil acts that she can claim its soul.

As much as she enjoys offering and enforcing her bargains, a hag rarely goes out looking for people to make deals with because she knows that someone coming to her puts her in a position of power. The visitor likely had to approach the hag in secret for fear of causing an uproar in town, and is probably eager to return home before being missed, which adds time pressure to the process and tips the balance more in the hag's favor. All these factors contribute to the hag's being able to set her terms for the bargain, presenting an offer that appears reasonable, and perhaps seems to have a tempting loophole or two that the mortal could exploit.

Hags understand mortal desires and vices, and know how to manipulate people by preying on those qualities. A hag's bargain might bring success and prosperity for a time, but eventually have a drawback or side effect that makes the mortal resent the agreement and seek to get out of it. The philandering spouse now happy to stay home might grow slothful, the mayor's father might turn violent after regaining his senses, and the merchant's child might relapse if not treated again every few months.

Even when a bargain turns sour for a mortal and other people in town hear about or see the person's misfortune, the hag will eventually attract new customers. Other people will come to believe that they can outsmart the hag, or that their need is simple and can't be perverted, or that the earlier victims got too greedy when they were proposing a deal. Even if only one or two people make deals with a hag every year, over time many unfortunates can come under her sway—and she remembers the exact terms of every one of those bargains.

MAKING A DEAL OUT OF DESIRE

Although it could be argued that there's no good time to make a bargain with a hag, mortals are more likely to get away in good shape if they offer up something a hag needs or wants. In such a case, the hag might even start the bidding.

A hag that faces a serious threat from enemies will not hesitate to use promises or bribes to defuse the situation. For instance, most treasures in a hag's lair are useless without her knowledge of how to identify and handle them, so she might offer to provide such information in return for her life. If an item later backfires on the one who uses it, or turns out to be cursed in some way, that's just another lesson in why never to never threaten or trust a hag.

Hags are curious about other creatures of power. They enjoy receiving news and gossip about other hags and influential creatures such as dragons, demons, genies, and certain mortals. Offering a hag accurate information of this sort as part of a bargain earns a small measure of her respect, and might make her more receptive to the idea of a "fair" deal.

When a hag bargains with other creatures of the Feywild, rather than mortals, she approaches the situation with a more respectful attitude. She realizes that the creatures of her native realm are more powerful than common humanoids and therefore more dangerous when disappointed or angered by a deal gone bad. Fey are also long-lived and thus have more time to retaliate against the hag, whereas most humanoids die within a few short decades. These considerations don't mean that hags are automatically pleasant in dealings with other fey, just that they aren't as blatant or demanding in the bargains they offer; hags know exactly how much they can get away with, and they like pushing the limits of what others will tolerate.

BARGAINER BEWARE

When a hag is generous with her help or requires only a simple task as payment, that's no guarantee that the deal will turn out as expected for both parties. By offering a proposal that seems, or actually is, fair, chances are that the hag is pursuing a hidden agenda. She still wants to set events into motion that benefit her or bring about the downfall of another, but she does so in an indirect way that has no obvious connection to her. A bargain as simple as a villager agreeing to deliver a mysterious letter at a crossroads at noon on a certain day could be the key to ruining the mortal's life. The hag's reasons might not become apparent for years or even decades, or won't be meaningful except under specific circumstances, such as an auspicious birth or a climactic encounter with a dangerous villain. Even when she's offering a deal that seems to have no downside, a hag is always secretive about her motivations, the reasons for the payments she requires, or how these things benefit her.

A hag that spends a long time in close proximity to a human settlement often depletes the community of good-hearted folk as they succumb to her evil and selfish plans. The mood of the town becomes unwelcoming, grim, moody, or outright hostile toward newcomers and travelers. Even after a hag has done her worst in such a place, she maintains leverage over her victims by holding out the prospect that someday she will undo the curses that she has lain on them. For that reason, the local leaders won't allow any outsiders to act against her (which includes sabotaging adventurers who might decide to confront her).

ROLEPLAYING A HAG

Even when a hag acts indifferently or friendly toward adventurers, inside she is still a twisted fey creature, and she doesn't give two coppers about what anyone else thinks or wants. She might casually comment about how easily a visitor would fit in her cauldron or make a blunt sexual comment about a guest. When a mortal visits a hag, the experience should be nerve-wracking, uncomfortable, and risky; at any point the hag might lose her temper and decide to pull out someone's fingernails with her iron teeth.

Hags look upon younger creatures from the perspective of a cantankerous grandparent who no longer cares what anyone thinks—set in her ways, free to speak her mind, and not afraid to bring down punishment if pushed too far. Hags enjoy meddling with other people's lives, like busybodies with cruel intentions. Any time a hag agrees to help someone, the bargain includes a price to be paid, plus a hidden plan by which she sets the mortal up to fail, or a way that she gains leverage (whether over the deal-maker or someone else).

When a hag is presented with an unusual spell, a rare magic item, or a person who has a strange magical gift, she will sniff it, shake it, listen to it, taste it, murmur odd statements to herself, and mentally place a value on the merchandise. Hags aren't subtle about showing their intent at such times, and one might snatch away the offering so she can examine it more closely, even if this makes it obvious she is interested. If she doesn't have anything else like it, or can think of a use for it, or if having it means a rival can't get her hands on it, she'll value the offering highly. A visitor who offers a desirable item as a bribe or a gift is more likely to get a fair deal from the hag, or at least likely to suffer less when the true price of the deal is revealed.

If a hag's life is threatened, she will pretend to be weak and helpless if she thinks it will spare her life or buy her time to retaliate or escape. She'll use dangerous treasures as bribes, not telling about their curses or side effects. She will lie and deceive and try to turn her enemies against each other, playing up their guilt and fear and jealousy to tear them apart from the inside. She is older, smarter, and more shrewd than any mortal who dares to threaten her.

Hags prefer to cajole and bargain rather than confront someone with actual violence; they reserve their aggressive outbursts for situations where they are overwhelmingly more powerful than their opponents (such as when attacking children) or have an unfair advantage (such as when their enemy is asleep). Although a hag can always resort to attacking with her claws, if it comes to that then something has gone very wrong with her plans.

Hag Personality Traits

d8	Personality Trait
1	I have made subtle insults into an art form.
2	I always act unpleasant so others never learn of my secret affections.
3	I enjoy wagers as parts of my bargains, which increase the risk and the stakes.
4	I laugh at my own jokes—the darker, the better.
5	I never volunteer information, and I respond only to questions.
6	I offer generous terms in my deals, but the cost for defaulting is exceedingly high.
7	I require all of my bargains to be put in writing and signed in the other party's blood.
8	I am very superstitious, and I see omens in every event and action around me.

Hag Ideals

d6	Ideal
1	**Change.** I will metamorphose into every kind of hag and live a century as each, becoming something even greater in the end. (Chaotic)
2	**Community.** Loneliness is the path to madness. That is why I have minions to keep me company. (Lawful)
3	**Greed.** I will acquire the rarest and most valuable holy treasures to keep them from being used for good. (Evil)
4	**Independence.** I neither require nor want a coven. I will not be someone's equal. (Neutral)
5	**Power.** I will become an auntie or a grandmother, even if I have to kill my own mother to do it. (Evil)
6	**Ugliness.** I want to be envied for my appearance and my cruel heart. (Evil)

Hag Bonds

d8	Bond
1	I hate a certain mortal family and steal one of their children each generation for my own purposes.
2	I am involved in a centuries-long feud with a rival of similar power and status.
3	My house holds everything that I hold dear. I can't abide visitors who threaten my hearth and home.
4	I owe a great favor to a hag grandmother.
5	I traded away something before I realized it was priceless, and now I want it back.
6	My daughter was taken from me, and I want to find her and train her.
7	My greatest rival and I know a secret word that will destroy both of us simultaneously.
8	The ones who looted and burned my home will pay for their offense.

Hag Flaws

d6	Flaw
1	I am too eager for gossip.
2	I can't resist flirting with a handsome man.
3	I have an allergy to a creature (such as cats or ravens) or a substance (such as apples or blood) that is important to my work.
4	I will not tell a lie, but I can still say nothing, nod suggestively, or bend the truth a little to suit my needs.
5	I am greatly weakened on the nights of the full moon.
6	I can't resist a clever riddle.

Hag Names

Hags have whimsical names, often with a dark twist. A hag gives her newborn daughter a name that the girl keeps during her childhood, but upon gaining her full hag powers the daughter chooses her own name, which might or might not relate to her birth name. Some hags use different names in different guises, but still prefer their original name as their favorite.

The Hag Names table allows you to generate a hag's name. You can also select from the table or use it as inspiration.

Hags always have a title followed by a first name, or a first name followed by a last name. You can randomly determine (equal chance of either) whether a hag has a title or a last name.

Hag Names

d12	Title	First Name	Last Name
1	Auntie	Agatha	Bonechewer
2	Black	Agnes	Frogwart
3	Cackling	Ethel	Greenteeth
4	Dismal	May	Gristlegums
5	Dread	Mathilda	Knucklebones
6	Driftwood	Morgan	Middenheap
7	Granny	Olga	Mudwallow
8	Old	Peggy	Pigtooth
9	Rickety	Polly	Titchwillow
10	Rotten	Sally	Toestealer
11	Turtleback	Ursula	Twigmouth
12	Wicked	Zilla	Wormwiggle

Weird Magic

Over the course of a seemingly endless lifetime, a hag typically discovers or creates several unusual ways to use magic. The weird magic that hags can call upon comes in a number of forms and with various means of activation. Even those who have read scholarly books about hag lore can't predict what a particular hag might have up her sleeve.

A grandmother or some other hag of great age and renown might know unique rituals that can temporarily or permanently alter or transform a creature, bring back the dead for a limited time, rewrite memories, or siphon emotions. At the other end of the spectrum, even a hag without lofty status is likely to have strange, single-use items that don't emulate common spells or even follow the normal rules of magic. For inspiration in devising the effects of such weird items, see "Charms" in chapter 7 of the *Dungeon Master's Guide*.

If you want a hag to use a weird object of this sort in a combat situation, provide her with an item that produces a CR-appropriate spell effect when the hag manipulates or activates it. The effect might be a benefit to herself or an attack against her enemies. For example, a green hag (CR 3) might smash an ornate hand mirror, producing a cloud of glass shards that damages creatures like *cloud of daggers* (a 2nd-level spell). She might instead uncork a bottle of wasps that surround her and stitch up her wounds with their stingers, healing her as *cure wounds* (cast as a 2nd-level spell). Or she could take a mummified toad from her pocket and throw it into her cauldron, which immediately spews out inky blackness equivalent to *darkness* (a 2nd-level spell).

A hag carefully shepherds her use of weird magic because the items in her repertoire are often impossible to duplicate or replace. To reflect this fact, a hag should be able to use weird magic only once or twice per encounter in her lair, or only once per encounter if she is elsewhere. A hag who is expecting a fight might be better prepared and able (or willing) to use weird magic one additional time per encounter.

If a hag is faced with mortal peril, all thoughts of conserving her resources vanish—she will use any weird magic at her disposal if it helps her stay alive. After all, a hag that's not dead has a virtually limitless lifetime to replace what was spent. No matter how hard it was to acquire that jar of death slugs, or that book on how to invoke the razor wind, or the runestone containing the three syllables for crystallizing blood, it is better to use such things than to risk death by not doing so.

Mounts and Vehicles

Many stories tell of hags using strange, enchanted creatures and objects for travel, and most of those stories are accurate.

Instead of the usual horse or pony, a hag might ride astride a giant pig, a goat, or a cow. It's not unknown for a hag to use a sentient creature as a mount, perhaps as the result of a bargain that creature struck with her. A hag that wants to humiliate a mortal hero might require that hero to serve as her mount for a year as part of fulfilling her bargain. The giant raven that carries a hag aloft could be in actuality one of the hag's victims transformed because that individual tried to go back on its deal with her.

Some hags prefer nonliving conveyances from time to time, and their imagination in this regard knows no bounds. A hag might happily animate and "spruce up" any sort of object she can tailor for the purpose, such as a clay statue, a huge woven basket, a cauldron, a butter churn, a giant bird's nest, a mortar and pestle, or a tombstone.

Usually only the hag that obtained or created them can use her mounts and vehicles. They obey only her commands, and their magic responds only to her will.

If a hag allows any other creature to use one of them as part of a bargain, she must be expecting an immense return on her investment.

Types of Hags

Each of the five common types of hags prefers a particular environment. It is possible to find a hag in unusual terrain, perhaps if she is traveling or is part of a coven along with two local hags. Grandmothers and aunties are more likely than other hags to take up permanent residence in unfriendly terrain, since their long-range plans sometimes require spending decades or years in a certain area before returning home.

Annis hags live in mountains or hills. The terrain is easy for them to navigate because they are the most physically capable hags. Even with her hunched posture, an annis hag is as tall as an ogre. Her skin is bruise-blue or black and her claws are like rusty blades. Annis hags love tormenting the weak and fearful, and seeing others feel fear. Statistics for the annis hag appear in chapter 3 of this book.

Bheur hags live in wintry lands, favoring snow-covered mountain peaks. They are gaunt, have blue-white skin, white hair, and are known for their gray wooden staffs that give them access to extraordinary ice magic. Bheur hags love seeing mortals freeze to death and have little if any room in their hearts for kin and community. Statistics for the bheur hag appear in chapter 3 of this book.

Green hags inhabit dismal forests, swamps, and moors. A green hag's body, whether broad, narrow, fat, or thin, is topped with a tangled mane of hair. A green hag thrives on creating despair and tragedy in the lives of her victims, using her skill with illusion magic to help in this goal. Destroying the hopes of others brings her unbridled joy.

Night hags have left behind the world of the fey to roam the Lower Planes. They have dark blue or purple-black skin with white or light-colored eyes and thin, curving horns. A night hag is as least as tall as a human, and most are stout or have a medium build rather than being thin or emaciated. Night hags enjoy corrupting the dreams of good people, compromising the ideals of their victims to get them to eventually perform evil acts. Then, when a victim dies, the hag can harvest its soul and bring it to Hades.

Sea hags live underwater or on the shore, favoring bleak and despoiled places. They have pale skin like that of a fish, covered in scales, with glassy dead eyes and hair like lank seaweed. Sea hags are emaciated, but one might be tall or short, frail or large-boned. A sea hag hates beauty in any form and seeks to attack, deface, or corrupt it so it has the opposite effect on its viewers. One is more likely to defile the inspiring statue in a town square, making it into a symbol of fear and sorrow, than to destroy it outright.

Solitary but Social

Hags are selfish by nature, and each one cherishes her independence—from the rest of the world as well as from other hags. At the same time, every hag recognizes

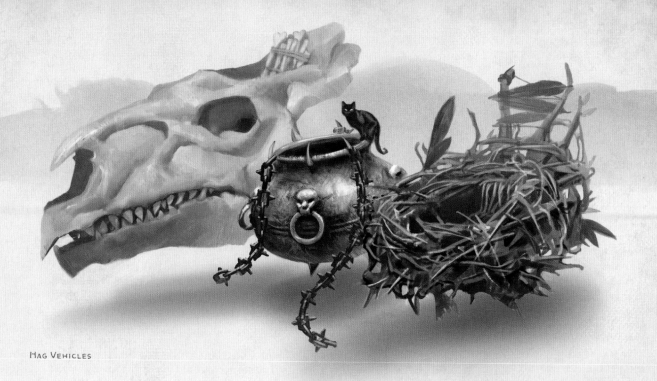

that she and her sisters are kindred souls, like the members of a dark sorority or sisterhood.

Even though hags don't like each other, they share knowledge and trade secrets, helping them to keep abreast of worldly events and possible dangers. Even a hag living in a remote, isolated location is aware of goings-on that involve her neighboring hags, whether through magical communication, personal visits, or mundane messengers such as birds. In most cases, these relationships with her sisters, though devoid of emotion, are the closest a hag comes to having friends.

When a hag is attacked or killed, other hags are likely to hear about it. If the victim was friendly with other hags, those responsible for her death might find themselves the target of retaliation. If the victim died while owing favors to another hag, that hag sees her killers as now responsible for the dead hag's debts. If the victim was unpopular or if other hags were indebted to her (and thus are happy to see her go), her killers might receive relatively cordial treatment from those other hags instead.

HAG METAMORPHOSIS

It's commonly believed that five kinds of hags exist in the world (and beyond it). What's not so widely known is that some hags can change from one kind to another during their lives.

A hag that lives long enough or has the necessary resources can alter her basic nature, leaving behind her old physiology and adopting that of a hag appropriate to the environment of her current home. She might accomplish this transformation through force of will over time, or faster with the help of a ritual or assistance from her coven. The reasons for making such a change are as varied as the personalities and goals of hags.

Every hag has a particular status relative to others of her kind and to hags of all sorts, based on age, abilities, influence, alliances, and experience, and is aware of her place (though not necessarily satisfied with it). The few grandmothers sit at the top of the hierarchy, a larger number of aunties are beneath that, and all other hags vie for prominence in a chaotic pecking order that no mortal can truly figure out. A hag that is known to associate with an auntie has a higher status than a similarly powerful hag without such a connection, and a young hag born of a grandmother begins her existence already benefiting from a greater measure of respect and status.

HAG COVENS

To a hag, the thought of sharing her home with other creatures—even other hags—is disgusting. She has nothing but dislike or disdain for anyone other than herself, and she loves being alone (except for the company of minions and other creatures under her sway). That's the ordinary state of affairs. But when a group of hags have a common goal or they seek greater power to combat a formidable threat, they suppress their basic nature and come together to do their work. The result is a coven.

Being part of a coven gives each individual hag more magic and spellcasting ability, and to her these benefits offset the inconvenience and bickering that goes with living and working with other hags.

If a member of a coven is killed and the surviving members intend to keep the group from dissolving, they immediately attempt to recruit a replacement. This process involves each prospective member committing cruel acts with the aim of impressing the remaining coven members. Adventurers who slay only one member of a coven might deal a blow to it in the short term, but later on the surrounding region is wracked with plagues, curses, and other disasters as the applicants attempt to outdo one another.

An unusually gifted mortal sorcerer, warlock, or wizard of a deeply evil nature might be invited to join a coven or allowed to compete for a vacancy. This arrangement is potentially a dangerous proposition for the mortal, but a pair of hags might agree to it if their needs are served. For instance, a human member of a coven makes an ideal spy and infiltrator in and around a humanoid settlement.

WELCOME TO THE FAMILY

Hags make more hags by snatching and devouring human infants, birthing daughters who turn into hags on entering the thirteenth year of their lives. Fortunately for humanity and the rest of the world, such an occurrence is rare.

Rarer still, but not unheard of, is for a hag to repeat this process twice or more in short succession, giving her multiple offspring of about the same age. She might do this to form a coven with two of her daughters, or to create a coven made up entirely of her offspring. Some hags cite ancient lore that suggests that if a hag consumes twins or triplets, her offspring might have additional, unusual abilities; similarly, devouring the seventh-born child of a seventh-born is said to be a way to pass on rare magic to the hag's daughter.

ALTERNATIVE COVEN SPELLS

Some covens gather for a specific purpose, such as to defeat a champion of good, to serve as oracles for the delivery of baleful prophecies, or to corrupt a pristine wilderness. In such a case, because the coven strives to bend its magic to a more directed purpose, the members have different spells available for use with their Shared Spellcasting trait, usually focusing on a theme related to

---

THE RULE OF THREE

They say that things come in threes. Good things. Bad things. Strange things. Hags and purveyors of witchcraft embrace the Rule of Three, as it is called: a coven has three members, they believe that good or evil magic returns upon its source threefold, and the casting of many spells requires the same words chanted three times.

Long ago, planar travelers came to recognize that many of the realms and layers of the multiverse are configured in multiples of three. It is possible that plane-traveling hags learned of this planar-based superstition and adapted it to their own uses, although some among the oldest hags claim to have invented the concept or at least named it.

---

that purpose. Three examples of themed hag coven spell lists are given below.

Death. For a coven whose members are obsessed with death and the ability to manipulate it, an appropriate spell list would be:

1st level (4 slots): *false life, inflict wounds*
2nd level (3 slots): *gentle repose, ray of enfeeblement*
3rd level (3 slots): *animate dead, revivify, speak with dead*
4th level (3 slots): *blight, death ward*
5th level (2 slots): *contagion, raise dead*
6th level (1 slot): *circle of death*

Nature. Hags might seek to exert control over their environment and the creatures in it by mastering the following group of spells:

1st level (4 slots): *entangle, speak with animals*
2nd level (3 slots): *flaming sphere, moonbeam, spike growth*
3rd level (3 slots): *call lightning, plant growth*
4th level (3 slots): *dominate beast, grasping vine*
5th level (2 slots): *insect plague, tree stride*
6th level (1 slot): *wall of thorns*

Prophecy. The power to affect the future or perceive things out of the norm could make these spells attractive to a coven:

1st level (4 slots): *bane, bless*
2nd level (3 slots): *augury, detect thoughts*
3rd level (3 slots): *clairvoyance, dispel magic, nondetection*
4th level (3 slots): *arcane eye, locate creature*
5th level (2 slots): *geas, legend lore*
6th level (1 slot): *true seeing*

HAG LAIRS

No matter what form it takes, a hag's home is a manifestation of her basic nature. It is ugly, eerie, or unnerving in some way, often incorporating some aspect of decay, such as a dead tree, a ruined tower, or a menacing cave entrance that resembles a skull.

Whether naturally or by manufactured means, the lair is well defended from intrusion. It might be reachable only by a steep mountain path, or it might be surrounded by a fence the hag builds out of posts capped with magically warded skulls. Often, a lair reflects the outlook of its primary inhabitant—a murderous hag's home might be crafted to look like a coffin or a mausoleum, and that of a gluttonous one might look like a tavern or a gingerbread house. Because such places are convenient for them, sea hags often establish their lairs inside the hulls of wrecked or abandoned ships.

BEST OF BOTH WORLDS

Many hags settle in places where the barriers between the mortal world and the Feywild are thin, making it easy for them to interact and bargain with creatures of both realms. Other popular choices are a place where the ambient energy augments certain kinds of magic, a site related to death such as a burial ground, and within a ring of fallen standing stones that still resonate with ancient power. In order to facilitate bargaining with mortals, the home must be near enough to a populated area that it attracts occasional visitors, but not so close that a community would see the hag's presence as a threat and try to defeat her or drive her off.

Treasure, Treasure Everywhere

A hag's home is cluttered with mundane items, caged creatures, oddities, objects that hint of a magical purpose, preserved specimens, scraps of lore, and curiosities that have a supernatural origin but aren't inherently magical. For a selection of strange hag treasures, see the "One-of-a-Kind Objects" section later in this chapter.

Exit Strategy

A hag always has an escape plan, in case ambitious do-gooders try to turn her home into her final resting place. If she is outmatched, or wants to vacate her lair quickly for some other reason, she uses a mix of her innate spellcasting, rare magic, guile, and the assistance of minions to get away. Most hags have three plans prepared: one for general threats and two others for specific likely scenarios, such as "They've set the house on fire" or "A necromancer with undead are attacking."

If a hag is forced to resort to such measures, she immediately begins to plot her retaliation against those that caused her to flee. Like a vampire or a demon, a hag has a long life over which to exact her vengeance, and no dish of revenge is sweeter than one served cold and to the next three generations of her enemy's family.

Hag Lair Actions

If a hag is a grandmother, she gains a set of lair actions appropriate to her nature, knowledge, and history. A coven that includes a grandmother can use her lair actions as well, but the grandmother's will prevails—if one of the coven attempts this sort of action and the grandmother disapproves, nothing happens. A powerful auntie (or her coven) might also have access to lair actions like these, but only at certain times of the year or when the influence of the Feywild is strong.

The following lair actions are options for grandmothers and powerful aunties. Grandmothers usually have three to five lair actions, aunties usually only one (if they have any at all). Unless otherwise noted, any lair action that requires a creature to make a saving throw uses the save DC of the hag's most powerful ability.

Lair Actions

On initiative count 20 (losing initiative ties), the hag can take a lair action to cause one of the following effects, but can't use the same effect two rounds in a row:

- Until initiative count 20 on the next round, the hag can pass through solid walls, doors, ceilings, and floors as if the surfaces weren't there.
- The hag targets any number of doors and windows that she can see, causing each one to either open or close as she wishes. Closed doors can be magically locked (requiring a successful DC 20 Strength check to force open) until she chooses to make them unlocked, or until she uses this lair action again to open them.

A powerful **annis hag** might have the following additional lair action:

- The hag creates a thick cloud of caustic black smoke that fills a 20-foot-radius sphere centered on a point she can see within 120 feet her. The cloud lasts un-

til initiative count 20 on the next round. Creatures and objects in or behind the smoke are heavily obscured. A creature that enters the cloud for the first time on a turn or starts its turn there takes 10 (3d6) acid damage.

A powerful **bheur hag** might have the following additional lair action:

- The hag creates a blizzard in a 40-foot-high, 20-foot radius cylinder centered on a point she can see within 120 feet of her. The effect lasts until initiative count 20 on the next round. The blizzard lightly obscures every creature and object in the area for the duration. A creature that enters the blizzard for the first time on a turn or starts its turn there is blinded until initiative count 20 on the next round.

A powerful **green hag** might have the following additional lair action:

- The hag creates an illusory duplicate of herself, which appears in its own space. As long as she can see her duplicate, the hag can move it a distance equal to her walking speed as well as make the illusion speak on her turn (no action required). The illusion has the same statistics as the hag but can't take actions or reactions. It can interact with its environment and even pick up and hold real objects. The illusion seems real in every way but disappears if it takes any amount of damage. Otherwise, it lasts until the hag dismisses it (no action required) or can no longer see it. If the hag uses this lair action to create a new duplicate, the previous one vanishes, dropping any real objects in its possession.

A powerful **night hag** might have the following additional lair actions:

- One creature the hag can see within 120 feet of her must succeed on a DC 15 Charisma saving throw or be banished to a prison demiplane. To escape, the creature must use its action to make a Charisma check contested by the hag's. If the creature wins, it escapes the demiplane. Otherwise, the effect ends on initiative count 20 on the next round. When the effect ends, the creature reappears in the space it left or in the nearest unoccupied space if that one is occupied.
- The hag targets up to three creatures that she can see within 60 feet of her. Each target must succeed on a DC 15 Constitution saving throw or be flung up to 30 feet through the air. A creature that strikes a solid object or is released in midair takes 1d6 bludgeoning damage for every 10 feet moved or fallen.

HAGS HATE TO BE IN DEBT TO SOMEONE WHO'S DONE THEM A FAVOR SPONTANEOUSLY, OUTSIDE OF ANY BARGAIN, AND SO WILL RETURN FAVORS UNEXPECTEDLY TO SUCH FOLK.

—ELMINSTER

HAG LAIRS

SKULL LAIR

UPPER LEVEL

SIDE VIEW

LOWER LEVEL

LOWER LEVEL

UPPER LEVEL

LOWER LEVEL

UPPER LEVEL

SIDE VIEW

N

TREE LAIR

SHIP LAIR

☐ = 10 FEET

BLANDO

A powerful **sea hag** might have the following additional lair actions:

- The hag fills up to four 10-foot cubes of water with ink. The inky areas are heavily obscured for 1 minute, although a steady, strong underwater current disperses the ink on initiative count 10. The hag ignores the obscuring effect of the ink.
- The hag chooses one humanoid within the lair and instantly creates a simulacrum of that creature (as if created with the *simulacrum* spell). This hideous simulacrum is formed out of seaweed, slime, half-eaten fish, and other garbage, but still generally resembles the creature it is imitating. This simulacrum obeys the hag's commands and is destroyed on initiative count 20 on the next round.

REGIONAL EFFECTS

A hag's foul nature slowly suffuses the environment around her lair, twisting it to evil.

Each hag's lair is the source of three to five regional effects; the home of a grandmother, an auntie, or a coven has more effects than the lair of a single hag, including some that can directly harm intruders. Any regional effect that requires a creature to make a saving throw uses the save DC of the hag's most powerful ability. These effects either end immediately if the hag dies or abandons the lair, or take up to 2d10 days to fade away.

REGIONAL EFFECTS

The region within 1 mile of a grandmother hag's lair is warped by the creature's fell magic, which creates one or more of the following effects:

- Birds, rodents, snakes, spiders, or toads (or some other creatures appropriate to the hag) are found in great profusion.
- Beasts that have an Intelligence score of 2 or lower are charmed by the hag and directed to be aggressive toward intruders in the area.
- Strange carved figurines, twig fetishes, or rag dolls magically appear in trees.

A powerful **annis hag** creates one or more of the following additional regional effects within 1 mile of her lair:

- The gravel stones on a safe-looking path, road, or trails occasionally become sharp for 100-foot intervals. Walking on these areas is like walking on caltrops.
- Small avalanches of rock intermittently fall, blocking a path or burying intruders. A buried creature is restrained and has to hold its breath until it is dug out.
- Strange laughter, sounding like that of children or the hag herself, occasionally pierces the silence.
- Small cairns appear along the route of travelers, containing anything from mysterious bones to nothing at all. These cairns might be haunted by skeletons, specters, or hostile fey.

A powerful **bheur hag** creates one or more of the following additional regional effects within 1 mile of her lair:

- Small avalanches of snow intermittently fall, blocking a path or burying intruders. A buried creature is restrained and has to hold its breath until it is dug out.
- Human-sized blocks of ice appear, containing frozen corpses. These corpses might break free and attack as zombies, or their spirits might attack as specters.
- Blizzards come without warning. A blizzard occurs once every 2d12 hours and lasts 1d3 hours. During a storm, creatures moving overland travel at half normal speed, and normal visibility is reduced to 30 feet.
- Roads, paths, and trails twist and turn back on themselves, making navigation in the area exceedingly difficult.

A powerful **green hag** creates one or more of the following additional regional effects within 1 mile of her lair:

- Illusory duplicates of the hag appear in random places at random times (but never more than one in any given location). An illusory duplicate has no substance, but it looks, sounds, and moves like the hag. The hag can sense when one or more creatures are within 60 feet of her duplicate and can interact with them as if she were present and standing in the duplicate's space. If the illusory duplicate takes any damage, it disappears.
- The region takes twice as long as normal to traverse, since the plants grow thick and twisted, and the swamps are thick with reeking mud.
- Trees transform into awakened trees and attack when hostile intruders are near.

A powerful **night hag** creates one or more of the following additional regional effects within 1 mile of her lair:

- Shadows seem abnormally gaunt and sometimes move on their own as though alive.
- Creatures are transported to a harmless but eerie demiplane filled with shadowy forms, waxy corpses, and cackling. The creatures are trapped there for a minute or two, and then returned to the place where they vanished from.
- Intelligent creatures see hallucinations of dead friends, family members, and even themselves littering the hag's realm. Any attempt to interact with a hallucinatory image causes it to disappear.

A powerful **sea hag** creates one or more of the following additional regional effects within 1 mile of her lair:

- Most surfaces are covered by a thin film of slime, which is slick and sticks to anything that touches it.
- Currents and tides are exceptionally strong and treacherous. Any ability check made to safely navigate or control a vessel moving through these waters has disadvantage.
- Shores are littered with dead, rotting fish. The hag can sense when one of the fish is handled and cause it to speak with her voice.

MINIONS AND PETS

Although they are solitary by nature, hags sometimes feel the need for companionship. Usually one scratches this itch by acquiring servants she can insult and

You will know Rickety Zilla's lair by its shape in the moonlight: a dead tree with a bent spine, its great roots reaching out for a boulder like a man for his severed head.

—Volo

slap around as she wishes. Such a creature might be charmed into compliance, or under a spell that stops its heart if it disobeys, or too afraid of nonmagical punishment for failure to do what she says. Most hags have some kind of slave or minion creature living with or near them as a defense against attackers, even if it's just a common animal.

Hags particularly delight in using mortals bound to their service as minions. A paladin might have no qualms about putting a hag coven to the sword, but her conviction falters if she must first fight through a crowd of innocent farmers that the hag has compelled to defend her. Ordinary folk are also useful as minions because they can serve the hag as her eyes and ears in a nearby settlement, either operating secretly or actively trying to persuade other townsfolk to pay her a visit.

The weird magic at a hag's disposal means that she might have almost any type of creature helping or serving her—fey, giant, undead, and so on. Even a creature much more powerful than she might be under her command, working off the debt of a bargain for itself or someone else. Favors beget favors, and under duress a hag might speak a magic word to call upon a blood debt from a dragon, a noble, or another hag, making her able to wield magical, political, or physical power in a way she can't do by herself.

Like the land near a hag's lair, over time her minions are altered by her presence, becoming twisted versions of their former selves (in a dark fey sort of way), but still recognizable as what they once were. She might alter them with magic, making them tireless, resistant to fire, able to transform into a flock of crows, or able to teleport through shadows—whatever the hag thinks best defends or serves her.

RANDOM HAG MINIONS

To determine the minions and helpers in a hag's retinue, roll once on the following tables or choose from the possibilities.

The Servants table includes faithful, trusted helpers that a hag uses to protect herself and her home. These creatures are either naturally wicked or warped by the hag to better serve her. In either case, a hag is confident that her servants will obey her orders without question.

The Brutes table gives examples of the muscle a hag might employ, mercenaries that serve the hag only so long as it benefits them. These creatures run errands and take care of roughing up enemies or patrolling areas that the hag considers beneath her personal attention. Hags prefer to employ clever, cruel creatures rather than dumb oafs.

SERVANTS

d8	Servant(s)
1	1d4 **flameskulls**
2	1d2 **flesh golems**
3	1d2 **helmed horrors**
4	1 **rug of smothering**
5	1d6 **scarecrows**
6	2d4 **shadow mastiffs***
7	2d4 **swarms of insects** or **swarms of rats**
8	1d6 **yeth hounds***

* See chapter 3 of this book for statistics.

BRUTES

d12	Servant(s)
1	2d6 + 2 **bugbears**
2	1d6 + 2 **doppelgangers**
3	1d6 + 2 **ettercaps**
4	2d6 + 2 **gargoyles**
5	2d4 + 2 **jackalweres**
6	2d6 + 4 **kenku**
7	2d6 + 2 **meenlocks***
8	1d4 **oni**
9	2d6 + 2 **quicklings***
10	2d4 + 2 **redcaps***
11	1d6 + 4 **wererats**
12	1d4 + 2 **werewolves**

* See chapter 3 of this book for statistics.

TREASURE

Much of a hag's treasure is strewn among all the clutter in her lair, making it difficult for intruders to quickly identify all the items that have use or value. But the hag knows what, and where, everything is.

Every hag is infallible when it comes to keeping track of her treasures and other possessions. Her organization and labeling, if such a system exists, is designed to foil thieves and serve as a final, vexing puzzle for anyone who tries to make use of an item without her consent.

A hag's treasure—like a gift from a fey being—should be doubted and even feared rather than simply being scooped up and carted away. Treasure-seekers are likely to fare better if they consider a hag's booty to be trapped, exercising caution rather than giving in to greed or curiosity. Manipulating a container or other item without knowing what's inside or what it does (or

without knowing the proper password or technique) is likely to be very dangerous. At best, whatever was held in a container merely escapes or dissipates. At worst, just about anything can happen, none of it good.

ONE-OF-A-KIND OBJECTS

Above and beyond the items of obvious value a hag has accumulated, she also has a few bizarre and unique items in her collection. The Hag Objects table provides a way to quickly add such weird items to a hag's home.

HAG OBJECTS

d10	Object
1	The eye of a cleric, preserved in a liquid-filled jar. When an undead creature comes within 100 feet of the jar, the eye darts about as if it is looking around in a panic. It otherwise remains motionless.
2	The leathery, preserved head of a dwarf. Anyone who holds its 5-foot-long beard can see through its eyes.
3	A perfectly smooth, round stone the size of a human's fist. If placed on the ground, it rolls 20 feet per round toward the nearest source of fresh water.
4	A sickly crow with clipped wings. The only sound it can make is to roar like a lion.
5	A seemingly empty, sealed jar. If opened, the person standing closest to the jar suddenly recalls 1d6 happy memories from the life of a long dead elf lord.
6	A seemingly mundane gold piece. Anyone who touches it gains the unshakable belief that this is the very first gold coin minted by humanity.
7	A black box, 3 feet on each side. Anyone who opens it finds a set of three wooden, articulated figures that are modeled after three members of the adventuring party. If the figures are stood on the ground, they act out insulting parodies of their duplicates' recent actions.
8	An oval-shaped disc made of an unknown metal. If it is tossed in the air, it flies in circles around the tosser for a minute, tiny lights winking on its surface, before settling to the ground nearby.
9	A thick, dusty tome, every page filled with tiny, barely legible writing. Careful study of the book reveals it to be a written transcript of every conversation that took place over the course of a year, three years ago, in a nearby village.
10	A small painting that depicts a placid field. Just after midnight each day, the painting changes to depict the following day's weather.

A hag always has some potion or amulet that puts the odds in her favor. If you're lucky, she only wants to make you miserable instead of just killing you.

—Volo

KOBOLDS: LITTLE DRAGONS

Kobolds are often dismissed as cowardly, foolish, and weak, but these little reptilian creatures actually have a strong social structure that stresses devotion to the tribe, are clever with their hands, and viciously work together in order to overcome their physical limitations.

In the kobolds' version of a perfect world, the creatures would be left alone to dig their tunnels and raise the next generation of kobolds, all the while seeking the magic that will free their imprisoned god (see the "Kurtulmak: God of Kobolds" sidebar). In the world they occupy, kobolds are often bullied and enslaved by larger creatures—or, when they live on their own, they are constantly fearful of invasion and oppression. Although individually they are timid and shy away from conflict, kobolds are dangerous if cornered, vicious when defending their eggs, and notorious for the dangerous improvised traps they use to protect their warrens.

EXPERT TUNNELERS

Kobolds are naturally skilled at tunneling. Similar to dwarves, they seem to have a near-instinctive sense of what sections of stone or earth are strong or weak, are bearing a load or are safe to excavate, or are likely to contain minerals or offer access to water. This ability enables them to fashion secure homes in places where other creatures wouldn't feel safe.

Kobolds take advantage of their size by creating small-diameter tunnels that they can easily pass through, but that require larger creatures to hunch over or even crawl to make progress. In places where a tunnel opens into a chasm and continues on the other side, the kobolds might connect the two passages with a rope bridge or some other rickety structure, designed to collapse under the weight of any creature heavier than a kobold. On occasion, the route through a kobold lair runs along a ledge that borders a cavern or a crevasse, and the kobolds might erect a railing or a wall that prevents them from falling off the edge—high enough to protect a kobold but low enough to serve as a tripping hazard for a larger creature.

Those of other humanoid races have little good to say about kobolds, but they do admit that the little reptilians do respectable tunnel work using simple tools. If a band of kobolds is enslaved by more powerful creatures, the kobolds are usually put to work enlarging their masters' living area and protecting vital areas of the lair with traps and other defenses.

Some human communities hire kobolds to dig their sewer tunnels, paying them with food and tools the kobolds wouldn't have access to on their own. If they are treated well and left alone to do the job, the kobolds work industriously and build a network of passages beneath the streets, connecting them to a nearby waterway and greatly improving the town's sanitation. If the kobolds like the area and aren't mistreated by the humans, they might build a warren and make a permanent home there, while continuing to expand the town's sewers as the community grows. These so-called "city kobolds" live underground but might make occasional nighttime forays up to the surface. Roughly one quarter of the towns and cities in the world have kobold communities living under them, but the kobolds are so good at staying hidden that the surface-dwelling citizens in the area often don't know what lies beneath them.

Because the kobolds make sure they stay out of the way of anyone more dangerous than themselves, grow their own subterranean food, and prefer to sneak about at night, the people of a town might go for weeks or months without noticing evidence that kobolds are in the area, and years between actual sightings.

ABLE SCAVENGERS

Kobolds are adept at identifying broken, misplaced, discarded, or leftover crafted items from other creatures that can still be put to use. They prefer to scavenge objects that have clearly been lost or thrown away, which is easy to do without attracting attention. At the same time, they don't automatically shy away from trying to grab items that are the property of other creatures, because such objects are more likely to be in good condition and thus more useful or valuable.

When they go after items that aren't free for the taking, kobolds try to remain undetected and don't give their targets reason to harm them. For example, a group of city kobolds might sneak into a cobbler's house at night to loot it of knives, leather bits, nails, and other useful items, but if they are at risk of discovery, they run away rather than attack anyone in the house. By fleeing before they can be seen or identified, they avoid getting into a situation where the townsfolk would try to hunt down all kobolds and put the tribe's survival at risk.

Some aggressive individual kobolds and tribes do exist, but in general kobolds don't purposely provoke retaliatory attacks from the creatures they steal from. It's better to be cautious and overlooked than to be considered dangerous and a threat.

In a couple of situations, kobolds might abandon this careful approach. First, because of their hatred of gnomes, city kobolds often go out of their way to target gnomes' houses and shops. Even in such cases, the kobolds' fear of retaliation usually prevents them from trying to directly harm the gnomes, but they might spit in the milk, balance dishes on tables so they're easily knocked over and broken, or scatter sewing needles all over the floor—petty, vengeful acts that humiliate, injure, or anger the gnomes, but not so much that the gnomes want to hunt down and kill the kobolds. Because of the kobolds' animosity, gnomes tend to avoid or abandon settlements that have a severe infestation of kobolds, and conversely kobolds are usually driven out of communities that have a large gnome population.

Second, kobolds are always on the lookout for magic that might help them free their imprisoned god, Kurtulmak. Typical kobolds don't know how to use a wand, a spellbook, or anything with more magical power than a potion, but they all believe that the tribal sorcerer can figure out how to use any such item they come across. When kobolds sense an opportunity to separate a magic item from its owner, they are often willing to take the chance of revealing themselves because the potential reward is worth the risk.

Dragon Servitors

Kobolds believe that they were created by Tiamat from the blood of dragons—a view supported by their reptilian (they would say draconic) appearance. In every kobold tribe, the legend of the creatures' origin is passed down from elder to hatchling, giving each individual and every generation a reason to feel pride and self-respect. The kobolds prefer to run away than fight, to live off the scraps of others, and they are often dominated by larger humanoids, but they know that there is greatness within them and they are proud that they were chosen to be the blood-kin of dragons.

Kobolds willingly serve chromatic dragons and worship them as if they were demigods—mighty beings of divine descent. This isn't a casual sort of worship or lip service; kobolds are awed in the presence of a dragon, as if an actual avatar of a deity were in their presence. Kobolds fall all over themselves to obey orders from a dragon, even if they are dangerous orders. Although kobolds usually don't worship Tiamat directly, they recognize her as the dragon-goddess of all chromatic dragons, and as the master of their racial god, Kurtulmak.

Kurtulmak: God of Kobolds

The god of kobolds was a vassal of Tiamat. When the gnome god Garl Glittergold stole a treasure from Tiamat's hoard, she sent Kurtulmak to retrieve it. Garl lured his pursuer into a maze-like cavern, then collapsed the exits behind him, trapping Kurtulmak for all eternity.

Kurtulmak is a hateful deity, one who despises all life except for kobolds. He especially hates Garl Glittergold, gnomes, and fey creatures that enjoy playing pranks. He taught the first kobolds how to mine, tunnel, hide, and ambush. He is dominated by his emotions—intelligent, but not wise. Arrogant and prone to gloating, he carries grudges, has a huge chip on his shoulder, and spends a lot of time fashioning elaborate revenge scenarios against those who have disrespected him.

Arcane Magic Users

Unlike some other humanoids, kobolds don't fear or shun arcane magic. They see magic as part of their connection to dragons, and are proud to be blessed with the ability to wield such power. Young kobold sorcerers are trained by elders, and the training has an almost religious significance. Most kobold sorcerers are of the draconic bloodline origin and specialize in either damaging magic (which can also be used in mining), augmentation (of materials or allies), or divination (to find raw materials and foresee threats to the tribe).

The main reason why kobolds depend on arcane magic rather than divine is Kurtulmak's imprisonment, which makes it difficult for him to grant spells to mortals and for those mortals to receive his favor. Furthermore, kobolds are so frail that a single hit from a human's weapon can kill one of them, so a tribe has little use for healing magic, and a sorcerer can meet most of the tribe's other magic-related needs. Kobold shamans are very rare; priests of Kurtulmak, when they reveal themselves, are easily recognized by orange garb (usually just a roughly torn sash or cloak) decorated with an image of a gnome's skull.

Life and Outlook

Kobolds have a tribal society in which they all take on specialized roles that protect and sustain the tribe. The strongest kobolds are trained to be hunters and warriors, the most clever are crafters and strategists, the toughest are miners and beast-wranglers, and so on. Even a stupid or physically weak kobold is given a role in the tribe, whether something as simple as picking mushrooms for food or watching over hatchlings, and they all understand that their actions contribute to the survival of the group. The tribe practices for the eventuality of defending the lair against intruders, and their plans always include knowing the best escape routes and who is responsible for blocking tunnels to deter pursuit.

Kobolds feel a cool affinity or something like kinship for other members of their tribe, but they are rarely affectionate with each other. Two kobolds who've known each other for over a decade might consider each other friends or enemies, but the strength of this sentiment is much fainter than any comparable human emotion. Since most of their waking time is spent working, adversarial kobolds rarely have opportunities to exchange insults, let alone come to blows over their differences.

Kobolds choose mates primarily for convenience. Their lack of emotional bonding means they have no concept of marriage or permanent family relationships. Their eggs are placed in a common tribal hatchery with no effort to keep track of who each one's mother is. This practice and the communal raising of the hatchlings mean that the tribe operates like a group of cousins.

Because they lay eggs, and the eggs don't require much tending, kobold females aren't exempted from war or work. Furthermore, kobolds can slowly change sex. If most males or females of a tribe are killed, some survivors change over several months until the tribe is balanced again. In this way, the tribe can quickly repopulate with just a few survivors. Because of these factors, kobolds don't have assigned gender roles for young or adults. A leader, sorcerer, miner, or crafter is as likely to be female as male.

Grow Fast, Die Early

Kobolds grow and mature much more swiftly than members of other humanoid races. At 6 years old a kobold is considered an adult. Most succumb to violence, accidents, or disease by age 20, but a kobold can live for up to 120 years—a longevity they attribute to being distantly related to dragons. A female can lay up to six eggs per year, and an egg matures for two to three months before it hatches.

Kobolds don't engage in funeral ceremonies; a dead kobold's body is burned or disposed of in some other convenient way (or, in a cannibalistic tribe, eaten). Kobolds believe that if they die in service to their tribe, Kurtulmak immediately sends each of them back to life as the next egg laid in the hatchery. If a particularly important or respected member of a tribe dies, the hatchery is closely monitored. The next egg laid is immediately separated from the rest and carefully protected. Once it hatches, the resultant young kobold is groomed to fill a position of importance.

Food and Cannibalism

Although their sharp teeth would suggest they are carnivores, kobolds are actually omnivores, and can eat just about anything, including meat, fruit, tree bark, bone, leather, and eggshells (a newly hatched kobold's first meal is usually its own shell). A hungry tribe leaves nothing behind from a kill, eating everything that's edible and using the rest to make tools or adornments.

Kobolds shed teeth as they wear out and grow new ones their entire lives. Many wear their own shed teeth as jewelry, with more teeth indicating an older—and wiser—kobold. Some unscrupulous individuals wear

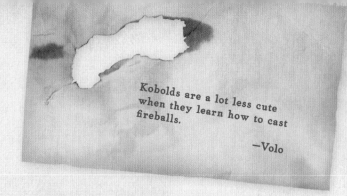

Kobolds are a lot less cute when they learn how to cast fireballs.

—Volo

teeth stolen or harvested from others in an attempt to make them seem older and more respectable.

Most kobold tribes avoid eating what they call "talking meat"—intelligent creatures—because such behavior prompts retaliation. The fear of starvation can make them flexible about this principle, however, and if their options are either attacking such creatures or going hungry, kobolds are practical. A few tribes, particularly those in lightly populated areas, practice cannibalism, believing it is foolish to waste good meat.

In any case, kobolds that eat humanoids don't simply start consuming corpses or prisoners right after a battle; they're more inclined to tie their victims to saplings and slowly roast them over a fire, or put them in a giant cook pot to make stew. Fortunately for the prisoners, the kobolds' almost comedic preparations sometimes give rescuers time to locate and free the captives before the kobolds settle down for the main course.

Hatred

Because the gnome god Garl Glittergold trapped the kobold god Kurtulmak in an inescapable maze, kobolds are bitterly hateful toward gnomes. Although they usually don't seek out gnomes to do them violence, if hostile kobolds encounter a mixed group of gnomes and other humanoids, the kobolds instinctively attack the gnomes. Kobolds in battle with gnomes are much less likely to run away because their hatred overrules their sense of self-preservation.

A kobold's cautious nature doesn't mean it can't get angry. The blood of dragons flows in its veins, and like a raging drake, a kobold that is pushed too far or has its back against the wall can become a miniature storm of fangs and claws as it desperately tries to defend its life. Likewise, kinship to their own tribe can prompt kobolds to battle another kobold tribe for resources or territory. Such conflicts aren't common, because two tribes will always prefer to expand in different directions if they come into contact, but they do happen.

For example, two neighboring tribes that want exclusive claim to a flock of mountain goats might skirmish with each other every few days. Eventually the leader of one warring tribe realizes it is losing due to attrition and moves its tribe to another area, ceding the contested territory to its more successful neighbors.

As demonstrated by their hatred of gnomes, kobolds have a persecution complex and easily take offense at the actions or deeds of other races. They aren't forgiving of other races, and they enjoy nursing their hatred until they get a chance to wreak revenge on a creature or a race that has wronged them.

Environment

Kobolds are cold-blooded and thus prefer temperate and tropical climates. Kobold tribes in colder regions tend to be smaller in population and more aggressive in their hunting, since food is relatively scarce in such areas.

Partly out of fear and partly because their eyes are sensitive to sunlight, kobolds prefer the security of a cave to living in the open air, and can be found in any sort of terrain that can support tunneling. In a swamp or along a coastline where digging into the soft ground is problematic, kobolds entrench themselves in dense woods, hills, or large rock outcroppings, creating warrens above the water line.

Kobolds reside most commonly in hilly or mountainous terrain. Such locations usually have natural caves suitable for living space, plenty of room to dig, and ready sources of food. Although lairing in these locations puts kobolds in competition with surface-dwelling humanoids, their ability to avoid detection often means their warrens go unnoticed by their larger rivals. If it's lucky, a tribe of kobolds that is discovered by a group of larger humanoids might form a mutually beneficial arrangement, relying on the humanoids for protection from invaders and in return providing services such as excavating new living spaces and disposing of trash. If it's unlucky, the tribe is enslaved by the other humanoids, and the kobolds serve similar roles but under threat of death.

Roleplaying a Kobold

A kobold acknowledges its weakness in the face of a hostile world. It knows it is puny, bigger creatures will exploit it, it will probably die at a young age, and its life will be full of toil. Although this outlook seems bleak, a kobold finds satisfaction in its work, the survival of its tribe, and the knowledge that it shares a heritage with the mightiest of dragons.

A kobold isn't clever, but it isn't as stupid as an orc. Someone can fool a kobold with smooth words or a quick wit, but when the kobold figures out it has been tricked, it remembers the affront. If it gets an opportunity to do so, it will retaliate against that person somehow, even if in merely a petty way.

A kobold doesn't like being cornered or alone. It wants to know it has a safe path for escape, or at least an ally nearby to improve its chances. A kobold without either of these options will be nervous, its behavior alternating between meek silence and hysteria.

Urds: Winged Kobolds

Winged kobolds, known as urds, hatch seemingly at random from kobold eggs, even in a tribe that has no adult urds. Although being able to fly is an incredible gift, and it would be expected for kobolds to interpret the wings as a blessing from Tiamat, ordinary kobolds resent urds and don't get along with them. Fragments of kobold legends speak of Kuraulyek, a winged godling servant of Kurtulmak, who betrayed his master in some way. Kobolds see urds as Kuraulyek's favorites, and they project their resentment of this traitor onto their winged kin.

Kobold Names

Kobold names are derived from the Draconic tongue and usually relate to a characteristic of the owner, such as scale color, distinctive body parts, or typical behavior. For example, "Red Foot," "White Claw," and "Scurry" are Common translations of often-used names. A kobold might change its name when it becomes an adult, or add additional word-syllables after important events such as completing its first hunt, laying its first egg, or surviving its first battle. The Kobold Names table presents kobold names suitable for any campaign.

Kobold Names

d20	Name	d20	Name
1	Arix	11	Molo
2	Eks	12	Ohsoss
3	Ett	13	Rotom
4	Galax	14	Sagin
5	Garu	15	Sik
6	Hagnar	16	Sniv
7	Hox	17	Taklak
8	Irtos	18	Tes
9	Kashak	19	Urak
10	Meepo	20	Varn

Physical Variations

Kobolds vary widely in how their scales are colored and patterned. Although a human might have difficulty telling two similar-looking kobolds apart, the kobolds themselves can easily recognize each other.

Most kobolds of the same tribe tend to have similar coloration. For example, the Copper Tooth tribe might be mostly gray with red stripes. Two tribes that merge eventually crossbreed enough to create a new look, although occasional outliers and throwbacks are born that bear the appearance of one of the original tribes.

Use the Scale Color table to randomly determine the predominant appearance of kobolds in a tribe. If the roll on the table indicates a patterned appearance, roll on the Scale Pattern table to determine how the two colors are combined.

Scale Color

d100	Scale Color
01–05	Black
06–10	Blue
11–25	Brown
26–30	Gray
31–35	Green
36–40	Orange
41–55	Orange-brown
56–60	Red
61–75	Red-brown
76–85	Tan
86–90	White
91–00	Patterned (roll twice, ignoring duplicate results and results of 91 or higher)

SCALE PATTERN

d20	Scale Pattern
1–4	Mottled
5–8	Reticulated
9–12	Shaded
13–16	Spotted
17–20	Striped

TACTICS

Because they are physically weak individually, kobolds know they have to use superior numbers and cunning to take down powerful foes. In addition to their Pack Tactics trait described in the *Monster Manual*, they use traps, ambushes, terrain, allied monsters, and any other advantage they can squeeze out of their environment. Essentially, the only way kobolds can win is not to play fair.

Kobolds work together to accomplish difficult tasks they couldn't manage alone. They carve intricate tunnel systems that enable them to hold off and discourage enemies several times their size. Without engaging in much verbal communication, each kobold knows what has to be done to succeed. Kobolds' ability to work together is remarkable, especially compared to the behavior of other small humanoids like goblins, which tend to squabble among themselves and cooperate only when threatened by a strong leader.

Kobolds avoid combat on a large scale, instead sticking to hit-and-run raids using smaller groups of warriors. If they have time, they prepare the battlefield with small bolt-holes for them to hide in and simple pit traps to hamper their opponents.

Standard kobold tactics include the following:

- Attacking light sources to extinguish them, so the kobolds can use their darkvision to best advantage.
- Leaving one defender in a room to lure invaders into a trap or an ambush. Often this bait is a sick or weak kobold who is otherwise unable to contribute to the tribe's needs.
- Using hit-and-run maneuvers, fleeing between attacks to better or more secure vantage points. Often their goal is to attract enemies and draw the foes into greater danger, which can be especially effective if the invaders have made camp, are injured, or are otherwise compromised (such as having to move by climbing or swimming).
- Using poison, usually harvested from vermin such as centipedes and spiders. They might extract the poison and use it on their weapons, or leave a chest or a clay pot full of the vermin in obvious places as false "treasure," prompting intruders to open the container and release a swarm.

In a combat involving large numbers of kobolds (such as ten or more), consider spreading out their attacks over the round instead of having them all act on the same initiative count. Doing this gives the kobolds more opportunities to react to what their enemies do, and makes it harder for players to coordinate their characters' attacks because not all the kobolds take their actions at the same time.

TREASURE

Because they live underground, kobolds have access to a remarkable amount of earth-based treasures such as metal ores and unpolished gems. They have the basic skill to extract metals found in their natural state and to polish raw gemstones. Although they don't create their own coinage, nuggets of raw metals used for trade, bribes, or crafting are commonly found in kobold lairs.

Kobolds are talented at crafting, so most tribes have a remarkable amount of treasure in the form of simple jewelry, such as armbands, rings, necklaces, and other items that are small or can be constructed out of small pieces. These adornments are always fashioned so that they don't make noise when the wearer moves, as that would make it difficult for a kobold to sneak anywhere.

Even though the jewelry they make has no functional purpose, kobolds savor these items, perhaps as some echo of a dragon's inclination to collect treasure. Because the tribe's wealth is portable, the kobolds can relocate quickly without needing to transport containers of nuggets and gems, and they can offer these items as bribes or tribute to more powerful creatures, or as religious offerings to a dragon.

ALLIES, MINIONS, AND PETS

Thanks to their lack of physical prowess and their small size, kobolds are rarely in a position to dominate other creatures, so they usually don't have minions. Even when the opportunity presents itself, kobolds would rather not try to enslave or hire any intelligent creatures because they can't trust such creatures to not turn on them.

Kobolds are good, however, at capturing and taming smaller animals and beasts, particularly rats, dire rats, and reptilian creatures like lizards that thrive in a cave or underground environment. The kobolds corral these pets or allow them to roam free, either feeding them scraps or allowing them to forage for insects and other morsels too small for the kobolds to care about. Much in the way that human villagers keep chickens, these animals help the kobolds with pest control and are occasionally used as food. Giant rats and similarly sized lizards are also used as pack animals and guardians.

Some tribes train giant weasels to serve as mounts or guardians, relying on their speed, keen senses, and ability to fit in kobold-sized tunnels. Other tribes use giant bats as mounts and guard animals, but the bats require a lot of space in which to move and are found only in lairs that feature large caves or close access to the surface world.

Kobolds are cautious and fearful of bears, since bears often seek to live in caves and the animals might wander into the outermost parts of the lair, particularly when they're about to begin hibernating. Kobolds are likely to panic when they see a bear animal companion in the company of another creature. This aversion extends to owlbears and other bear-like creatures.

Kobold Lairs

The lair of a kobold tribe is usually a maze of twisty little passages, sometimes stretching for hundreds of yards, and frequently guarded by traps. The area has a host of intersections, abrupt dead-ends, tunnels that cross over or under one another, concealed passages, and other features that make the lair difficult for outsiders to navigate.

Creatures larger than a kobold have to squat or crawl in order to fit through the tunnels of a kobold warren, which by itself is enough to deter most hostile humanoids (such as orcs or hobgoblins) from trying to invade the kobolds' territory. Adventurers trying to eradicate a kobold infestation often find themselves stuck in low passages too narrow to turn around in, forcing them to move in single file and putting the burden of combat on the first and last people in line.

The layout of a kobold tribe's lair changes over time. The inhabitants regularly collapse or seal off tunnels and caves as they carve new ones. As such, any information that might be gleaned about the layout or location of areas within the lair becomes increasingly inaccurate as the kobolds "migrate" through the rock to meet the needs and ensure the safety of the community.

Kobolds riddle their lairs with traps, using their gift for tunneling in conjunction with their skill at repurposing found items. Even though these traps are often far more deadly than the kobolds themselves, the kobolds don't feel threatened by having these devices in their home, any more than a human is afraid of its vicious but loyal guard dog.

The most common traps in a lair are deadfalls, which the kobolds set up either to kill intruders or to block off key areas of the warren as invaders approach those places. Since the tribe is continually migrating and expanding its tunnel system, older tunnels are often employed in these traps. A tunnel can be rigged to collapse by pulling a rope connected to a support beam; a fleeing kobold can yank the rope, or the beam might be in a space so tight that a larger creature can't keep from dislodging it as the creature moves through area. Even if a deadfall traps some kobolds in an enclosed space, they and their fellows can usually chisel open an air vent within an hour, and create an opening large enough for the trapped kobolds to squeeze through in a few more.

Any place where a tunnel takes a sharp turn or becomes exceedingly narrow is a natural choke point that forces invaders to fight from a disadvantaged position. Such a location usually includes a small chamber in the ceiling that features murder holes, allowing the kobolds to drop rocks, poisonous vermin, and other annoyances on those below.

Escape Tunnels

A kobold warren always has at least one escape tunnel that leads to a concealed surface exit, and the residents always know the shortest path to that tunnel. Usually an escape tunnel is rigged with traps to slow pursuers and ends in a narrow opening that requires even kobolds to squeeze through, to keep larger creatures from following them out.

Kiln and Crafting Areas

A chamber that contains a kiln is usually one of the uppermost areas of the warren, because the fire needs to be vented to the surface in order to keep it from depleting the breathable air in the lair. Kobold crafters spend their time in this area, using the kiln to bake mud bricks and harden pottery. The room is also used for other noisy activities.

Mines

Any chamber in the kobolds' underground complex that isn't immediately needed for another purpose is mined and excavated, both to extract usable ore and minerals and to provide room for later expansion of the den.

Mushroom Farms

Kobolds aren't good at agriculture, but they can get sustenance from subterranean mushrooms and hardy plant life that can live underground. A farm area might be completely underground, or a cavern near the surface with holes in the ceiling to let in some sunlight.

Root Cellars

Much as humans do in their dwellings, kobolds set aside rooms with deep pits in which they preserve food for lean times.

Sleeping Areas

Every lair has one or more spaces for living and sleeping, each large enough to comfortably hold ten to thirty adult kobolds. Individual kobolds might rest in a shallow pit or a personal-sized alcove, depending on the customs of the tribe. These spaces are used primarily for resting, although some kobolds might quietly work on crafts while others sleep. The creatures' sanitary needs, such as they are, are served by a deep pit near each sleeping area where refuse is deposited.

Most of the sleeping areas in the lair also double as hatcheries. Kobolds tend to their eggs by nesting them in a shallow pit lined with earth and dried grass. Because the eggs are susceptible to cold, they are kept near a slow-burning fire, or are protected by an insulating layer of dung and decomposing matter around the eggs.

Throne Room

A warren's throne room is always protected by traps and features a shrine to Kurtulmak in the form of a carved idol behind the throne. Rather than entering the chamber to pay homage, kobolds offer prayers at its entrance with the belief that their god hears them. The location might include a basin where offerings such as metal nuggets, raw gems, and teeth can be left.

Traps

Kobolds are amazingly creative at building traps, especially when adapting natural hazards and salvaged materials. They pound nails or spikes through a sapling and bend it to create a spring-arm, line pits or pools with sharp stones, rig platforms to collapse under anything more than a kobold's weight, and so on. Kobold traps might look flimsy or poorly designed, but a creature that gets hit with a bent sapling adorned with sharpened

KOBOLD·LAIR

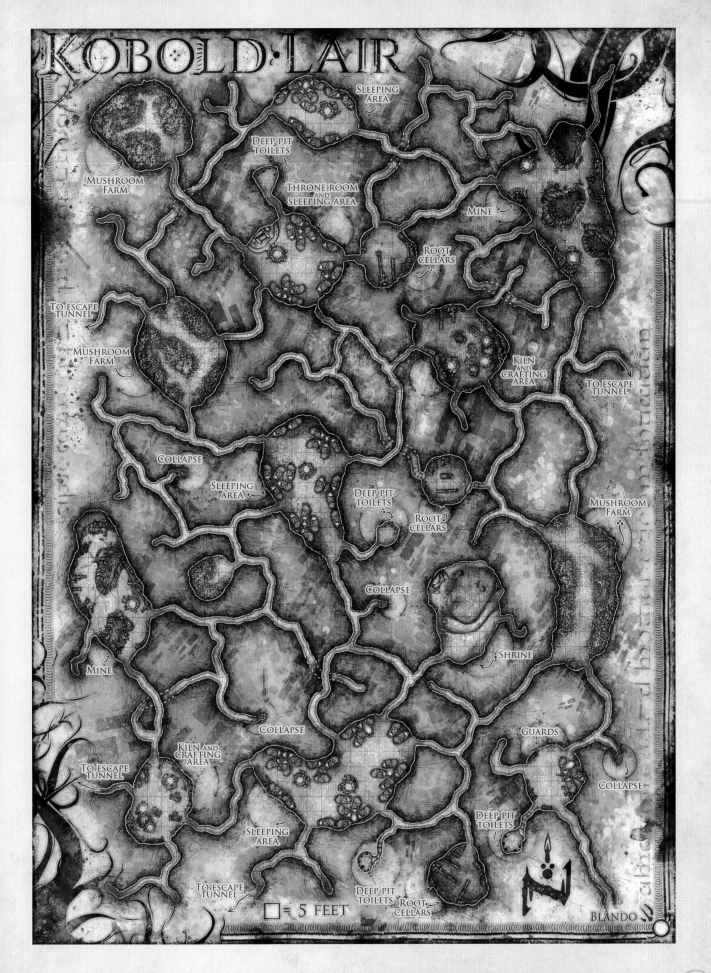

MUSHROOM FARM

SLEEPING AREA

DEEP PIT TOILETS

THRONE ROOM AND SLEEPING AREA

MINE

ROOT CELLARS

TO ESCAPE TUNNEL

MUSHROOM FARM

KILN AND CRAFTING AREA

TO ESCAPE TUNNEL

COLLAPSE

SLEEPING AREA

DEEP PIT TOILETS

ROOT CELLARS

MUSHROOM FARM

COLLAPSE

MINE

SHRINE

COLLAPSE

GUARDS

TO ESCAPE TUNNEL

KILN AND CRAFTING AREA

COLLAPSE

DEEP PIT TOILETS

SLEEPING AREA

TO ESCAPE TUNNEL

DEEP PIT TOILETS

ROOT CELLARS

☐ = 5 FEET

BLANDO

butter knives is liable to come away with a newfound respect for the little creatures.

The following are examples of common kobold traps:

- Barrels or small pots of oil (to be boiled, spilled, lit, or both)
- Bear traps that fall on tall creatures' heads
- Bells to announce intruders
- Block-and-tackle mine elevators rigged to fall
- Caltrops in shallow mud or soft dirt (light kobolds can walk on them without trouble)
- Collapsing ceilings
- Crates of centipedes
- Falling blocks
- Moats full of pitch or oil, which the kobolds can retreat behind and ignite
- Nets attached to ropes that pull creatures up vertical shafts far away from anyone who can help
- Pipes/shafts that dump boiling water (either from cookpots or from cooling the kiln)
- Pits with disease-covered spikes
- Pots of green slime
- Rolling boulders
- Small-size bridges and ladders rigged to break if there is too much weight on them
- Snares
- Tripwires, either connected to traps or just for tripping creatures
- Volleys of needles

SURVIVAL SKILLS

Nearly every activity in a kobold lair contributes to the tribe's survival. Guarding the lair keeps all of them safe from harm. Setting snares, farming mushrooms, and hunting provide food. Building traps deters intruders. Training guard animals helps protect the lair. Mining provides gems and ore for bribing enemies to leave them alone. Carving tunnels and rooms creates spaces for the next generation to live and improves the opportunity for the tribe to escape an overwhelming force.

The kobolds in a lair sleep in shifts, and all activities in the warren go on around the clock. Kobolds tend to be more active at night than during daylight hours, but unlike in a human settlement, there is no time when most of the inhabitants are resting. Warrens are built so that sleeping areas are somewhat isolated from the noise of work areas, enabling miners and crafters to do their work without awakening the sleepers. Kobolds learn at a young age to fall asleep to the noise of hammering nearby, but they still wake quickly at the sound of unusual activity.

Survival of the tribe is more important than the life of any particular individual. Even a cowardly kobold might sacrifice itself to give its fellows time to collapse a nearby tunnel and prevent invaders from getting to the rest of the tribe. All kobolds know that fleeing from danger, especially against bad odds, is the smart thing to do, but they are smart enough to realize that the strategic death of an individual can buy valuable time for the rest of the tribe, and each individual reluctantly accepts this need for sacrifice when it presents itself. This practice contributes to the reason why most common folk (and adventurers) think kobolds are stupid as well as weak; they've seen or heard of a lone kobold trying to hold off a group of armed attackers and attribute the act either to idiocy or the creature's ridiculously inflated idea of its prospects for success. The truth is that the lone kobold—persuaded into this role by its peers—is just hoping to slow down the invaders long enough to give the rest of the tribe time to prepare a lethal trap, an ambush, or a quick getaway.

The tribe's leader is usually the oldest and smartest kobold; the other kobolds respect the old one's ability to survive so long, and they assume the leader will use that knowledge to help the tribe survive. In some cases, the best lesson a kobold leader can teach is "I don't have to be faster than the bear. I just have to be faster than you."

MIND FLAYERS: SCOURGE OF WORLDS

Mind flayers, also known as illithids, are horrific, alien humanoids that lurk deep within the Underdark. Masters of psionic energy, they use their mental powers to dominate other creatures. The fortunate among their victims are slain, their brains devoured. The unlucky ones have their psyches warped, leaving them as mindless slaves with little hope of being rescued.

A CULTURE OF FUGITIVES

Despite all their unique and overwhelming abilities, the mind flayers are a race on the edge of extinction.

Thousands of years ago, the illithids were the dominant power of the Inner Planes. From their astral domains, they launched flying vessels called nautiloids, able to cross between planes, so that they could harvest intelligent humanoids from hundreds of worlds.

The mind flayers relied on a slave race, the gith, to provide physical labor and sustenance when other sources of food grew thin. Eventually, the gith revolted. Whether the mind flayers became decadent or the gith discovered a weakness, none can say. What is known is that after centuries of domination, the mind flayer empire collapsed in less than a year. The gith rose up, slaughtered their masters, and destroyed almost all traces of the illithids' astral domains.

Only the mind flayers that had infiltrated the worlds of the Material Plane survived, and their safety was short-lived. Both the githzerai and the githyanki, two factions that arose from the victorious gith, sent hunting parties to root out and slaughter the remaining mind flayers.

To this day, isolated clutches of mind flayers remain in hiding, seeking ways to recapture their former glory but hampered by their paranoia of being discovered and destroyed by their enemies.

LOST COLONIES
Speculation persists concerning mind flayer realms yet adrift in the Astral Plane. Though no one has discovered such a place, it is beyond dispute that an empire as vast as the illithids' built great cities and other edifices. Most sages, however, believe that the gith tore apart every last bit of mind flayer artifice, ensuring that no evidence remained of the mind flayers' reign.

A few skeptics suggest that the entire narrative of the gith victory rings false. How could a slave race overpower the mind flayers? Where are the signs of this great struggle? Perhaps the gith didn't actually win. Perhaps, instead, the mind flayers moved themselves and their works into the future to avoid being overrun. That theory would explain the mind flayers' disappearance and the absence of any ruins from their empire.

Few folk take such talk seriously, yet no one can be sure exactly what the illithids are and are not capable of.

THE IMPORTANCE OF BRAINS

Because of their dietary needs and their otherworldly biology, mind flayers must remain within hunting distance of intelligent humanoids, even if doing so makes them vulnerable to attack from their enemies. They use the brains of such creatures as food, of course, but they also need sentient humanoids to propagate.

FOOD FOR THOUGHT
When a mind flayer devours a brain, it acquires stray memories from its victim and shares them with the other members of its colony. Mind flayers also receive a degree of sustenance from the physical substance of a brain, but subsist primarily on the psionic energy that they extract from it in its final moments of activity.

Through some quirk of the illithids' parasitic nature, the cultural sophistication of a mind flayer depends upon what sorts of brains are in its diet. For example, members of a colony that feed on grimlocks are no less intelligent than a colony that feeds on elves, but the former will pay almost no attention to crafting clothes to wear, and the latter will dress in elaborate robes. This phenomenon extends to all displays of culture, from modes of architecture to the decorations that adorn illithid funerary brain jars.

> ONE MIND FLAYER SEES YE, AND THEY ALL SEE.
> ONE MIND. ONE NASTY, SUSPICIOUS MIND.
> —ELMINSTER

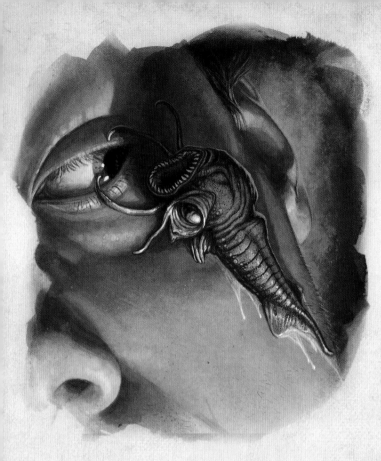

ences, and skills of all of its members and stored within the elder brain.

In some ways, a mind flayer colony is like a great library of lore stored within its members' minds, with the elder brain as its librarian. Each individual illithid represents a category or subsection within the library. One mind flayer might specialize in biology, while another is an expert in defending the colony. Given that an individual mind flayer has a near-genius intellect, the extent of its knowledge is equivalent to the highest levels of scholarship attainable by humans.

There are limits to a colony's reach. An illithid can be part of its colony's network of minds only while it is within five miles of the elder brain. Beyond that distance, it is on its own. Mind flayers that venture away from the colony do so only under strict orders from the elder brain. Although such missions risk attracting unwanted attention, they can yield a treasure trove of knowledge and insights to be shared throughout the entire colony when a roaming mind flayer returns.

It is convenient for humanoids to understand a mind flayer colony by thinking of it as a single individual—the elder brain—directing a number of subservient, remote minds, which are the individual mind flayers. Perhaps at one time each mind flayer was independent, but now the elder brain is the only true power. The illithids know that their continued survival and their eventual return to power are possible only though perfect coordination and absolute obedience to the elder brain.

An elder brain is arrogant, scheming, and power hungry, yet quick to flee or beg for mercy in the face of a powerful foe. It has no conception of joy, sympathy, or charity, but is well acquainted with fear, anger, and curiosity. It is an intellect utterly incapable of empathy or concern for creatures other than itself.

An elder brain has a perfect recollection of its race's history. Consequently, it views itself as both a refugee and a victim, forced into hiding by barbaric monsters. An elder brain also sees itself as a savior of the mind flayer race and a living memorial that preserves the memories of the mind flayers' prey. By its twisted logic, humanoids whose brains are devoured by the colony are rendered immortal, their memories preserved forever in the elder brain's labyrinthine mind.

When a mind flayer grows old, becomes infirm, or is grievously injured, the elder brain absorbs it—another form of immortality, as the mind flayer's mind dwells within the hive mind forever after.

See chapter 3 for more information on elder brains.

CEREMORPHOSIS

Mind flayers don't reproduce in the traditional sense. Instead, they lay eggs from which hatch tadpole-like creatures that are used to make more of their kind through a process called ceremorphosis. First, a captured humanoid is rendered docile by a blast of psionic power. A newly hatched tadpole is inserted into the victim's cranium, usually through a nostril or ear canal. The tadpole grows as it devours the humanoid's brain, attaching to the victim's brain stem and becoming its new brain. Over the course of a week, the humanoid body changes form, and a new mind flayer comes into being. The emergent mind flayer often retains a few dim memories from its previous form, but these vague recollections seldom have any bearing on its new life as a brain-eating monster.

THE ELDER BRAIN

Mind flayers use telepathy to communicate with each other and with other creatures. Among their own kind, they form a network of minds. Each mind flayer is an individual node of the network, taking on specific tasks, sharing information, and so on. At the center of this network is the elder brain. The elder brain is the most powerful member of a mind flayer colony. Just as mind flayers treat thralls made from captured humanoids, an elder brain expects perfect obedience from the illithids that dwell in its colony.

If a single mind flayer in a colony sees or hears something, the elder brain and the rest of the illithids in the colony learn of it immediately. The colony relies on a collective memory, composed from the knowledge, experi-

RENEGADE ILLITHIDS

Sometimes a mind flayer that's away from its colony breaks free from the elder brain. Perhaps it ran into a situation where its bonds of obedience were broken, or perhaps the colony was destroyed while it was away. In such a case, the mind flayer becomes free-willed for as long as it avoids contact with an elder brain.

A renegade illithid remains fearful of gith attacks, and likely sets about creating a sort of colony of its own, the better to remain undetected. It gathers minions, establishes a lair, and makes defense of its territory a top priority. Unlike colonial mind flayers, rogue illithids

develop a healthy respect for those not of their kind. They treat especially powerful creatures and individuals as equals, not adversaries, and seek to cooperate with them. A renegade mind flayer might become a trusted advisor or a powerful ally, so long as it is kept well fed. Any alliance it makes, however, collapses if the mind flayer falls under the sway of an elder brain once more.

Enemies Everywhere

Elder brains seek stability and safety for their colonies, and a colony can remain in a relatively peaceful state for decades if it can evade discovery while it acquires food.

Two kinds of events can disrupt the tranquility of a colony: an invasion and the appearance of an ulitharid.

The Gith Never Rest

Githzerai and githyanki remember the mind flayers' enslavement of their ancestors. They dispatch hunting parties to the Material Plane to root out and slaughter illithids wherever they can find them. After centuries of hunting, they have grown very skilled at it. Every mind flayer colony is constantly on the alert for an incursion of gith, even if it has never had to fight them off before.

Underdark predators, adventurers, and other kinds of formidable creatures are just as much of a threat to a colony. Although the mind flayers and their elder brain are incredibly powerful, they aren't invincible: highly accomplished heroes, drow raiding parties, rampant demons, and other hazards of the Underdark can decimate a colony even if they don't succeed in destroying the elder brain.

Rise of a Ulitharid

Rarely, the process of ceremorphosis yields an ulitharid, a more powerful mind flayer that isn't beholden to the elder brain's whims.

The appearance of an ulitharid causes a surge in the colony's collective intelligence, creativity, and strength. As the ulitharid gains power by devouring brains and honing its psionic abilities, the colony becomes more aggressive, seeking to gather more and more thralls.

Eventually, if the colony grows to sufficient size, the ulitharid strikes out on its own. Half the mind flayers and thralls in the colony undertake a great migration, seeking a new lair at least 100 miles away from the old one. Once the ulitharid finds a suitable spot, its followers construct a new lair while it transforms into an elder brain.

Although a creature as arrogant and ambitious as an elder brain might resent an ulitharid's rise, it understands that the mind flayers can't rebuild their shattered empire without expanding their reach. It might resent its new rival, but it can take comfort that soon enough the ulitharid will strike out on its own and the colony will return to normal.

The Grand Design

The first priority of any mind flayer colony is to survive. The elder brain and its servants seek to remain hidden, typically deep within the earth, while harvesting enough intelligent humanoids to nourish themselves and allow for slow but steady growth.

Once a colony is secure, it focuses on the Grand Design—the mind flayers' plan to rebuild their lost empire. The illithids know that reclaiming their rightful place in the world is possible only after the githzerai and githyanki have been eliminated and the remaining humanoids have been turned into docile slaves. To that end, each colony conducts research into the nature of the world and the creatures that inhabit it. The mind flayers examine all facets of reality, seeking any knowledge that could give them the edge they need to confront, defeat, and subjugate their enemies.

Every colony investigates a wide variety of topics and phenomena. A few members might focus on straightforward projects such as developing new uses for psionic power or how to breed savage creatures to serve as foot soldiers. Others pursue more theoretical subjects. A mind flayer might study musical tones, for example, in hopes of finding a way to manipulate the emotions of humanoids. Another might research the food humanoids eat to see if their diet or agricultural practices can be exploited. No line of inquiry is too esoteric if it might provide the next step in enacting the Grand Design.

Strategic Principles

Since mind flayers need to settle near a source of food, they must determine how best to interact with the humanoids they intend to conquer. A colony usually adopts one of three approaches to dealing with its neighbors.

Control. A colony that desperately needs to increase its population concentrates on capturing humanoids to turn them into thralls and illithids. Operating individually or in small groups, its members use stealth and deception to infiltrate the humanoid community while keeping their presence secret. Lacking the numbers or the ability to overwhelm and dominate the entire population, a colony turns its research toward more effective ways to exert control, such as finding a way to amplify an elder brain's power to enable it to exert influence over a greater distance.

Destruction. Because mind flayers are physically weak, they can't rely on simple combat to stand up against their enemies. If a colony finds itself in circumstances where it can be outwardly aggressive, its members likely focus their research on ways to cause mass casualties with minimal risk to themselves, such as plagues or methods to bring about famine and other natural disasters. A mind flayer colony using this strategy collects and feeds on humanoids mainly to use the knowledge they gain to understand their victims' strengths and weaknesses, with the ultimate goal of finding a way to dispense with all of them at once.

Subversion. As a compromise between control and destruction, a colony might attempt to seize control of a few key elements of a humanoid community, and then mix in a few, calculated destructive acts to send the humanoids into an inexorable decline. If the illithids can engineer the collapse of a society's central authority, such as by inciting years of famine while driving the local nobility to bouts of madness through psionic assaults, they can create widespread unrest that the colony can use to its advantage. The mind flayers can become more expansion-minded, confident that any response from the humanoids will be too scattered to threaten them.

Special Goals

Many of the esoteric research topics pursued by a colony reflect the ambitions and priorities of the elder brain that controls it. Each one has particular ideas about how best to contribute to the ultimate success of the Grand Design, including these possibilities:

- The discovery and destruction of all githyanki crèches
- Collecting creatures and instigating insanity in them to create new flavors of thought
- Fostering a school of wizardry to attract intelligent minds for the colony to feed upon
- Rediscovering the secrets of nautiloid manufacture to take to the sky
- Drawing a surface city into the Underdark so as to have a population of ready victims

Roleplaying a Mind Flayer

Mind flayers are inhuman monsters that typically exist as part of a collective colony mind. Yet illithids aren't drones to an elder brain. Each has a brilliant mind, personality, and motivations of its own.

Mind Flayer Personality Traits

d8	Personality Trait
1	I never let pass an opportunity to show my contempt for lesser beings.
2	I like to flavor my meals by engendering positive emotions in my victims before feeding on them.
3	So as not to taint my thoughts, I avoid telepathically communicating with lesser beings when possible.
4	I never eat unless the victim is conscious and aware.
5	I'm very picky. I feed only on the brains of a specific kind of humanoid.
6	I'm curious about how other races live and how their societies function.
7	I find battle stimulating.
8	I'm curious about the limits of other creatures' intelligence and devise situations to test them.

Mind Flayer Ideals

d6	Ideal
1	**Knowledge.** All information is of value. (Neutral)
2	**Obedience.** Nothing is more important than following orders. (Lawful)
3	**Selfishness.** I do my best work when motivated by my own self-interest. (Chaotic)
4	**Truth.** Truth is the foundation of knowledge, so I never lie. (Lawful)
5	**Superiority.** Nothing can be gained from the study of lesser beings. (Neutral)
6	**Domination.** All others should submit to my control. (Evil)

Mind Flayer Bonds

d6	Bond
1	I think the elder brain is wrong about something, and I want to convince it.
2	I have a secret I wish to keep even from other mind flayers.
3	The more the colony grows, the more powerful we all become.
4	Nothing is more important than rebuilding our lost empire.
5	Persistence of my colony is the greatest good.
6	I have important research that must be protected at all costs.

Mind Flayer Flaws

d6	Flaw
1	I am oblivious to the emotions expressed by others.
2	I believe my minions will always do precisely as I intend.
3	I never assume others understand and always explain everything.
4	I have a memory that isn't mine. I obsess about it.
5	It is inconceivable that another creature could out-smart me.
6	I sometimes confuse others' thoughts with my own.

Mind Flayer Names

Among mind flayers, thoughts aren't communicated in language per se, but are instead transmitted telepathically as concepts and associations, which other humanoids interpret in their own language.

Telepathic communication with a mind flayer is frequently accompanied by a mental static that "sounds" to the receiver like an underlying sussuration peppered with guttural clicks. The intensity of this static increases when a mind flayer refers to itself, because with the saying of its name, the illithid is communicating far more information about itself than other humanoids can comprehend. The syllables that make up mind flayer names as expressed in other languages are thus weak approximations of the sound that others hear in their minds when illithids refer to themselves.

An illithid might adopt a name that is easier for minions and allies to speak or that makes it seem more fearsome to enemies, but each begins its life with a thought-name such as the examples in the Mind Flayer Names table, which are suitable for any campaign.

Mind Flayer Names

d12	Name	d12	Name
1	Aurangaul	7	Ralayan
2	Cephalossk	8	Sardsult
3	Drukt	9	S'venchen
4	Drusiss	10	Tharcereli
5	Lugribossk	11	Tobulux
6	Quoor	12	Zellix

Speech

The physiology of mind flayers doesn't leave them well equipped for typical humanoid speech, and most use telepathy exclusively. At times, however, they find it necessary to speak, such as when casting a divine spell, voicing the command word of a magic item, or communicating with multiple creatures at once. A mind flayer accomplishes such vocal feats by forcing one of its tentacles down its own throat and curling the tip to act as a tongue. The process is uncomfortable to the mind flayer, can be disquieting for other creatures to witness, and results in a sound that is often harrowing to the ear. Despite the difficulty, some mind flayers make a study of spoken communication and manage consistently intelligible (if not melodious) speech.

Qualith

The "writing" of mind flayers, known as Qualith, isn't as simple as a set of symbols representing sounds or ideas. An inscription in Qualith captures the thoughts of its creator and psionically transmits the thoughts to a mind flayer who later reads the inscription by touching it with its tentacles. Mind flayers write in Qualith by psionically imprinting their messages on nonmagical, nonliving material they grasp or caress with their tentacles. The imprinting causes imperceptible surface changes to the object, and abrasion or degradation of the material can cause the inscription to fade and fail.

An expression in Qualith is made up of four-line stanzas packed into interlocking blocks, creating complex patterns that are indecipherable by other creatures. Someone that touches a Qualith inscription, however, can receive fragmentary insight into the multilayered thoughts contained within it. A non-illithid that wants to understand a Qualith inscription can make an Intelligence check (DC based on the complexity of the contained thoughts) to try to derive some of the inscription's meaning. Multiple successful attempts might uncover different aspects about the illithid author, its intended meaning, and its intended audience. A failed attempt results in a crushing headache and, in extreme cases, madness. A *comprehend languages* spell provides understanding of the inscription roughly equivalent to what a mind flayer would get from it.

Mind Flayer Thralls

Mind flayers never truly ally with any creatures. They either attempt to seize control of a population by subverting its leaders, or they use psionics to dominate a humanoid and turn it into a thrall.

Illithids sometimes infiltrate an Underdark tribe of humanoids and use their superstitions and traditions as tools to make them useful followers. A mind flayer might use its psionic ability to send visions to a humanoid shaman, causing it to proclaim the mind flayers as emissaries of the gods. With that ruse in place, the "gods" then dictate strict rules that cause some members of the tribe to be branded as heretics, to provide the pretense for occasionally seizing a humanoid and devouring its brain. After the colony depletes and demoralizes the popula-

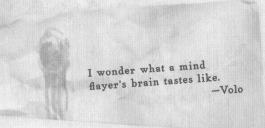

tion sufficiently, the illithids might move in en masse and attempt to turn the remaining followers into thralls.

The process of transforming a creature into a thrall requires the entire colony's energy and attention, making it no small matter. Although it takes only one mind flayer to perform the process, any illithid not directly involved in the process is required to donate its psionic power to the effort while otherwise remaining inactive.

A thrall-to-be is first rendered docile through psionic means. Using a low-power version of its Mind Blast ability, the mind flayer bombards the victim with energy that washes through its synapses like acid, clearing away its former personality and leaving it a partially empty shell. This step takes 24 hours. Over the next 48 hours, the illithids rebuild the victim's memories and personality, and the victim gains the skills and talents it needs to perform its intended function.

The process that creates a thrall changes almost everything about the victim. The creature retains its Hit Dice, hit points, racial traits (but not proficiencies granted by race), and all of its ability scores except for Intelligence. After the first stage of the process, the creature's Intelligence is halved; when the second stage is over, its Intelligence score increases by 1d6.

To complete the process, the thrall receives a new set of proficiencies, a new alignment, and a new personality. Some colonies have learned how to salvage a victim's psionic abilities during the process or how to implant psionic powers into their thralls. Also, some colonies know how to leave a victim's persona intact while infusing it with a fanatical loyalty to the colony's elder brain as well as telepathic power that allows the victim to communicate with its new masters as if it were a mind flayer. This sort of thrall makes a perfect spy, since most would never suspect its true nature.

A thrall can be restored to its former self through a combination of spells and ministration. The thrall must have *regeneration*, *heal*, and *greater restoration* cast on it once per day for three consecutive days. The victim is restored to normal when the final round of spells is cast.

Mind flayers vastly prefer to use humanoids as thralls, since they have a good balance of physical attributes and proper anatomy. Animals, in contrast, require a lot of direct oversight and lack the ability to use tools to help maintain the colony. Among the variety of humanoids available to the illithids, they have some preferences and tendencies.

DUERGAR

Mind flayers have hated duergar ever since the gray dwarves revolted against them, but consider their brains a delicacy. Duergar serve as a constant reminder to the illithids that any creatures that serve them must be kept dimwitted and easily controlled. The clever duergar threw off the long-ago attempt by the mind flayers to rule them and have been enemies of the illithids ever since.

GRIMLOCKS

The first grimlocks were descended from humans corrupted by mind flayers in ancient times, and today these sightless humanoids are among the illithids' preferred servants. Grimlocks are easily cowed by mind flayers, because their culture still centers on worship of and subservience to the illithids. Strong but dimwitted, they lack the initiative and the cunning to rebel as long as they are provided with food, shelter, and the opportunity to pillage and slay. Also, the grimlocks' inability to see gives their brains an exotic flavor that mind flayers love.

KUO-TOA

Illithids once used kuo-toa as slaves extensively, since they proved quite easy to control. In time, though, repeated exposure to the mind flayers' psionic intrusions drove the kuo-toa mad. Nowadays, kuo-toa don't make for good thralls because their insanity makes them difficult to control. Mind flayers consider kuo-toa brains a great treat, but they prefer to eat them raw, unsullied by psionic alteration. Thus, they tend to eat kuo-toa soon after capturing them, rather than attempting to keep them penned up or docile.

QUAGGOTHS

Mind flayers find that the quaggoths' innate, though rarely manifested, talent for psionics makes them excellent thralls. When possible, they manipulate a tribe's thonot (a psionic shaman) into pledging allegiance to a colony. Quaggoths are naturally strong and quick, making them ideal shock troops without any additional modifications. The quaggoths' chaotic tendencies eventually motivate most colonies to convert them into thralls or food, rather than relying on the quaggoth thonot to keep them under control.

HUMANOIDS

Only the most desperate colonies bother using goblins, kobolds, gnomes, and other small humanoids for anything except food. Small humanoids do make a good food source because they tend to gather in large groups, and their fear and despair in the face of a mind flayer incursion make their brains tasty to the illithid palate. They are also relatively easy for larger, stronger humanoid thralls to control. Small humanoids are only rarely transformed into thralls or otherwise kept under firm control.

Almost any humanoid creature can end up as a thrall, and mind flayers sometimes work with whatever victims fall into their grasp. Aside from the exceptions discussed above, they tend to see orcs, bugbears, humans, and other similar humanoids as largely interchangeable. Their brains all have a similar taste, and their utility as thralls is roughly equal.

Mind Flayer Monsters

Mind flayers hardly ever use non-humanoid creatures as thralls or develop other relationships with them. Most of them are either too big and strong to keep penned up for long or too limited in intellect to complete anything but the simplest tasks. In general, non-humanoids found in the company of mind flayers are those that the illithids have created or bred for specific purposes. A few types of these creatures warrant special mention.

Intellect Devourers
Almost every mind flayer colony creates intellect devourers and seeds the areas around its lair with a few to keep watch, slay intruders, and lure fresh victims to their doom.

Mindwitnesses
A mindwitness represents an exception to the typical mind flayer pattern of reproduction. If a colony succeeds in capturing and subduing a beholder, it can use a tadpole to convert the creature into a bizarre hybrid known as a mindwitness. A mindwitness is a sort of psychic hub, able to collect and amplify the illithids' psionic power.

See chapter 3 of this book for more information on mindwitnesses.

Neothelids
These horrors, hated by mind flayers, sometimes come into being when those ignorant of mind flayer lore destroy a colony. A neothelid arises when a tadpole pool is left untended. The tadpoles turn against each other, and the survivor grows to immense size. Comparable to purple worms, these behemoths devour everything in their path.

See chapter 3 of this book for more information on neothelids.

Mind Flayer Lairs

In the lair of a mind flayer colony, the safety and security of its residents is all-important. As a result, illithid lairs are always well hidden and well defended, almost always underground, and within easy reach of humanoids and their succulent brains.

No two lairs are the same, as the resident elder brain drives the form and function of each one. The lair shown in the accompanying map is typical and includes many elements found in every colony's stronghold.

The illithids, with their ability to levitate, design major portions of their lairs so as to make movement as difficult as possible for ordinary two-legged creatures. In such locations, thralls must climb or use ropes to move from place to place.

Brain Chamber
Mind flayers sometimes preserve extracted brains in a magical liquid. Still fully alive, they are kept in the brain chamber. The mind flayers use these brains to advance the study of how psionics affects their enemies. They also enjoy the babble of confused, horrified thoughts that emanates from these sources, and sometimes sit here in quiet, comfortable contemplation. Brains that

prove boring or dull are eventually consumed, while the most interesting ones are added to the brain library.

Brain Library

Extracted brains that are exceptional in some way are kept in the colony's brain library. Here, the mind flayers continue their examinations at a much greater depth.

Cleansing Chambers

Freshly captured victims are processed in the cleansing chambers. Their gear is removed and either destroyed or kept if it is of interest, their hair is shaved to prevent parasites, and any sickly ones are disposed of.

Common Room

The lair's common room serves as a gathering spot for the colony's thralls. As they complete tasks, they come here to rest, eat, and wait for new orders. Any mind flayer in need of assistance can visit this room to obtain the needed muscle power. In the event of an attack, the thralls gather here to arm themselves and ready for battle.

Elder Brain Resting Pool

Usually centrally located, the lair's resting pool is where the elder brain holds court in its brine pool, protected by a nearly impenetrable layer of a glass-like substance that blocks all attacks except for psionic abilities. The elder brain relaxes here, and often assembles the colony members to engage in debates on philosophy and the nature of the planes. This particular colony's elder brain is something of a bully, and has been known to destroy illithids that outwit it in discussions.

Guardrooms

Chambers on the perimeter of the lair are continually staffed by heavily armed thralls, constructs, and other watchers. The inhabitants of these rooms attack strangers on sight and sound an alarm. Any entrance to a lair is always hidden by a secret door, an illusion, or some other barrier.

Illithid Quarters

Each member of the colony claims a single room or a small series of chambers at its own and uses the space to conduct its personal research. One illithid's quarters might contain musical instruments and thralls with melodious voices; another might have cages of specimens that teem with a variety of diseases the mind flayers are studying.

Library (and Dissection Chamber)

The library in a mind flayer lair isn't a collection of books, but an array of still-living organs kept in the same fluid that enables them to keep brains alive. The mind flayers study the organs to refine their experiments. Failed experiments from the transformation chamber eventually are brought here to be dissected so that their organs can be added to the library's contents.

Prison

The results of failed experiments from the transformation chamber are dumped into cages and cells in the prison, to prevent them from getting underfoot elsewhere in the lair. They are eventually processed in the nearby library.

Tadpole Chambers

The elder brain dictates that populations of tadpoles be kept in smaller pools under guard, away from the brine pool. Should the brine pool be destroyed in an attack, these tadpoles stand a better chance of survival.

Transformation Chamber

The transformation chamber contains a number of small cells. The subjects of promising experiments are kept here, bombarded with psionic energy in an effort to warp their physical development. Most creatures that undergo this process are turned into twisted, crippled wretches, but a few emerge stronger and tougher than before.

Nautiloids

Mind flayers employ bizarre flying ships called nautiloids. Able to move through the Astral Plane, nautiloids can also transport mind flayers between the various worlds of the Material Plane.

A nautiloid looks like an enormous conch shell fitted with an exterior deck and a large mass of rubbery tentacles. Ages ago, when the mind flayers could fly through the worlds of the Material Plane without resistance, they used the nautiloid's tentacles to scour the surface for interesting creatures to take back home for study or a feasting.

The most notable feature of a nautiloid is its ability to move directly from one world to another in the Material Plane. Normally, travelers must venture to Sigil, a city in the Outer Planes, and find a doorway leading to the specific world they seek. But mind flayers can use nautiloids to move between worlds without going through Sigil. By this means, they have been able to spread themselves out into almost every corner of the multiverse.

Nowadays, a nautiloid is an incredibly rare sight. A colony in possession of one takes great care to keep it hidden, taking to the sky only out of necessity. Word of a nautiloid seen soaring through the air travels quickly in almost every world and is likely to attract the attention of vengeful githyanki and githzerai. A gith hunting party counts a nautiloid as the greatest prize it can claim, above even an elder brain.

The illithids have lost the secret of manufacturing nautiloids, meaning that the loss of any vessel brings them one step closer to remaining trapped on the Material Plane.

Offensive and Defensive Uses

A colony that has access to a nautiloid uses it as a weapon only in rare circumstances, perhaps as part of the final phase of a plan to subvert, destroy, or control an enemy. Nautiloids move quietly and are almost impossible to detect in the darkness. A sudden strike, with the ship disgorging mind flayers and thralls to finish the assault after it lands, can reduce an enemy settlement to ruins in a single night.

GUARDROOM

ILLITHID QUARTERS

COMMON ROOM

CLEANSING CHAMBERS

ELDER BRAIN CHAMBER

BRAIN LIBRARY

RESTING POOL

TRANSFORMATION CHAMBER

PRISON

TADPOLE CHAMBERS

LIBRARY/DISSECTION CHAMBER

ESCAPE SHAFT

GUARDROOM

UNDERCAVERN

MIND FLAYER COLONY

50 FEET

BLANDO

Most colonies that possess a nautiloid save it for use as an emergency escape vehicle. If pressed by attackers, the surviving illithids and the elder brain move into the vessel and immediately shift to another world, leaving the attackers in their wake.

Mobile Lairs

A few nautiloids are large enough to hold an entire colony, serving as a mobile lair. A colony that uses a nautiloid in this way is much more aggressive than other colonies, since it can effectively carry out hit-and-run attacks and can vacate an area that has been depleted of victims.

These immense vessels invariably have protections that enable them to survive in extreme environments. As such, the illithids typically locate their lair on a mountaintop, beneath the surface of the ocean, or at the upper levels of the atmosphere—places where raids by their enemies are almost impossible.

Mind Flayer Magic

From their perspective as masters of psionic energy, mind flayers view magic as a wild, unpredictable, and primitive source of power. After all, anything that simple humanoids can learn to use must be ineffectual compared to what illithids are capable of.

Arcane Magic

Mind flayers consider arcane magic to be an abomination, a twisted cousin of psionic power that will be erased from the multiverse when the illithids' empire rises again. Some sages speculate that this attitude arose among the mind flayers because magic played an important role in the rebellion of the gith.

In any case, a few renegade mind flayers do pursue arcane magic. Using some of the items or spells they discover, they can shield their minds as they aspire to break free of the elder brain's control.

Eventually, a mind flayer thus separated from the hive turns to the path of lichdom. Just as the elder brain offers immortality to its faithful illithids, so does becoming a lich ensure life everlasting. The feeling of freedom that comes from this change is liberating, but the specter of death forever after colors the mind flayer's actions. An undead mind flayer is hated and hunted by other illithids, but many are powerful enough to stand on their own against attackers.

See the alhoon entry in chapter 3 of this book for more information on undead mind flayers.

Funerary Brain Jars

When a mind flayer dies, other mind flayers try to salvage the dead illithid's brain and bring it to the colony's brine pool for the elder brain to consume. For this purpose, mind flayers craft funerary brain jars made of stone. Every jar is made for an individual, inscribed with Qualith and artwork that relate the mind flayer's accomplishments. Often a mind flayer's funerary brain jar is created long before the illithid's death and updated as the years pass, with the jar serving as a diary of sorts for the one whose brain will eventually fill it. After it is filled with brine, a funerary brain jar can preserve a brain without spoiling for 1d4 + 10 days.

Divine Magic

Illithids acknowledge the existence of divine entities, but it is unusual for any but a deviant mind flayer to actively worship such a power. Since they are capable of planar travel, illithids don't view the afterlife and the Outer Planes in the mythic way that most other races do. Illithids don't believe they possess souls whose eternal fate is governed by the gods. Instead, when a mind flayer's brain is returned to the elder brain to be consumed, the creature's intelligence lives on. Only if an illithid's brain isn't retrieved after death would its consciousness be cast into oblivion.

Two divine entities have long been associated with mind flayers by the scholars of other races. These aren't deities, but rather manifestations of ideal psionic and philosophical mental states that mind flayers revere. Illithids occasionally meditate on these ideals while performing physical movements meant to help them achieve the proper attitude—actions that have often been misinterpreted by observers as worship.

Maanzecorian. The entity/concept called Maanzecorian embodies a complete comprehension of knowledge. It is a state wherein memories, thoughts, and aptitudes are dredged up from one's mind not one at a time as needed, but are all laid bare and brought to the fore at once. The perfect memories exhibited by aboleths have long fascinated mind flayers that emulate Maanzecorian, leading to frequent conflict between the two races.

Ilsensine. Ilsensine is a broader philosophical ideal than Maanzecorian, leading many sages to assume it must be the more important or more powerful of the two "gods." Ilsensine represents not just mastery of one's own mind but a psionic union between oneself and the realm of universal knowledge. Different elder brains have different interpretations of what this state consists of and how to achieve it. Elder brains and illithids that devote themselves to Ilsensine sometimes pursue ways to dominate gods of knowledge or even aspire to supplant those gods on the way to attaining the state of full incorporation into the universal consciousness.

Mind Flayer Magic Items

Some mind flayer colonies have developed the ability to create or modify certain kinds of gear, imbuing them with psionic energy. Mind flayers craft magic items that only they or their thralls can use—a sensible security measure to keep enemies from turning the illithids' own creations against them.

Mind Blade

Weapon (any sword), rare (requires attunement by a specific individual)

Mind flayers can turn any nonmagical sword into a *mind blade*. Only one creature can attune to it: either a specific mind flayer or one of its thralls. In the hands of any other creature, the *mind blade* functions as a normal sword of its kind. In the hands of its intended wielder, the *mind blade* is a magic weapon that deals an extra 2d6 psychic damage to any target it hits.

Mind Carapace Armor

Armor (any heavy armor), uncommon (requires attunement by a specific individual)

Any nonmagical suit of heavy armor can be turned by mind flayers into *mind carapace armor*. Only one creature can attune to it: either a specific mind flayer or one of its thralls. While worn by any other creature, the *mind carapace armor* functions as normal armor of its kind. To its intended wearer, the armor grants advantage on Intelligence, Wisdom, and Charisma saving throws and makes its wearer immune to the frightened condition.

Mind Lash

Weapon (whip), rare (requires attunement by a mind flayer)

In the hands of a creature other than a mind flayer, a *mind lash* functions as a normal whip. In the hands of an illithid, this magic weapon strips away a creature's will to survive as it also strips away flesh, dealing an extra 2d4 psychic damage to any target it hits. Any creature that takes psychic damage from the *mind lash* must also succeed on a DC 15 Wisdom saving throw or have disadvantage on Intelligence, Wisdom, and Charisma saving throws for 1 minute. The creature can repeat the saving throw at the end of each of its turns, ending the effect on itself on a success.

Shield of Far Sight

Armor (shield), rare

A mind flayer skilled at crafting magic items creates a *shield of far sight* by harvesting an eye from an intelligent humanoid and magically implanting it on the outer surface of a nonmagical shield. The shield becomes a magic item once the eye is implanted, whereupon the mind flayer can give the shield to a thrall or hang it on a wall in its lair. As long as the shield is on the same plane of existence as its creator, the mind flayer can see through the shield's eye, which has darkvision out to a range of 60 feet. While peering through this magical eye, the mind flayer can use its Mind Blast action as though it were standing behind the shield.

If a *shield of far sight* is destroyed, the mind flayer that created it is blinded for 2d12 hours.

Mind Flayer Augmentations

Some mind flayer colonies augment their thralls with nonmagical gear to make them more effective as lair guardians and bodyguards. Two examples of mind flayer augmentations are presented here.

Flensing Claws

Illithids don't always provide their thralls with normal weapons, such as swords and axes. Sometimes they improve the natural capabilities of thralls by giving them new anatomy. Flensing claws take the form of articulated digits that extend into long metal blades. The claws are knitted into the flesh and bones of a creature's arms and can't be removed without surgical amputation.

Each set of flensing claws is designed for a specific creature and can't be used by anyone else. A creature equipped with flensing claws can use its action to make one melee weapon attack with the claws. The claws deal slashing damage based on the creature's size: Small, 1d8; Medium, 1d10; Large, 1d12; or Huge, 2d8. The creature adds its proficiency bonus and Strength modifier to any attack roll made with the claws, and its Strength modifier to its damage roll when it hits a target with the claws. Tiny and Gargantuan creatures can't be fitted with flensing claws.

Survival Mantle

This carapace-like augmentation encases portions of the wearer's shoulders, neck, and chest. A survival mantle is equivalent to a suit of nonmagical half plate armor and takes just as long to don or doff. It can't be worn with other kinds of armor.

A creature wearing a survival mantle can breathe normally in any environment (including a vacuum) and has advantage on saving throws against harmful gases (such as those created by a *cloudkill* spell, a *stinking cloud* spell, inhaled poisons, and the breath weapons of some dragons).

Treasure

Mind flayers don't hoard coins, gemstones, jewelry, and other sorts of treasure. However, a colony obsessed with the study of biology would consider a new, alien specimen a great prize, especially a living creature. One concerned with improving its war machinery might seek out new gear, weapons, and armor it can use. A colony that collects gold coins or gemstones might do so not to become rich but to contaminate them with a psychic effect it wants to spread through the surface world.

Adventurers who are motivated by the prospect of vast wealth are best off avoiding mind flayer colonies. Although illithids are evil, and defeating them makes the world a safer place, they don't accumulate material wealth the way many other powerful creatures do. Because of their disdain for arcane and divine power, they discount most magic items as trivial baubles, unless they are useful to the colony for a particular reason. A mind flayer might ignore a bag of diamonds it is offered as a bribe, but might listen to a proposal if a bargaining creature offers it news of a new construction technique developed by the dwarves of a faraway kingdom.

Mind flayers know that humans, orcs, and other primitive creatures love shiny baubles and mysterious devices. They might use such objects they come across the way a rat catcher uses a lump of cheese—a lure to draw quarry into a trap.

ORCS: THE GODSWORN

To feel the thunder of orcish war drums outside the gate and to hear a chorus of voices growling, "Gruumsh!" is the nightmare of every civilized place in the world. For no matter how thick its walls, skilled its archers, or brave its knights, few settlements have ever withstood a full-scale onslaught of orcs.

Every soldier who lives through a fight with orcs tells of confronting a hulking foe that can cleave through a warrior with a single blow, part of a force that can cut down enemies as though they were trembling stalks of wheat before the scythe. Only a skilled and determined hero can hope to survive single combat with an orc.

Savage and fearless, orc tribes are ever in search of elves, dwarves, and humans to destroy. Motivated by their hatred of the civilized races of the world and their need to satisfy the demands of their deities, the orcs know that if they fight well and bring glory to their tribe, Gruumsh will call them home to the plane of Acheron. It is there in the afterlife where the chosen ones will join Gruumsh and his armies in their endless extraplanar battle for supremacy.

GODS OF THE ORCS

Orcs believe their gods to be invincible. They see the principles that define them and their deities at work every day in the world around them—nature rewards the strong and mercilessly eliminates the weak and the infirm. Orcs don't revere their gods as much as they fear them; every tribe has superstitions about how to avert their wrath or bring their favor. This deep-seated uncertainty and fear comes forth in the form of savagery and relentlessness, as orcs ravage and kill to appease the gods in order to avoid their terrible retribution.

At the pinnacle of the orc pantheon is Gruumsh One-Eye, who created the orcs and continues to direct their destiny. He is aided and abetted by the other warrior deities, Bahgtru and Ilneval, who bring strength and cunning to the battlefield. The followers of all three gods are a tribe's raiders and ravagers—often the only part of an orc tribe that its victims ever see.

Deep within the den of a tribe, far away from the warhearth where warriors gather and celebrate, dwell the followers of Yurtrus, the god of disease and death, and Shargaas, the god of darkness and the unknown. Orcs too weak for battle (because of bodily weakness, malformation, injury, or age) often join these cults instead of facing daily humiliation, exile, or death.

Serving as the bridge between the two parts of the tribe are the priestesses of Luthic, the orc goddess who represents both life and the grave. It is her worshipers that raise young orcs to be warriors, and then, at the end of their lives, take them to Yurtrus and Shargaas to be carried into death and the great unknown.

GRUUMSH, "HE WHO WATCHES"

Gruumsh, the undisputed ruler of the orc pantheon, pushes his children to increase their numbers so they may be his instrument of revenge against the realms of elves, humans, and dwarves. In order to spite the gods who spurned him, Gruumsh leads his orcs on a mission

Lord Dagult Neverember once told me, during a drunken tirade, that orcs are fearful of their gods, and, if one plays one's cards right, they can be controlled through that fear and made to dance to any tune.

—Volo

of ceaseless slaughter, fueled by an unending rage that seeks to lay waste to the civilized world and revel in its anguish.

Orcs are naturally chaotic and unorganized, acting on their emotions and instincts rather than out of reason and logic. Only certain charismatic orcs, those who have been directly touched by the will and might of Gruumsh, have the capacity to control the other orcs in a tribe.

A Chosen Few. Orcs don't become renowned in their tribes by choosing Gruumsh; he chooses them. An orc might claim its allegiance to Gruumsh, but only those who have proven themselves through feats of strength and ferocity in war are considered worthy of being true worshipers. Gruumsh singles out these individuals by bestowing upon each one a powerful dream or vision that signifies acceptance into his inner circle.

Those who are visited by Gruumsh are transformed psychologically and often physically by the experience. Some are driven to the brink of madness, reduced to muttering about omens and prophecies, while others become imbued with supernatural power and rise to positions of leadership.

NISHREK AND THE ETERNAL WAR

Orcs believe that if they die with honor, their spirits go to the plane of Acheron, the Infinite Battlefield—specifically the layer of Nishrek, where they join Gruumsh's army and fight on his behalf in the endless war against the goblinoid followers of Maglubiyet. Gruumsh sees this conflict as a chance to pit his people against an eager foe and enable them to prove their worth before their deities. He relishes every short-term triumph and swears revenge for every setback.

Luthic, though, takes a longer view. She understands the cosmic implications of Maglubiyet's attacks. To prevent the goblinoids from outstripping her people in population, she urges the orcs to have many offspring and teach them the ways of battle not only for survival in the material world, but to keep Maglubiyet at bay in the conflict on the planes. Her children will remain in her care, and if need be she wouldn't hesitate to take to the field herself and claw Maglubiyet's beady eyes from his face to prevent him from taking them from her.

The cosmic battle between the two pantheons has raged for eons without resolution, leading those who study its ebb and flow to expect the stalemate to continue. A different view is put forth by the archmage Tzunk, who notes that Maglubiyet has never faced a foe as ferocious and protective as Luthic. He predicts that the war will end with Luthic the only deity standing, as the cave mother ascends to rule her warrior children.

Eyes of Gruumsh. A few of the orcs touched by the power of Gruumsh are given the ultimate honor of carrying a small part of the god's overwhelming rage into battle, in the form of magic that augments their weapons and helps the tribe succeed. To become an eye of Gruumsh, an orc that has been chosen by Gruumsh must gouge out one of its eyes as a sign of devotion, sacrificing half of its mortal vision in return for divine power. These god-touched orcs are revered as living connections to Gruumsh, and are treated with respect even when they are old and infirm.

ILNEVAL, "THE WAR MAKER"

Ilneval is the loyal right hand of Gruumsh. He is the god who plans the attacks and devises the strategies that allow the forces of Gruumsh to dominate the battle and fill their war wagons with plunder and severed heads. Ilneval stands with his bloody sword, calling to those who understand the ebb and flow of combat to sit around his council fire and learn the ways of warfare.

Skilled Strategists. Orcs that show aptitude for the nuances of warfare at an early age are considered chosen by Ilneval and are groomed to serve as blades of Ilneval. These individuals are battle captains that follow the orders of the tribe's chief, leading a portion of the tribe's warriors into the thick of battle and bringing a measure of strategy to the assault. Blades of Ilneval are fearsome opponents, seeming to have an uncanny sense of when to move and when to strike, able to exploit the weakness of their enemy like a pack of hungry wolves.

BAHGTRU, "THE LEG BREAKER"

Despite the influence of Ilneval, orcs are and will forever be brutal and feral in how they wage war. Bahgtru is the deity who epitomizes the physical might and ruthlessness that orcs use to overwhelm their foes. He is the one who drives every thrust of an orc's weapon, so that it does as much harm as possible.

Fearless and Mighty. In the myths, it is said that Bahgtru was out hunting when he was surprised by the mightiest of the behirs, one with hundreds of legs. In a flash, Bahgtru was wrapped in the creature's coils and gripped by its legs. No one had ever escaped the grasp of the behir, but Bahgtru saw this as the ultimate test of his strength, and laughed at his good fortune. One by one, Bahgtru broke the behir's legs, and freed himself from its clutches. The creature's shrieks became the lightning of the storm, and its broken femur became the symbol of Bahgtru's followers, reminding them that anything can be broken and defeated by superior strength.

Competing in Cruelty. Most young orcs that an explorer or an adventurer might encounters are followers of Bahgtru. Orcs of Bahgtru continually try to prove their superior strength and endurance through cruel contests against their tribe mates, acts of unprovoked belligerence, and great success in battle. It is through these tests of strength that Bahgtru's followers prove which among them will eventually be worthy of Gruumsh's unwavering gaze.

The Sacred Bull. Orcs of Bahgtru sometimes enter battle astride aurochs, large creatures that resemble

Not all orc weaklings are taken by those who serve Yurtrus and Shargaas. Some are sent forth into the cities dominated by humans, on dark missions. Beware them.

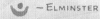 — Elminster

oxen or cattle but are much more ferocious (see appendix B for their statistics). By doing so they honor the creatures as well as their deity, because legends tell that Bahgtru also rode a great bull into battle. No orc will eat or harm one of these sacred beasts, which are believed to be imbued with Bahgtru's spirit.

LUTHIC, "THE CAVE MOTHER"

While Gruumsh is the external force that pushes the orcs to victory over their enemies, it is the influence of Luthic, his wife, that binds them together and makes the orcs internally cohesive. She is the force that keeps the explosive rage of Gruumsh from bursting the orcs apart. If it was not for the followers of Luthic, it is possible that the race of orcs would be no more than small bands of warrior-nomads, scratching out a meager existence, rather than a force capable of great destruction.

Far from the den's war hearth, within the protective depths of the caves, the followers of Luthic tend the orc brood, raising them to be strong and cruel like their progenitors. By invoking the power of superstitions, omens, and traditions, these claws of Luthic hold the tribe together through ritual, fear and, if necessary, force.

Talons of the Bear. Luthic is often thought to take the guise of an enormous cave bear. Her followers honor this aspect of her by keeping cave bears as pets to guard the whelping pens that are filled with squabbling young. Luthic's devoted also grow their claws long and paint them black to mimic the fearsome talons of their goddess. Luthic rewards them by making their claws as strong and tough as iron.

Holding the Fort. Along with protecting the young and the tribe's food stores, the worshipers of Luthic also serve as the crafters, engineers, and builders of an orc tribe. They fashion crude weapons, armor, and the few manufactured items that the orcs need for daily life. When the tribe is away on raids, they are expected to dig deeper into the caverns of the den to create more living space for the ever-increasing population.

YURTRUS, "THE WHITE HAND"

Yurtrus is often depicted as consumed by rot and covered in oozing pustules, utterly repulsive except for his hands, which are pure white and free of any blemish. Yurtrus has no mouth and never utters a sound, so that he may come in absolute silence for his chosen.

The followers of Yurtrus are allowed to dwell on the fringes of the tribe, but are looked upon with distaste and unease. They interact with the tribe mostly on occasions of death, claiming the bones of fallen warriors to add to the ossuary shrines of Yurtrus, and sometimes during shamanic rites when contact with spirits occurs.

The White Hands. Shamans who heed the telepathic whispers of Yurtrus walk the perilous line between the living and the dead, and gain uncanny powers from doing so. Through this nonverbal communion, they begin to comprehend how to use the magic of death. These shamans, known as White Hands, cover their hands in white ash or wear pale gloves made of elf skin to symbolize their connection to the power of Yurtrus. The necromancy practiced by the shamans of Yurtrus is a force considered taboo by orcs, which makes them both revered and feared by the rest of the tribe.

Traffickers of the Dead. Orcs who die "a good death" are sent to Gruumsh by the priests of Yurtrus. The priests seek out the bodies of such fallen heroes and sever their heads, boil or smoke them to rid them of most of the flesh, and then use a ritual punch to break out the bridge of the nose and leave the skull with a single eye. Orcs that appreciate the strength and ferocity of a foe might choose to honor that enemy by giving it the same treatment. The bodies of orcs that die in a failed battle are left behind; they were weak and don't deserve to join Gruumsh. Those that die of old age have typically already been taken into Yurtrus's fold, and their bones are used to build furnishings and structures in the area of the lair dedicated to the worship of Yurtrus.

Chosen of Yurtrus. Orcs that suffer from gruesome diseases are brought into Yurtrus's fold and tended like prized cattle. These orcs are called nurtured ones, and they are considered the chosen of Yurtrus because they have been picked for the special purpose of spreading his virulent message among the enemy. At night, or during a heavy fog, these infected orcs rush toward an enemy's encampment, often through a hail of arrows, in order to spread their affliction within their foe's ranks.

SHARGAAS, "THE NIGHT LORD"

Shargaas is a god of darkness and the unknown. He is a secretive and murderous deity, dangerous to all except Gruumsh. His realm is the darkness that no creatures but those devoted to him can see through.

To other orcs, the followers of Shargaas are depraved and twisted creatures that have no honor and skulk in the shadows. Rejected by Yurtrus as too unsuitable to serve as custodians of the dead, these orcs live even deeper inside the lair, close to where the entrance to Shargaas's realm is located. There in the darkness, orcs exiled to meet their fate are either brought into the fold as members of the tribe's Shargaas cult, or are torn to pieces and devoured as sacrificial tributes by the worshipers of the Night Lord.

Culling the Weak. Although most followers of Shargaas are exiles, living in the farthest reaches of the lair away from the rest of the tribe, others remain within the main body, posing as ordinary warriors. These agents single out the weakest members of the fighting force, because removing these weak links strengthens the rest of the group. Soon after being born, an orc must be able to show that it will grow into a capable warrior, or else it will be visited by the cultists of Shargaas. The cultists also waylay orcs that have proved themselves ineffectual in leadership or combat, then drag them into Shargaas's dark caverns to be ritually murdered and devoured.

This culling of the weak and the unworthy is accepted as necessary by the tribe, but speaking about it is taboo.

Those that disappear are simply said to be "with Shargaas" and are spoken of no more.

Alliance of Convenience. When faced with a particularly skilled foe able to withstand direct assaults, a war chief might call upon the cultists of Shargaas to assassinate an enemy leader, kidnap an influential hostage, or steal a valuable item.

Gruumsh doesn't always look kindly on acts of subterfuge and indirectness, because orcs are meant to take and do what they want through straightforward assault and brutality. Nonetheless, when the chief seeks the aid of Shargaas to accomplish such a task, the leader of the cult is willing to comply—for a price. In exchange for its less than honorable services, the leader will strike a deal with the war chief to provide food, tools, slaves, or some other commodity that the cult prizes.

LIFE IN THE TRIBE

Orcs survive through savagery and force of numbers. Theirs is a life that has no place for weakness, and every warrior must be strong enough to take what is needed by force. Orcs aren't interested in treaties, trade negotiations or diplomacy. They care only for satisfying their insatiable desire for battle, to smash their foes and appease their gods.

BOOMING BIRTH RATE

In order to replenish the casualties of their endless warring, orcs breed prodigiously (and they aren't choosy about what they breed with, which is why such creatures as half-orcs and ogrillons are found in the world). Females that are about to give birth are relieved of their other roles and taken to the lair's whelping pens, where they are tended to by Luthic's followers.

Orcs don't take mates, and no pair-bonding occurs in a tribe other than at the moment when coupling takes place. At other times, males and females are more or less indifferent toward one another. All orcs consider mating to be a mundane necessity of life, and no special significance beyond that is imparted to it.

At 4 years old an orc is considered a juvenile, and by age 12 it is a fully functioning adult. Most orcs don't live past the age of 25 due to battle or illness, but an orc can live to about 40, remaining healthy almost up until the end. Luthic's divine blessing can further extend an orc's life, though Gruumsh is never happy when she uses this power and tends to frown upon the one so "blessed."

FUTURE WARRIORS

Young orcs must mature quickly in order to survive their perilous upbringing. Their early years are fraught with tests of strength, fierce competition and nothing in the way of maternal or paternal love. From the time a child can wield a stick or a crude knife, it asserts itself and defends itself while learning to fight, to survive in the wild, and to fear the gods.

The children that can't endure the rigors of a life of combat are culled from the main body of the tribe, taken into the depths of the lair, and left for the followers of Yurtrus or Shargaas to accept or reject. A fully grown orc warrior is well prepared for a lifetime of combat.

SEARCH, DESTROY, REPEAT

When a tribe is on the move, orc warriors are commanded to scour the surrounding landscape for any opportunity to spill blood and bring glory to their gods. Often, bands of warriors work on a rotation, with one group heading out on a raid just as another group returns, laden with severed heads, sacks of loot, and armfuls of food. Warriors also serve as scouts, bringing back detailed reports about the surrounding area so that the chief can plan where to send raiders next.

The territory that orc war parties cover can extend for many miles around the lair, and any encampment or settlement of elves, dwarves, or humans in that area is at risk. If orcs come upon a target that is too large to assault directly, they will lurk along supply routes, taking out their frustration on caravans and travelers. Left unchecked, a tribe can subsist on this sort of prey and booty for quite some time.

WAR WAGONS

Orcs pillage and scavenge wherever they go—everything is loot, and loot is always something to be proud of. In order to haul as much food and booty as possible back to the tribe's den, every tribe has a sturdy war wagon. Since orcs are poor crafters, most of their wagons are stolen from human or dwarven strongholds, and then decorated with uniquely orcish accessories.

A war wagon is a source of great pride for a war chief, comparable to a human army's banner or flag. Many are clad in armor and festooned with garish trinkets and grisly trophies that hang from hooks and spikes. A war wagon makes a good shield against arrows when orcs besiege an elven fortress, and a heavily modified wagon could serve as a battering ram if a settlement dares to close its gates, blocking the way to the treasures and tasty food that lie within.

A heavily laden wagon that requires the strongest orcs to return it to the lair is a sign of great success. One that can be moved by the runts of the tribe is proof of a shameful performance.

The loss of a tribe's war wagon can undermine the chieftain's authority and cause the tribe to collapse into chaos, with the survivors scattering either to join new tribes or to strike out on their own. At the other extreme, warriors that return home with a heavily laden wagon or after heroically defending it from thieves gain great respect and advance higher in the tribe's pecking order.

ALL ARE FIGHTERS

Most of the orcs that stay behind when the warriors go on their raids are weaker than their tribe mates or otherwise not suited for a life of battle. Worshipers of Luthic fall into this category, as do some of those that revere Yurtrus or Shargaas. But even these orcs are trained in combat, and all of them are expected to act like warriors if the lair is attacked or threatened. Their numbers are augmented by any orogs in the tribe, which are primarily responsible for making sure that the lair is protected from intruders.

SPECIAL ENEMIES

When orcs attack a settlement of humans or halflings, they will kill anyone who presents a threat, but they are more interested in grabbing plunder and food rather than in wanton slaughter. The elderly, children, and any who seem weak or meek enough might escape death. If they leave the population more or less intact, the orcs leave themselves the option of returning to raid the community over and over.

When orcs fight elves, all of that changes. The enmity between the two races cuts to the core, and no orc will leave an elf alive. Orcs become so frenzied in combat against elves that they forget all about taking loot and valuables back to the tribe—the only trophies of any worth are the heads of their enemies.

Orcs treat dwarves somewhat differently from other foes, because they covet the homes that dwarves fashion for themselves. If a tribe succeeds in fighting its way into a dwarfhold, the orcs will butcher any dwarf that stands against them, but it's really all about the property—they would be just as happy if all the dwarves ran away.

STRENGTH RESPECTS STRENGTH

Orcs appreciate physical prowess and formidable combat ability in any form. As such, they might accept other creatures into their ranks from time to time. Orcs have been known to associate with wereboars and ettins, both creatures that can markedly improve a tribe's murderous efficiency. For a promise of sufficient food and loot, a troll might accompany a tribe temporarily.

A group of orcs can be dominated by evil creatures of immense power, and they accept this subservient role either because they are forced to or because it offers them a measure of security while they engage in their savagery. Green dragons, for instance, sometimes use orcs as sentinels or shock troops. Orcs are sometimes attracted to the service of frost giants or fire giants, who then "reward" their loyalty by turning them into slaves.

If a tribe is defeated and driven from its lair, the survivors might come under the sway of a strong but dimwitted creature, such as a hill giant or an ogre. It is also not unheard of for an exceptionally strong and charismatic evil human to lead stray orcs that no longer have a tribe to call their own.

WHEN TRIBES TEAM UP

An orc tribe typically has no more than a few hundred members, because a larger group would need a prohibitive amount of resources to remain strong. As a rule, a tribe is violently hostile toward any other tribe it meets, seeing the rival orcs first and foremost as competitors for food and victims.

On some occasions, though, tribes that have a common concern band together. The result is an orc horde—a sea of slavering killers that washes over the countryside and leaves vast tracts of devastation in its wake. Such an event is rare in the extreme, but its consequences can lay low entire nations that are unable to stand against the wave.

ORC CULTURE AND BELIEFS

Orcs live in constant fear of their gods, and their behavior is rooted in that mentality. They believe that they can see the influence of the gods everywhere in the world around them, and the priests of a tribe are entrusted with the responsibility of identifying these signs and omens—both good and bad—and deciding how the tribe should react to them.

As a race, orcs have no noteworthy universal social traits, but some commonality does exist in the crude written communication that all orcs employ and in the way that they use pigments to decorate and distinguish themselves and their lairs.

OMENS AND SUPERSTITIONS

Orcs believe that any seemingly unimportant discovery or event—a bear's claw marks on a tree, a flock of crows, or a sudden gust of wind—might be a communication from the gods. If the tribe has encountered a similar omen before, the priests understand how to interpret it, but if a sign from the gods has no clear explanation, the priests might have to meditate for hours or days to get a vision of its meaning.

Every group of orcs has particular superstitions and recognizes certain omens. These tenets vary from tribe to tribe, and are often based on events that the tribe has experienced. Here are a few examples:

- If a dwarf or a human invokes its god upon dying, you must carry the corpse's ears for three days to ward off any retribution, and then bury or burn them.
- Three ravens is always a good sign.
- It is good luck to spit where you are about to sleep.
- Gnome bones can ward off diseases if they are worn.
- Don't stand inside a ring of stones, mushrooms, or any other kind of circle.
- Seeing a shooting star before a battle is bad luck. To ward it off, you must swallow a stone.
- A tribute of elf ears brings favor from Gruumsh.
- If you bury five stones at dawn before a long journey, you will always find your way back to the war hearth.
- Stomping your foot three times and uttering "Gruumsh" wards off bad magic.

SYMBOLIC COMMUNICATION

Orcs have a written language adapted from that of the dwarves, but they aren't a literate culture and rarely keep records or write down their thoughts. When orcs need to communicate in writing, they use crude symbols to convey basic information, such as "food stored here," "danger close," or "go this way." A orc raiding party might leave such a sign in its wake, as an aid to other warriors that travel through the same area later on. Mountain guides, druids, and rangers might be familiar with many of these symbols, enabling them to keep their charges from inadvertently stumbling into a tribe's territory.

ORCS AS UNDERLINGS

With their culturally ingrained tendency to bow before superior strength, orcs can be subjugated by a powerful and charismatic individual. Evil human spellcasters and rulers in particular have a penchant for enslaving or deceiving orcs into service. A leader backed by a great military force could swoop down upon a tribe, kill its leaders, and cow the rest of the orcs into submission.

A spellcaster typically takes a more devious approach, using magic to conjure up false omens that strike fear into the tribe and make it obedient. A wizard might manipulate a few of the orcs that rank just below the war chief, using them as pawns to help overthrow the leader. The wizard validates the change in command with signs supposedly delivered by the gods (which are in truth nothing but a few well-cast illusions), and turns the tribe into a strike force eager to do the bidding of its new chief.

The survivors of a tribe scattered by defeat sometimes fall back on their fighting skills to find employment, individually or in small groups, with whoever is willing to hire them. These mercenaries, while they might pride themselves on their seeming independence, nevertheless strive to follow through on their end of a bargain, because being paid by one's employer is better than being hunted down for breaking a deal.

COLORS OF CONQUEST

Three colors have special meaning to all orcs, and they adorn their bodies, possessions, and lairs with pigments that produce those hues. Red ochre is used to represent blood, grayish-white ash to represent death, and charcoal to represent darkness.

The unwritten laws that govern the status of individual orcs within a tribe are manifested to a degree in how each orc uses these colors on itself and its personal items. For instance, the chief of one tribe might be the only one that has the right to stain its tusks with red ochre, while the warriors of another tribe rub streaks of ash into their garments to signify their safe return from a raid.

ROLEPLAYING AN ORC

Most orcs have been indoctrinated into a life of destruction and slaughter. But unlike creatures who by their very nature are evil, such as gnolls, it's possible that an orc, if raised outside its culture, could develop a limited capacity for empathy, love, and compassion.

No matter how domesticated an orc might seem, its blood lust flows just beneath the surface. With its instinctive love of battle and its desire to prove its strength, an orc trying to live within the confines of civilization is faced with a difficult task.

ORC PERSONALITY TRAITS

d6	Personality Trait
1	I never relinquish my weapon.
2	I welcome any chance to prove my battle skills.
3	I always appear like I am about to kill everyone around me.
4	I love a good brawl.
5	I drink the blood of monsters to consume their power.
6	I chant orcish war dirges during combat.

ORC IDEALS

d6	Ideal
1	**Strength.** Showing superior strength brings honor to Gruumsh. (Any)
2	**Prowess.** Killing all your enemies is the path to greatness. (Evil)
3	**Dominance.** I will have achieved glory when all cower before my might. (Evil)
4	**Intimidation.** I can get what I want from weaklings that fear me. (Evil)
5	**Glory.** The goals of the tribe don't concern me. Personal glory is what I crave. (Chaotic)
6	**Savagery.** I will not be controlled. (Chaotic)

Orc Bonds

d6	Bond
1	I will defend my tribe to the death.
2	Every serious choice I make must be decided by signs or omens from the gods.
3	I carry the teeth of a great warrior. They inspire me to commit great deeds in battle.
4	To avenge Gruumsh, I will kill every elf I see.
5	I will seek and destroy those who murdered my tribe.
6	I owe my survival to a non-orc.

Orc Flaws

d6	Flaw
1	I have a calm temperament and let insults roll off my back.
2	I don't fear the gods and have no patience for superstitions.
3	I am slow to anger, but when I do become enraged I fight until my enemies are dead, no matter the cost.
4	I understand the value of civilization and the order that society brings.
5	I don't trust anyone.
6	I believe in living to fight another day.

Orc Names

Orc names don't always have meaning in the Orc language, and most noteworthy orcs are given epithets by their tribe mates.

Orc Names

d12	Male Name	Female Name	Epithet
1	Grutok	Kansif	The Filthy
2	Lortar	Ownka	Skull Cleaver
3	Abzug	Emen	Eye Gouger
4	Shugog	Sutha	Iron Tusk
5	Urzul	Myev	Skin Flayer
6	Ruhk	Neega	Bone Crusher
7	Mobad	Baggi	Flesh Ripper
8	Shamog	Shautha	Doom Hammer
9	Mugrub	Ovak	Elf Butcher
10	Bajok	Vola	Spine Snapper
11	Rhorog	Engong	Death Spear
12	Jahrukk	Volen	The Brutal

Half-Orcs

The lore of humans depicts orcs as rapacious fiends, intent on coupling with other humanoids to spread their seed far and wide. In truth, orcs mate with non-orcs only when they think such a match will strengthen the tribe. When orcs encounter human who match them in prowess and ferocity, they sometimes strike an alliance that is sealed by mingling the bloodlines of the two groups.

A half-orc in an orc tribe is often just as strong as a full-blooded orc and also displays superior cunning. Thus, half-orcs are capable of gaining status in the tribe more quickly than their fellows, and it isn't unusual for a half-orc to rise to leadership of a tribe.

Orogs

Orcs believe that an orog's exceptional strength and intelligence are a gift from the goddess Luthic to ensure that her brood survives and flourishes. So, when an orog is born, a tremor goes throughout the tribe, for the event is seen as a great blessing from the goddess, but it brings tension as well.

An orog within the tribe poses a potential problem for an orc war chief: will the orog grow up to be a powerful ally or a dangerous adversary? Most war chiefs treasure their positions so highly that they would refuse to relinquish the title, even to a clearly superior creature. Thus, a chief might be tempted to kill the orog while it is still young and weak, but such an act would most certainly incur the wrath of Luthic.

To raise an orog within the tribe, from the chief's point of view, is to take a risk that the orog won't one day rise up and usurp power from the chief. Because of this sentiment, orogs are secreted away by priestesses of Luthic and raised out of the sight of the chief.

Keeping the Balance

What most war chiefs don't realize, or trust in, is the fact that orogs aren't a direct threat to their rule. By nothing more than their presence, orogs serve as a balancing force. Indoctrinated by the priestesses of Luthic, they see to it that Luthic's followers are protected from the more aggressive members of the tribe. Most orogs don't go on raids, because their main responsibility is the safety of the tribe members that remain in the lair—ensuring that the tribe remains intact even if a raid goes badly and many warriors are killed. In times of internal strife, such as after the death of the chief, orogs move in to oversee the selection of a new leader and keep the tribe from splintering due to infighting. Orogs strive not to lead their tribe, but to keep the tribe together—which is often the more difficult of the two tasks.

Breaking the Mold

An orc lives on the edge of chaos and rage, and orogs are no exception. At times, an orog goes rogue and becomes a force of destruction in the tribe, seeking to fracture the group along lines of loyalty to the gods. If those who worship Luthic and those who worship Gruumsh split, the tribe can be torn apart by the schism.

At the other extreme, an orog might accept a role in battle or leadership under special circumstances. If a tribe finds itself up against formidable or unexpected resistance, the endurance and superior intellect of an orog serving as chief or battle master can be enough to win the day when a less capable leader would have failed.

Tanarukks

A tanarukk is an abyssal creation infused with demonic power. Half demon, half orc, it wanders the world in a murderous haze. Its dimly glowing red eyes burn under thick, horn-like brows, and its tusks and claws are razor-sharp. Because the skin of tanarukks is unnaturally tough, they rarely wear armor, preferring to rush into battle unencumbered, smashing their foes with a demon-forged maul or tearing them apart.

A tanarukk is spawned when an orc tribe turns away from its gods and makes sacrifices to the demon lord Baphomet. The lords of the Abyss are always eager to claim more followers, and the violent orcs are prime candidates for corruption. A tribe pushed to the edge of destruction, its faith in its deities shattered, might beseech Baphomet to bless its next generation of warriors. In so doing, Baphomet imbues the tribe's unborn with demonic might, yielding a generation of tanarukks.

The orc deities consider such a betrayal of their worship as a crime punishable by obliteration, and orcs faithful to their gods view tanarukks as horrid blasphemies that must be attacked on sight.

On rare occasions, a non-orc that has gained control over a tribe performs a ritual to Baphomet in hopes of spawning tanarukks to serve as a squad of shock troops. Only the strongest warlords and spellcasters can keep such a force in line, meaning that often the would-be conqueror is slain by its own creations.

Orc Lairs

An orc tribe needs a home base of sorts—a place where warriors can reconnoiter after a raid, and ideally also a site that can be easily defended to ensure the safety of the tribe's noncombatants. Orcs establish their encampments mainly in mountainous areas, around and within deep caves or large crevasses in the rock. Although they prefer such terrain for strategic purposes, they can adapt and thrive in almost any environment.

Every encampment is divided along lines of worship. Those who revere Gruumsh, Ilneval, Bahgtru, and Lu-

thic are given the best parts of the lair, while the followers of Yurtrus and Shargaas are relegated to the deep, dark recesses of the site, away from the rest of the tribe.

At the center of the camp is the tribe's war hearth. Once a war hearth is lit, the priests of Gruumsh keep it continually burning, for it represents the rage within Gruumsh's unblinking eye. The orcs converge on the hearth to celebrate victory and to feast after a kill. If a tribe moves its camp, coals from the hearth are kept glowing within shells and pots so they can be used to start the war hearth at the new encampment.

Given a choice between occupying a site on the surface and one that is wholly or partly underground, an orc chieftain typically opts for the latter. If the surface location happens to be a ruin left behind by another race, orcs are more likely to use it as a temporary campsite. The ruins of elven settlements are the exception to this rule. If orcs come across such a place, they desecrate it and leave it unfit for any sort of habitation.

A tribe uses its home base for as long as the resources in the surrounding area hold out—enough food for the foragers and hunters, and enough victims for the warriors. The orcs might have to range farther and farther from their lair as prey becomes more scarce, and after a few months or a year or two, the tribe will be forced to move on and find more fertile hunting grounds.

On occasion, a tribe finds itself in a best-of-both-worlds situation, able to take over occupancy of an underground space voluminous enough to accommodate all the factions in the tribe and within raiding distance of a steady supply of prey.

The orc stronghold depicted and described here is an example of such a place, which could suit the needs of a tribe for several years or even decades. It has several subterranean chambers, conveniently configured to provide every group of worshipers with appropriate quarters, and it is accessible from the surface through only one well-guarded passageway.

Main Chamber

The warriors that worship Gruumsh and Ilneval occupy the main area of the complex, a large cavern that has the war hearth at its center and a shrine to Ilneval along the perimeter. The focal point of the shrine is a blood-covered sword mounted on the wall.

The area also includes a pile of broken femurs that represents a shrine to Bahgtru. The worshipers of Bahgtru are mostly young, brash orc warriors, eager to prove their strength and bravery to the elders of the tribe. Even if space is available in the stronghold, they often live outside the entrance in crude bivouacs and roughshod fortifications, protecting their elders by guarding the stronghold's vulnerable spot.

Off to one side of the chamber, away from where the warriors are quartered, is the fighting pit, a sunken and fenced-off area where orcs settle their differences or engage in contests of strength.

War Chief's Quarters

Adjacent to the main chamber is the room where the war chief resides, holds council, and hands out blessings or punishments from Gruumsh. The best loot and trophies of triumph are piled in this room and considered to be the property of the chief. A fire, not as large as the war hearth, burns in its center.

Next to the chief's enclosed sleeping area is a shrine to Gruumsh consisting of a crude stone effigy of He Who Watches, surrounded by bloody offerings.

Caves for Followers of Luthic

Orcs who worship Luthic are sequestered in a cavern off the main chamber, where they protect the young and supervise food stores. These orcs take control of prisoners brought back from raids, using them as slave labor to dig out new living space and do other menial tasks.

Most of Luthic's faithful reside in this area, close to the whelping pens where young orcs are kept until they grow old enough to contribute to the tribe. When they're not being worked, slaves are housed in a small adjoining chamber and watched over by a group of cave bears that Luthic's worshipers keep as pets.

Many of Luthic's priestesses have their quarters in a nearby cavern that holds the tribe's shrine to Luthic. She is represented by a crude stone statue with claws covered in charcoal and a body smeared with red ochre.

Caves for Followers of Yurtrus

Followers of Yurtrus reside on the threshold of where the deep area of the cavern system begins. They are the keepers of the dead, and the entrance to their realm is festooned with piles of bones and skulls. An altar to Yurtrus, made of stone with a hand painted in ash and tallow on it, stands in a cramped chamber apart from the main living area that is lined with skulls and bones.

Caves for Followers of Shargaas

Followers of Shargaas dwell within the most remote area of the stronghold, immersed in darkness and feared by the rest of the tribe. The tribe's altar to Shargaas is a bloodstained rock.

The stronghold depicted in the map features a number of small passages that lead away from the depths of the lair and eventually provide egress to the surface. The members of the tribe's Shargaas cult, which call themselves the Red Fang of Shargaas, take advantage of these secret tunnels to raid the outside world and bring back prisoners.

The members of the Red Fang use giant, carnivorous bats as mounts, that allow them to gain silent access to any location. Those who think they can hide under cover of darkness or escape invisibly are easy marks for the Red Fang's bats, which locate their prey with high-pitched clicks and shrieks, then swoop down and snatch up their prey with razor sharp claws.

Bat riders of the Red Fang return from their raids the same way they exited—through a crack in the cliff face far away from their lair. A tunnel leads through layers of damp stone and crystallized minerals before eventually opening out into their subterranean domain. Captives are used as food for the brood of giant bats that roost in the rookery or are kept as slaves to be worked or used for barter.

Treasure

Orcs are consummate raiders. When they attack and overwhelm, they claim as booty anything of value that they can carry—and an orc's definition of "value" can be very loose indeed.

The strongest or most dominant orcs will always claim the best loot after a successful raid, and since the pecking order in the group is almost always firmly established, there are usually no squabbles over who gets what. If the tribe's war wagon is available, it is used to transport large or especially treasured items.

Each orc warrior carries its personal loot from the raid in a sack. These are the trophies of victory that orcs brandish and boast about when they return to the den. A loot sack might contain something of demonstrable worth or usefulness, something that's edible (or used to be), or something that was acquired at great risk. In any case, once the bragging is over, the loot is eaten, put to use, or otherwise disposed of.

The Orc Trophies table provides a selection of items that might be found in an orc's loot sack.

Orc Trophies

d10	Trophy	d10	Trophy
1	1d12 elf ears	6	1d20 severed fingers
2	1d4 dwarf beards	7	1d8 eyeballs
3	1d6 human heads	8	Flayed elf skin
4	Skulls and bones	9	Dire wolf hide
5	Cave bear paw	10	Random trinket*

* Roll on the Trinkets table in chapter 5 of the *Player's Handbook*.

Orc Stronghold

BAHGTRU BONE PIT

WARRIOR CAMP

MAIN GATE

OUTER GUARDROOM

AMBUSH PORTAL

FIRE PIT

S

WAR HEARTH

WARRIOR CAMP

WARRIOR CAMP

OFFERING TO LUTHIC

OFFAL PIT

SLAVE PENS

S

S

OFFAL PIT

CAVE BEARS

N

SLEEPING AREA

FOOD STORAGE

SHRINE TO ILNEVAL

FIGHTING PIT

WHELPING PIT

LUTHIC DEN

FIRE PIT

LIVESTOCK

FOOD STORAGE

YURTRUS CAMP

YURTRUS SHRINE

OFFAL PIT

TROPHIES

LOOT

CHIEFTAIN'S HUT

ALTAR TO GRUUMSH

SHRINE TO LUTHIC

LOOT

PRISONERS

SHARGAAS LAIR

PRIESTESS QUARTERS

PIT TRAP
T

PIT TRAP
T

PIT TRAP
T

GUARD ROOM

GIANT BAT ROOKERY

T

PIT TRAP

BAT FOOD

OFFAL PIT

ALTAR TO SHARGAAS

□ = 10 FEET

BLANCO

Yuan-ti: Snake People

The serpent creatures known as yuan-ti are all that remains of an ancient, decadent human empire. Ages ago their dark gods taught them profane, cannibalistic rituals to mix their flesh with that of snakes, producing a caste-based society of hybrids in which the most snake-like are the leaders and the most humanlike are spies and agents in foreign lands.

Humans Transformed

The people who became yuan-ti were one of the original human civilizations. Their society built great temples of stone and forged metal into armor, tools, and weapons. In their ceremonies they paid homage to the snake as the embodiment of the qualities they most appreciated. They developed a philosophy of separating emotion from intellectual pursuits, allowing them to focus their energy on personal advancement and expanding their territory. They believed themselves to be the most enlightened mortals in the world, and in their hubris they sought to become ever greater.

The serpent gods of the primordial world heeded the prayers of these people and hissed dark demands into their ears. The people tainted their souls by performing human sacrifices in the name of the gods, debased their flesh by cannibalizing their victims, and then performed a sorcerous ritual while writhing in pools filled with living snakes that enabled them to mix their flesh with that of serpents, becoming like the gods in body, thought, and emotion. Freed from the limitations of their human bodies, the yuan-ti used their new abilities to conquer new lands and expand their borders.

One Race, Many Forms

The bodies of all yuan-ti have a mix of humanlike and snakelike parts, but the proportion varies from individual to individual. After the initial metamorphosis of the humans, their society quickly coalesced into a caste system based on how complete a person's transformation was. The vast majority of yuan-ti fall into three categories—abominations, malisons, and purebloods—while the mutated broodguards and exceedingly rare anathemas have their place in the hierarchy as well.

All yuan-ti can interbreed. Females usually lay clutches of eggs, which are stored in a common hatchery, although live births aren't uncommon. A mating between yuan-ti of different types almost always produces eggs that hatch into yuan-ti of the weaker parent, so most choose partners of the same type in the interest of maintaining the strength of their personal bloodline.

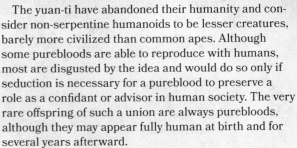

Ye cannot goad one of the serpent folk into hatred or fear, or evoke in it love or friendship. They may feign such things to cozen ye, but within they are always coldly, calmly calculating.

—Elminster

The yuan-ti have abandoned their humanity and consider non-serpentine humanoids to be lesser creatures, barely more civilized than common apes. Although some purebloods are able to reproduce with humans, most are disgusted by the idea and would do so only if seduction is necessary for a pureblood to preserve a role as a confidant or advisor in human society. The very rare offspring of such a union are always purebloods, although they may appear fully human at birth and for several years afterward.

The yuan-ti know rituals that can transform an individual into a more powerful type. The cost and time required to perform the ritual is prohibitive, and as a result most yuan-ti never get the opportunity to undergo such a transformation. Every use of the ritual must be modified to suit the individual undergoing transformation, and requires rare herbs, exotic magical substances, snakes, and one or more humans to be sacrificed and eaten as part of the procedure.

Undercover Empire

The human civilization that gave rise to the yuan-ti was among the richest in the mortal world. It rapidly progressed in metalworking, using keen intellect and magic to discover the secrets of making steel. Its military shattered rival tribes and developed advanced tactics for fighting in forests and open plains.

The civilization grew into a cluster of allied city-states. Conquered neighbors were allowed to keep their leaders and culture so long as they paid tribute, swore allegiance to the victors, and incorporated their conquerors' serpent gods into their religions. These victories sent a constant influx of food, ore, and slaves back to the home cities.

The wealth of the empire allowed the ruling elite plenty of time to focus on intellectual pursuits. These nobles turned to philosophy and prayer, offering gifts of magic and animal sacrifices to their serpent gods, paying homage to the perfection of the ophidian form. The serpent gods taught the humans how to take on aspects of the snake, but the cost of the change was high, requiring many sacrifices for each person to be transformed. Entire households of slaves in one city-state were killed and eaten to create the first yuan-ti, and once the news of how to perform these rituals spread to other leaders, the call for slaves to fuel the process increased. As the serpent gods began to demand more and more sacrifices, the yuan-ti stepped up their raids on bordering settlements to meet this need.

The physical and magical prowess of the yuan-ti empire allowed the former humans to retain their holdings for several hundred years, until a combination of drought, attacks by enemies (including dragons and nagas), civil war, torpor among the serpent gods, and the development of iron weapons by the some of their conquered enemies finally loosened the yuan-ti's hold over nearby lands. The serpent people withdrew to their fortified cities and underground temples, ceding the rest of their territory to their former minions. The yuan-ti crawled away and hid in a matter of weeks, all but disappearing from the world. Yuan-ti structures throughout the land were torn down to celebrate liberation from the snake-bodied oppressors, and within a few generations the yuan-ti were all but forgotten by the new humanoid civilizations.

For over a thousand years after their empire fell, the yuan-ti remained ensconced in their hidden strongholds, biding their time until they were ready to strike again. Today, with their numbers greatly depleted and their enemies much stronger than in ages past, the yuan-ti know they can't resort to direct attacks in order to reclaim their rightful place in the world. Operating out of the subterranean ruins of their buildings in foreign lands, yuan-ti agents infiltrate enemy governments to discover weaknesses that their leaders can exploit. The yuan-ti look forward to the day when their empire rises again and spreads across the world like venom through the blood, as it once did.

Because their population is so small, the yuan-ti are aware they are vulnerable in open warfare. Instead, their current plans assume they will never rule outwardly in human society, so they gain influence by controlling enemy rulers—and those close to them—through blackmail, drugs, magic, and the subterfuge of disguised purebloods.

Gods of the Yuan-ti

The detached, intellectual nature of the yuan-ti doesn't lend itself to fervent or devout worship in the manner that others revere their deities. Nonetheless, they acknowledge a wide range of supernatural and divine entities. Some of these are true deities, some are primordial spirits as powerful as gods, and some are creatures of questionable origin.

In addition to the three primary deities discussed below, the yuan-ti worship over a dozen other "serpent gods"—lesser beings such as animal spirits, ascended heroes, divine servants of more powerful gods, and demon lords. Many of the cults devoted to these lesser gods are unique to a particular city, and followers of the three main yuan-ti deities usually consider these religious practices quaint rather than threatening.

Dendar

The Night Serpent came into being before recorded history, spawned from the feverish dreams of the first intelligent creatures. She subsists and grows stronger by feeding on the fears that plague the folk of the world. Her followers believe that Dendar is a harbinger of the end of things, which will come when she amasses enough power to consume the world. Another legend concerning her speaks of an iron door to the underworld behind which she lurks; when the time is right, she will tear it down, then eat the sun, plunging the world into darkness before she finally devours it.

Yuan-ti worshipers of Dendar are led by nightmare speakers, malison warlocks that honor their deity through acts of terror and receive magical power in return. Rather than killing enemies, these followers of the Night Serpent prefer to threaten and torture them, the better to feed and strengthen the goddess. See chapter 3 of this book for more information on yuan-ti malison nightmare speakers.

Calm long-view schemers, innate deceivers, and immune to poison—yuan-ti make perfect courtiers. And, worse for the rest of us, rulers.

—Elminster

Merrshaulk

Though the Master of the Pit is not conscious, neither is he entirely dormant. Mirroring the fate of yuan-ti in the world, Merrshaulk entered a deep slumber when the serpent folk left the surface and went into hiding in ages past. It is unclear if declining worship caused him to fall asleep, or if his prolonged torpor caused his worshipers to abandon him. Even in his compromised state, Merrshaulk grants spells to his clergy in response to their invocations. Rousing him for advice or direct intervention is possible, but requires many ritual murders to be performed in his name, and his return to consciousness lasts only a short time.

The leaders of Merrshaulk's worshipers, called pit masters, are malison warlocks that uphold and advance the age-old yuan-ti traditions. They sense that it has become easier to wake him in recent decades, and believe this to be a sign that he will soon fully awaken, shed his skin, and—renewed by transformation—restore the yuan-ti to their rightful place as masters of the mortal world. See chapter 3 of this book for more information on yuan-ti malison pit masters.

Sseth

In the last years before the yuan-ti empire collapsed, Sseth appeared to the serpent folk in the form of a winged yuan-ti. He promised to lead the yuan-ti away from the brink of defeat and back to the pinnacle of world domination in return for their veneration. Many of Merrshaulk's devout turned to the worship of the Sibilant Death, believing him to be an avatar of their deity. They granted him enough power to mount a brief recovery, but those actions were too little and too late to prevent the collapse of the empire. Sseth chose to rest and gather strength during the years of decline, as more and more of the yuan-ti adopted his worship.

Gods of Other Worlds

In worlds other than the Forgotten Realms, yuan-ti make pacts with deities of the pantheons presented in appendix B of the *Player's Handbook*. The following are suggested yuan-ti deities for each pantheon.

Greyhawk. Erythnul, Iuz, Tharizdun, Vecna.
Dragonlance. Chemosh, Sargonnas.
Eberron. The Fury, the Keeper, the Mockery, the Shadow, the Traveler.
Celtic. Math Mathonwy, Morrigan.
Greek. Ares, Hecate.
Egyptian. Apep, Set.
Norse. Hel, Loki.

His most devout followers, known as mind whisperers, use their god-given magic to emulate Sseth's tactics and principles. They strive to succeed by offering an alternative choice to contesting viewpoints or plans, and in so doing they exude an air of self-importance that gives them a less than savory reputation among yuan-ti that follow other gods. See chapter 3 of this book for more information on yuan-ti malison mind whisperers.

Serpent Gods

The yuan-ti's dispassionate attitude toward religion is especially evident among the powerful yuan-ti that take one of the lesser serpent gods as an object of worship. The worshiper of a serpent god pays homage not out of respect or fear, but because it aspires to emulate the entity, beseeching it to reveal the secret of transcending mortality. Then, once armed with that knowledge, the yuan-ti sets out to supplant its deity and become a new serpent god.

The serpent gods don't wish to be brought low, or to be bled of power as Merrshaulk was, so they mollify their worshipers with pronouncements that hint at what the supplicants seek. The truth is never easy to ferret out, but rarely an exceptionally clever yuan-ti succeeds in attaining divine form and vanquishing its benefactor. This cannibalistic pressure from mortals means that the lower ranks of the serpent gods experience a change every century or so, although often it is the newest yuan-ti godling that falls prey to the next one's ambitions.

YUAN-TI RELICS

STRUCTURED SOCIETY

The goal of every yuan-ti is to transform itself into the ideal combination of snake and humanoid. This attitude is reflected in yuan-ti society by a caste system, with status predicated on where a particular form of yuan-ti lies along the ladder of transformation.

The basic form of yuan-ti society is a pyramid with abominations at the top, malisons in the middle level, and purebloods at the base. The outliers are the anathemas, the most powerful yuan-ti of all, and two castes that lie beneath all yuan-ti: broodguards and slaves.

Statistics for yuan-ti anathemas, yuan-ti broodguards, and new kinds of yuan-ti malisons appear in chapter 3. Two new malison variants are presented in the "Yuan-ti Malison Variants: Types 4 and 5" sidebar in this chapter.

YUAN-TI ANATHEMAS

The exceedingly rare yuan-ti known as anathemas look much like abominations, but larger, with clawed hands, and six snake heads sprouting from where the head should be. Each anathema is the product of a unique ritual that alters its original abomination form, increasing its size, power, and intelligence. Other yuan-ti treat anathemas like demigods, and they naturally assume a leadership position over all others in the area.

An anathema's aggressive presence brings about a transformation in a yuan-ti city, pushing it to become more warlike and expansionistic. The anathema directs the yuan-ti to wage small-scale wars on humanoids, usually through proxies such as cults and allied creatures, and uses these conflicts to gather riches and slaves until it has enough resources to establish the yuan-ti as the rulers of a region.

YUAN-TI ABOMINATIONS

Mostly ophidian, but with humanlike arms that can wield weapons and use tools, abominations closely resemble the perfect form that the serpent gods envisioned. Absent the presence of an anathema, yuan-ti abominations are the leaders in most yuan-ti cities.

YUAN-TI MALISONS

The various kinds of malisons are imperfect compared to abominations but still a step above humankind in the eyes of the serpent gods. Malisons tend to be receptive to religion, seeking insight about how they can improve toward the serpent ideal, and many of them become leaders in the worship of one of the serpent gods.

YUAN-TI PUREBLOOD

The most numerous of the yuan-ti, purebloods are also the most humanlike, exhibiting only one or two snakelike features such as slitted pupils or patches of scales on the skin.

In yuan-ti cities, purebloods are treated fairly but live in an environment where their wants and needs are eclipsed by those of the malisons and abominations.

Because purebloods can easily pass as human, their most important function is as agents of the yuan-ti in the outside world. They can live incognito among humans as diplomats, infiltrators, and spies. Because they get

From Calimshan and the Lake of Steam out along the trade routes to cross the world, yuan-ti poisons and potent liquors are covertly sold. Beware! Some of the latter slowly and subtly bring imbibers under the sway of the next pureblood serpent-spy or yuan-ti malison to meet with them unlooked-for.

— ELMINSTER

to wield power and influence while playing such roles, some purebloods surround themselves with luxury in their human guises and then become resentful when they have to return home and live under the caste system again.

YUAN-TI BROODGUARDS

The devolved creatures known as broodguards are created by feeding humanoids a special elixir, which gives them scaly skin and a compulsion to follow orders. Because their minds are crippled by their transformation, broodguards are less useful than slaves for many tasks, but because of their unwavering loyalty they make capable guardians for yuan-ti eggs.

Broodguards are technically slaves, but because of their loyalty and the expense of the potion that creates them, they have slightly higher status than common slaves—meaning that a pureblood is more likely to give a suicidal order to a slave than to a broodguard.

SLAVES

Every yuan-ti settlement has a number of other creatures under its control, including intelligent humanoids, charmed or trained beasts, and even undead or conjured minions. Regardless of their nature, all are treated as slaves: no creature that is not a yuan-ti is fit for anything other than menial labor and subservience. Slaves that fail to follow orders or lag in their duties are dispatched or turned into broodguards.

EMOTIONLESS EVIL

During their ascension ages ago, the yuan-ti freed themselves from the yoke of their human emotions. Now they view the world from a pragmatic and dispassionate perspective. They understand emotional connections in a detached, intellectual way, and recognize that these feelings in others can be exploited through bribes, favors, or threats.

As creatures devoid of emotion, yuan-ti exhibit behavior and use tactics that exemplify that outlook (or lack of one). Whether in combat or in daily life, the following principles guide the yuan-ti in all they do.

Other Lives Are Cheap

Yuan-ti put little value on humanoid lives, even those of their own slaves and cultists. They would poison children to carry out a threat against their parents, or turn one person into a broodguard in order to show her family the consequence of resistance. They might refrain from provoking others' feelings if doing so could adversely affect the yuan-ti's plans, but they understand humanoid psychology well enough to know that they can get away with this casual disregard for life almost anytime.

Furthermore, in the yuan-ti caste system, a greater yuan-ti's life is worth far more than a lesser one's. Weaker citizens are expected to lay down their lives to protect their betters. Leaders rely on this zealotry in their plans, and although they don't needlessly waste the lives of purebloods on futile actions, most strategies include a fallback option in which mobs of purebloods and slaves are thrown at opposing forces in the hope of allowing the malisons and abominations time to escape.

Survival First

Yuan-ti are likely to retreat or flee from conflict if they don't believe they have a reasonable chance of success. This reaction isn't out of cowardice, but practicality—yuan-ti value their own lives much too highly to risk them when the odds aren't in their favor. A short retreat might be just the thing to reach a better tactical position, find allies, or to allow the yuan-ti the opportunity to study their opponents and implement better tactics. Any enemy who chases a group of fleeing yuan-ti might be on the victorious side of a rout or could be heading into a trap; if the enemy has been encountered before, it is likely that the yuan-ti have prepared a special ambush at the end of the pursuit.

Capture, Not Kill

The objective of the yuan-ti as a race is to conquer and enslave others; they don't espouse the sort of evil that calls for them to butcher or eradicate all who oppose them. In keeping with their goal of domination, the yuan-ti would rather capture potentially useful opponents than kill them. They use many methods for capturing enemies, such as poisoning, knocking out an opponent instead of making a killing blow, throwing nets, using magic such as *suggestion*, or restraining them in the coils of a giant snake.

To force their compliance, enemies might be brainwashed, charmed, tortured, or transformed into broodguards. Those that prove intractable still have their uses, either as sacrifices to the gods or as food.

Depend on Deceit

Yuan-ti have no sense of honorable combat. They are naturally stealthy, and if they can sneak up on enemies, either in an ambush or to murder them in their sleep, the yuan-ti will do so—and they actually prefer these tactics to open warfare. Because abominations and malisons can change into the shapes of snakes, they can keep their presence hidden and get into places their normal forms couldn't enter.

Their immunity to poison gives all yuan-ti a tactical advantage in dealing with other creatures. A pureblood serving as a food taster for a royal family could poison a meal and declare it "safe" after taking a bite.

Serpent Cults

Some humans believe that not only are the yuan-ti superior to humans and worthy of emulation, but they are also the blessed emissaries of the serpent gods. From these entwined beliefs are born the serpent cults, groups of devout mortals who serve the yuan-ti either directly or in foreign outposts. Fanatical in their ideals, these cultists are willing to die for the yuan-ti and their gods, whether from an enemy's weapon or at the point of a sacrificial knife.

The yuan-ti use the cults devoted to them as a steady supply of willing minions and sycophants. Many yuan-ti establish or encourage cults to gather the special herbs and magic they need to perform the ritual for evolving into a more powerful form. And just as the yuan-ti have rituals to transform their own bodies, they have a ritual that can change a human into a pureblood. They sometimes use the promise of this ritual as an enticement for power-hungry followers or a reward for their most devoted cultists.

In civilized society, cultists ingratiate themselves into the local populace, usually by promising perfection of the flesh (sometimes including the healing of afflictions), freedom from the ideas of sin and guilt, and hedonistic delights to those who join the cult. The leader of a cult is usually advised by a pureblood that relays orders and information between the cult and a yuan-ti city.

YUAN-TI MALISON VARIANTS: TYPES 4 AND 5

A malison is a yuan-ti that has a blend of human and serpentine features. Three different types of malisons are described in the *Monster Manual*, and two rarer types are described here. Type 4 and type 5 malisons are the lowest-ranking members of the malison caste, and neither type is venomous in its yuan-ti form.

For a type 4 or type 5 malison, use the **yuan-ti malison** stat block in the *Monster Manual*, but replace the Malison Type trait and the monster's action options with the following:

Malison Type. The yuan-ti has one of the following types:

Type 4: Human form with one or more serpentine tails
Type 5: Human form covered in scales

Actions for Type 4 or Type 5

Multiattack (Yuan-ti Form Only). The yuan-ti makes two melee attacks or two ranged attacks.

Bite (Snake Form Only). *Melee Weapon Attack:* +5 to hit, reach 5 ft., one target. *Hit:* 5 (1d4 + 3) piercing damage plus 7 (2d6) poison damage.

Scimitar (Yuan-ti Form Only). *Melee Weapon Attack:* +5 to hit, reach 5 ft., one target. *Hit:* 6 (1d6 + 3) slashing damage.

Longbow (Yuan-ti Form Only). *Ranged Weapon Attack:* +4 to hit, range 150/600 ft., one target. *Hit:* 6 (1d8 + 2) piercing damage.

PHYSICAL VARIATIONS

No two yuan-ti look exactly the same. Both the snake-like and the humanlike portions of a yuan-ti's anatomy exhibit a wide variety of shapes and colorations. Because a yuan-ti's appearance is mostly inherited, in small settlements all the yuan-ti look somewhat alike, while larger settlements see more intermixing, which produces a wider range of results.

There are legends of certain yuan-ti infiltrating human cities and forming deadly covert societies that sell drugs and spell scrolls, blackmail merchants, and influence kings. But lacking any proof, I can't believe such tales.

—Volo

YE SHOULD.
—ELMINSTER

YUAN-TI SNAKE BODY TYPE

d20	Snake Body Shape
1–5	Thick
6–15	Normal
16–20	Sleek

YUAN-TI HUMANOID SKIN COLOR

d20	Humanoid Skin Color
1–4	Dark brown
5	Green-brown
6–9	Light brown
10–15	Medium brown
16	Pale brown
17–18	Red-brown
19–20	Yellow-brown

YUAN-TI SCALE COLOR

d100	Scale Color	d100	Scale Color
01–06	Black	49–51	Blue and gray
07–12	Black and brown	52–54	Blue and yellow
13–18	Black and green	55–60	Brown
19–23	Black and red	61–66	Brown and green
24–26	Black and white	67–73	Green
27–30	Black and yellow	74–79	Green and tan
31–36	Black, gold, and red	80–84	Green and white
37–42	Black, red, and white	85–90	Green and yellow
43–45	Blue	91–96	Red and tan
46–48	Blue and black	97–00	Albino

YUAN-TI SCALE PATTERN

d20	Scale Pattern
1–5	Mottled
6–7	Random
8–10	Reticulated
11–15	Speckled
16–20	Striped

YUAN-TI TONGUE COLOR

d6	Tongue Color
1	Black
2	Blue
3	Orange
4	Pale
5–6	Red

YUAN-TI EYE COLOR

d6	Eye Color	d6	Eye Color
1	Blue	4	Red
2	Brown	5	Tan
3	Green	6	Yellow

YUAN-TI SNAKE HEAD SHAPE

d20	Snake Head Shape
1–5	Broad and rounded
6–9	Flattened
10–11	Hooded
12–15	Slender
16–20	Triangular

TYPE 2 MALISON: ARMS

d10	Malison Type 2 Arm*
1–4	Cluster of small snakes
5–9	One large snake
10	Scaly humanoid with snake head for a hand

* Roll once for each arm.

TYPE 4 MALISON: LOWER BODY

d20	Malison Type 4 Lower Body
1–7	Human legs and large snake tail
8–10	Human legs and multiple small snake tails
11–16	Scaly human legs and large snake tail
17–20	Scaly human legs and multiple small snake tails

PUREBLOOD CHARACTERISTICS

d20	Pureblood Characteristic
1–3	Fangs
4–5	Forked tongue
6–9	Scaly arms and hands
10–11	Scaly face
12–15	Scaly torso
16–18	Serpentine eyes
19–20	Roll twice, re-rolling results of 19 or 20

Unusual Abilities

The variety among yuan-ti doesn't end with their physical characteristics. Some of them are born with powers that are unusual or even unique among their kind. High-ranking yuan-ti might have one or more of the following abilities, either replacing or augmenting what a normal yuan-ti can do.

Traits

You can customize a yuan-ti by giving it one or more of the following traits.

Acid Slime (Abomination, Anathema, or Malison Only). As a bonus action, the yuan-ti can coat its body in a slimy acid that lasts for 1 minute. A creature that touches the yuan-ti, hits it with a melee attack while within 5 feet of it, or is hit by its constrict attack takes 5 (1d10) acid damage.

Chameleon Skin. The yuan-ti has advantage on Dexterity (Stealth) checks made to hide.

Shapechanger (Pureblood Only). The yuan-ti can use its action to polymorph into a Medium **giant poisonous snake**, or into a Large **constrictor snake**, or back into its true form. Its statistics are the same in each form, except for the size change noted. Any equipment it is wearing or carrying isn't transformed. It doesn't change form if it dies.

Shed Skin (1/Day). The yuan-ti can shed its skin as a bonus action to free itself from a grapple, shackles, or other restraints. If the yuan-ti spends 1 minute eating its shed skin, it regains hit points equal to half its hit point maximum.

Action Options

The following action options are restricted to certain kinds of yuan-ti.

Bite (Pureblood Only). *Melee Weapon Attack:* +3 to hit, reach 5 ft., one creature. *Hit:* 3 (1d4) piercing damage plus 3 (1d6) poison damage. If the pureblood uses Multiattack, it can make two melee attacks, but can use its bite only once.

Polymorph into Snake (Abomination or Malison Only; Recharge 6). The yuan-ti targets a creature it can see within 60 feet of it. The target must succeed on a Wisdom saving throw or be transformed into a Tiny **poisonous snake**, as if affected by the *polymorph* spell. The save DC is the same as that of the yuan-ti's Innate Spellcasting ability.

Snake Antipathy (Abomination or Malison Only; Recharge 6). The yuan-ti targets a creature it can see within 60 feet of it. The target must succeed on a Wisdom saving throw or feel an intense urge to avoid snakes and snakelike creatures (including yuan-ti), as if affected by the antipathy effect of an *antipathy/sympathy* spell. The save DC is the same as that of the yuan-ti's Innate Spellcasting ability.

Sticks to Snakes (Abomination or Malison Only; Recharge 6). The yuan-ti transforms a pile of sticks, arrows, or similar-sized pieces of wood into a **swarm of poisonous snakes**. The swarm acts as an ally of the yuan-ti and obeys its spoken commands. The swarm remains for 1 minute, after which it turns back into the original materials.

Roleplaying a Yuan-ti

Yuan-ti are emotionless, yet feel completely superior to humanoids, in the same way that a human can feel superior to chickens or rabbits—in a matter-of-fact, completely objective way that doesn't brook any second-guessing. To a yuan-ti, there are only three categories of creature: threat, yuan-ti, or meat. Threats are powerful creatures such as demons, dragons, and genies. Yuan-ti are any of their own kind, regardless of caste; although a rival yuan-ti might be dangerous, and a weak or dead one might be potential food, it is first and foremost one of the true people and deserving of some respect. Meat includes any creature that is neither a threat nor a yuan-ti, possibly useful for a base purpose but not worthy of other consideration.

Most yuan-ti consider it beneath themselves to speak to meat. Abominations and malisons rarely communicate directly with slaves except in emergencies (such as for giving battle orders); at other times, slaves are expected to constantly be aware of the master's mood, anticipate the master's needs, and recognize subtle gestures of hands, head, and tail that indicate commands.

Only purebloods—which walk among humanoids and therefore have to learn how to speak to them civilly—practice interacting with meat-creatures. Much of their training involves suppressing their innate annoyance at having to speak to lesser beings as though they were equals, or being obliged to kowtow to a humanoid ruler as if the pureblood were merely an advisor. Pureblood spies feel a sort of aloof contempt toward meat-creatures, but they can affect a pleasant tone, and speak to such creatures with a silver tongue that disguises their true feelings.

Under normal circumstances, yuan-ti are always calmly deferential to those of higher rank. They tend to be curt and formal with those of lower rank, for the differences between them aren't a source of anger or disgust (emotions that the yuan-ti don't feel anyway), merely a fact of the natural order, and their culture long ago realized that treating the lower castes with a measure of detached respect prevents rebellion and advances the cause of the entire race.

Yuan-ti Personality Traits

d8	Personality Trait
1	I see omens in every event and action. The serpent gods continue to advise us.
2	I have very high standards for food, drink, and physical pleasures.
3	I prefer to be alone rather than among other creatures, including my own kind.
4	I sometimes become consumed by philosophy.
5	I believe I am superior to others of my caste.
6	I am driven by wanderlust and want to explore lands far from our cities.
7	I am interested in modern human culture, even as primitive as it is.
8	I await the day when we again conquer lands by force, as we did in the old times.

Yuan-ti Ideals

d6	Ideal
1	**Greed.** I display my wealth as a sign of my power and prosperity. (Evil)
2	**Aspiration.** I strive to follow the path toward becoming an anathema. (Evil)
3	**Unity.** No leader shall put personal goals above those of our race. (Any)
4	**Kinship.** My allegiance is to my caste and my city. Other settlements can burn for all I care. (Any)
5	**Inspiration.** My actions set an example for the lesser castes to emulate. (Any)
6	**Power.** Everything I choose to do is determined by whether it will make me smarter and stronger. (Evil)

Yuan-ti Bonds

d6	Bond
1	I will see our empire rise again and, in so doing, win the favor of the serpent gods.
2	I am enamored with the culture and trappings of another society and wish to be part of it.
3	I respect my superiors and obey them without question. My fate is theirs to decide.
4	I have an interest in an unsuitable mate, which I can't suppress.
5	I respect and emulate a great hero or ancestor.
6	An enemy destroyed something of value to me, and I will find where it lives and kill the offender.

Yuan-ti Flaws

d6	Flaw
1	I feel twinges of emotion, and it shames me that I am imperfect in this way.
2	I put too much credence in the dictates of a particular god.
3	I frequently overindulge in food and wine, and I am impaired and lethargic for days afterward.
4	I worship a forbidden god.
5	I secretly believe things would be better if I was in charge.
6	If I could get away with it, I would gladly kill and eat a superior yuan-ti.

Yuan-ti Names

Yuan-ti names have meanings that have been passed down through the generations, although spellings and inflections have changed over time.

Some yuan-ti add more sibilants to their birth names to create an exaggerated hissing sound, based on one's personal preference and whether an individual's anatomy can more easily pronounce the name in this altered form. An adopted name of this sort is recognized as a variant of the birth name, rather than a unique name unto itself. A yuan-ti might refer to itself by its birth name, by its adopted name, or (especially among purebloods) by a name it borrows from the local populace.

The Yuan-ti Names table provides yuan-ti birth names suitable for any campaign.

Yuan-ti Names

d20	Name	d20	Name
1	Asutali	11	Shalkashlah
2	Eztli	12	Sisava
3	Hessatal	13	Sitlali
4	Hitotee	14	Soakosh
5	Issahu	15	Ssimalli
6	Itstli	16	Suisatal
7	Manuya	17	Talash
8	Meztli	18	Teoshi
9	Nesalli	19	Yaotal
10	Otleh	20	Zihu

Yuan-ti Cities

Most yuan-ti cities were built during the height of their empire centuries ago. Since they no longer have the vast number of expendable slaves necessary for large work projects, the yuan-ti content themselves with maintaining these ancient places rather than building new ones for their needs. Although these sites are hundreds or even thousands of years old, they don't look or feel primitive—the yuan-ti empire was once very advanced, and although it has declined, its culture is still thriving on a smaller scale.

Because the yuan-ti were previously human, their architecture reflects human ideas about art and beauty. Over time this perspective was skewed toward the concept that the snake is the perfect form, so serpents are a common theme in their aesthetic.

The major buildings in a city usually have four sides and a sloped or staggered pyramid-like exterior. It is customary for stone buildings to have a series of tiles or carvings of snakes encircling the ground level at head height. These features are sometimes trapped or

---

Cannibalism and Sacrifice

The ritual that produced the first yuan-ti required the human subjects to butcher and eat their human slaves and prisoners. This act of cannibalism had several ramifications. It broke a long-standing taboo among civilized humanoids and set the yuan-ti apart from other civilizations as creatures not beholden to moral values. It corrupted their flesh, making the yuan-ti receptive to dark magic. It emulated the dispassionate viewpoint of the reptilian mind, a trait the yuan-ti admired.

Today, cannibalism is practiced by the most fervent of yuan-ti cultists, including those who aspire to transform into yuan-ti themselves. In yuan-ti cities, the activity persists in the form of human sacrifice—not strictly cannibalism anymore, but still serving as a repudiation of what it is to be human and a glorification of what it is to be yuan-ti.

Yuan-ti don't have a taboo against eating their own kind; a starving yuan-ti would kill and eat a lesser without a second thought, and a group of them would choose the weakest among them to be killed and eaten. Under normal circumstances, however, they bury or cremate their dead rather than eating them, but a great hero or someone of status might be ritually consumed as a form of tribute.

magically warded to prevent anyone from climbing the building's exterior. Interior walls usually have floor-level holes or tunnels that a Medium or Large snake could pass through, allowing the yuan-ti's serpentine pets, as well as abominations and malisons in snake form, to bypass human-style doors for convenience or in order to respond quickly to invaders. In well-traveled areas, ramps replace stairs, making it easier to snake-bodied yuan-ti to move between levels.

A yuan-ti settlement usually has a paved plaza, and major roads are also paved. Fountains, gardens, and carved, freestanding columns are common elements. Six-foot-high walls high divide the community into city blocks or districts, with open arches allowing traffic to pass through.

Yuan-ti lairs in human settlements are nothing like the accommodations in their own cities. Because these locations are used mainly by humanoid purebloods and cultists (or were built by humanoids and taken over by yuan-ti), stairs and humanoid architecture are the norm. Each of these sites resembles the headquarters of a spy ring, a thieves' guild, or a hedonistic cult rather than the outpost of an evil empire bent on cannibalism and world domination, but it usually has a sacrificial slab tucked away in a corner for special events.

Particularly in their cities, yuan-ti rely on poison traps to keep intruders, spies, and rebellious slaves out of sensitive areas. Traps are commonly placed on door locks, chests, and fake objects designed to attract looters. One insidious delivery method uses blocks of special incense to fill a room with poisonous faint smoke that disguises the presence of the poison until it takes effect.

Pyramid Temple

In a typical yuan-ti city, one of the busiest and most prominent buildings is the temple complex that houses yuan-ti and their followers while it provides facilities for worship, sacrifice, and all the other hallmarks of daily life. The accompanying map is an example of such a location.

Cultist Level

The lowest level of the temple includes sleeping and living quarters for favored or high-ranking cultists, as well as a shrine and a separate temple where the cultists can conduct their own ceremonies. The area has two ground-level entrances that are always well concealed and usually trapped, plus a guard room nearby that offers additional security.

Pureblood Level

Beginning with the second level, the accommodations in the rest of the temple are meant for yuan-ti only, and access is limited accordingly. Purebloods live and work on this tier, which features cages for slaves, special quarters for the current slave master, and a centrally located torture chamber. A pair of staircases offer access to the next level up.

Abomination Level

The yuan-ti at the top of the social hierarchy reside in the most insulted level of the pyramid, within quick

YUAN-TI TEMPLE

Level 5: Temple Mount

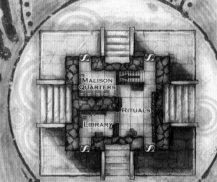

ALTAR

PATIO

N

Level 3: Abomination Level

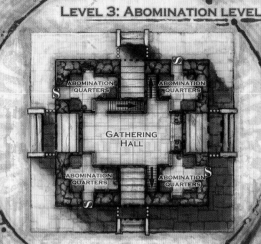

ABOMINATION QUARTERS

ABOMINATION QUARTERS

GATHERING HALL

ABOMINATION QUARTERS

ABOMINATION QUARTERS

Level 2: Pureblood Level

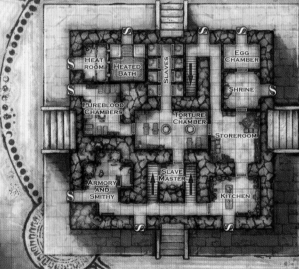

HEAT ROOM

HEATED BATH

SLAVES

EGG CHAMBER

PUREBLOOD CHAMBERS

TORTURE CHAMBER

SHRINE

STOREROOM

ARMORY AND SMITHY

SLAVE MASTER

KITCHEN

Level 4: Malison Level

MALISON QUARTERS

RITUALS

LIBRARY

Level 1: Cultist Level

KITCHEN

GUARD

CULTIST QUARTERS

CULTIST QUARTERS

BATH

TEMPLE

SHRINE

GUARD

CULTIST QUARTERS

CULTIST QUARTERS

SIDE VIEW

LEVEL 5
LEVEL 4
LEVEL 3
LEVEL 2
LEVEL 1

☐ = 10 FEET

striking distance of the levels above and below. On this level, substantially sized quarters for abominations are laid around the perimeter of the temple's largest chamber, a hall where the entire population of the place can assemble.

MALISON LEVEL

Of all yuan-ti, the malisons have the strongest proclivity for worship of their deities. As such, they occupy the uppermost residential level in the pyramid, one step below the mount. This level contains a library where the yuan-ti store the knowledge of their transformation rituals, and a chamber where those rituals are performed.

TEMPLE MOUNT

At the apex of the pyramid, reachable by ascending the exterior steps from ground level but not through an interior staircase, is a plateau surrounded by viewing areas. The center holds an elaborately decorated altar, where many a sacrifice meets its end as yuan-ti witnesses pay homage to their gods.

ALLIES AND MINIONS

Yuan-ti have been controlling and manipulating lesser creatures for hundreds of years. They enslave beasts and intelligent creatures to serve them and guard their homes, and they blackmail, enchant, or enthrall others to be their agents in humanoid lands.

RANDOM YUAN-TI SERVANTS

Yuan-ti employ a variety of creatures as spies and protectors. The Yuan-ti Agents table lists groups of creatures that work for the yuan-ti, representing their masters' interests. Agents of the serpent folk might roam the countryside on a specific mission or operate secretly inside a humanoid community. The Yuan-ti Protectors table includes creatures that serve as guardians either within a yuan-ti city or in a yuan-ti hideout inside a humanoid city.

YUAN-TI AGENTS

d100	Agents	d100	Agents
01–20	4d6 cultists	51–60	1d4 nobles
21–30	2d6 cult fanatics	61–72	1d4 priests
31–34	2d4 doppelgangers	73–86	2d6 scouts
35–50	2d10 guards	87–00	1d4 spies

YUAN-TI PROTECTORS

d100	Protector(s)
01–10	1d3 bandit captains and 3d10 bandits
11–12	1d6 basilisks
13–18	4d6 constrictor snakes
19–26	1d6 cult fanatics and 4d10 cultists
27–28	3d10 flying snakes
29–35	3d6 giant constrictor snakes
36–45	3d6 giant poisonous snakes
46–50	2d6 gladiators
51–55	2d6 guards
56–58	1d2 hydras
59–60	1d3 medusas
61	2d6 mummies*
62–63	6d10 poisonous snakes
64–68	2d6 priests
69–70	4d10 skeletons
71	1d2 stone golems
72–81	3d6 swarms of poisonous snakes
82–91	4d10 tribal warriors
92–97	2d8 veterans
98–00	4d8 zombies

* The mummies are the undead remains of yuan-ti malisons or purebloods. Each has the statistics of a normal mummy.

> The pyramids, plazas, and fountains were all made of stone and decorated with snake carvings. All of it felt old—as old as an elven city—and foreboding in its strange beauty.
>
> —Volo

CHAPTER 2: CHARACTER RACES

EROES COME IN MANY SHAPES AND
sizes. This chapter presents character
races that are some of the more distinctive race options in the D&D multiverse. They supplement the options in
the *Player's Handbook* and are more
rare in the worlds of D&D than the
races in that book are.

If you're a player, consult with your DM before using
any of the races here. Many DMs like to consider the implications for their world before adding a new race. Your
DM may say yes or no to you using a race or may modifiy
it in some way.

The following races are detailed in this chapter:

Aasimar are humanoids with an angelic spark in their
souls, which grants them supernatural power.

Firbolgs are forest guardians who prefer peaceful methods to protect their homes but take up arms they must.

Goliaths are hulking wanderers who dwell at the highest mountain reaches.

Kenku are cursed bird folk, who still pay the price for
an ancient betrayal. Dwelling in human cities, they
have a sinister reputation for working as criminals.

Lizardfolk sometimes venture from their swamp homes
in search of treasure and glory. Inscrutable to their
mammalian companions, they prove to be stout allies.

Tabaxi are curious cat folk, who have journeyed from
their distant homeland in search of interesting treasures and lore.

Tritons are guardians of the ocean depths, who sometimes join people on land in the battle against evil.

The chapter also includes a section of monstrous character options that a DM can add to a campaign: **bugbear, goblin, hobgoblin, kobold, orc**, and **yuan-ti pureblood**, the stories of which are explored in chapter 1.

At the end of the chapter is a section that you can use
to determine the height and weight of a character who is
a member of one of the races in this chapter.

If you're the DM, including any of these races in your
campaign is a storytelling opportunity, a chance for you
to decide the roles that different peoples play in the tales
you weave. You might decide that a race in this chapter
is common in your world, that only a few members of
it still live, or that it doesn't exist at all. Whatever you
decide about the races, consider how they can enhance
your stories.

Aasimar

*I SAW HER, WREATHED IN WINGS OF PURE LIGHT, HER
eyes blazing with the fury of the gods. The bone devils
stopped in their tracks, shielding their faces. Her blade,
now a brand of light, swept once, twice, three times. The
devils' heads hit the ground, one after another. And thus we
learned that an aasimar traveled in our ragtag band.*

—Geldon Parl, *Of the Tyranny of Dragons*

Aasimar bear within their souls the light of the heavens. They are descended from humans with a touch of the power of Mount Celestia, the divine realm of many lawful good deities. Aasimar are born to serve as champions of the gods, their births hailed as blessed events. They are a people of otherworldly visages, with luminous features that reveal their celestial heritage.

Celestial Champions

Aasimar are placed in the world to serve as guardians of law and good. Their patrons expect them to strike at evil, lead by example, and further the cause of justice.

From an early age, an aasimar receives visions and guidance from celestial entities via dreams. These dreams help shape an aasimar, granting a sense of destiny and a desire for righteousness.

Each aasimar can count a specific celestial agent of the gods as a guide. This entity is typically a deva, an angel who acts as a messenger to the mortal world.

Hidden Wanderers

While aasimar are strident foes of evil, they typically prefer to keep a low profile. An aasimar inevitably draws the attention of evil cultists, fiends, and other enemies of good, all of whom would be eager to strike down a celestial champion if they had the chance.

When traveling, aasimar prefer hoods, closed helms, and other gear that allows them to conceal their identities. They nevertheless have no compunction about striking openly at evil. The secrecy they desire is never worth endangering the innocent.

Aasimar Guides

An aasimar, except for one who has turned to evil, has a link to an angelic being. That being—usually a deva—provides guidance to the aasimar, though this connection functions only in dreams. As such, the guidance is not a direct command or a simple spoken word. Instead, the aasimar receives visions, prophecies, and feelings.

The angelic being is far from omniscient. Its guidance is based on its understanding of the tenets of law and good, and it might have insight into combating especially powerful evils that it knows about.

As part of fleshing out an aasimar character, consider the nature of that character's angelic guide. The Angelic Guide tables offer names and natures that you can use to flesh out your character's guide.

Note to the DM: Playing an Angelic Guide

As DM, you take on the role of an aasimar's angelic guide and decide what kind of advice or omens to send in dreams.

The deva, or other celestial being, is your chance to add special roleplaying opportunities to the game. Remember, a deva lives in a realm of absolute law and good. The deva might not understand the compromises and hard choices that mortals must grapple with in the world. To the deva, an aasimar is a prized student who must live up to high, sometimes inflexible standards.

Angelic Guide

d6	Name
1	Tadriel
2	Myllandra
3	Seraphina
4	Galladia
5	Mykiel
6	Valandras

d6	Nature
1	Bookish and lecturing
2	Compassionate and hopeful
3	Practical and lighthearted
4	Fierce and vengeful
5	Stern and judgmental
6	Kind and parental

Conflicted Souls

Despite its celestial origin, an aasimar is mortal and possesses free will. Most aasimar follow their ordained path, but some grow to see their abilities as a curse. These disaffected aasimar are typically content to turn away from the world, but a few become agents of evil. In their minds, their exposure to celestial powers amounted to little more than brainwashing.

Evil aasimar make deadly foes. The radiant power they once commanded becomes corrupted into a horrid, draining magic. And their angelic guides abandon them.

Even aasimar wholly dedicated to good sometimes feel torn between two worlds. The angels that guide them see the world from a distant perch. An aasimar who wishes to stop and help a town recover from a drought might be told by an angelic guide to push forward on a greater quest. To a distant angel, saving a few commoners might pale in comparison to defeating a cult of Orcus. An aasimar's guide is wise but not infallible.

Aasimar Names

Most aasimar are born from human parents, and they use the same naming conventions as their native culture.

Aasimar Traits

Your aasimar character has the following racial traits.

Ability Score Increase. Your Charisma score increases by 2.

Age. Aasimar mature at the same rate as humans, but they can live up to 160 years.

Alignment. Imbued with celestial power, most aasimar are good. Outcast aasimar are most often neutral or even evil.

Size. Aasimar have the same range of height and weight as humans.

Speed. Your base walking speed is 30 feet.

Darkvision. Blessed with a radiant soul, your vision can easily cut through darkness. You can see in dim light within 60 feet of you as if it were bright light, and in darkness as if it were dim light. You can't discern color in darkness, only shades of gray.

Celestial Resistance. You have resistance to necrotic damage and radiant damage.

Healing Hands. As an action, you can touch a creature and cause it to regain a number of hit points equal to your level. Once you use this trait, you can't use it again until you finish a long rest.

Light Bearer. You know the *light* cantrip. Charisma is your spellcasting ability for it.

Languages. You can speak, read, and write Common and Celestial.

Subrace. Three subraces of aasimar exist: protector aasimar, scourge aasimar, and fallen aasimar. Choose one of them for your character.

PROTECTOR AASIMAR

Protector aasimar are charged by the powers of good to guard the weak, to strike at evil wherever it arises, and to stand vigilant against the darkness. From a young age, a protector aasimar receives advice and directives that urge to stand against evil.

Ability Score Increase. Your Wisdom score increases by 1.

Radiant Soul. Starting at 3rd level, you can use your action to unleash the divine energy within yourself, causing your eyes to glimmer and two luminous, incorporeal wings to sprout from your back.

Your transformation lasts for 1 minute or until you end it as a bonus action. During it, you have a flying speed of 30 feet, and once on each of your turns, you can deal extra radiant damage to one target when you deal damage to it with an attack or a spell. The extra radiant damage equals your level.

Once you use this trait, you can't use it again until you finish a long rest.

SCOURGE AASIMAR

Scourge aasimar are imbued with a divine energy that blazes intensely within them. It feeds a powerful desire to destroy evil—a desire that is, at its best, unflinching and, at its worst, all-consuming. Many scourge aasimar wear masks to block out the world and focus on containing this power, unmasking themselves only in battle.

Ability Score Increase. Your Constitution score increases by 1.

Radiant Consumption. Starting at 3rd level, you can use your action to unleash the divine energy within yourself, causing a searing light to radiate from you, pour out of your eyes and mouth, and threaten to char you.

Your transformation lasts for 1 minute or until you end it as a bonus action. During it, you shed bright light in a 10-foot radius and dim light for an additional 10 feet,

and at the end of each of your turns, you and each creature within 10 feet of you take radiant damage equal to half your level (rounded up). In addition, once on each of your turns, you can deal extra radiant damage to one target when you deal damage to it with an attack or a spell. The extra radiant damage equals your level.

Once you use this trait, you can't use it again until you finish a long rest.

FALLEN AASIMAR

An aasimar who was touched by dark powers as a youth or who turns to evil in early adulthood can become one of the fallen—a group of aasimar whose inner light has been replaced by shadow.

Ability Score Increase. Your Strength score increases by 1.

Necrotic Shroud. Starting at 3rd level, you can use your action to unleash the divine energy within yourself, causing your eyes to turn into pools of darkness and two skeletal, ghostly, flightless wings to sprout from your back. The instant you transform, other creatures within 10 feet of you that can see you must each succeed on a Charisma saving throw (DC 8 + your proficiency bonus + your Charisma modifier) or become frightened of you until the end of your next turn.

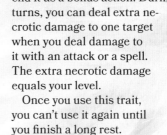

Your transformation lasts for 1 minute or until you end it as a bonus action. During it, once on each of your turns, you can deal extra necrotic damage to one target when you deal damage to it with an attack or a spell. The extra necrotic damage equals your level.

Once you use this trait, you can't use it again until you finish a long rest.

> ### FALLING FROM GRACE OR RISING TO IT
>
> With your DM's consent, you can change your character's subrace to fallen aasimar if your protector/scourge aasimar turns to evil. To do so, replace your subrace benefits, including the ability score increase, with those of a fallen aasimar.
>
> Similarly, if your fallen aasimar turns to good, your DM might allow you to become a protector or scourge aasimar.

FIRBOLG

WE SPENT THREE MONTHS TRACKING THE GREEN DRAGON
before locating the forest in which it sought refuge. On our
second day in that place, we woke to find the dragon's head
placed in the center of our camp. Soveliss told me that
firbolgs must have claimed the forest, and they wanted to
show us we had no further business there. If we lingered, he
assured me, our heads would be next.

—Gimble, *Notes from a Treasure Hunter*

Firbolg tribes cloister in remote forest strongholds,
preferring to spend their days in quiet harmony with the
woods. When provoked, firbolgs demonstrate formidable skills with weapons and druidic magic.

HUMBLE GUARDIANS

Firbolgs love nothing more than a peaceful day spent
among the trees of an old forest. They see forests as
sacred places, representing the heart of the world and
monuments to the durability of life.

In their role as caretakers, firbolgs live off the land
while striving to remain in balance with nature. Their
methods reflect common sense and remarkable resourcefulness. During a bountiful summer, they store
away excess nuts, fruit, and berries. When winter arrives, they scatter everything they can spare to ensure
the animals of the wood survive until springtime.

In a firbolg's eyes, there is no greater fault than greed.
The firbolgs believe that the world remains healthiest
when each creature takes only what it needs. Material
goods, especially precious gems and gold, have little
appeal to them. What use are such things when winter
lingers and food runs short?

NATURAL DRUIDS

Firbolgs have a talent for druidic magic. Their cultural
reverence for nature, combined with their strong and
insightful minds, makes learning such magic an instinctive part of their development. Almost every firbolg
learns a few spells, typically those used to mask their
presence, and many go on to master nature magic.

Firbolgs who become druids serve as stronghold leaders. With every action the tribe takes, the druids weigh
not only the group's needs, but the effect each action will
have on the forest and the rest of the natural world. Firbolg tribes would rather go hungry than strain the land
during a famine.

HIDDEN SHEPHERDS

As caretakers of the land, firbolgs prefer to remain out
of sight and out of mind. They don't try to dominate
nature, but rather seek to ensure that it prospers and
survives according to its own laws.

Firbolgs use their magic to keep their presence in a
forest secret. This approach allows them to avoid the
politics and struggles of elves, humans, and orcs. Such
events concern the firbolgs only when the events affect
the forest.

Even in the face of an intrusion, firbolgs prefer a
subtle, gentle approach to prevent damage to their territory. They employ their magic to make the forest an
unappealing place to explore by temporarily diverting
springs, driving away game, stealing critical tools,
and altering trails to leave hunting or lumber parties
hopelessly lost. The firbolgs' presence is marked by an
absence of animals and a strange quiet, as if the forest
wishes to avoid attracting attention to itself. The faster
travelers decide to move on, the better.

If these tactics fail, the firbolgs take more direct
action. Their observations of a settlement determine
what happens next. If the outsiders seem peaceful, the
firbolgs approach and gently ask them to leave, even
offering food and other supplies to aid their departure.
If those who insist on remaining respect nature, take
only what they need, and live in harmony with the wood,
firbolgs explore the possibility of friendship with them,
as long as the outsiders vow to safeguard the forest. If
the settlers clearly display evil intentions, however, the
firbolgs martial their strength and magic for a single
overwhelming attack.

OUTCAST ADVENTURERS

As guardians of the wood, few firbolgs would dream
of leaving their homes or attempting to fit into human
society. An exiled firbolg, or one whose clan has been
destroyed, might not have a choice in the matter. Most
adventuring firbolgs fall into this latter category.

Outcast firbolgs can never return home. They committed some unforgivable deed, usually something that put
their homeland at risk, such as starting a forest fire or
killing a rare or beautiful wild creature. These firbolgs
are loners who wander the world in hope of finding a
new place to call home.

Orphaned firbolgs are those whose clans or homelands have been destroyed. They become crusaders for
nature, seeking to avenge their loss and prevent the further destruction of the natural world.

A few rare firbolgs are entrusted by their clan with an
important mission that takes them beyond their homes.
These firbolgs feel like pilgrims in a strange land, and
usually they wish only to complete their quests and return home as quickly as possible.

The Firbolg Adventurers table can serve as inspiration
for determining why a firbolg character leaves home.

FIRBOLG ADVENTURERS

d8	Reason for Adventuring
1	Outcast for murder
2	Outcast for severely damaging home territory
3	Clan slain by invading humanoids
4	Clan slain by a dragon or demon
5	Separated from the tribe and lost
6	Homeland destroyed by natural disaster
7	Personal quest ordained by omens
8	Dispatched on a quest by tribe leaders

Firbolg Names

Firbolg adopt elven names when they must deal with outsiders, although the concept of names strikes them as strange. They know the animals and plants of the forest without formal names, and instead identify the forest's children by their deeds, habits, and other actions.

By the same token, their tribe names merely refer to their homes. When dealing with other races, firbolgs refer to their lands by whatever name the surrounding folk use, as a matter of tact and hospitality, but among their own kind they simply call it "home."

Sometimes firbolgs adopt the nicknames or titles outsiders give them under the assumption that those who need names can call them whatever they wish.

Firbolg Traits

Your firbolg character has the following racial traits.

Ability Score Increase. Your Wisdom score increases by 2, and your Strength score increases by 1.

Age. As humanoids related to the fey, firbolg have long lifespans. A firbolg reaches adulthood around 30, and the oldest of them can live for 500 years.

Alignment. As people who follow the rhythm of nature and see themselves as its caretakers, firbolg are typically neutral good. Evil firbolg are rare and are usually the sworn enemies of the rest of their kind.

Size. Firbolg are between 7 and 8 feet tall and weigh between 240 and 300 pounds. Your size is Medium.

Speed. Your base walking speed is 30 feet.

Firbolg Magic. You can cast *detect magic* and *disguise self* with this trait, using Wisdom as your spellcasting ability for them. Once you cast either spell, you can't cast it again with this trait until you finish a short or long rest. When you use this version of *disguise self*, you can seem up to 3 feet shorter than normal, allowing you to more easily blend in with humans and elves.

Hidden Step. As a bonus action, you can magically turn invisible until the start of your next turn or until you attack, make a damage roll, or force someone to make a saving throw. Once you use this trait, you can't use it again until you finish a short or long rest.

Powerful Build. You count as one size larger when determining your carrying capacity and the weight you can push, drag, or lift.

Speech of Beast and Leaf. You have the ability to communicate in a limited manner with beasts and plants. They can understand the meaning of your words, though you have no special ability to understand them in return. You have advantage on all Charisma checks you make to influence them.

Languages. You can speak, read, and write Common, Elvish, and Giant.

Firbolg Classes

Most firbolgs are druids, rangers, or fighters. Among their kind, these vocations are passed down from one generation to the next. The firbolgs' magical heritage also expresses itself in other ways; those who become bards preserve the clan's lore, and firbolg sorcerers defend their communities. Firbolg wizards arise when a clan becomes friendly with elves.

Firbolg rogues are typically scouts tasked with spying on neighboring folk to determine their intentions. They are most common among firbolgs whose homes border human settlements.

Firbolg barbarians are rare except among clans that face constant threats from evil humanoids and other invaders.

Firbolg clerics and paladins are usually dedicated to nature gods and are seen as enforcers of that god's will.

Firbolg warlocks are rare, but some clans forge alliances and arcane pacts with powerful fey beings.

Firbolg monks are almost entirely unheard of, though a monastery might take in the young survivors of a devastated firbolg clan.

Goliath

Goliaths can prove useful allies, but never turn to them in weakness. They are as hard and unforgiving as the mountain stone, as cold and pitiless as its bitter, cold winds. If you approach them in strength, they might consider you worthy of an alliance.

—Tordek, *A Guide to the Peaks*

At the highest mountain peaks—far above the slopes where trees grow and where the air is thin and the frigid winds howl—dwell the reclusive goliaths. Few folk can claim to have seen a goliath, and fewer still can claim friendship with one. Goliaths wander a bleak realm of rock, wind, and cold. Their bodies look as if they are carved from mountain stone and give them great physical power. Their spirits take after the wandering wind, making them nomads who wander from peak to peak. Their hearts are infused with the cold regard of their frigid realm, leaving each goliath with the responsibility to earn a place in the tribe or die trying.

Driven Competitors

Every day brings a new challenge to a goliath. Food, water, and shelter are rare in the uppermost mountain reaches. A single mistake can bring doom to an entire tribe, while an individual's heroic effort can ensure the entire group's survival.

Goliaths thus place a premium on self-sufficiency and individual skill. They have a compulsion to keep score,

counting their deeds and tallying their accomplishments to compare to others. Goliaths love to win, but they see defeat as a prod to improve their skills.

This dedication to competition has a dark side. Goliaths are ferocious competitors, but above all else they are driven to outdo their past efforts. If a goliath slays a dragon, he or she might seek out a larger, more powerful wyrm to battle. Few goliath adventurers reach old age, as most die attempting to surpass their past accomplishments.

Fair Play

For goliaths, competition exists only when it is supported by a level playing field. Competition measures talent, dedication, and effort. Those factors determine survival in their home territory, not reliance on magic items, money, or other elements that can tip the balance one way or the other. Goliaths happily rely on such benefits, but they are careful to remember that such an advantage can always be lost. A goliath who relies too much on them can grow complacent, a recipe for disaster in the mountains.

This trait manifests most strongly when goliaths interact with other folk. The relationship between peasants and nobles puzzles goliaths. If a king lacks the intelligence or leadership to lead, then clearly the most talented person in the kingdom should take his place. Goliaths rarely keep such opinions to themselves, and mock folk who rely on society's structures or rules to maintain power.

Survival of the Fittest

Among goliaths, any adult who can't contribute to the tribe is expelled. A lone goliath has little chance of survival, especially an older or weaker one. Goliaths have little pity for adults who can't take care of themselves, though a sick or injured individual is treated, as a result of the goliath concept of fair play.

A permanently injured goliath is still expected to pull his or her weight in the tribe. Typically, such a goliath dies attempting to keep up, or the goliath slips away in the night to seek the cold will of fate.

In some ways, the goliath drive to outdo themselves feeds into the grim inevitability of their decline and death. A goliath would much rather die in battle, at the peak of strength and skill, than endure the slow decay of old age. Few folk have ever meet an elderly goliath, and even those goliaths who have left their people grapple with the urge to give up their lives as their physical skills decay.

Because of their risk-taking, goliath tribes suffer from a chronic lack of the experience offered by long-term leaders. They hope for innate wisdom in their leadership, for they can rarely count on a wisdom grown with age.

Goliath Names

Every goliath has three names: a birth name assigned by the newborn's mother and father, a nickname assigned by the tribal chief, and a family or clan name. A birth name is up to three syllables long. Clan names are five syllables or more and end in a vowel.

Birth names are rarely linked to gender. Goliaths see females and males as equal in all things, and they find societies with roles divided by gender to be puzzling or worthy of mockery. To a goliath, the person who is best at a job should be the one tasked with doing it.

A goliath's nickname is a description that can change on the whim of a chieftain or tribal elder. It refers to a notable deed, either a success or failure, committed by the goliath. Goliaths assign and use nicknames with their friends of other races, and change them to refer to an individual's notable deeds.

Goliaths present all three names when identifying themselves, in the order of birth name, nickname, and clan name. In casual conversation, they use their nickname.

Birth Names: Aukan, Eglath, Gae-Al, Gauthak, Ilikan, Keothi, Kuori, Lo-Kag, Manneo, Maveith, Nalla, Orilo, Paavu, Pethani, Thalai, Thotham, Uthal, Vaunea, Vimak

Nicknames: Bearkiller, Dawncaller, Fearless, Flint-finder, Horncarver, Keeneye, Lonehunter, Long-leaper, Rootsmasher, Skywatcher, Steadyhand, Threadtwister, Twice-Orphaned, Twistedlimb, Wordpainter

Clan Names: Anakalathai, Elanithino, Gathakanathi, Kalagiano, Katho-Olavi, Kolae-Gileana, Ogolakanu, Thuliaga, Thunukalathi, Vaimei-Laga

GOLIATH TRAITS

Goliaths share a number of traits in common with each other.

Ability Score Increase. Your Strength score increases by 2, and your Constitution score increases by 1.

Age. Goliaths have lifespans comparable to humans. They enter adulthood in their late teens and usually live less than a century.

Alignment. Goliath society, with its clear roles and tasks, has a strong lawful bent. The goliath sense of fairness, balanced with an emphasis on self-sufficiency and personal accountability, pushes them toward neutrality.

Size. Goliaths are between 7 and 8 feet tall and weigh between 280 and 340 pounds. Your size is Medium.

Speed. Your base walking speed is 30 feet.

Natural Athlete. You have proficiency in the Athletics skill.

Stone's Endurance. You can focus yourself to occasionally shrug off injury. When you take damage, you can use your reaction to roll a d12. Add your Constitution modifier to the number rolled, and reduce the damage by that total. After you use this trait, you can't use it again until you finish a short or long rest.

Powerful Build. You count as one size larger when determining your carrying capacity and the weight you can push, drag, or lift.

Mountain Born. You're acclimated to high altitude, including elevations above 20,000 feet. You're also naturally adapted to cold climates, as described in chapter 5 of the *Dungeon Master's Guide*.

Languages. You can speak, read, and write Common and Giant.

KENKU

THE MAP WE FOUND SHOWED THE ENTRANCE TO THE *Priest King's treasure cache right in the middle of the ruined section of the city. We approached our destination without issue, but as we arrived at the burned-out building, a sudden cacophony erupted around us. Birds squawked, cats hissed, and dogs growled. Lidda hustled us back to the city's safer avenues. Only when we were back within the area patrolled by the guard did she explain that the noises indicated that the wingless folk had claimed that area, and that to trespass would be to court death.*

—Gimble, *Notes from a Treasure Hunter*

Haunted by an ancient crime that robbed them of their wings, the kenku wander the world as vagabonds and burglars who live at the edge of human society. Kenku suffer from a sinister reputation that is not wholly unearned, but they can prove to be valuable allies.

AN ANCIENT CURSE

The kenku once served a mysterious, powerful entity on another plane of existence. Some believe they were minions of Grazz't, while others say that they were scouts and explorers for the Wind Dukes of Aaqa. Whatever the truth, according to legend, the kenku betrayed their master. Unable to resist the lure of a beautiful sparkling treasure, the kenku plotted to steal the item and escape to the Material Plane.

Unfortunately for the kenku, their master discovered their plan before they could enact it. Enraged, the entity imposed three dreadful curses upon them. First, the kenku's beloved wings withered and fell away from their bodies, leaving them bound to the earth. Second, because their ingenuity and skill had turned toward scheming against their patron, the spark of creativity was torn from their souls. Finally, to ensure that the kenku could never divulge any secrets, their master took away their voices. Once the entity was satisfied that they had been sufficiently punished, the kenku were set loose on the Material Plane.

Since then, the kenku have wandered the world. They settle in places that accept them, usually bleak cities that have fallen on hard times and are overrun with crime.

DREAMS OF FLIGHT

Above all else, kenku wish to regain their ability to fly. Every kenku is born with a desire to take to the air, and those who learn spellcasting do so in hope of mastering spells that will allow them to fly. Rumors of magic items such as flying carpets, brooms capable of flight, and similar objects provoke a great desire for the kenku to acquire the items for themselves.

Despite their lack of wings, kenku love dwelling in towers and other tall structures. They seek out ruins that reach to the sky, though they lack the motivation and creativity to make repairs or fortify such places.

items with exceptional skill, allowing them to become excellent artisans and scribes. They can copy books, make replicas of objects, and otherwise thrive in situations where they can produce large numbers of identical items. Few kenku find this work satisfying, since their quest for the freedom of flight makes them ill-suited to settle into a routine.

IDEAL MINIONS

Kenku gather in groups called flocks. A flock is led by the oldest and most experienced kenku with the widest store of knowledge to draw on, often called Master.

Although kenku can't create new things, they have a talent for learning and memorizing details. Thus, ambitious kenku can excel as superb spies and scouts. A kenku who learns of clever schemes and plans devised by other creatures can put them to use. The kenku lack the talent to improvise or alter a plan, but a wise Master sets multiple plans in motion at once, confident that underlings can follow orders to the letter.

For this reason, many kenku make an easy living serving as messengers, spies, and lookouts for thieves' guilds, bandits, and other criminal cartels. A network of kenku can relay a bird call or similar noise across the city, alerting their allies to the approach of a guard patrol or signaling a prime opportunity for a robbery.

Since kenku can precisely reproduce any sound, the messages they carry rarely suffer degradation or shifts in meaning. Human messengers might switch words or phrases and garble a message inadvertently, but the kenku produce perfect copies of whatever they hear.

KENKU ADVENTURERS

Kenku adventurers are usually the survivors of a flock that has sustained heavy losses, or a rare kenku who has grown weary of a life of crime. These kenku are more ambitious and daring than their fellows. Others strike out on their own in search of the secrets of flight, to master magic, or to uncover the secret of their curse and find a method to break it.

Kenku adventurers, despite their relative independence, still have a tendency to seek out a companion to emulate and follow. A kenku loves to mimic the voice and words of its chosen companion.

KENKU NAMES

Given that kenku can duplicate any sound, their names are drawn from a staggering variety of noises and phrases. Kenku names tend to break down into three categories that make no distinction between male and female names.

Kenku thugs, warriors, and toughs adopt noises made by weapons, such as the clang of a mace against armor or the sound made by a breaking bone. Non-kenku refer to the kenku by describing this noise. Examples of this type of name include Smasher, Clanger, Slicer, and Basher.

Kenku thieves, con artists, and burglars adopt animal noises, typically those common in urban settings. In this manner, kenku can call out to each other while those who overhear them mistake them for common animals.

Even so, their light weight and size allow them to dwell in rickety structures that would collapse beneath a human or an orc.

Some thieves' guilds use kenku as lookouts and messengers. The kenku dwell in the tallest buildings and towers the guild controls, allowing them to lurk in the highest levels and to keep watch on the city below.

HOPELESS PLAGIARISTS

As a result of their lack of creativity, kenku function comfortably as minions of a powerful master. Flock leaders enforce discipline and minimize conflicts, but they fail at effective planning or crafting long-term schemes.

Although unable to speak in their own voices, kenku can perfectly mimic any sound they hear, from a halfling's voice to the noise of rocks clattering down a hillside. However, kenku cannot create new sounds and can communicate only by using sounds they have heard. Most kenku use a combination of overheard phrases and sound effects to convey their ideas and thoughts.

By the same token, kenku have no ability to invent new ideas or create new things. Kenku can copy existing

Non-kenku use names that refer to the sound made or the animal a kenku mimics, such as Rat Scratch, Whistler, Mouser, and Growler.

Some kenku turn their back on crime to pursue legitimate trades. These kenku adopt noises made as part of their craft. A sailor duplicates the sound of a fluttering sail, while a smith mimics the clanging of a hammer on metal. Non-kenku describe these folk by their trade sounds, such as Sail Snap, Hammerer, and Cutter.

Kenku Traits

Your kenku character has the following racial traits.

Ability Score Increase. Your Dexterity score increases by 2, and your Wisdom score increases by 1.

Age. Kenku have shorter lifespans than humans. They reach maturity at about 12 years old and can live to 60.

Alignment. Kenku are chaotic creatures, rarely making enduring commitments, and they care mostly for preserving their own hides. They are generally chaotic neutral in outlook.

Size. Kenku are around 5 feet tall and weigh between 90 and 120 pounds. Your size is Medium.

Speed. Your base walking speed is 30 feet.

Expert Forgery. You can duplicate other creatures' handwriting and craftwork. You have advantage on all checks made to produce forgeries or duplicates of existing objects.

Kenku Training. You are proficient in your choice of two of the following skills: Acrobatics, Deception, Stealth, and Sleight of Hand.

Mimicry. You can mimic sounds you have heard, including voices. A creature that hears the sounds you make can tell they are imitations with a successful Wisdom (Insight) check opposed by your Charisma (Deception) check.

Languages. You can read and write Common and Auran, but you can speak only by using your Mimicry trait.

> ### Roleplaying a Kenku
> If you're playing a kenku, constant attempts to mimic noises can come across as confusing or irritating rather than entertaining. You can just as easily describe the sounds your character makes and what they mean. Be clear about your character's intentions unless you're deliberately aiming for inscrutable or mysterious.
>
> You might say, "Snapper makes the noise of a hammer slowly and rhythmically tapping a stone to show how bored he is. He plays with his dagger and studies the Lords' Alliance agent sitting at the bar." Creating a vocabulary of noises for the other players to decode might sound like fun, but it can prove distracting and could slow down the game.

Lizardfolk

IF YOU'RE CONSIDERING TAKING A SCALED ONE ALONG *on an adventure, remember this important fact. The strange, inhuman glint in its eyes as it looks you over is the same look you might give a freshly grilled steak.*

—Tordek, *dwarf fighter and adventurer*

Only a fool looks at the lizardfolk and sees nothing more than scaly humanoids. Their physical shape notwithstanding, lizardfolk have more in common with iguanas or dragons than they do with humans, dwarves, or elves. Lizardfolk possess an alien and inscrutable mindset, their desires and thoughts driven by a different set of basic principles than those of warm-blooded creatures. Their dismal swamp homes might lie hundreds of miles from the nearest human settlement, but the gap between their way of thinking and that of the smooth-skins is far greater.

Despite their alien outlook, some lizardfolk make an effort to understand and, in their own manner, befriend people of other races. Such lizardfolk make faithful and skilled allies.

Alien Minds

The lizardfolk's reptilian nature comes through not only in their appearance, but also in how they think and act. Lizardfolk experience a more limited emotional life than other humanoids. Like most reptiles, their feelings largely revolve around fear, aggression, and pleasure.

Lizardfolk experience most feelings as detached descriptions of creatures and situations. For example, humans confronted by an angry troll experience fear on a basic level. Their limbs shake, their thinking becomes panicked and jumbled, and they react by instinct. The emotion of fear takes hold and controls their actions. In contrast, lizardfolk see emotions as traits assigned to other creatures, objects, and situations. A lizardfolk doesn't think, "I'm scared." Instead, aggressive, stronger creatures register to the lizardfolk as fearsome beings to be avoided if possible. If such creatures attack, lizardfolk flee, fighting only if cornered. Lizardfolk aren't scared of a troll; instead, they understand that a troll is a fearsome, dangerous creature and react accordingly.

Lizardfolk never become angry in the way others do, but they act with aggression toward creatures that they could defeat in a fight and that can't be dealt with in some other manner. They are aggressive toward prey they want to eat, creatures that want to harm them, and so on.

Pleasurable people and things make life easier for lizardfolk. Pleasurable things should be preserved and protected, sometimes at the cost of the lizardfolk's own safety. The most pleasurable creatures and things are ones that allow lizardfolk to assess more situations as benign rather than fearsome.

UTILITY AND SURVIVAL

The lizardfolk mindset might seem unnecessarily cruel, but it helps them survive in a hostile environment. The swamps they inhabit are filled with a staggering variety of threats. Lizardfolk focus on survival above all, without sentiment.

Lizardfolk assess everyone and everything in terms of utility. Art and beauty have little meaning for them. A sharp sword serves a useful and good purpose, while a dull sword is a dead weight without a whetstone.

Lizardfolk see little need to plan more than a season or so into the future. This approach allows them to maintain their current level of influence in the world, but it limits their growth. Lizardfolk have no interest in developing writing, making long-term plans, or cultivating other methods to progress beyond their simple existence as hunters and gatherers.

HAPLESS SOFT ONES

At their core, lizardfolk view other humanoids with an indifference verging on pity. Born into the world lacking stout scales and sharp teeth, it's a wonder they have managed to survive for so long. The typical human would barely make it through a day in the swamps.

Still, if other creatures prove useful to lizardfolk, those creatures can trigger a protective response made all the stronger by their apparent weakness. The lizardfolk assess such beings as hatchlings, young ones incapable of protecting themselves but who might prove useful in the future if they receive care.

LIZARDFOLK PERSONALITY

You can use the Lizardfolk Quirks table to determine a personality quirk for a lizardfolk character or to inspire a unique mannerism.

LIZARDFOLK QUIRKS

d8	Quirk
1	You hate waste and see no reason not to scavenge fallen enemies. Fingers are tasty and portable!
2	You sleep best while mostly submerged in water.
3	Money is meaningless to you.
4	You think there are only two species of humanoid: lizardfolk and meat.
5	You have learned to laugh. You use this talent in response to all emotional situations, to better fit in with your comrades.
6	You still don't understand how metaphors work. That doesn't stop you from using them at every opportunity.
7	You appreciate the soft humanoids who realize they need chain mail and swords to match the gifts you were born with.
8	You enjoy eating your food while it's still wriggling.

COLD AND CALCULATING

Most humanoids describe cold-blooded people as lacking in emotion and empathy. The same label serves as an apt depiction of lizardfolk.

Lacking any internal emotional reactions, lizardfolk behave in a distant manner. They don't mourn fallen comrades or rage against their enemies. They simply observe and react as a situation warrants.

Lizardfolk lack meaningful emotional ties to the past. They assess situations based on their current and future utility and importance. Nowhere does this come through as strongly as when lizardfolk deal with the dead. To a lizardfolk, a comrade who dies becomes a potential source of food. That companion might have once been a warrior or hunter, but now the body is just freshly killed meat.

A lizardfolk who lives among other humanoids can, over time, learn to respect other creatures' emotions. The lizardfolk doesn't share those feelings, but instead assesses them in the same clinical manner. Yes, the fallen dwarf might be most useful as a meal, but hacking the body into steaks provokes aggression in the other humanoids and makes them less helpful in battle.

Lizardfolk Names

Lizardfolk take their names from the Draconic language. They use simple descriptives granted by the tribe based on an individual's notable deeds or actions. For example, Garurt translates as "axe," a name given to a lizardfolk warrior who defeated an orc and claimed his foe's weapon. A lizardfolk who likes to hide in a stand of reeds before ambushing an animal might be called Achuak, which means "green" to describe how she blends into the foliage.

Lizardfolk make no distinction between male and female in their naming conventions. Each example name includes its translation in parenthesis.

Lizardfolk Names: Achuak (green), Aryte (war), Baeshra (animal), Darastrix (dragon), Garurt (axe), Irhtos (secret), Jhank (hammer), Kepesk (storm), Kethend (gem), Korth (danger), Kosj (small), Kothar (demon), Litrix (armor), Mirik (song), Othokent (smart), Sauriv (eye), Throden (many), Thurkear (night), Usk (iron), Valignat (burn), Vargach (battle), Verthica (mountain), Vutha (black), Vyth (steel)

Lizardfolk Traits

Your lizardfolk character has the following racial traits.

Ability Score Increase. Your Constitution score increases by 2, and your Wisdom score increases by 1.

Age. Lizardfolk reach maturity around age 14 and rarely live longer than 60 years.

Alignment. Most lizardfolk are neutral. They see the world as a place of predators and prey, where life and death are natural processes. They wish only to survive, and prefer to leave other creatures to their own devices.

Size. Lizardfolk are a little bulkier and taller than humans, and their colorful frills make them appear even larger. Your size is Medium.

Speed. Your base walking speed is 30 feet, and you have a swimming speed of 30 feet.

Bite. Your fanged maw is a natural weapon, which you can use to make unarmed strikes. If you hit with it, you deal piercing damage equal to 1d6 + your Strength modifier, instead of the bludgeoning damage normal for an unarmed strike.

Cunning Artisan. As part of a short rest, you can harvest bone and hide from a slain beast, construct, dragon, monstrosity, or plant creature of size Small or larger to create one of the following items: a shield, a club, a javelin, or 1d4 darts or blowgun needles. To use this trait, you need a blade, such as a dagger, or appropriate artisan's tools, such as leatherworker's tools.

Hold Breath. You can hold your breath for up to 15 minutes at a time.

Hunter's Lore. You gain proficiency with two of the following skills of your choice: Animal Handling, Nature, Perception, Stealth, and Survival.

Natural Armor. You have tough, scaly skin. When you aren't wearing armor, your AC is 13 + your Dexterity modifier. You can use your natural armor to determine your AC if the armor you wear would leave you with a lower AC. A shield's benefits apply as normal while you use your natural armor.

> **Lizardfolk Speech**
>
> Lizardfolk can master Common, but their mindset results in a speech pattern distinct from other humanoids.
>
> Lizardfolk rarely use metaphors. Their speech is almost always literal. They might pick up idioms, but only with some difficulty.
>
> Names confuse them, unless they are descriptive. They tend to apply their own naming conventions to other creatures using Common words.
>
> Lizardfolk use active verbs to describe the world. A lizardfolk in cold weather might say, "This wind brings cold" rather than "I feel cold." Lizardfolk tend to define things in terms of actions, rather than effects.

Hungry Jaws. In battle, you can throw yourself into a vicious feeding frenzy. As a bonus action, you can make a special attack with your bite. If the attack hits, it deals its normal damage, and you gain temporary hit points (minimum of 1) equal to your Constitution modifier, and you can't use this trait again until you finish a short or long rest.

Languages. You can speak, read, and write Common and Draconic.

Tabaxi

WE HAD A TABAXI COME THROUGH ONCE, A FEW WINTERS *back. She kept the taproom packed each night with her stories and spent most days napping in a chair in front of the fireplace. We thought she was lazy, but when Linene came around looking for a missing broach, she was out the door before I could blink an eye.*

—Toblen Stonehill, *innkeeper*

Hailing from a strange and distant land, wandering tabaxi are catlike humanoids driven by curiosity to collect interesting artifacts, gather tales and stories, and lay eyes on all the world's wonders. Ultimate travelers, the inquisitive tabaxi rarely stay in one place for long. Their innate nature pushes them to leave no secrets uncovered, no treasures or legends lost.

Wandering Outcasts

Most tabaxi remain in their distant homeland, content to dwell in small, tight clans. These tabaxi hunt for food, craft goods, and largely keep to themselves.

However, not all tabaxi are satisfied with such a life. The Cat Lord, the divine figure responsible for the creation of the tabaxi, gifts each of his children with one specific feline trait. Those tabaxi gifted with curiosity are compelled to wander far and wide. They seek out stories, artifacts, and lore. Those who survive this period of wanderlust return home in their elder years to share news of the outside world. In this manner, the tabaxi remain isolated but never ignorant of the world beyond their home.

Barterers of Lore

Tabaxi treasure knowledge rather than material things. A chest filled with gold coins might be useful to buy food or a coil of rope, but it's not intrinsically interesting.

In the tabaxi's eyes, gathering wealth is like packing rations for a long trip. It's important to survive in the world, but not worth fussing over.

Instead, tabaxi value knowledge and new experiences. Their ears perk up in a busy tavern, and they tease out stories with offers of food, drink, and coin. Tabaxi might walk away with empty purses, but they mull over the stories and rumors they collected like a miser counting coins.

Although material wealth holds little attraction for the tabaxi, they have an insatiable desire to find and inspect ancient relics, magical items, and other rare objects. Aside from the power such items might confer, a tabaxi takes great joy in unraveling the stories behind their creation and the history of their use.

FLEETING FANCIES

Wandering tabaxi are mercurial creatures, trading one obsession or passion for the next as the whim strikes. A tabaxi's desire burns bright, but once met it disappears to be replaced with a new obsession. Objects remain intriguing only as long as they still hold secrets.

A tabaxi rogue could happily spend months plotting to steal a strange gem from a noble, only to trade it for passage on a ship or a week's lodging after stealing it. The tabaxi might take extensive notes or memorize every facet of the gem before passing it on, but the gem holds no more allure once its secrets and nature have been laid bare.

TINKERS AND MINSTRELS

Curiosity drives most of the tabaxi found outside their homeland, but not all of them become adventurers. Tabaxi who seek a safer path to satisfy their obsessions become wandering tinkers and minstrels.

These tabaxi work in small troupes, usually consisting of an elder, more experienced tabaxi who guides up to four young ones learning their way in the world. They travel in small, colorful wagons, moving from settlement to settlement. When they arrive, they set up a small stage in a public square where they sing, play instruments, tell stories, and offer exotic goods in trade for items that spark their interest. Tabaxi reluctantly accept gold, but they much prefer interesting objects or pieces of lore as payment.

These wanderers keep to civilized realms, preferring to bargain instead of pursuing more dangerous methods of sating their curiosity. However, they aren't above a little discreet theft to get their claws on a particularly interesting item when an owner refuses to sell or trade it.

TABAXI NAMES

Each tabaxi has a single name, determined by clan and based on a complex formula that involves astrology, prophecy, clan history, and other esoteric factors. Tabaxi names can apply to both males and females, and most use nicknames derived from or inspired by their full names.

Clan names are usually based on a geographical feature located in or near the clan's territory.

The following list of sample tabaxi names includes nicknames in parenthesis.

Tabaxi Names: Cloud on the Mountaintop (Cloud), Five Timber (Timber), Jade Shoe (Jade), Left-Handed Hummingbird (Bird), Seven Thundercloud (Thunder), Skirt of Snakes (Snake), Smoking Mirror (Smoke)

Tabaxi Clans: Bright Cliffs, Distant Rain, Mountain Tree, Rumbling River, Snoring Mountain

TABAXI PERSONALITY

A tabaxi might have motivations and quirks much different from a dwarf or an elf with a similar background. You can use the following tables to customize your character in addition to the trait, ideal, bond, and flaw from your background.

The Tabaxi Obsession table can help hone your character's goals. For extra fun, roll a new result every few days that pass in the campaign to reflect your ever-changing curiosity.

TABAXI OBSESSIONS

d8	My curiosity is currently fixed on ...
1	A god or planar entity
2	A monster
3	A lost civilization
4	A wizard's secrets
5	A mundane item
6	A magic item
7	A location
8	A legend or tale

TABAXI QUIRKS

d10	Quirk
1	You miss your tropical home and complain endlessly about the freezing weather, even in summer.
2	You never wear the same outfit twice, unless you absolutely must.
3	You have a minor phobia of water and hate getting wet.
4	Your tail always betrays your inner thoughts.
5	You purr loudly when you are happy.
6	You keep a small ball of yarn in your hand, which you constantly fidget with.
7	You are always in debt, since you spend your gold on lavish parties and gifts for friends.
8	When talking about something you're obsessed with, you speak quickly and never pause and others can't understand you.
9	You are a font of random trivia from the lore and stories you have discovered.
10	You can't help but pocket interesting objects you come across.

Size. Tabaxi are taller on average than humans and relatively slender. Your size is Medium.

Speed. Your base walking speed is 30 feet.

Darkvision. You have a cat's keen senses, especially in the dark. You can see in dim light within 60 feet of you as if it were bright light, and in darkness as if it were dim light. You can't discern color in darkness, only shades of gray.

Feline Agility. Your reflexes and agility allow you to move with a burst of speed. When you move on your turn in combat, you can double your speed until the end of the turn. Once you use this trait, you can't use it again until you move 0 feet on one of your turns.

Cat's Claws. Because of your claws, you have a climbing speed of 20 feet. In addition, your claws are natural weapons, which you can use to make unarmed strikes. If you hit with them, you deal slashing damage equal to 1d4 + your Strength modifier, instead of the bludgeoning damage normal for an unarmed strike.

Cat's Talent. You have proficiency in the Perception and Stealth skills.

Languages. You can speak, read, and write Common and one other language of your choice.

TRITON

AH, THE TRITONS. IMAGINE IF THE ELVES SPENT A FEW centuries far beneath the sea, where their arrogance and pretension could grow undisturbed. At least the tritons spent that time fighting sahuagin and worse, so you know you can count on them in a fight.

—Brego Stoneheart, *sea captain*

Tritons guard the ocean depths, building small settlements beside deep trenches, portals to the elemental planes, and other dangerous spots far from the eyes of land-bound folk. Long-established guardians of the deep ocean floor, in recent years the noble tritons have become increasingly active in the world above.

AQUATIC CRUSADERS

Centuries ago, tritons entered the world in response to the growing threat of evil elementals. Tritons waged many wars against their enemies on the Plane of Water, driving them into the Darkened Depths where they escaped into the crushing pressure and utter darkness. In time, the tritons noticed that their ancient elemental foes had grown quiet. Expeditions to the depths revealed that krakens, sahuagin, and far worse foes had fled the Plane of Water for the Material Plane.

The tritons, driven by a sense of duty and responsibility, would not allow their foes to escape so easily. A great conclave of tritons chose volunteers skilled in weapons and magic as part of an expeditionary force to enter the Material Plane and seek out their enemies.

Those tritons spread across the world's oceans and established protectorates to watch over deep sea trenches, portals, undersea caves, and other locations where their enemies might lurk. They defeated their foes when they found them and drove the rest into hiding.

TABAXI TRAITS

Your tabaxi character has the following racial traits.

Ability Score Increase. Your Dexterity score increases by 2, and your Charisma score increases by 1.

Age. Tabaxi have lifespans equivalent to humans.

Alignment. Tabaxi tend toward chaotic alignments, as they let impulse and fancy guide their decisions. They are rarely evil, with most of them driven by curiosity rather than greed or other dark impulses.

> ### TABAXI IN THE FORGOTTEN REALMS
>
> In the Forgotten Realms, tabaxi hail from Maztica, a realm located far across the ocean west of the Sword Coast. The tabaxi of Maztica are known for their isolation, and until recently they never ventured from their homeland. The tabaxi say little of why that has changed, though rumors persist of strange happenings in that distant land.

allowance for such ignorance and are delighted to expound upon the great debt others owe them.

Tritons also have a tendency to emerge from their isolation under the assumption that other folk will welcome them as respected allies and mentors. Again, distance drives much of this attitude. The tritons' limited view of the world leaves them ignorant of the kingdoms, wars, and other struggles of the surface world. Tritons readily see such concerns as minor events, a sideshow to the tritons' role as the world's true protectors.

STAUNCH CHAMPIONS

Despite their off-putting manners, tritons are benevolent creatures at heart, convinced that other civilized races deserve their protection. Their attitude might grate, but when pirate fleets prowl the waves or a kraken awakens from its slumber, they are among the first to take up arms to protect others.

Tritons readily sacrifice themselves for the common good. They will fight and die for humans, merfolk, and other creatures without question. Their self-absorbed nature makes them overlook the history of other creatures, but they also endure a sense of guilt over allowing the evils of the Plane of Water to enter the Material Plane and threaten its inhabitants. The tritons believe they owe a debt of honor to the world, and they will fight and die to pay it.

At times their fervor and ignorance of the world can lead them astray. Tritons encountering other creatures for the first time can underestimate them, leaving the tritons vulnerable to deception. With their strong martial tradition, tritons can sometimes be too eager to leap into a fight.

STRANGERS TO THE SURFACE

Given their isolation, most tritons have never been to the surface world. They struggle with the idea that they can't easily move up and down out of water, and the changing of the seasons mystifies them.

With their foes banished to the deepest reaches of the sea, tritons settled in to watch for any sign of their return. Over time, the tritons extended their stewardship over the sea floor from their initial settlements and built outposts to create trade with other races. Despite this expansion, few folk know of them. Their settlements are so remote even merfolk and sea elves rarely encounter them.

HAUGHTY NOBLES

As a result of their isolation and limited understanding of the Material Plane, tritons can come across as haughty and arrogant. They see themselves as caretakers of the sea, and they expect other creatures to pay them deep respect, if not complete deference.

This attitude might grate on others, but it arises from a seed of truth. Few know of the tritons' great victories over dreadful undersea threats. The tritons make little

---

SPELL: WALL OF WATER
3rd-level evocation

Casting Time: 1 action
Range: 60 feet
Components: V, S, M (a drop of water)
Duration: Concentration, up to 10 minutes

You conjure up a wall of water on the ground at a point you can see within range. You can make the wall up to 30 feet long, 10 feet high, and 1 foot thick, or you can make a ringed wall up to 20 feet in diameter, 20 feet high, and 1 foot thick. The wall vanishes when the spell ends. The wall's space is difficult terrain.

Any ranged weapon attack that enters the wall's space has disadvantage on the attack roll, and fire damage is halved if the fire effect passes through the wall to reach its target. Spells that deal cold damage that pass through the wall cause the area of the wall they pass through to freeze solid (at least a 5-foot square section is frozen). Each 5-foot-square frozen section has AC 5 and 15 hit points. Reducing a frozen section to 0 hit points destroys it. When a section is destroyed, the wall's water doesn't fill it.

Tritons also find the variety of social institutions, kingdoms, and other customs bewildering. For all their proud culture, they remain innocent of the surface world. The typical triton protectorate is tightly regimented, organized, and unified around a common cause. A triton on the surface becomes easily confused by the bewildering array of alliances, rivalries, and petty grievances that prevent the surface folk from truly unifying.

At its worst, a triton's arrogance compounds the tendency for the triton not to understand the ways of the surface world. It's easy for a triton to blame baffling social practices on what the triton perceives as the barbarism, weakness, or cowardice of surface folk.

Triton Personality

Far from flawless, these champions of good mean well, but they are easily frustrated by others. You can select, roll, or adapt a triton-specific quirk from the Triton Quirks table. Use the quirk to inform how you portray your character.

Triton Quirks

d6	Quirk
1	You phrase requests as orders that you expect to be obeyed.
2	You are quick to boast of the greatness of your civilization.
3	You learned an antiquated version of Common and drop "thee" and "thou" into your speech.
4	You assume that people are telling you the truth about local customs and expectations.
5	The surface world is a wondrous place, and you catalog all its details in a journal.
6	You mistakenly assume that surface folk know about and are impressed by your people's history.

Triton Names

Most triton names have two or three syllables. Male names typically end with a vowel and the letter *s*, and female names traditionally end with an *n*. Tritons use their home protectorate as a surname, with the name formed by adding a vowel followed by a "th" to the end of the protectorate's name.

Female Triton Names: Aryn, Belthyn, Duthyn, Feloren, Otanyn, Shalryn, Vlaryn, Wolyn

Male Triton Names: Corus, Delnis, Jhimas, Keros, Molos, Nalos, Vodos, Zunis

Triton Surnames: Ahlorsath, Pumanath, Vuuvaxath

Triton Traits

Your triton character has the following racial traits.

Ability Score Increase. Your Strength, Constitution, and Charisma scores each increase by 1.

Age. Tritons reach maturity around age 15 and can live up to 200 years.

Alignment. Tritons tend toward lawful good. As guardians of the darkest reaches of the sea, their culture pushes them toward order and benevolence.

Size. Tritons are slightly shorter than humans, averaging about 5 feet tall. Your size is Medium.

Speed. Your base walking speed is 30 feet, and you have a swimming speed of 30 feet.

Amphibious. You can breathe air and water.

Control Air and Water. A child of the sea, you can call on the magic of elemental air and water. You can cast *fog cloud* with this trait. Starting at 3rd level, you can cast *gust of wind* with it, and starting at 5th level, you can also cast *wall of water* with it (see the spell in the sidebar). Once you cast a spell with this trait, you can't cast that spell with it again until you finish a long rest. Charisma is your spellcasting ability for these spells.

Emissary of the Sea. Aquatic beasts have an extraordinary affinity with your people. You can communicate simple ideas with beasts that can breathe water. They can understand the meaning of your words, though you have no special ability to understand them in return.

Guardians of the Depths. Adapted to even the most extreme ocean depths, you have resistance to cold damage, and you ignore any of the drawbacks caused by a deep, underwater environment.

Languages. You can speak, read, and write Common and Primordial.

Monstrous Adventurers

In some campaigns, humanoids normally regarded as sinister threats can emerge to adventure alongside humans and the other standard races. This section is aimed at DMs who wish to expand the race selections for their campaigns beyond the typical folk of D&D.

Why a Monstrous Character?

Creating characters as creatures normally cast as villains offers up some interesting roleplaying possibilities. Whether played for comedy, as a tragic story of betrayal and loss, or as an antihero, a monstrous character gives a player a chance to take on an unusual challenge in the campaign. Before allowing monstrous characters in your campaign, consider the following three questions.

Rare or Mundane?

Consider how common orc, goblin, and similar adventurers are in your setting. Are they regarded as no stranger than elves or dwarves? Are they met with suspicion? The role these races play in your setting should determine the kinds of reactions that such characters meet.

Don't be afraid to push things to an extreme. An orc character might have to venture into town in disguise or remain in the wilderness, for fear of imprisonment or mob violence. Be sure to talk to the group about how such characters can expect the world to treat them. Some players like the challenge of taking on an outcast, but don't set up one expectation and deliver another.

You can establish a monstrous creature as just another culture in your campaign, one that has alliances and rivalries with humans, elves, and dwarves. A hobgoblin kingdom might serve as a buffer between a human kingdom and a blighted region overrun by the spawn of Kyuss. Kobolds might be city builders, the ar-

chitects of grand, heavily fortified edifices, which other folk dwell in for a price. The cultural notes in chapter 1 are the standard D&D depiction of these creatures, but by no means do they define them for your campaign. Use them as a starting point for your own ideas.

Outcast or Ambassador?

Consider how a monstrous character's native culture views the character. Is the character an outcast, a spy, an ambassador, or something else? Work with the player to determine how the character ended up as an adventurer.

The character's bond is a great starting point to consider for this question. How did the bond drive the character to adventure? The character's trait, flaw, and ideal can also play a role in fleshing out the story.

Friends or Enemies?

Figure out what special ties the character has to other members of the adventuring party. An orc warlock might be the dwarf ranger's sworn enemy, but the two are forced to work together to defeat a mutual foe. Perhaps the kobold sorcerer was the tiefling wizard's familiar, transformed by an irate archmage in return for some petty insult. The hobgoblin paladin might have been human once, but crossed the wrong hag and was cursed to take on an evil guise. A creative tie between a monstrous character and the rest of the party helps make for a memorable campaign.

The Monstrous Origin table gives a number of ideas for adding a monstrous character to the campaign.

Monstrous Origin

d8	Origin
1	You are a spy sent to undermine your enemies from within.
2	You are the victim of a curse or polymorph spell.
3	You were raised by humans, elves, or dwarves and have adopted their culture.
4	At a young age, you adopted a human religion and now serve it faithfully.
5	You received divine insight that sent you on your path, and occasionally receive new visions that guide you.
6	Your sworn enemy is an ally of your people, forcing you to leave your tribe to gain vengeance.
7	An evil entity corrupted your people's society.
8	An injury or strange event caused you to lose all memory of your past, but occasional flashes of it return to you.

Racial Traits

The game traits of the monstrous races are given here. Refer to chapter 1 for their cultural and roleplaying notes. Some of these races are unusual in that they have a reduction to an ability score, and some are more or less powerful than the typical D&D races—additional reasons for the monstrous races to be used in a campaign with care.

BUGBEAR TRAITS

Your bugbear character has the following racial traits.

Ability Score Increase. Your Strength score increases by 2, and your Dexterity score increases by 1.

Age. Bugbears reach adulthood at age 16 and live up to 80 years.

Alignment. Bugbears endure a harsh existence that demands each of them to remain self-sufficient, even at the expense of their fellows. They tend to be chaotic evil.

Size. Bugbears are between 6 and 8 feet tall and weigh between 250 and 350 pounds. Your size is Medium.

Speed. Your base walking speed is 30 feet.

Darkvision. You can see in dim light within 60 feet of you as if it were bright light, and in darkness as if it were dim light. You can't discern color in darkness, only shades of gray.

Long-Limbed. When you make a melee attack on your turn, your reach for it is 5 feet greater than normal.

Powerful Build. You count as one size larger when determining your carrying capacity and the weight you can push, drag, or lift.

Sneaky. You are proficient in the Stealth skill.

Surprise Attack. If you surprise a creature and hit it with an attack on your first turn in combat, the attack deals an extra 2d6 damage to it. You can use this trait only once per combat.

Languages. You can speak, read, and write Common and Goblin.

GOBLIN TRAITS

Your goblin character has the following racial traits.

Ability Score Increase. Your Dexterity score increases by 2, and your Constitution score increases by 1.

Age. Goblins reach adulthood at age 8 and live up to 60 years.

Alignment. Goblins are typically neutral evil, as they care only for their own needs. A few goblins might tend toward good or neutrality, but only rarely.

Size. Goblins are between 3 and 4 feet tall and weigh between 40 and 80 pounds. Your size is Small.

Speed. Your base walking speed is 30 feet.

Darkvision. You can see in dim light within 60 feet of you as if it were bright light, and in darkness as if it were dim light. You can't discern color in darkness, only shades of gray.

Fury of the Small. When you damage a creature with an attack or a spell and the creature's size is larger than yours, you can cause the attack or spell to deal extra damage to the creature. The extra damage equals your level. Once you use this trait, you can't use it again until you finish a short or long rest.

Nimble Escape. You can take the Disengage or Hide action as a bonus action on each of your turns.

Languages. You can speak, read, and write Common and Goblin.

HOBGOBLIN TRAITS

Your hobgoblin character has the following racial traits.

Ability Score Increase. Your Constitution score increases by 2, and your Intelligence score increases by 1.

Age. Hobgoblins mature at the same rate as humans and have lifespans similar in length to theirs.

Alignment. Hobgoblin society is built on fidelity to a rigid, unforgiving code of conduct. As such, they tend toward lawful evil.

Size. Hobgoblins are between 5 and 6 feet tall and weigh between 150 and 200 pounds. Your size is Medium.

Speed. Your base walking speed is 30 feet.

Darkvision. You can see in dim light within 60 feet of you as if it were bright light, and in darkness as if it were dim light. You can't discern color in darkness, only shades of gray.

Martial Training. You are proficient with two martial weapons of your choice and with light armor.

Saving Face. Hobgoblins are careful not to show weakness in front of their allies, for fear of losing status. If you miss with an attack roll or fail an ability check or a saving throw, you can gain a bonus to the roll equal to the number of allies you can see within 30 feet of you (maximum bonus of +5). Once you use this trait, you can't use it again until you finish a short or long rest.

Languages. You can speak, read, and write Common and Goblin.

KOBOLD TRAITS

Your kobold character has the following racial traits.

Ability Score Increase. Your Dexterity score increases by 2, and your Strength score is reduced by 2.

Age. Kobolds reach adulthood at age 6 and can live up to 120 years but rarely do so.

Alignment. Kobolds are fundamentally selfish, making them evil, but their reliance on the strength of their group makes them trend toward law.

Size. Kobolds are between 2 and 3 feet tall and weigh between 25 and 35 pounds. Your size is Small.

Speed. Your base walking speed is 30 feet.

Darkvision. You can see in dim light within 60 feet of you as if it were bright light, and in darkness as if it were dim light. You can't discern color in darkness, only shades of gray.

Grovel, Cower, and Beg. As an action on your turn, you can cower pathetically to distract nearby foes. Until the end of your next turn, your allies gain advantage on attack rolls against enemies within 10 feet of you that can see you. Once you use this trait, you can't use it again until you finish a short or long rest.

Pack Tactics. You have advantage on an attack roll against a creature if at least one of your allies is within 5 feet of the creature and the ally isn't incapacitated.

Sunlight Sensitivity. You have disadvantage on attack rolls and on Wisdom (Perception) checks that rely on sight when you, the target of your attack, or whatever you are trying to perceive is in direct sunlight.

Languages. You can speak, read, and write Common and Draconic.

Yuan-ti Pureblood Traits

Your yuan-ti pureblood character—called a pureblood for short—has the following racial traits.

Ability Score Increase. Your Charisma score increases by 2, and your Intelligence score increases by 1.

Age. Purebloods mature at the same rate as humans and have lifespans similar in length to theirs.

Alignment. Purebloods are devoid of emotion and see others as tools to manipulate. They care little for law or chaos and are typically neutral evil.

Size. Purebloods match humans in average size and weight. Your size is Medium.

Speed. Your base walking speed is 30 feet.

Darkvision. You can see in dim light within 60 feet of you as if it were bright light, and in darkness as if it were dim light. You can't discern color in darkness, only shades of gray.

Innate Spellcasting. You know the *poison spray* cantrip. You can cast *animal friendship* an unlimited number of times with this trait, but you can target only snakes with it. Starting at 3rd level, you can also cast *suggestion* with this trait. Once you cast it, you can't do so again until you finish a long rest. Charisma is your spellcasting ability for these spells.

Magic Resistance. You have advantage on saving throws against spells and other magical effects.

Poison Immunity. You are immune to poison damage and the poisoned condition.

Languages. You can speak, read, and write Common, Abyssal, and Draconic.

Height and Weight

You may roll for your character's height and weight on the Random Height and Weight table. The roll in the Height Modifier column adds a number (in inches) to the character's base height. To get a weight, multiply the number you rolled for height by the roll in the Weight Modifier column and add the result (in pounds) to the base weight.

Random Height and Weight

Race	Base Height	Base Weight	Height Modifier	Weight Modifier
Aasimar	4'8"	110 lb.	+2d10	× (2d4) lb.
Bugbear	6'0"	200 lb.	+2d12	× (2d6) lb.
Firbolg	6'2"	175 lb.	+2d12	× (2d6) lb.
Goblin	3'5"	35 lb.	+2d4	× 1 lb.
Goliath	6'2"	200 lb.	+2d10	× (2d6) lb.
Hobgoblin	4'8"	110 lb.	+2d10	× (2d4) lb.
Kenku	4'4"	50 lb.	+2d8	× (1d6) lb.
Kobold	2'1"	25 lb.	+2d4	× 1 lb.
Lizardfolk	4'9"	120 lb.	+2d10	× (2d6) lb.
Orc	5'4"	175 lb.	+2d8	× (2d6) lb.
Tabaxi	4'10"	90 lb.	+2d10	× (2d4) lb.
Triton	4'6"	90 lb.	+2d10	× (2d4) lb.
Yuan-ti	4'8"	110 lb.	+2d10	× (2d4) lb.

Orc Traits

Your orc character has the following racial traits.

Ability Score Increase. Your Strength score increases by 2, your Constitution score increases by 1, and your Intelligence score is reduced by 2.

Age. Orcs reach adulthood at age 12 and live up to 50 years.

Alignment. Orcs are vicious raiders, who believe that the world should be theirs. They also respect strength above all else and believe the strong must bully the weak to ensure that weakness does not spread like a disease. They are usually chaotic evil.

Size. Orcs are usually over 6 feet tall and weigh between 230 and 280 pounds. Your size is Medium.

Speed. Your base walking speed is 30 feet.

Darkvision. You can see in dim light within 60 feet of you as if it were bright light, and in darkness as if it were dim light. You can't discern color in darkness, only shades of gray.

Aggressive. As a bonus action, you can move up to your speed toward an enemy of your choice that you can see or hear. You must end this move closer to the enemy than you started.

Menacing. You are trained in the Intimidation skill.

Powerful Build. You count as one size larger when determining your carrying capacity and the weight you can push, drag, or lift.

Languages. You can speak, read, and write Common and Orc.

CHAPTER 3: BESTIARY

ITHIN THIS BESTIARY, YOU WILL FIND game statistics and lore for nearly one hundred monsters suitable for any D&D campaign. Many of these monsters, such as the froghemoth and the morkoth, have been around since the earliest editions of the game. Others, such as the banderhobb and the vargouille, came later but are equally beloved. Some of the new creatures found herein are variants of the monsters discussed in chapter 1.

This chapter is a continuation of the *Monster Manual* and adopts a similar presentation. If you are unfamiliar with the monster stat block format, read the introduction of the *Monster Manual* before proceeding further. It explains stat block terminology and gives rules for various monster traits—information that isn't repeated here.

As with the monsters in the *Monster Manual*, we've tried to capture the essence of each creature and focus on those traits that make it unique or that encourage DMs to use it. You can do what you will with these monsters and change their lore to suit your game. Nothing we say here is meant to curtail your creativity.

The creatures in this bestiary are organized alphabetically. A few are grouped under a banner heading; for example, the "Orcs" section contains stat blocks for various kinds of orcs, including tanarukks (demonic orcs). Immediately following this chapter are two appendices that contain additional stat blocks. Appendix A gathers a handful of beasts that don't warrant longer entries. Appendix B provides generic NPCs whose statistics can be customized to serve your campaign.

This chapter and appendices A and B are meant to be used in conjunction with the rest of this book. Appendix C contains lists of creatures by type, challenge rating, and environment. These lists can help you find monsters that are appropriate for your adventure or campaign. If you're looking for ways to use the variant beholders, giants, gnolls, goblinoids, hags, kobolds, mind flayers, orcs, and yuan-ti described in this chapter, the lore and maps in chapter 1 might inspire you. Similarly, the racial traits in chapter 2 can be applied to the stat blocks in appendix B to create such memorable NPCs as goliath champions, kenku master thieves, and tabaxi bards.

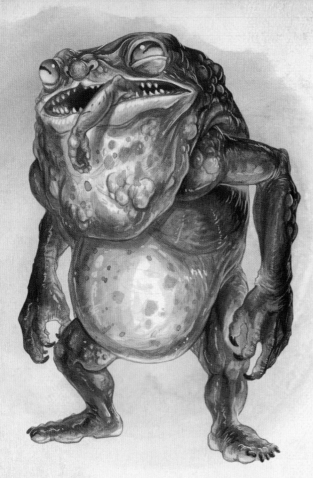

other object connected to the target. Possession of such an item allows it to sense the creature's location from as far as a mile away.

A banderhobb fulfills its duties until its existence ends. When it expires, usually several days after its birth, it leaves behind only tarry goo and wisps of shadow. Legends tell of a dark tower in the Shadowfell where the shadows sometimes reform, and banderhobbs roam.

BANDERHOBB

A banderhobb is a hybrid of shadow and flesh. Through dark magic, these components take on an enormous and vile humanoid shape, resembling a bipedal toad. In this form, a banderhobb temporarily serves its creator as a thug, a thief, and a kidnapper.

Birthed by Hags. In the earliest days of the world, a coven of night hags devised a ritual that led to the creation of the first banderhobb. A hag that knows the ritual might be willing to teach it for the right price. Some other dark fey and powerful fiends also know of the process, as do a few mortal mages. Instructions might also be found in a tome devoted to debased wizardry.

Silent and Deadly. When the ritual to create a banderhobb is complete, flesh, spirit, and shadow combine to produce a creature as big as an ogre. The newly formed monstrosity has spindly limbs that belie great strength. Its broad maw holds a long tongue and rows of fangs, both of which it uses to grab and swallow a creature or perhaps an object the banderhobb intends to steal. Despite its size, a banderhobb makes little noise, moving as silently as the shadows that infuse it. A banderhobb isn't capable of speech, but it can understand orders given to it by its creator and communicates with nearby banderhobbs in a psychic manner.

Agents of Evil. During its brief existence, a banderhobb attempts to carry out the bidding of the one who birthed it. It accomplishes its mission with no concern for the harm it suffers or creates. Its only desire is to serve and succeed. A banderhobb that is assigned to track down a target is particularly dangerous when it is provided with a lock of hair, a personal belonging, or

---

BANDERHOBB
Large monstrosity, neutral evil

Armor Class 15 (natural armor)
Hit Points 84 (8d10 + 40)
Speed 30 ft.

STR	DEX	CON	INT	WIS	CHA
20 (+5)	12 (+1)	20 (+5)	11 (+0)	14 (+2)	8 (−1)

Skills Athletics +8, Stealth +7
Condition Immunities charmed, frightened
Senses darkvision 120 ft., passive Perception 12
Languages understands Common and the languages of its creator, but can't speak
Challenge 5 (1,800 XP)

Resonant Connection. If the banderhobb has even a tiny piece of a creature or an object in its possession, such as a lock of hair or a splinter of wood, it knows the most direct route to that creature or object if it is within 1 mile of the banderhobb.

Shadow Stealth. While in dim light or darkness, the banderhobb can take the Hide action as a bonus action.

ACTIONS

Bite. *Melee Weapon Attack:* +8 to hit, reach 5 ft., one target. *Hit:* 22 (5d6 + 5) piercing damage, and the target is grappled (escape DC 15) if it is a Large or smaller creature. Until this grapple ends, the target is restrained, and the banderhobb can't use its bite attack or tongue attack on another target.

Tongue. *Melee Weapon Attack:* +8 to hit, reach 15 ft., one creature. *Hit:* 10 (3d6) necrotic damage, and the target must make a DC 15 Strength saving throw. On a failed save, the target is pulled to a space within 5 feet of the banderhobb, which can use a bonus action to make a bite attack against the target.

Swallow. The banderhobb makes a bite attack against a Medium or smaller creature it is grappling. If the attack hits, the creature is swallowed, and the grapple ends. The swallowed creature is blinded and restrained, it has total cover against attacks and other effects outside the banderhobb, and it takes 10 (3d6) necrotic damage at the start of each of the banderhobb's turns. A creature reduced to 0 hit points in this way stops taking the necrotic damage and becomes stable.

The banderhobb can have only one creature swallowed at a time. While the banderhobb isn't incapacitated, it can regurgitate the creature at any time (no action required) in a space within 5 feet of it. The creature exits prone. If the banderhobb dies, it likewise regurgitates a swallowed creature.

Shadow Step. The banderhobb magically teleports up to 30 feet to an unoccupied space of dim light or darkness that it can see. Before or after teleporting, it can make a bite or tongue attack.

Barghest

Long ago, Maglubiyet, master of the goblinoid gods, bargained with the General of Gehenna for aid. The General provided yugoloths that died to serve the cause of the goblin god. Yet when the time came to honor his part of the compact, Maglubiyet reneged on the deal. As an act of vengeance, the General of Gehenna created the soul-devouring barghests to devour goblinoid souls and deprive Maglubiyet of troops for his army in the afterlife.

Consumers of Souls. A barghest is born to goblin parents just as normal offspring are. The creature emerges in the form of a goblin, then develops the ability to assume its true form: that of a large, fiendish canine.

The mission of every barghest, implanted in it by the General of Gehenna, is to consume seventeen goblinoid souls by devouring the bodies of those it kills. Souls consumed in this way are prevented from joining Maglubiyet's forces in Acheron. Why seventeen? Because the oaths Maglubiyet broke in his compact with the General totaled seventeen.

A barghest hungers for the day when it can complete its mission, return to Gehenna, and serve the General directly in his yugoloth legions, but it doesn't kill goblinoids indiscriminately. By devouring the souls of goblinoid leaders and other powerful individuals, rather than lowly goblins, a barghest earns elevated status in the afterlife. Barghests typically keep their true nature secret, preying upon a goblin or two when the opportunity arises, until they reach adult age and are old and strong enough to seek out stronger prey. When goblins discover that a barghest is among them, they react with groveling obeisance, each member of the tribe eager to show the barghest that it isn't worthy of being devoured.

Banished by Fire. A barghest avoids contact with large, open fires. Any conflagration larger than its body acts as a gateway to Gehenna and banishes the fiend to that plane, where it is likely to be slain or enslaved by a yugoloth for its failure.

SOUL FEEDING

A barghest can feed on the corpse of a humanoid that it killed that has been dead for less than 10 minutes, devouring both flesh and soul in doing so. This feeding takes at least 1 minute, and it destroys the victim's body. The victim's soul is trapped in the barghest for 24 hours, after which time it is digested. If the barghest dies before the soul is digested, the soul is released.

While a humanoid's soul is trapped in a barghest, any form of revival that could work has only a 50 percent chance of doing so, freeing the soul from the barghest if it is successful. Once a creature's soul is digested, however, no mortal magic can return that humanoid to life.

BARGHEST
Large fiend (shapechanger), neutral evil

Armor Class 17 (natural armor)
Hit Points 90 (12d10 + 24)
Speed 60 ft. (30 ft. in goblin form)

STR	DEX	CON	INT	WIS	CHA
19 (+4)	15 (+2)	14 (+2)	13 (+1)	12 (+1)	14 (+2)

Skills Deception +4, Intimidation +4, Perception +5, Stealth +4
Damage Resistances cold, fire, lightning; bludgeoning, piercing, and slashing from nonmagical attacks
Damage Immunities acid, poison
Condition Immunities poisoned
Senses blindsight 60 ft., darkvision 60 ft., passive Perception 15
Languages Abyssal, Common, Goblin, Infernal, telepathy 60 ft.
Challenge 4 (1,100 XP)

Shapechanger. The barghest can use its action to polymorph into a Small goblin or back into its true form. Other than its size and speed, its statistics are the same in each form. Any equipment it is wearing or carrying isn't transformed. The barghest reverts to its true form if it dies.

Fire Banishment. When the barghest starts its turn engulfed in flames that are at least 10 feet high or wide, it must succeed on a DC 15 Charisma saving throw or be instantly banished to Gehenna. Instantaneous bursts of flame (such as a red dragon's breath or a *fireball* spell) don't have this effect on the barghest.

Keen Smell. The barghest has advantage on Wisdom (Perception) checks that rely on smell.

Innate Spellcasting. The barghest's innate spellcasting ability is Charisma (spell save DC 12). The barghest can innately cast the following spells, requiring no material components:

At will: *levitate, minor illusion, pass without trace*
1/day each: *charm person, dimension door, suggestion*

ACTIONS

Bite. *Melee Weapon Attack* (true form only): +6 to hit, reach 5 ft., one target. *Hit:* 13 (2d8 + 4) piercing damage.

Claws. *Melee Weapon Attack.* +6 to hit, reach 5 ft., one target. *Hit:* 8 (1d8 + 4) slashing damage.

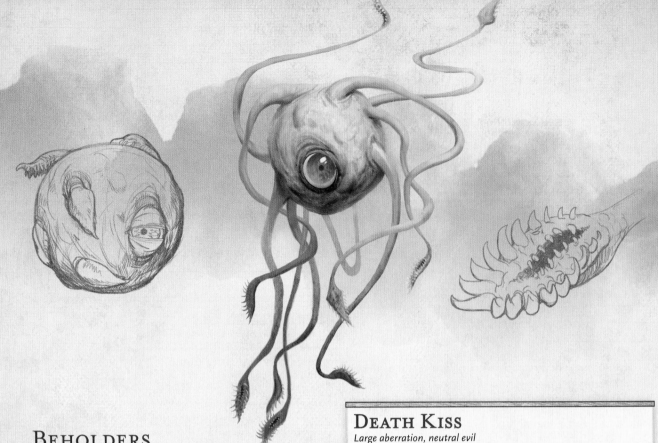

BEHOLDERS

True beholders are isolationists that despise others of
their kind, but their dreams can give rise to a variety of
lesser beholder-like creatures, a few of which are described here.

DEATH KISS

A death kiss is a lesser beholder that might come into
being when a beholder has a vivid nightmare about
losing blood. Instead of magical eye rays, it has ten
long tentacles, each ending in a mouth full of teeth. In
coloration and shape it is similar to the beholder that
dreamed it into existence, but its hue is more muted.

Blood Drinker. A death kiss survives solely on in-
gested blood, which it uses to generate electrical energy
inside its body. Paranoid about dying from starvation,
it obsessively drains even little creatures such as rats
in an effort to stave off this fate for as long as possible.
After it drains its prey, it abandons the corpse to scavengers. A death kiss prefers to hunt alone. If it meets
another death kiss, it might fight, flee, or team up, depending on its health and pride. When underground, it
uses its tentacles as feelers, prodding and examining
the environment in all directions. Above ground, it usually keeps its tentacles retracted when on the hunt, then
lashes out and extends them to their full length to catch
opponents off guard.

False Tyrant. In poor lighting and with its tentacles
extended, a death kiss can be mistaken for a true beholder. It might purposely present itself as a beholder
to an ignorant creature, but this behavior is rare, since
it usually is focused on hunting and lacks the self-importance and paranoia of a true beholder. It can speak
through any of its tentacle-throats, and its voice sounds
nasal and high-pitched. A true beholder has little to fear

DEATH KISS
Large aberration, neutral evil

Armor Class 16 (natural armor)
Hit Points 161 (17d10 + 68)
Speed 0 ft., fly 30 ft. (hover)

STR	DEX	CON	INT	WIS	CHA
18 (+4)	14 (+2)	18 (+4)	10 (+0)	12 (+1)	10 (+0)

Saving Throws Con +8, Wis +5
Skills Perception +5
Damage Immunities lightning
Condition Immunities prone
Senses darkvision 120 ft., passive Perception 15
Languages Deep Speech, Undercommon
Challenge 10 (5,900 XP)

Lightning Blood. A creature within 5 feet of the death kiss takes
5 (1d10) lightning damage whenever it hits the death kiss with
a melee attack that deals piercing or slashing damage.

ACTIONS

Multiattack. The death kiss makes three tentacle attacks. Up
to three of these attacks can be replaced by Blood Drain, one
replacement per tentacle grappling a creature.

Tentacle. *Melee Weapon Attack:* +8 to hit, reach 20 ft., one target. *Hit:* 14 (3d6 + 4) piercing damage, and the target is grappled (escape DC 14) if it is a Huge or smaller creature. Until
this grapple ends, the target is restrained, and the death kiss
can't use the same tentacle on another target. The death kiss
has ten tentacles.

Blood Drain. One creature grappled by a tentacle of the death
kiss must make a DC 16 Constitution saving throw. On a failed
save, the target takes 22 (4d10) lightning damage, and the
death kiss regains half as many hit points.

GAUTH
Medium aberration, lawful evil

Armor Class 15 (natural armor)
Hit Points 67 (9d8 + 27)
Speed 0 ft., fly 20 ft. (hover)

STR	DEX	CON	INT	WIS	CHA
10 (+0)	14 (+2)	16 (+3)	15 (+2)	15 (+2)	13 (+1)

Saving Throws Int +5, Wis +5, Cha +4
Skills Perception +5
Condition Immunities prone
Senses darkvision 120 ft., passive Perception 15
Languages Deep Speech, Undercommon
Challenge 6 (2,300 XP)

Stunning Gaze. When a creature that can see the gauth's central eye starts its turn within 30 feet of the gauth, the gauth can force it to make a DC 14 Wisdom saving throw if the gauth isn't incapacitated and can see the creature. A creature that fails the save is stunned until the start of its next turn.

Unless surprised, a creature can avert its eyes at the start of its turn to avoid the saving throw. If the creature does so, it can't see the gauth until the start of its next turn, when it can avert its eyes again. If the creature looks at the gauth in the meantime, it must immediately make the save.

Death Throes. When the gauth dies, the magical energy within it explodes, and each creature within 10 feet of it must make a DC 14 Dexterity saving throw, taking 13 (3d8) force damage on a failed save, or half as much damage on a successful one.

ACTIONS

Bite. *Melee Weapon Attack:* +6 to hit, reach 5 ft., one target. *Hit:* 9 (2d8) piercing damage.

Eye Rays. The gauth shoots three of the following magical eye rays at random (reroll duplicates), choosing one to three targets it can see within 120 feet of it:

1. *Devour Magic Ray.* The targeted creature must succeed on a DC 14 Dexterity saving throw or have one of its magic items lose all magical properties until the start of the gauth's next turn. If the object is a charged item, it also loses 1d4 charges. Determine the affected item randomly, ignoring single-use items such as potions and scrolls.

2. *Enervation Ray.* The targeted creature must make a DC 14 Constitution saving throw, taking 18 (4d8) necrotic damage on a failed save, or half as much damage on a successful one.

3. *Pushing Ray.* The targeted creature must succeed on a DC 14 Strength saving throw or be pushed up to 15 feet directly away from the gauth and have its speed halved until the start of the gauth's next turn.

4. *Fire Ray.* The targeted creature must succeed on a DC 14 Dexterity saving throw or take 22 (4d10) fire damage.

5. *Paralyzing Ray.* The targeted creature must succeed on a DC 14 Constitution saving throw or be paralyzed for 1 minute. The target can repeat the saving throw at the end of each of its turns, ending the effect on itself on a success.

6. *Sleep Ray.* The targeted creature must succeed on a DC 14 Wisdom saving throw or fall asleep and remain unconscious for 1 minute. The target awakens if it takes damage or another creature takes an action to wake it. This ray has no effect on constructs and undead.

from a death kiss, since it can easily kill or subdue the death kiss long before the death kiss gets into melee range. Thus, out of self-preservation, a death kiss usually submits to the rule of a beholder that it encounters, though it might attempt to escape as soon as its master is preoccupied.

Simple Tactics. A death kiss lacks the combat finesse and intelligence of a beholder. It might attempt an unusual maneuver to control its prey (such as flying up while grappling), but in most cases, it attaches one or more of its tentacles to a creature and drains blood until its prey collapses. If it is in a superior position and its opponent poses no threat, it might toy with its food, slowly squeezing and draining the life out of a creature.

GAUTH

A gauth is a hungry, tyrannical beholder-like creature that eats magic and tries to exact tribute from anything weaker than itself. Its body is about 4 feet in diameter, with six eyestalks, a central eye (sometimes surrounded by multiple smaller eyes), and four small grasping tentacles near its mouth. It has color and texture variations similar to a true beholder.

Magical Metabolism. A gauth can survive on meat but prefers to sustain itself with power drained from magic objects. If starved of magic for several weeks, it is forced back to its home plane, so it constantly seeks new items to drain. A gauth might employ creatures to serve it by bringing it items that provide it with sustenance.

Accidental Summoning. When the ritual to summon a spectator goes wrong, a gauth might push itself through the flawed connection, arriving immediately or several minutes later. It might present itself as a beholder to ignorant creatures in an attempt to intimidate them, or as a spectator to its summoner in order to drain magic items it is expected to guard.

B

> I met a wizard in the Yawning Portal tavern who had a tiny beholder pet. A gazer, she called it. When I reached to pet it, the creature struck me with one of its eye beams and flung me back against a wall with such force that I almost spilled my ale.
>
> —Volo

Inferior Tyrant. A beholder usually drives away or kills any gauths that enter its territory, but it might choose to enslave them and use them as lieutenants. Gauths are less xenophobic than beholders, so they might form small clusters and work together, though they're just as likely to ignore each other entirely.

GAZER

A gazer is a tiny manifestation of a beholder's dreams. It resembles the beholder who dreamed it into existence, but its body is only 8 inches wide, and it has only four eyestalks. It follows its creator like a devoted, aggressive puppy, and sometimes small packs of these creatures patrol their master's lair for vermin to kill and lone creatures to harass.

Nuisance Pet. A gazer can't speak any languages but can approximate mimicking words and sentences in a high-pitched, mocking manner. Beholders find gazers amusing and tolerate their presence like spoiled pets. A gazer can't be tamed by anyone but its creator, except through the use of magic or by bonding with a spellcaster (see sidebar). Some beholders with wizard minions insist they take a gazer as a familiar because they can see through the eyes of these creatures.

Aggressive Vermin-Eater. A wild gazer (one living separately from a beholder) is territorial, eats bugs and small animals, and is known for playing with its food. A lone gazer avoids picking fights with creatures that are Medium or larger, but a pack of them might take on larger prey. A gazer might follow humanoids in its territory, noisily mimicking their speech and generally being a nuisance, until they leave the area, but it flees if confronted by something it can't kill.

VARIANT: GAZER FAMILIAR

Spellcasters who are interested in unusual familiars find that gazers are eager to serve someone who has magical power, especially those who make a point of bullying and harassing others. The gazer behaves aggressively toward creatures smaller than itself, and it tends to randomly attack house pets, farm animals, and even children in town unless its master is very strict. A gazer serving as a familiar has the following trait.

Familiar. The gazer can serve another creature as a familiar, forming a telepathic bond with its willing master, provided that the master is at least a 3rd-level spellcaster. While the two are bonded, the master can sense what the gazer senses as long as they are within 1 mile of each other. If its master causes it physical harm, the gazer will end its service as a familiar, breaking the telepathic bond.

GAZER
Tiny aberration, neutral evil

Armor Class 13
Hit Points 13 (3d4 + 6)
Speed 0 ft., fly 30 ft. (hover)

STR	DEX	CON	INT	WIS	CHA
3 (−4)	17 (+3)	14 (+2)	3 (−4)	10 (+0)	7 (−2)

Saving Throws Wis +2
Skills Perception +4, Stealth +5
Condition Immunities prone
Senses darkvision 60 ft., passive Perception 14
Languages —
Challenge 1/2 (100 XP)

Aggressive. As a bonus action, the gazer can move up to its speed toward a hostile creature that it can see.

Mimicry. The gazer can mimic simple sounds of speech it has heard, in any language. A creature that hears the sounds can tell they are imitations with a successful DC 10 Wisdom (Insight) check.

ACTIONS

Bite. *Melee Weapon Attack:* +5 to hit, reach 5 ft., one target. *Hit:* 1 piercing damage.

Eye Rays. The gazer shoots two of the following magical eye rays at random (reroll duplicates), choosing one or two targets it can see within 60 feet of it:

1. *Dazing Ray.* The targeted creature must succeed on a DC 12 Wisdom saving throw or be charmed until the start of the gazer's next turn. While the target is charmed in this way, its speed is halved, and it has disadvantage on attack rolls.

2. *Fear Ray.* The targeted creature must succeed on a DC 12 Wisdom saving throw or be frightened until the start of the gazer's next turn.

3. *Frost Ray.* The targeted creature must succeed on a DC 12 Dexterity saving throw or take 10 (3d6) cold damage.

4. *Telekinetic Ray.* If the target is a creature that is Medium or smaller, it must succeed on a DC 12 Strength saving throw or be moved up to 30 feet directly away from the gazer.

If the target is an object weighing 10 pounds or less that isn't being worn or carried, the gazer moves it up to 30 feet in any direction. The gazer can also exert fine control on objects with this ray, such as manipulating a simple tool or opening a container.

Bodak

A bodak is the undead remains of someone who revered Orcus. Devoid of life and soul, it exists only to cause death.

Marked by Orcus. A worshiper of Orcus can take ritual vows while carving the demon lord's symbol on its chest over the heart. Orcus's power flays body, mind, and soul, leaving behind a sentient husk that sucks in all life energy near it. Most bodaks come into being in this way, then unleashed to spread death in Orcus's name.

Orcus created the first bodaks in the Abyss from seven devotees, called the Hierophants of Annihilation. These figures, as mighty as balors, have free will but serve the Prince of Undeath directly. Any one of these bodaks can turn a slain mortal into a bodak with its gaze. Like each Hierophant of Annihilation, every bodak bears the mark of Orcus as a chest wound, an opening where a mortal humanoid's heart would be.

Orcus can recall anything a bodak sees or hears. If he so chooses, he can speak through a bodak to address his enemies and followers directly. Bodaks are extensions of Orcus's will outside the Abyss, serving the demon prince's aims and other minions.

Unhallowed Fragments. A bodak retains vague impressions of its past life. It seeks out both its former allies and its former enemies to destroy them, as its warped soul seeks to erase anything connected to its former life. Minions of Orcus are the one exception to this compulsion; a bodak recognizes them as kindred souls and spares them from its wrath. Anyone who knew the individual before its transformation into a bodak can recognize mannerisms or other subtle clues to its original identity.

Even nature despises bodaks. The sun burns away a bodak's tainted flesh. The creature's gaze lays waste to the living. Anyone a bodak slays with its gaze withers, its face frozen in a mask of terror. The monster's mere presence is so unnatural that it chills the soul. Animals untrained for war instinctively flee just before a bodak arrives.

Ravaged Soul. The soul of a creature that becomes a bodak is so damaged that it is unfit for most forms of magical resurrection. Only a *wish* spell or similar magic can return a bodak to its former life.

Undead Nature. A bodak doesn't require air, food, drink, or sleep.

Bodak
Medium undead, chaotic evil

Armor Class 15 (natural armor)
Hit Points 58 (9d8 + 18)
Speed 30 ft.

STR	DEX	CON	INT	WIS	CHA
15 (+2)	16 (+3)	15 (+2)	7 (−2)	12 (+1)	12 (+1)

Skills Perception +4, Stealth +6
Damage Resistances cold, fire, necrotic; bludgeoning, piercing, and slashing from nonmagical attacks
Damage Immunities lightning, poison
Condition Immunities charmed, frightened, poisoned
Senses darkvision 120 ft., passive Perception 14
Languages Abyssal, the languages it knew in life
Challenge 6 (2,300 XP)

Aura of Annihilation. The bodak can activate or deactivate this feature as a bonus action. While active, the aura deals 5 necrotic damage to any creature that ends its turn within 30 feet of the bodak. Undead and fiends ignore this effect.

Death Gaze. When a creature that can see the bodak's eyes starts its turn within 30 feet of the bodak, the bodak can force it to make a DC 13 Constitution saving throw if the bodak isn't incapacitated and can see the creature. If the saving throw fails by 5 or more, the creature is reduced to 0 hit points, unless it is immune to the frightened condition. Otherwise, a creature takes 16 (3d10) psychic damage on a failed save.

Unless surprised, a creature can avert its eyes to avoid the saving throw at the start of its turn. If the creature does so, it has disadvantage on attack rolls against the bodak until the start of its next turn. If the creature looks at the bodak in the meantime, it must immediately make the saving throw.

Sunlight Hypersensitivity. The bodak takes 5 radiant damage when it starts its turn in sunlight. While in sunlight, it has disadvantage on attack rolls and ability checks.

Actions

Fist. *Melee Weapon Attack:* +5 to hit, reach 5 ft., one target. *Hit:* 4 (1d4 + 2) bludgeoning damage plus 9 (2d8) necrotic damage.

Withering Gaze. One creature that the bodak can see within 60 feet of it must make a DC 13 Constitution saving throw, taking 22 (4d10) necrotic damage on a failed save, or half as much damage on a successful one.

Boggle

Boggles are the little bogeys of fairy tales. They lurk in the fringes of the Feywild and are also found on the Material Plane, where they hide under beds and in closets, waiting to frighten and bedevil folk with their mischief.

A boggle is born out of feelings of loneliness, materializing in a place where the Feywild touches the world in proximity to an intelligent being that feels isolated or abandoned. For example, a forsaken child might unintentionally conjure a boggle and see it as a sort of imaginary friend. A boggle might also appear in the attic of a lonely widower's house or in the caves of a hermit.

Irksome Pests. Boggles engage in petty pranks to amuse themselves, passing the time at their hosts' expense. A boggle isn't above breaking dishes, hiding tools, making frightening sounds to startle cows and sour their milk, or hiding a baby in an attic. Although a boggle's antics might cause distress and unintentional harm, mischief—not mayhem—is usually its intent. If threatened, a boggle flees rather than stand and fight.

Oily Excretions. A boggle excretes an oil from its pores and can make its oil slippery or sticky. The oil dries up and disappears an hour later.

Twisting Space. A boggle can create magical openings to travel short distances or to pilfer items that would otherwise be beyond its reach. To create such a rift in space, a boggle must be adjacent to a space defined by a frame, such as an open window or a doorway, a gap between the bars of a cage, or the opening between the feet of a bed and the floor. The rift is invisible and disappears after a few seconds—enough time for the boggle to step, reach, or attack through it.

Unreliable Allies. A boggle makes a decent servant for a strong-willed master, and wicked creatures such as fomorians and hags sometimes shelter boggles in their lairs. Warlocks who form pacts with archfey have also been known to command boggles, and charismatic individuals who make the right offers have enjoyed temporary alliances with these little tricksters. A bored boggle always finds some way to entertain itself.

Boggle
Small fey, chaotic neutral

Armor Class 14
Hit Points 18 (4d6 + 4)
Speed 30 ft., climb 30 ft.

STR	DEX	CON	INT	WIS	CHA
8 (−1)	18 (+4)	13 (+1)	6 (−2)	12 (+1)	7 (−2)

Skills Perception +3, Sleight of Hand +6, Stealth +6
Damage Resistances fire
Senses darkvision 60 ft., passive Perception 13
Languages Sylvan
Challenge 1/8 (25 XP)

Boggle Oil. The boggle excretes nonflammable oil from its pores. The boggle chooses whether the oil is slippery or sticky and can change the oil on its skin from one consistency to another as a bonus action.

Slippery Oil: While coated in slippery oil, the boggle gains advantage on Dexterity (Acrobatics) checks made to escape bonds, squeeze through narrow spaces, and end grapples.

Sticky Oil: While coated in sticky oil, the boggle gains advantage on Strength (Athletics) checks made to grapple and any ability check made to maintain a hold on another creature, a surface, or an object. The boggle can also climb difficult surfaces, including upside down on ceilings, without needing to make an ability check.

Dimensional Rift. As a bonus action, the boggle can create an invisible and immobile rift within an opening or frame it can see within 5 feet of it, provided that the space is no bigger than 10 feet on any side. The dimensional rift bridges the distance between that space and any point within 30 feet of it that the boggle can see or specify by distance and direction (such as "30 feet straight up"). While next to the rift, the boggle can see through it and is considered to be next to the destination as well, and anything the boggle puts through the rift (including a portion of its body) emerges at the destination. Only the boggle can use the rift, and it lasts until the end of the boggle's next turn.

Uncanny Smell. The boggle has advantage on Wisdom (Perception) checks that rely on smell.

Actions

Pummel. *Melee Weapon Attack:* +1 to hit, reach 5 ft., one target. *Hit:* 2 (1d6 − 1) bludgeoning damage.

Oil Puddle. The boggle creates a puddle of oil that is either slippery or sticky (boggle's choice). The puddle is 1 inch deep and covers the ground in the boggle's space. The puddle is difficult terrain for all creatures except boggles and lasts for 1 hour.

If the oil is slippery, any creature that enters the puddle's area or starts its turn there must succeed on a DC 11 Dexterity saving throw or fall prone.

If the oil is sticky, any creature that enters the puddle's area or starts its turn there must succeed on a DC 11 Strength saving throw or be restrained. On its turn, a creature can use an action to try to extricate itself from the sticky puddle, ending the effect and moving into the nearest safe unoccupied space with a successful DC 11 Strength check.

CATOBLEPAS

The catoblepas is as loathsome as the vile swamplands in which it lives. Like such wastelands, this conglomeration of bloated buffalo, dinosaur, warthog, and hippopotamus parts has few redeeming qualities. Few travelers willingly traverse the territory of a catoblepas.

Animalistic Nature. Despite their ungainly physiology, catoblepases resemble natural beasts. A catoblepas behaves much like an animal, too, ambling through its marshy home, munching choice vegetation, eating the occasional bit of carrion, and wallowing in mire. A catoblepas might be found with the one mate it chooses for life and, on occasion, a calf. Especially if it's guarding its young, a catoblepas attacks anyone that moves too close.

Stench of Death. A catoblepas's stink, like that of death mixed with swamp gas and skunk musk, gives it away as being much more ghastly than its appearance suggests. When it is on the attack, a catoblepas reveals the extent of its horrific nature. The creature's serpentine neck has trouble lifting its head, but one glare from its bloodshot eyes can rot flesh. At the end of its tail is a club that can rattle body and soul if it strikes true, leaving a victim unable to act. If the target of its attacks dies, the catoblepas feasts on the fresh remains.

Blighted Territory. A catoblepas's nature as a creature of disease and decay brings out similar characteristics in the creature's swampy habitat. Such a wetland becomes gloomy, tangled, and more fetid than it was before. Beneficial qualities of the environment, such as healing herbs and clean water, diminish when a catoblepas lives nearby. Swamp gases have a hint of the catoblepas's foulness to them. Animals in the area are more aggressive and liable to be diseased. Degenerate creatures are likely to take up residence near a catoblepas's territory, as are those seeking to avoid notice.

Sinister Folklore. Ordinary folk rarely see a catoblepas, but the creature has such a feared reputation that stories about it are ingrained in the popular culture. Any rumor of a catoblepas taking up residence nearby is taken to be a bad omen, even if the rumor is proven false. The silhouette of a catoblepas, with its tail extended over its body and its head held low, is a baleful heraldic figure signifying death or doom.

Sages say that gods of pestilence and rot created catoblepases as embodiments of their influence. Whatever the origin of the creature, stories link the catoblepas to misfortune, and many of these yarns have elements of truth. Some such tales claim that hags tend catoblepases like cattle, and that a swamp that contains a catoblepas might also be home to a hag that drinks the monster's milk. Although a particular catoblepas might not be linked to a hag, a coven of hags might keep one or more of these beasts as guardians or pets. Other legends say that those of impure heart can tame a catoblepas. Indeed, some tales have circulated of malevolent warlocks and dark knights who have discovered how to domesticate the beasts and use them as mounts.

CATOBLEPAS
Large monstrosity, unaligned

Armor Class 14 (natural armor)
Hit Points 84 (8d10 + 40)
Speed 30 ft.

STR	DEX	CON	INT	WIS	CHA
19 (+4)	12 (+1)	21 (+5)	3 (−4)	14 (+2)	8 (−1)

Senses darkvision 60 ft., passive Perception 12
Languages —
Challenge 5 (1,800 XP)

Keen Smell. The catoblepas has advantage on Wisdom (Perception) checks that rely on smell.

Stench. Any creature other than a catoblepas that starts its turn within 10 feet of the catoblepas must succeed on a DC 16 Constitution saving throw or be poisoned until the start of the creature's next turn. On a successful saving throw, the creature is immune to the stench of any catoblepas for 1 hour.

Actions

Tail. *Melee Weapon Attack:* +7 to hit, reach 10 ft., one target. *Hit:* 21 (5d6 + 4) bludgeoning damage, and the target must succeed on a DC 16 Constitution saving throw or be stunned until the start of the catoblepas's next turn.

Death Ray (Recharge 5–6). The catoblepas targets a creature that it can see within 30 feet of it. The target must make a DC 16 Constitution saving throw, taking 36 (8d8) necrotic damage on a failed save, or half as much damage on a successful one. If the saving throw fails by 5 or more, the target instead takes 64 necrotic damage. The target dies if reduced to 0 hit points by this ray.

C

CAVE FISHER

A cave fisher is a subterranean arachnid with a long snout that houses spinnerets, enabling the creature to produce sticky filament, much like the strands of a spider's webbing, which the creature uses to snag prey.

Ambushers. A cave fisher usually hunts small animals and is fond of bats, so it stretches its filament over an opening that such prey might travel through. It then climbs to a hiding spot and adheres itself to the surface to rest and wait. When prey blunders into the filament, the cave fisher reels in its meal. A group of cave fishers might work together to cover a large area with filaments, but as soon as one captures potential food, every cave fisher in the area competes for the prize. If a victim escapes from the initial ambush, a cave fisher can reclaim its prey by shooting a filament out to capture it again.

Moving Up in the World. Scarce food might draw a group of cave fishers up to the surface, into a shadowy canyon or a gloomy forest that features both native animal prey and creatures such as explorers or travelers occasionally moving through the area.

A cave fisher instinctively knows that larger targets such as humanoids are more difficult to overcome, so the creatures shy away from attacking such prey unless they come across a solitary target. They might try to pick off a scout moving ahead of a group of travelers or a straggler lagging behind, rather than attracting the attention of the entire group.

Valuable Innards. Nearly every part of a cave fisher is useful after the creature has been dispatched. Its blood is alcoholic and tastes like strong liquor. Several dwarven spirits include cave fisher blood as part of the recipe, and some dwarves, especially berserkers, drink the blood straight. If they are gathered after being extruded, cave fisher filaments can be woven into rope that is thin, tough, and nearly invisible. Cave fisher meat is edible, tasting much like crab cooked in strong wine. The creature's shell is used in the manufacture of tools, armor, and jewelry.

Reluctant Servants. While some folk hunt cave fishers to kill them for their filaments and their blood, others capture cave fisher eggs and rear the hatchlings. Cave fishers have a natural aversion to fire, since their blood is flammable. As such, chitines and hobgoblins sometimes use the threat of fire to train cave fishers, then employ them to guard passages or as beasts of war.

CAVE FISHER
Medium monstrosity, unaligned

Armor Class 16 (natural armor)
Hit Points 58 (9d8 + 18)
Speed 20 ft., climb 20 ft.

STR	DEX	CON	INT	WIS	CHA
16 (+3)	13 (+1)	14 (+2)	3 (−4)	10 (+0)	3 (−4)

Skills Perception +2, Stealth +5
Senses blindsight 60 ft., passive Perception 12
Languages —
Challenge 3 (700 XP)

Adhesive Filament. The cave fisher can use its action to extend a sticky filament up to 60 feet, and the filament adheres to anything that touches it. A creature adhered to the filament is grappled by the cave fisher (escape DC 13), and ability checks made to escape this grapple have disadvantage. The filament can be attacked (AC 15; 5 hit points; immunity to poison and psychic damage), but a weapon that fails to sever it becomes stuck to it, requiring an action and a successful DC 13 Strength check to pull free. Destroying the filament deals no damage to the cave fisher, which can extrude a replacement filament on its next turn.

Flammable Blood. If the cave fisher drops to half its hit points or fewer, it gains vulnerability to fire damage.

Spider Climb. The cave fisher can climb difficult surfaces, including upside down on ceilings, without needing to make an ability check.

ACTIONS

Multiattack. The cave fisher makes two attacks with its claws.

Claw. *Melee Weapon Attack:* +5 to hit, reach 5 ft., one target. *Hit:* 10 (2d6 + 3) slashing damage.

Filament. One creature grappled by the cave fisher's adhesive filament must make a DC 13 Strength saving throw, provided that the target weighs 200 pounds or less. On a failure, the target is pulled into an unoccupied space within 5 feet of the cave fisher, and the cave fisher makes a claw attack against it as a bonus action. Reeling up the target releases anyone else who was attached to the filament. Until the grapple ends on the target, the cave fisher can't extrude another filament.

Chitines

Chitines are multiarmed humanoids with arachnid qualities that serve Lolth. They operate in well-organized colonies that prove to be effective fighters in the war against the enemies of the Demon Queen of Spiders. On occasion, Lolth pits chitines against dark elves—even though both groups worship her—as a way of punishing the drow, who created the chitines but displeased their goddess by doing so.

Unnatural Origin. Long ago, the drow first subjected elf prisoners to horrible rituals that transformed the captives into creatures with both humanoid and spider traits, which their creators dubbed chitines. The dark elves' intention was to create slaves dedicated first of all to the drow and, by association with them, to Lolth. As the drow ultimately discovered, the goddess found this arrangement unacceptable.

The creation process required cooperation between magical disciplines. Drow wizards and warlocks used arcane magic and demonic powers, and drow priestesses invoked Lolth's aid for the divine spark needed to ensure the subject's survival. Lolth watched, expecting at some part of the process to see these new abominations dedicated to her, but no such ritual was performed. In retribution for this lack of respect, the Spider Queen twisted the drow's creation rituals to serve her own purposes.

Lolth's Revenge. As the drow continued to perform the rituals, the process usually transformed the subject into the spindly, stunted creature they expected. Occasionally, though, the elf changed into a monstrosity that was more spider than elf, resembling Lolth in her spider form, and more cunning than a chitine, that the drow dubbed a choldrith.

At first, the drow were unaware that the new creatures were signs of Lolth's displeasure with them. Instead, they were pleased, because choldriths could lay eggs that birthed more chitines (and the rare choldrith) and could direct the chitines in their work. But the dark elves came to realize their mistake—choldriths belonged to Lolth, body and soul. They whispered to the chitines of their adoration of the Spider Queen and their enmity of the drow, and the seeds of a rebellion took root and grew. The chitines and choldriths rose up against their would-be masters; soon afterward most of the creatures were free, and a number of the drow who helped breed and tend them were dead.

Nowadays, drow still create chitines when they have need to. Outside the presence of a choldrith, chitines make good workers for the drow, and they can be useful if the drow find an independent chitine colony and want to infiltrate it. If the creation process yields a choldrith, though, the drow destroy the creature immediately.

Lolth's Chosen. Choldriths are born with a fanatical devotion to Lolth, which leads them to develop some skill in divine magic. They preach that chitines are Lolth's favored people, and that choldriths are the Spider Queen's rightful worldly representatives sent to

---

Chitine
Small monstrosity, chaotic evil

Armor Class 14 (hide armor)
Hit Points 18 (4d6 + 4)
Speed 30 ft., climb 30 ft.

STR	DEX	CON	INT	WIS	CHA
10 (+0)	14 (+2)	12 (+1)	10 (+0)	10 (+0)	7 (–2)

Skills Athletics +4, Stealth +4
Senses darkvision 60 ft., passive Perception 10
Languages Undercommon
Challenge 1/2 (100 XP)

Fey Ancestry. The chitine has advantage on saving throws against being charmed, and magic can't put the chitine to sleep.

Sunlight Sensitivity. While in sunlight, the chitine has disadvantage on attack rolls, as well as on Wisdom (Perception) checks that rely on sight.

Web Sense. While in contact with a web, the chitine knows the exact location of any other creature in contact with the same web.

Web Walker. The chitine ignores movement restrictions caused by webbing.

Actions

Multiattack. The chitine makes three attacks with its daggers.

Dagger. *Melee or Ranged Weapon Attack:* +4 to hit, reach 5 ft. or range 20/60 ft., one target. *Hit:* 4 (1d4 + 2) piercing damage.

free the chitines from slavery. Although choldriths and chitines lack sexual characteristics, and choldriths need no mate to lay eggs, these creatures choose the gender identity of their goddess. Choldriths also believe and teach that Lolth's spider form, much like that of a choldrith, is her truest shape. Any idol to Lolth in a chitine colony depicts Lolth in this way.

As servants of Lolth, choldriths and chitines love spiders and spiderlike creatures. They rear spiders and similar arachnids, such as cave fishers. Chitine colonies erect shrines to Lolth that serve as beacons, attracting spiders and other evil, brutish beings that serve her. Anywhere chitines set up a colony quickly becomes a web-shrouded, gloomy, and treacherous place.

Communal Spiders. Chitines and choldriths resemble spiders, but they behave more like social insects such as ants. Chitines are divided into worker and warrior castes, and choldriths occupy the top levels of a colony's hierarchy. Each chitine has a social position that comes with duties related to that rank, and all chitines are expected to willingly sacrifice themselves to protect the choldriths. Every chitine has spinnerets and slowly produces webbing that is used to build floors, walls, structures, objects, and traps that benefit and protect the colony. A warrior might be responsible for crafting web armor (which is as tough as hide or leather), while a group of workers might be tasked to dig a pit trap and cover it with fragile webbing disguised with loose dirt to appear as a solid surface.

A colony can support numerous choldriths, which serve as commanders, priests, and supervisors. The choldriths continually jockey for position, although they rarely confront one another in a way that puts the colony at risk. The colony is ruled by a singular sovereign that determines which colony members perform which tasks, including whether she or any other choldrith is permitted to lay eggs. If this supreme ruler receives a vision from Lolth, she might change her colony's entire course of action. At such times, chitines have emerged from the Underdark to settle in remote, gloomy places on the surface, from where they can wage war on other species, especially drow and elves.

CHOLDRITH

Medium monstrosity, chaotic evil

Armor Class 15 (studded leather armor)
Hit Points 66 (12d8 + 12)
Speed 30 ft., climb 30 ft.

STR	DEX	CON	INT	WIS	CHA
12 (+1)	16 (+3)	12 (+1)	11 (+0)	14 (+2)	10 (+0)

Skills Athletics +5, Religion +2, Stealth +5
Senses darkvision 60 ft., passive Perception 12
Languages Undercommon
Challenge 3 (700 XP)

Fey Ancestry. The choldrith has advantage on saving throws against being charmed, and magic can't put the choldrith to sleep.

Spellcasting. The choldrith is a 4th-level spellcaster. Its spellcasting ability is Wisdom (save DC 12, +4 to hit with spell attacks). The choldrith has the following cleric spells prepared:

Cantrips (at will): *guidance, mending, resistance, thaumaturgy*
1st level (4 slots): *bane, healing word, sanctuary, shield of faith*
2nd level (3 slots): *hold person, spiritual weapon* (dagger)

Spider Climb. The choldrith can climb difficult surfaces, including upside down on ceilings, without needing to make an ability check.

Sunlight Sensitivity. While in sunlight, the choldrith has disadvantage on attack rolls, as well as on Wisdom (Perception) checks that rely on sight.

Web Sense. While in contact with a web, the choldrith knows the exact location of any other creature in contact with the same web.

Web Walker. The choldrith ignores movement restrictions caused by webbing.

ACTIONS

Dagger. *Melee or Ranged Weapon Attack:* +5 to hit, reach 5 ft. or range 20/60 ft., one target. *Hit:* 5 (1d4 + 3) piercing damage plus 10 (3d6) poison damage.

Web (Recharge 5–6). *Ranged Weapon Attack:* +5 to hit, range 30/60 ft., one Large or smaller creature. *Hit:* The target is restrained by webbing. As an action, the restrained target can make a DC 11 Strength check, bursting the webbing on a success. The webbing can also be attacked and destroyed (AC 10; 5 hit points; vulnerability to fire damage; immunity to bludgeoning, poison, and psychic damage).

A rat separated from the swarm becomes an ordinary cranium rat with an Intelligence of 15. It loses 1 point of Intelligence each day that it remains separated from the swarm. Its Intelligence can't drop below 4 and becomes 15 again if it rejoins the swarm or another one.

Telepathic Vermin. A single, low-intelligence cranium rat uses its natural telepathy to communicate hunger, fear, and other base emotions. A swarm of cranium rats communicating telepathically "speaks" as one creature, often referring to itself using the collective pronouns "we" and "us."

Spies for an Elder Brain. Mind flayer colonies use cranium rats as spies. The rats invade surface communities and act as eyes and ears for the elder brain, transmitting their thoughts when they swarm and are within range of the elder brain's telepathy.

Cranium rats occasionally spread beyond the elder brain's range of influence. Whatever these rats do is of no concern to the elder brain, and the illithids can always make more if they so desire.

CRANIUM RATS

Mind flayers create cranium rats by bombarding normal rats with psionic energy.

Evil Collectives. Cranium rats are no smarter than ordinary rats and behave as such. However, if enough cranium rats come together to form a swarm, they merge their minds into a single intelligence with the accumulated memories of all the swarm's constituents. The rats become smarter as a result, and they retain their heightened intelligence for as long as the swarm persists. The swarm also awakens latent psionic abilities implanted within each cranium rat by its mind flayer creators, bestowing upon the swarm psionic powers similar to spells.

CRANIUM RAT

Tiny beast, lawful evil

Armor Class 12
Hit Points 2 (1d4)
Speed 30 ft.

STR	DEX	CON	INT	WIS	CHA
2 (−4)	14 (+2)	10 (+0)	4 (−3)	11 (+0)	8 (−1)

Senses darkvision 30 ft., passive Perception 10
Languages telepathy 30 ft.
Challenge 0 (10 XP)

Illumination. As a bonus action, the cranium rat can shed dim light from its brain in a 5-foot radius or extinguish the light.

Telepathic Shroud. The cranium rat is immune to any effect that would sense its emotions or read its thoughts, as well as to all divination spells.

ACTIONS

Bite. *Melee Weapon Attack:* +4 to hit, reach 5 ft., one target. *Hit:* 1 piercing damage.

SWARM OF CRANIUM RATS

Medium swarm of Tiny beasts, lawful evil

Armor Class 12
Hit Points 36 (8d8)
Speed 30 ft.

STR	DEX	CON	INT	WIS	CHA
9 (−1)	14 (+2)	10 (+0)	15 (+2)	11 (+0)	14 (+2)

Damage Resistances bludgeoning, piercing, slashing
Condition Immunities charmed, frightened, grappled, paralyzed, petrified, prone, restrained, stunned
Senses darkvision 30 ft., passive Perception 10
Languages telepathy 30 ft.
Challenge 5 (1,800 XP)

Illumination. As a bonus action, the swarm can shed dim light from its brains in a 5-foot radius, increase the illumination to bright light in a 5- to 20-foot radius (and dim light for an additional number of feet equal to the chosen radius), or extinguish the light.

Innate Spellcasting (Psionics). The swarm's innate spellcasting ability is Intelligence (spell save DC 13). As long as it has more than half of its hit points remaining, the swarm can innately cast the following spells, requiring no components:

At will: *command, comprehend languages, detect thoughts*
1/day each: *confusion, dominate monster*

Swarm. The swarm can occupy another creature's space and vice versa, and the swarm can move through any opening large enough for a Tiny rat. The swarm can't regain hit points or gain temporary hit points.

Telepathic Shroud. The swarm is immune to any effect that would sense its emotions or read its thoughts, as well as to all divination spells.

ACTIONS

Bites. *Melee Weapon Attack:* +5 to hit, reach 0 ft., one target in the swarm's space. *Hit:* 14 (4d6) piercing damage, or 7 (2d6) piercing damage if the swarm has half of its hit points or fewer.

C

DARKLINGS

Ancient legends speak of a seelie fey who betrayed the Summer Queen. His true name has been stricken from history, but the stories call him Dubh Catha ("Dark Crow" in Common). So great was the Summer Queen's wrath that she cursed every member of his house. Other fey refer to the descendants of Dubh Catha's house as the dubh sith—or, in Common, "darklings." Darklings most often settle in secluded caverns and chambers beneath the towns of other species. From such enclaves, they quietly ply their trade as thieves and assassins.

The Killing Light. The Summer Queen's curse causes a darkling's body to absorb light, and doing so wizens the creature, much like the effect of rapid aging. For this reason, darklings cover every part of their body with clothing when exposure to light is a risk. The light a darkling absorbs over the course of its lifetime explodes outward when the darkling dies, incinerating the creature and much of its possessions.

Love of Art. Despite their curse, darklings retain a fondness for the beauty of art. A darkling might risk taking a peek at a sunset or lighting a tiny candle to glimpse the colors in a painting or a jewel.

Elder Transformation. A wise and respected darkling can qualify to undergo a ritual to become an elder. Other elders mark the supplicant with glowing tattoos, channeling some of the darkling's absorbed light away from its body. If the ritual succeeds, the darkling grows into a tall and fair form, like that of a gray-skinned elf. The darkling perishes if the ritual fails.

DARKLING
Small fey, chaotic neutral

Armor Class 14 (leather armor)
Hit Points 13 (3d6 + 3)
Speed 30 ft.

STR	DEX	CON	INT	WIS	CHA
9 (−1)	16 (+3)	12 (+1)	10 (+0)	12 (+1)	10 (+0)

Skills Acrobatics +5, Deception +2, Perception +5, Stealth +7
Senses blindsight 30 ft., darkvision 120 ft., passive Perception 15
Languages Elvish, Sylvan
Challenge 1/2 (100 XP)

Death Flash. When the darkling dies, nonmagical light flashes out from it in a 10-foot radius as its body and possessions, other than metal or magic objects, burn to ash. Any creature in that area and able to see the bright light must succeed on a DC 10 Constitution saving throw or be blinded until the end of the creature's next turn.

Light Sensitivity. While in bright light, the darkling has disadvantage on attack rolls, as well as on Wisdom (Perception) checks that rely on sight.

ACTIONS

Dagger. *Melee or Ranged Weapon Attack:* +5 to hit, reach 5 ft. or range 20/60 ft., one target. *Hit:* 5 (1d4 + 3) piercing damage. If the darkling has advantage on the attack roll, the attack deals an extra 7 (2d6) piercing damage.

DARKLING ELDER
Medium fey, chaotic neutral

Armor Class 15 (studded leather armor)
Hit Points 27 (5d8 + 5)
Speed 30 ft.

STR	DEX	CON	INT	WIS	CHA
13 (+1)	17 (+3)	12 (+1)	10 (+0)	14 (+2)	13 (+1)

Skills Acrobatics +5, Deception +3, Perception +6, Stealth +7
Senses blindsight 30 ft., darkvision 120 ft., passive Perception 16
Languages Elvish, Sylvan
Challenge 2 (450 XP)

Death Burn. When the darkling elder dies, magical light flashes out from it in a 10-foot radius as its body and possessions, other than metal or magic objects, burn to ash. Any creature in that area must make a DC 11 Constitution saving throw. On a failure, the creature takes 7 (2d6) radiant damage and, if the creature can see the light, is blinded until the end of its next turn. If the saving throw is successful, the creature takes half the damage and isn't blinded.

ACTIONS

Multiattack. The darkling elder makes two melee attacks.

Shortsword. *Melee Weapon Attack:* +5 to hit, reach 5 ft., one target. *Hit:* 6 (1d6 + 3) piercing damage. If the darkling elder had advantage on the attack roll, the attack deals an extra 10 (3d6) piercing damage.

Darkness (Recharges after a Short or Long Rest). The darkling elder casts *darkness* without any components. Wisdom is its spellcasting ability.

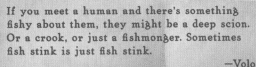

Cold-Hearted Killers. The training to which a deep scion is subjected rids it of empathy for those whom it spies on. Though one might behave as though infatuated, laugh at the joke of a friend, or appear incensed at some injustice, each of these acts is artificial to the deep scion, a means to an end. It believes that its true form is the shape it takes when it returns to the sea that it thinks of as home. Ironically, however, a deep scion that is killed when in its piscine form is stripped of the magic that robbed it of emotion, leaving behind the corpse of the person the deep scion once was.

DEEP SCION

Medium humanoid (shapechanger), neutral evil

Armor Class 11
Hit Points 67 (9d8 + 27)
Speed 30 ft. (20 ft. and swim 40 ft. in hybrid form)

STR	DEX	CON	INT	WIS	CHA
18 (+4)	13 (+1)	16 (+3)	10 (+0)	12 (+1)	14 (+2)

Saving Throws Wis +3, Cha +4
Skills Deception +6, Insight +3, Sleight of Hand +3, Stealth +3
Senses darkvision 120 ft., passive Perception 11
Languages Aquan, Common, thieves' cant
Challenge 3 (700 XP)

Shapechanger. The deep scion can use its action to polymorph into a humanoid-piscine hybrid form, or back into its true form. Its statistics, other than its speed, are the same in each form. Any equipment it is wearing or carrying isn't transformed. The deep scion reverts to its true form if it dies.

Amphibious (Hybrid Form Only). The deep scion can breathe air and water.

ACTIONS

Multiattack. In humanoid form, the deep scion makes two melee attacks. In hybrid form, the deep scion makes three attacks: one with its bite and two with its claws.

Battleaxe (Humanoid Form Only). *Melee Weapon Attack:* +6 to hit, reach 5 ft., one target. *Hit:* 8 (1d8 + 4) slashing damage, or 9 (1d10 + 4) slashing damage if used with two hands.

Bite (Hybrid Form Only). *Melee Weapon Attack:* +6 to hit, reach 5 ft., one creature. *Hit:* 6 (1d4 + 4) piercing damage.

Claw (Hybrid Form Only). *Melee Weapon Attack:* +6 to hit, reach 5 ft., one target. *Hit:* 7 (1d6 + 4) slashing damage.

Psychic Screech (Hybrid Form Only; Recharges after a Short or Long Rest). The deep scion emits a terrible scream audible within 300 feet. Creatures within 30 feet of the deep scion must succeed on a DC 13 Wisdom saving throw or be stunned until the end of the deep scion's next turn. In water, the psychic screech also telepathically transmits the deep scion's memories of the last 24 hours to its master, regardless of distance, so long as it and its master are in the same body of water.

DEEP SCION

Deep scions began life as people who were stolen from shore or saved from sinking ships and offered a terrible bargain by an undersea power: surrender, body and soul, or drown. Those who submit are subjected to an ancient ritual widespread among evil aquatic creatures. Its methods are painful and the result never certain, but when it works, the magic transforms an air-breathing person into a shapechanger that can take a form that is fully at home beneath the waves.

Spies from the Sea. A deep scion emerges from the depths in service to its underwater master, which is likely a kraken or some other ancient being of the deep. While wearing the mind and body of the person it once was as a sort of mask, the creature is bent on fulfilling its master's desires. Sometimes a deep scion returns to its former home and a hero's welcome—unexpectedly found alive when all hope was lost. At other times the deep scion takes on a new identity. In any case, it is the deep scion's duty to infiltrate the air-breathing world and report back to its master. When set to its task, a deep scion worms its way into the life of an unsuspecting enemy as a new best friend, an irresistible lover, the perfect candidate for a job, or in some other role that enables the minion to carry out its master's commands.

Maw demons appear among gnoll war bands, usually summoned as part of ritual offerings of freshly slain humanoids made to Yeenoghu. The gnolls don't command them, but these demons accompany the war band and attack whatever creatures the gnolls fall upon.

SHOOSUVA

A shoosuva is a hyena-demon gifted by Yeenoghu to an especially powerful gnoll (typically as a fang of Yeenoghu). A shoosuva manifests shortly after a war band achieves a great victory, emerging from a billowing, fetid cloud of smoke as it arrives from the Abyss. In battle, the demon wraps its slavering jaws around one victim while lashing out with the poisonous stinger on its tail to bring down another one. A creature immobilized by the poison becomes easy pickings for any gnolls nearby.

Each shoosuva is bonded to a particular gnoll and fights alongside its master. A gnoll that has been gifted with a shoosuva is second only to a flind in status within a war band.

DEMONS

Demon lords create lesser demons for the purpose of spreading chaos and terror throughout the multiverse. Three such demons are described here.

BABAU

Demons and devils clash endlessly for control of the Lower Planes. One of these battles pitted the legions of the archdevil Glasya against the screaming hordes of the demon lord Graz'zt. It is said that Glasya wounded Graz'zt with her sword, and the first babaus arose where his blood struck the ground. Their sudden appearance helped rout Glasya and secured Graz'zt's place as one of the preeminent demon lords of the Abyss.

A babau demon possesses the cunning of a devil and the bloodthirstiness of a demon. It has leathery black skin pulled tight over its gaunt frame, and a curved horn protruding from the back of its elongated skull. A babau's baleful glare can weaken a creature.

MAW DEMON

Maw demons share Yeenoghu's ceaseless hunger for carnage and mortal flesh. After a maw demon rests for 8 hours, anything devoured by it is transported directly into the Lord of Savagery's gullet.

BABAU
Medium fiend (demon), chaotic evil

Armor Class 16 (natural armor)
Hit Points 82 (11d8 + 33)
Speed 40 ft.

STR	DEX	CON	INT	WIS	CHA
19 (+4)	16 (+3)	16 (+3)	11 (+0)	12 (+1)	13 (+1)

Skills Perception +5, Stealth +5
Damage Resistances cold, fire, lightning; bludgeoning, piercing, and slashing from nonmagical attacks
Damage Immunities poison
Condition Immunities poisoned
Senses darkvision 120 ft., passive Perception 15
Languages Abyssal
Challenge 4 (1,100 XP)

Innate Spellcasting. The babau's innate spellcasting ability is Wisdom (spell save DC 11). The babau can innately cast the following spells, requiring no material components:

At will: *darkness, dispel magic, fear, heat metal, levitate*

ACTIONS

Multiattack. The babau makes two melee attacks. It can also use Weakening Gaze before or after making these attacks.

Claw. *Melee Weapon Attack:* +6 to hit, reach 5 ft., one target. *Hit:* 8 (1d8 + 4) slashing damage.

Spear. *Melee or Ranged Weapon Attack:* +6 to hit, reach 5 ft. or range 20/60 ft., one target. *Hit:* 7 (1d6 + 4) piercing damage, or 8 (1d8 + 4) piercing damage when used with two hands to make a melee attack.

Weakening Gaze. The babau targets one creature that it can see within 20 feet of it. The target must make a DC 13 Constitution saving throw. On a failed save, the target deals only half damage with weapon attacks that use Strength for 1 minute. The target can repeat the saving throw at the end of each of its turns, ending the effect on itself on a success.

SHOOSUVA
Large fiend (demon), chaotic evil

Armor Class 14 (natural armor)
Hit Points 110 (13d10 + 39)
Speed 40 ft.

STR	DEX	CON	INT	WIS	CHA
18 (+4)	13 (+1)	17 (+3)	7 (−2)	14 (+2)	9 (−1)

Saving Throws Dex +4, Con +6, Wis +5
Damage Resistances cold, fire, lightning; bludgeoning, piercing, and slashing from nonmagical attacks
Damage Immunities poison
Condition Immunities charmed, frightened, poisoned
Senses darkvision 60 ft., passive Perception 12
Languages Abyssal, Gnoll, telepathy 120 ft.
Challenge 8 (3,900 XP)

Rampage. When it reduces a creature to 0 hit points with a melee attack on its turn, the shoosuva can take a bonus action to move up to half its speed and make a bite attack.

ACTIONS

Multiattack. The shoosuva makes two attacks: one with its bite and one with its tail stinger.

Bite. *Melee Weapon Attack:* +7 to hit, reach 5 ft., one target. *Hit:* 26 (4d10 + 4) piercing damage.

Tail Stinger. *Melee Weapon Attack:* +7 to hit, reach 15 ft., one creature. *Hit:* 13 (2d8 + 4) piercing damage, and the target must succeed on a DC 14 Constitution saving throw or become poisoned. While poisoned, the target is also paralyzed. The target can repeat the saving throw at the end of each of its turns, ending the effect on itself on a success.

MAW DEMON
Medium fiend (demon), chaotic evil

Armor Class 13 (natural armor)
Hit Points 33 (6d8 + 6)
Speed 30 ft.

STR	DEX	CON	INT	WIS	CHA
14 (+2)	8 (−1)	13 (+1)	5 (−3)	8 (−1)	5 (−3)

Damage Resistances cold, fire, lightning
Damage Immunities poison
Condition Immunities charmed, frightened, poisoned
Senses darkvision 60 ft., passive Perception 9
Languages understands Abyssal but can't speak
Challenge 1 (200 XP)

Rampage. When it reduces a creature to 0 hit points with a melee attack on its turn, the maw demon can take a bonus action to move up to half its speed and make a bite attack.

ACTIONS

Bite. *Melee Weapon Attack:* +4 to hit, reach 5 ft., one target. *Hit:* 11 (2d8 + 2) piercing damage.

D

a horrible transformation, springing forth from the devourer's body to begin its new existence as an undead servitor of the monster that spawned it.

Fiendish Nature. A devourer doesn't require air, food (other than souls), drink, or sleep.

DEVOURER
Large fiend, chaotic evil

Armor Class 16 (natural armor)
Hit Points 178 (17d10 + 85)
Speed 30 ft.

STR	DEX	CON	INT	WIS	CHA
20 (+5)	12 (+1)	20 (+5)	13 (+1)	10 (+0)	16 (+3)

Damage Resistances cold, fire, lightning
Damage Immunities poison
Condition Immunities poisoned
Senses darkvision 120 ft., passive Perception 10
Languages Abyssal, telepathy 120 ft.
Challenge 13 (10,000 XP)

ACTIONS

Multiattack. The devourer makes two claw attacks and can use either Imprison Soul or Soul Rend.

Claw. *Melee Weapon Attack:* +10 to hit, reach 5 ft., one target. *Hit:* 12 (2d6 + 5) slashing damage plus 21 (6d6) necrotic damage.

Imprison Soul. The devourer chooses a living humanoid with 0 hit points that it can see within 30 feet of it. That creature is teleported inside the devourer's ribcage and imprisoned there. A creature imprisoned in this manner has disadvantage on death saving throws. If it dies while imprisoned, the devourer regains 25 hit points, immediately recharges Soul Rend, and gains an additional action on its next turn. Additionally, at the start of its next turn, the devourer regurgitates the slain creature as a bonus action, and the creature becomes an undead. If the victim had 2 or fewer Hit Dice, it becomes a **zombie**. If it had 3 to 5 Hit Dice, it becomes a **ghoul**. Otherwise, it becomes a **wight**. A devourer can imprison only one creature at a time.

Soul Rend (Recharge 6). The devourer creates a vortex of life-draining energy in a 20-foot radius centered on itself. Each humanoid in that area must make a DC 18 Constitution saving throw, taking 44 (8d10) necrotic damage on a failed save, or half as much damage on a successful one. Increase the damage by 10 for each living humanoid with 0 hit points in that area.

DEVOURER

Of all the abominations Orcus has unleashed, devourers are among the most feared. These tall, mummy-like fiends wander the planes, consuming souls and, by example, spreading Orcus's creed of replacing all life with everlasting death.

Instruments of Orcus. A lesser demon that proves itself to Orcus might be granted the privilege of becoming a devourer. The Prince of Undeath transforms such a demon into an 8-foot-tall, desiccated humanoid with a hollowed-out ribcage, then fills the new creature with a hunger for souls. Orcus grants each new devourer the essence of a less fortunate demon to power the devourer's first foray into the planes. Most devourers remain in the Abyss, or on the Astral or Ethereal Plane, pursuing Orcus's schemes and interests in those realms. When Orcus sends devourers to the Material Plane, he often sets them on a mission to create, control, and lead a plague of undead. Skeletons, zombies, ghouls and ghasts, and shadows are particularly attracted to the presence of a devourer.

Tormentors of Souls. Devourers hunt humanoids, with the intent of consuming them body and soul. After a devourer brings a target to the brink of death, it pulls the victim's body in and traps the creature within its own ribcage. As the victim tries to stave off death (usually without success), the devourer tortures its soul with telepathic noise. When the victim expires, it undergoes

Dinosaurs

The *Monster Manual* has statistics for several kinds of dinosaurs. This section provides several more.

Brontosaurus

This massive four-legged dinosaur is large enough that most predators leave it alone. Its deadly tail can drive away or kill smaller threats.

Deinonychus

This larger cousin of the velociraptor kills by gripping its target with its claws and feeding while the creature is still alive.

Dimetrodon

This sail-backed reptile is commonly found in areas where dinosaurs live. It hunts on shores and in shallow water, filling a similar role as a crocodile.

Hadrosaurus

A hadrosaurus is a semi-quadrupedal herbivore recognizable by its bony head crests. If raised as a hatchling, it can be trained to carry a Small or Medium rider.

Quetzalcoatlus

This giant relative of the pteranodon has a wingspan exceeding 30 feet. Although it can move on the ground like a quadruped, it is more comfortable in the air.

Stegosaurus

This heavily built dinosaur has rows of plates on its back and a flexible, spiked tail held high to strike predators. It tends to travel in herds of mixed ages.

Velociraptor

This feathered dinosaur is about the size of a large turkey. It is an aggressive predator and often hunts in packs to bring down larger prey.

Dimetrodon
Medium beast, unaligned

Armor Class 12 (natural armor)
Hit Points 19 (3d8 + 6)
Speed 30 ft., swim 20 ft.

STR	DEX	CON	INT	WIS	CHA
14 (+2)	10 (+0)	15 (+2)	2 (–4)	10 (+0)	5 (–3)

Skills Perception +2
Senses passive Perception 12
Languages —
Challenge 1/4 (50 XP)

Actions

Bite. *Melee Weapon Attack:* +4 to hit, reach 5 ft., one target. *Hit:* 9 (2d6 + 2) piercing damage.

Brontosaurus
Gargantuan beast, unaligned

Armor Class 15 (natural armor)
Hit Points 121 (9d20 + 27)
Speed 30 ft.

STR	DEX	CON	INT	WIS	CHA
21 (+5)	9 (–1)	17 (+3)	2 (–4)	10 (+0)	7 (–2)

Saving Throws Con +6
Senses passive Perception 10
Languages —
Challenge 5 (1,800 XP)

Actions

Stomp. *Melee Weapon Attack:* +8 to hit, reach 20 ft., one target. *Hit:* 27 (5d8 + 5) bludgeoning damage, and the target must succeed on a DC 14 Strength saving throw or be knocked prone.

Tail. *Melee Weapon Attack:* +8 to hit, reach 20 ft., one target. *Hit:* 32 (6d8 + 5) bludgeoning damage.

Deinonychus
Medium beast, unaligned

Armor Class 13 (natural armor)
Hit Points 26 (4d8 + 8)
Speed 40 ft.

STR	DEX	CON	INT	WIS	CHA
15 (+2)	15 (+2)	14 (+2)	4 (–3)	12 (+1)	6 (–2)

Skills Perception +3
Senses passive Perception 13
Languages —
Challenge 1 (200 XP)

Pounce. If the deinonychus moves at least 20 feet straight toward a creature and then hits it with a claw attack on the same turn, that target must succeed on a DC 12 Strength saving throw or be knocked prone. If the target is prone, the deinonychus can make one bite attack against it as a bonus action.

Actions

Multiattack. The deinonychus makes three attacks: one with its bite and two with its claws.

Bite. *Melee Weapon Attack:* +4 to hit, reach 5 ft., one target. *Hit:* 6 (1d8 + 2) piercing damage.

Claw. *Melee Weapon Attack:* +4 to hit, reach 5 ft., one target. *Hit:* 6 (1d8 + 2) slashing damage.

HADROSAURUS

Large beast, unaligned

Armor Class 11 (natural armor)
Hit Points 19 (3d10 + 3)
Speed 40 ft.

STR	DEX	CON	INT	WIS	CHA
15 (+2)	10 (+0)	13 (+1)	2 (–4)	10 (+0)	5 (–3)

Skills Perception +2
Senses passive Perception 12
Languages —
Challenge 1/4 (50 XP)

ACTIONS

Tail. *Melee Weapon Attack:* +4 to hit, reach 5 ft., one target. *Hit:* 7 (1d10 + 2) bludgeoning damage.

QUETZALCOATLUS

Huge beast, unaligned

Armor Class 13 (natural armor)
Hit Points 30 (4d12 + 4)
Speed 10 ft., fly 80 ft.

STR	DEX	CON	INT	WIS	CHA
15 (+2)	13 (+1)	13 (+1)	2 (–4)	10 (+0)	5 (–3)

Skills Perception +2
Senses passive Perception 12
Languages —
Challenge 2 (450 XP)

Dive Attack. If the quetzalcoatlus is flying and dives at least 30 feet toward a target and then hits with a bite attack, the attack deals an extra 10 (3d6) damage to the target.

Flyby. The quetzalcoatlus doesn't provoke an opportunity attack when it flies out of an enemy's reach.

ACTIONS

Bite. *Melee Weapon Attack:* +4 to hit, reach 10 ft., one creature. *Hit:* 12 (3d6 + 2) piercing damage.

STEGOSAURUS

Huge beast, unaligned

Armor Class 13 (natural armor)
Hit Points 76 (8d12 + 24)
Speed 40 ft.

STR	DEX	CON	INT	WIS	CHA
20 (+5)	9 (–1)	17 (+3)	2 (–4)	11 (+0)	5 (–3)

Senses passive Perception 10
Languages —
Challenge 4 (1,100 XP)

ACTIONS

Tail. *Melee Weapon Attack:* +7 to hit, reach 10 ft., one target. *Hit:* 26 (6d6 + 5) piercing damage.

VELOCIRAPTOR

Tiny beast, unaligned

Armor Class 13 (natural armor)
Hit Points 10 (3d4 + 3)
Speed 30 ft.

STR	DEX	CON	INT	WIS	CHA
6 (–2)	14 (+2)	13 (+1)	4 (–3)	12 (+1)	6 (–2)

Skills Perception +3
Senses passive Perception 13
Languages —
Challenge 1/4 (50 XP)

Pack Tactics. The velociraptor has advantage on an attack roll against a creature if at least one of the velociraptor's allies is within 5 feet of the creature and the ally isn't incapacitated.

ACTIONS

Multiattack. The velociraptor makes two attacks: one with its bite and one with its claws.

Bite. *Melee Weapon Attack:* +4 to hit, reach 5 ft., one creature. *Hit:* 5 (1d6 + 2) piercing damage.

Claws. *Melee Weapon Attack:* +4 to hit, reach 5 ft., one target. *Hit:* 4 (1d4 + 2) slashing damage.

These drow house pets are as graceful and nimble as
Waterdhavian stage dancers. Only they're slayers and enforcers,
four-armed brutes built like an ogre. Life isn't fair.

—Volo

DRAEGLOTH

A draegloth is a half-drow, half-glabrezu demon, born
of a drow high priestess in an unholy, dangerous ritual.
Gifted with innate magic and physical might, it usually
remains in the service of its mother's house, lending its
thirst for destruction to that house's plans to triumph
over its rivals.

A draegloth is an ogre-sized, four-armed humanoid
with purple-black skin and yellow-white hair. Two of its
arms are huge and muscular, tipped with sharp claws;
the other two are the size and shape of drow arms, capable of delicate movements. Although the creature is
heavily muscled, it is graceful and quiet like a drow. Its
face is clearly demonic, with bestial features, glowing
red eyes, an elongated doglike snout, and a mouth full of
sharp teeth.

Blessing on the House. The ritual to create a draegloth succeeds only rarely, but when it does, it is a great
event that is seen by the drow of the house as a sign
of the demon lord Lolth's favor—and a sign of Lolth's
disregard for the family's rivals, which were not thus
gifted. The birth prompts the leaders of the house to
begin crafting new plans to strike at its rivals when the
draegloth is fully grown. These plans always use the
draegloth in a significant role, because its abilities can
turn the tide in a battle against a house that doesn't have
a draegloth of its own.

Subservient Enforcers. Although it plays an important part in the welfare of its house, a draegloth can't
rise above the status of a favored slave or a consort to
a priestess. Before a draegloth is given any duties, it receives instruction in accepting the role set for it and not
challenging authority. Draegloths instinctively resist this
sort of treatment, but most of them take out their frustration on their house's enemies. A draegloth that can't
suppress its ambitions might abandon its house and
strike out on its own. Whether these rebellious draegloths are part of Lolth's plan for sowing even greater
chaos is unclear.

Brute Cunning and Dark Magic. A draegloth loves
the feeling of tearing opponents apart with its claws and
teeth and of wielding the magic that courses through its
veins. Most are too impatient to bother with complicated
tactics, but a few go on to learn more destructive magic.

DRAEGLOTH
Large fiend (demon), chaotic evil

Armor Class 15 (natural armor)
Hit Points 123 (13d10 + 52)
Speed 30 ft.

STR	DEX	CON	INT	WIS	CHA
20 (+5)	15 (+2)	18 (+4)	13 (+1)	11 (+0)	11 (+0)

Skills Perception +3, Stealth +5
Damage Resistances cold, fire, lightning
Damage Immunities poison
Condition Immunities poisoned
Senses darkvision 120 ft., passive Perception 13
Languages Abyssal, Elvish, Undercommon
Challenge 7 (2,900 XP)

Fey Ancestry. The draegloth has advantage on saving throws
against being charmed, and magic can't put it to sleep.

Innate Spellcasting. The draegloth's innate spellcasting ability
is Charisma (spell save DC 11). The draegloth can innately cast
the following spells, requiring no material components:

At will: *darkness*
1/day each: *confusion, dancing lights, faerie fire*

ACTIONS

Multiattack. The draegloth makes three attacks: one with its
bite and two with its claws.

Bite. *Melee Weapon Attack:* +8 to hit, reach 5 ft., one creature.
Hit: 16 (2d10 + 5) piercing damage.

Claws. *Melee Weapon Attack:* +8 to hit, reach 10 ft., one target.
Hit: 16 (2d10 + 5) slashing damage.

D

Firenewts

In regions that contain hot springs, volcanic activity, or similar hot and wet conditions, firenewts might be found. These humanoid amphibians live in a militaristic theocracy that reveres elemental fire in its worst incarnation.

Heat Seekers. Firenewts need hot water to live and breed. A firenewt becomes sluggish, mentally and physically, after spending a week away from an external source of moist heat. A prolonged lack of heat can shut down a firenewt community, as the creatures within go into hibernation and their eggs stop developing.

Firenewts delve for sources of heat in the earth, such as boiling mud and hot springs, that make ideal places to settle. Through excavation and mining in the area, they fashion living space and obtain an ample supply of minerals for other uses, such as smelting, smithing, and alchemy. A firenewt lair features a network of channels and sluices to circulate hot liquid through the settlement.

The alchemy practiced by firenewts focuses on fire. One of their favorite mixtures is a paste of sulfur, mineral salts, and oil. Firenewts chew this blend habitually, because doing so produces a pleasant internal heat and it enables a firenewt to vomit forth a small ball of flame. Most firenewts carry a container with this mixture in it.

Religious Militants. Firenewt society and culture are based on the worship of Imix, the Prince of Evil Fire. This veneration of Imix leads firenewts to be aggressive, wrathful, and cruel. Firenewt warlocks of Imix teach that by demonstrating these qualities, a firenewt warrior in combat can become "touched by the Fire Lord," entering a nearly unstoppable battle rage.

Warlocks of Imix command warriors to prove their worth by going on raids to bring back treasure and captives. The warlocks take the choicest loot as a tithe to Imix, and then those who participated in the raid divide the rest according to merit. Prisoners that have no apparent usefulness are sacrificed to Imix and then eaten. Those that are deemed capable of mining and performing other chores around the lair are kept as slaves for a while before meeting the same fate.

When firenewts muster for war, rather than merely staging occasional raids, they take no prisoners. Their goal is nothing less than the annihilation of their foes—and they reserve their greatest animosity for others of their kind. If two groups of firenewts come upon each other, it's likely that they're in competition for the same territory, and a bloody battle is the usual result.

Giant Striders. Firenewts have a close relationship with a type of monstrous beast they believe Imix sent to aid them—borne out by the creatures' ability to send a gout of flame against distant enemies. Called giant striders, these monsters appear birdlike and reptilian, but are truly neither. Firenewts provide shelter, food, and breeding grounds in their lairs for giant striders, and the striders voluntarily serve as mounts for elite firenewt soldiers.

Firenewt Warrior

Medium humanoid (firenewt), neutral evil

Armor Class 16 (chain shirt, shield)
Hit Points 22 (4d8 + 4)
Speed 30 ft.

STR	DEX	CON	INT	WIS	CHA
10 (+0)	13 (+1)	12 (+1)	7 (−2)	11 (+0)	8 (−1)

Damage Immunities fire
Senses passive Perception 10
Languages Draconic, Ignan
Challenge 1/2 (100 XP)

Amphibious. The firenewt can breathe air and water.

Actions

Multiattack. The firenewt makes two attacks with its scimitar.

Scimitar. *Melee Weapon Attack:* +3 to hit, reach 5 ft., one target. *Hit:* 4 (1d6 + 1) slashing damage.

Spit Fire (Recharges after a Short or Long Rest). The firenewt spits fire at a creature within 10 feet of it. The creature must make a DC 11 Dexterity saving throw, taking 9 (2d8) fire damage on a failed save, or half as much damage on a successful one.

'TIS ALWAYS A FIGHT TO DEATH FOR THEM, SO 'TIS ALSO ONE FOR YE.

—ELMINSTER

GIANT STRIDER
Large monstrosity, neutral evil

Armor Class 14 (natural armor)
Hit Points 22 (3d10 + 6)
Speed 50 ft.

STR	DEX	CON	INT	WIS	CHA
18 (+4)	13 (+1)	14 (+2)	4 (−3)	12 (+1)	6 (−2)

Damage Immunities fire
Senses passive Perception 11
Languages —
Challenge 1 (200 XP)

Fire Absorption. Whenever the giant strider is subjected to fire damage, it takes no damage and regains a number of hit points equal to half the fire damage dealt.

ACTIONS

Bite. *Melee Weapon Attack:* +6 to hit, reach 5 ft., one target. *Hit:* 8 (1d8 + 4) piercing damage.

Fire Burst (Recharge 5–6). The giant strider hurls a gout of flame at a point it can see within 60 feet of it. Each creature in a 10-foot-radius sphere centered on that point must make a DC 12 Dexterity saving throw, taking 14 (4d6) fire damage on a failed save, or half as much damage on a successful one. The fire spreads around corners, and it ignites flammable objects in that area that aren't being worn or carried.

FIRENEWT WARLOCK OF IMIX
Medium humanoid (firenewt), neutral evil

Armor Class 10 (13 with *mage armor*)
Hit Points 33 (6d8 + 6)
Speed 30 ft.

STR	DEX	CON	INT	WIS	CHA
13 (+1)	11 (+0)	12 (+1)	9 (−1)	11 (+0)	14 (+2)

Damage Immunities fire
Senses darkvision 120 ft. (penetrates magical darkness), passive Perception 10
Languages Draconic, Ignan
Challenge 1 (200 XP)

Amphibious. The firenewt can breathe air and water.

Innate Spellcasting. The firenewt's innate spellcasting ability is Charisma. It can innately cast *mage armor* (self only) at will, requiring no material components.

Spellcasting. The firenewt is a 3rd-level spellcaster. Its spellcasting ability is Charisma (spell save DC 12, +4 to hit with spell attacks). It regains its expended spell slots when it finishes a short or long rest. It knows the following warlock spells:

Cantrips (at will): *fire bolt*, *guidance*, *light*, *mage hand*, *prestidigitation*
1st–2nd level (2 2nd-level slots): *burning hands*, *flaming sphere*, *hellish rebuke*, *scorching ray*

Imix's Blessing. When the firenewt reduces an enemy to 0 hit points, the firenewt gains 5 temporary hit points.

ACTIONS

Morningstar. *Melee Weapon Attack:* +3 to hit, reach 5 ft., one target. *Hit:* 5 (1d8 + 1) piercing damage.

F

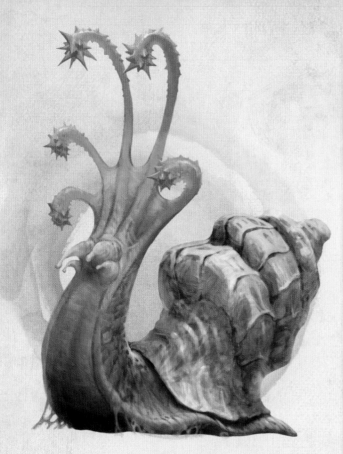

Flail Snail

A flail snail is a creature of elemental earth that is prized for its multihued shell. Hunters might be lulled into a false sense of confidence upon sighting this ponderous, seemingly nonhostile creature. If any other creature large enough to be a threat approaches too close, though, the snail unleashes a flash of scintillating light and then attacks with its mace-like tentacles.

Trail of Treasure. Left undisturbed, a flail snail moves slowly along the ground, consuming everything on the surface, including rocks, sand, and soil, stopping to relish crystal growths and other large mineral deposits. It leaves behind a shimmering trail that quickly solidifies into a thin layer of a nearly transparent substance inedible to the snail. This glassy residue can be harvested and cut to form window panes of varying clearness. It can also be heated and spun into glass objects of other sorts. Some humanoids make a living from trailing flail snails to collect this glass.

Using the Shell of a Flail Snail

A flail snail shell, which weighs about 250 pounds, has numerous uses. One intact shell can sell for 5,000 gp.

Many hunters seek the shell for its antimagic properties. A skilled armorer can make three shields from one shell. For 1 month, each shield gives its wielder the snail's Antimagic Shell trait. When the shield's magic fades, it leaves behind an exotic shield that is the perfect item from which to make a *spellguard shield*.

A flail snail shell can also be used to make a *robe of scintillating colors*. The shell is ground and added to the dye while the garment is being fashioned. The powder is also a material component of the ritual that enchants the robe.

Flail Snail
Large elemental, unaligned

Armor Class 16 (natural armor)
Hit Points 52 (5d10 + 25)
Speed 10 ft.

STR	DEX	CON	INT	WIS	CHA
17 (+3)	5 (−3)	20 (+5)	3 (−4)	10 (+0)	5 (−3)

Damage Immunities fire, poison
Condition Immunities poisoned
Senses darkvision 60 ft., tremorsense 60 ft., passive Perception 10
Languages —
Challenge 3 (700 XP)

Antimagic Shell. The snail has advantage on saving throws against spells, and any creature making a spell attack against the snail has disadvantage on the attack roll. If the snail succeeds on its saving throw against a spell or a spell attack misses it, an additional effect might occur, as determined by rolling a d6:

1–2. If the spell affects an area or has multiple targets, it fails and has no effect. If the spell targets only the snail, it has no effect on the snail and is reflected back at the caster, using the spell slot level, spell save DC, attack bonus, and spellcasting ability of the caster.

3–4. No additional effect.

5–6. The snail's shell converts some of the spell's energy into a burst of destructive force. Each creature within 30 feet of the snail must make a DC 15 Constitution saving throw, taking 1d6 force damage per level of the spell on a failed save, or half as much damage on a successful one.

Flail Tentacles. The flail snail has five flail tentacles. Whenever the snail takes 10 damage or more on a single turn, one of its tentacles dies. If even one tentacle remains, the snail regrows all dead ones within 1d4 days. If all its tentacles die, the snail retracts into its shell, gaining total cover, and it begins wailing, a sound that can be heard for 600 feet, stopping only when it dies 5d6 minutes later. Healing magic that restores limbs, such as the *regenerate* spell, can halt this dying process.

Actions

Multiattack. The flail snail makes as many Flail Tentacle attacks as it has flail tentacles, all against the same target.

Flail Tentacle. *Melee Weapon Attack:* +5 to hit, reach 10 ft., one target. *Hit:* 6 (1d6 + 3) bludgeoning damage.

Scintillating Shell (Recharges after a Short or Long Rest). The snail's shell emits dazzling, colored light until the end of the snail's next turn. During this time, the shell sheds bright light in a 30-foot radius and dim light for an additional 30 feet, and creatures that can see the snail have disadvantage on attack rolls against it. In addition, any creature within the bright light and able to see the snail when this power is activated must succeed on a DC 15 Wisdom saving throw or be stunned until the light ends.

Shell Defense. The flail snail withdraws into its shell, gaining a +4 bonus to AC until it emerges. It can emerge from its shell as a bonus action on its turn.

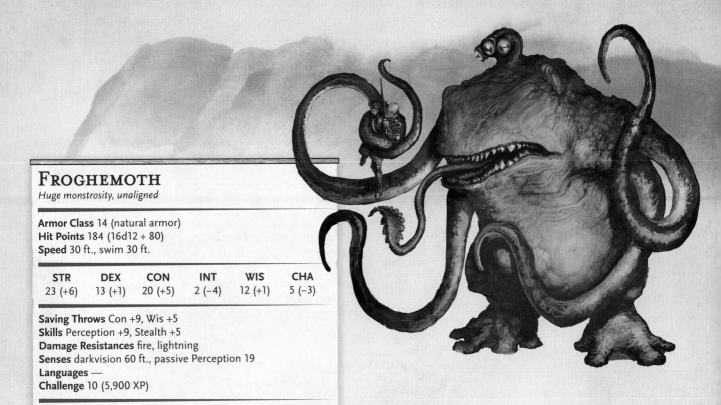

FROGHEMOTH

Huge monstrosity, unaligned

Armor Class 14 (natural armor)
Hit Points 184 (16d12 + 80)
Speed 30 ft., swim 30 ft.

STR	DEX	CON	INT	WIS	CHA
23 (+6)	13 (+1)	20 (+5)	2 (–4)	12 (+1)	5 (–3)

Saving Throws Con +9, Wis +5
Skills Perception +9, Stealth +5
Damage Resistances fire, lightning
Senses darkvision 60 ft., passive Perception 19
Languages —
Challenge 10 (5,900 XP)

Amphibious. The froghemoth can breathe air and water.

Shock Susceptibility. If the froghemoth takes lightning damage, it suffers several effects until the end of its next turn: its speed is halved, it takes a –2 penalty to AC and Dexterity saving throws, it can't use reactions or Multiattack, and on its turn, it can use either an action or a bonus action, not both.

ACTIONS

Multiattack. The froghemoth makes three attacks: two with its tentacles and one with its tongue or bite.

Tentacle. *Melee Weapon Attack:* +10 to hit, reach 20 ft., one target. *Hit:* 19 (3d8 + 6) bludgeoning damage, and the target is grappled (escape DC 16) if it is a Huge or smaller creature. Until the grapple ends, the froghemoth can't use this tentacle on another target. The froghemoth has four tentacles.

Bite. *Melee Weapon Attack:* +10 to hit, reach 5 ft., one target. *Hit:* 22 (3d10 + 6) piercing damage, and the target is swallowed if it is a Medium or smaller creature. A swallowed creature is blinded and restrained, has total cover against attacks and other effects outside the froghemoth, and takes 10 (3d6) acid damage at the start of each of the froghemoth's turns.

The froghemoth's gullet can hold up to two creatures at a time. If the froghemoth takes 20 damage or more on a single turn from a creature inside it, the froghemoth must succeed on a DC 20 Constitution saving throw at the end of that turn or regurgitate all swallowed creatures, each of which falls prone in a space within 10 feet of the froghemoth. If the froghemoth dies, a swallowed creature is no longer restrained by it and can escape from the corpse using 10 feet of movement, exiting prone.

Tongue. The froghemoth targets one Medium or smaller creature that it can see within 20 feet of it. The target must make a DC 18 Strength saving throw. On a failed save, the target is pulled into an unoccupied space within 5 feet of the froghemoth, and the froghemoth can make a bite attack against it as a bonus action.

FROGHEMOTH

A froghemoth is an amphibious predator as big as an elephant. It lairs in swamps and has four tentacles, a thick rubbery hide, a fang-filled maw with a prehensile tongue, and an extendable stalk sporting three bulbous eyes that face in different directions.

Otherworldly Entities. Froghemoths are creatures not of this world. A journal purportedly written long ago by the wizard Lum the Mad describes strange, cylindrical chambers of metal buried in the ground from which froghemoths emerged, but no reliable reports of the location of such places exist.

Hungry from Birth. Every few years, a froghemoth can lay a fertile egg without mating. The froghemoth cares nothing for its egg, and might eat the hatchling. A young froghemoth's survival is most often predicated on its parent leaving it behind in indifference. A newborn froghemoth grows to full size over a period of months by indiscriminately preying on other creatures in its swampy domain. It learns to hide its enormous body in murky pools, keeping only its eyestalk above water to watch for passing creatures. When food comes within reach, the froghemoth erupts from its pool, tentacles and tongue flailing. It can grab several targets at once, keeping them at bay while it wraps its tongue around another one and pulls it in to be devoured.

Revered by Bullywugs. If a bullywug tribe comes across a froghemoth, the bullywugs treat the froghemoth as a god and do all they can to coax the monster into their den. A froghemoth can be tamed (after a fashion) by offering it food, and bullywugs can communicate with it on a basic level, so the creature might eat only a few bullywugs before following the rest. Bullywugs gather food as tribute for it, provide it with a comfortable lair, fanatically protect it from harm, and try to ensure that any young froghemoth reaches maturity.

Giants

The giants presented here are more powerful than others of their kind, either because their gods have shown them favor or because fate has dealt them a bad hand and forced them to seek out other paths to power.

Cloud Giant Smiling One

Cloud giants aren't, on the whole, religious. They tolerate many conflicting ideas about their patron deity, Memnor. The smiling ones strain that tolerance.

Smiling ones are cloud giants who honor and emulate Memnor's craftiness and deceit above all else. They are tricksters supreme who use sleight of hand, deception, misdirection, and magic in their pursuit of wealth. They also possess a flair for unpredictability and a wicked sense of humor.

While cloud giants expect a certain amount of trickery and deceit in their dealings with others of their kind, smiling ones overstep the bounds of decorum with their behavior, doing and saying things that nobler cloud giants consider beneath the dignity of their kind.

Mysterious Masks. Smiling ones take their name from the strange two-faced masks they wear. The smiling half of the face often looks more like a smirk or a triumphant sneer than a pleasant grin. The frowning half represents the displeasure smiling ones feel about their place in the ordning—second to the storm giants. The masks serve as symbols of their devotion, but they also conceal their wearers' true facial expressions.

Cloud Giant Smiling One

Huge giant (cloud giant), chaotic neutral

Armor Class 15 (natural armor)
Hit Points 262 (21d12 + 126)
Speed 40 ft.

STR	DEX	CON	INT	WIS	CHA
26 (+8)	12 (+1)	22 (+6)	15 (+2)	16 (+3)	17 (+3)

Saving Throws Con +10, Int +6, Cha +7
Skills Deception +11, Insight +7, Perception +7, Sleight of Hand +9
Senses passive Perception 17
Languages Common, Giant
Challenge 11 (7,200 XP)

Innate Spellcasting. The giant's innate spellcasting ability is Charisma (spell save DC 15). It can innately cast the following spells, requiring no material components:

At will: *detect magic, fog cloud, light*
3/day each: *feather fall, fly, misty step, telekinesis*
1/day each: *control weather, gaseous form*

Spellcasting. The giant is a 5th-level spellcaster. Its spellcasting ability is Charisma (spell save DC 15, +7 to hit with spell attacks). The giant has the following bard spells prepared:

Cantrips (at will): *minor illusion, prestidigitation, vicious mockery*
1st level (4 slots): *cure wounds, disguise self, silent image, Tasha's hideous laughter*
2nd level (3 slots): *invisibility, suggestion*
3rd level (2 slots): *major image, tongues*

Keen Smell. The giant has advantage on Wisdom (Perception) checks that rely on smell.

Actions

Multiattack. The giant makes two attacks with its morningstar.

Morningstar. *Melee Weapon Attack:* +12 to hit, reach 10 ft., one target. *Hit:* 21 (3d8 + 8) bludgeoning damage. The attack deals an extra 14 (4d6) damage if the giant has advantage on the attack roll.

Rock. *Ranged Weapon Attack:* +12 to hit, range 60/240 ft., one target. *Hit:* 30 (4d10 + 8) bludgeoning damage. The attack deals an extra 14 (4d6) damage if the giant has advantage on the attack roll.

Change Shape. The giant magically polymorphs into a beast or humanoid it has seen, or back into its true form. Any equipment the giant is wearing or carrying is absorbed by the new form. Its statistics, other than its size, are the same in each form. It reverts to its true form if it dies.

Fire Giant Dreadnought

The ordning for fire giants emphasizes not just strength but also skill at forgecraft. The foundry is the heart of any fire giant community. It is temple, school, proving ground, and political hub rolled into one.

Those who have brawn but little brain are usually consigned to the lowliest of tasks such as working forge bellows or moving coal. However, there is one role at which the strongest among them can excel and gain rank: the dreadnought.

FIRE GIANT DREADNOUGHT

Huge giant (fire giant), lawful evil

Armor Class 21 (plate, shields)
Hit Points 187 (15d12 + 90)
Speed 30 ft.

STR	DEX	CON	INT	WIS	CHA
27 (+8)	9 (−1)	23 (+6)	8 (−1)	10 (+0)	11 (+0)

Saving Throws Dex +4, Con +11, Cha +5
Skills Athletics +13, Perception +5
Damage Immunities fire
Senses passive Perception 15
Languages Giant
Challenge 14 (11,500 XP)

Dual Shields. The giant carries two shields, each of which is accounted for in the giant's AC. The giant must stow or drop one of its shields to hurl rocks.

ACTIONS

Multiattack. The giant makes two fireshield attacks.

Fireshield. *Melee Weapon Attack:* +13 to hit, reach 5 ft., one target. *Hit:* 22 (4d6 + 8) bludgeoning damage plus 7 (2d6) fire damage plus 7 (2d6) piercing damage.

Rock. *Ranged Weapon Attack:* +13 to hit, range 60/240 ft., one target. *Hit:* 30 (4d10 + 8) bludgeoning damage.

Shield Charge. The giant moves up to 30 feet in a straight line and can move through the space of any creature smaller than Huge. The first time it enters a creature's space during this move, it makes a fireshield attack against that creature. If the attack hits, the target must also succeed on a DC 21 Strength saving throw or be pushed ahead of the giant for the rest of this move. If a creature fails the save by 5 or more, it is also knocked prone and takes 18 (3d6 + 8) bludgeoning damage, or 29 (6d6 + 8) bludgeoning damage if it was already prone.

Weapons of War. Dreadnoughts are massively powerful fire giants who wield two huge shields like plow blades. These shields bear spikes on their exterior and have hollow interiors into which the dreadnought pours hot coals at the first sign of danger. Armed with its two shields, the dreadnought can present a fiery wall to any attacker. When the dreadnought has finished, often all that is left of a foe is a smoking smear on the floor.

When not called on to fight, dreadnoughts maintain their strength by using their shields to shove huge quantities of coal, stone, or ore about the foundry. Occasionally, dreadnoughts are called on by their superiors to accompany a war or diplomatic delegation, The presence of the dreadnoughts presents a fierce face in either case.

FROST GIANT EVERLASTING ONE

To hold its place or rise within the ordning, a frost giant must routinely face mighty foes in single combat. Some seek out magic that will aid them, but enchanted objects can be taken or lost. True greatness relies on personal prowess. Faced with this truth, a frost giant might seek a supernatural gift from Vaprak the Destroyer.

Troll Eater. Frost giants mainly turn to Vaprak, a rapacious god of strength and hunger worshiped by ogres and trolls, out of desperation. Vaprak likes to tempt frost giants with dreams of glory followed by nightmares of bloody cannibalism. Those who don't shrink from such visions or report them to priests of Thrym receive more of the same. If a frost giant comes to relish these dreams and nightmares, as some do, Vaprak sets a troll upon a sacred quest to find the frost giant and meet it in secret. The troll offers up its own body to be devoured in Vaprak's name. Only the boldest and most determined frost giants can finish such a gory feast.

Vaprak's Blessing. After devouring the troll sent by Vaprak, bones and all, a frost giant becomes an everlasting one, gaining tremendous strength, an ill temper, and a troll's regenerative ability. With these gifts, the frost giant can swiftly claim the title of jarl and easily fend off rivals for decades. However, if the frost giant doesn't give enough honor to Vaprak or fails to heed Vaprak's visions, injuries the frost giant sustains heal wrong, often resulting in discolored skin, warty scars, and vestigial body parts, such as extra digits, limbs, and even extra heads. The touch of Vaprak can no longer be hidden then, and the everlasting one is either killed or exiled by its clan. Sometimes small communities of everlasting ones gather and even reproduce, passing the "blessing" and worship of Vaprak from one generation to the next.

FROST GIANT EVERLASTING ONE

Huge giant (frost giant), chaotic evil

Armor Class 15 (patchwork armor)
Hit Points 189 (14d12 + 98)
Speed 40 ft.

STR	DEX	CON	INT	WIS	CHA
25 (+7)	9 (−1)	24 (+7)	9 (−1)	10 (−0)	12 (+1)

Saving Throws Str +11, Con +11, Wis +4
Skills Athletics +11, Perception +4
Damage Immunities cold
Senses darkvision 60 ft., passive Perception 14
Languages Giant
Challenge 12 (8,400 XP)

Extra Heads. The giant has a 25 percent chance of having more than one head. If it has more than one, it has advantage on Wisdom (Perception) checks and on saving throws against being blinded, charmed, deafened, frightened, stunned, or knocked unconscious.

Regeneration. The giant regains 10 hit points at the start of its turn. If the giant takes acid or fire damage, this trait doesn't function at the start of its next turn. The giant dies only if it starts its turn with 0 hit points and doesn't regenerate.

Vaprak's Rage (Recharges after a Short or Long Rest). As a bonus action, the giant can enter a rage at the start of its turn. The rage lasts for 1 minute or until the giant is incapacitated. While raging, the giant gains the following benefits:

- The giant has advantage on Strength checks and Strength saving throws
- When it makes a melee weapon attack, the giant gains a +4 bonus to the damage roll.
- The giant has resistance to bludgeoning, piercing, and slashing damage.

ACTIONS

Multiattack. The giant makes two attacks with its greataxe.

Greataxe. *Melee Weapon Attack:* +11 to hit, reach 10 ft., one target. *Hit:* 26 (3d12 + 7) slashing damage, or 30 (3d12 + 11) slashing damage while raging.

Rock. *Ranged Weapon Attack:* +11 to hit, range 60/240 ft., one target. *Hit:* 29 (4d10 + 7) bludgeoning damage.

MOUTH OF GROLANTOR

Hill giants know the kinds of foods that make them fatter, and they understand that exerting themselves too much tends to make them thinner. What the lazy brutes don't comprehend are the things that make them sick. They consume spoiled food and diseased carcasses with as much enthusiasm as children eating dessert. Fortunately for hill giants, they have a vulture's constitution and rarely suffer for such eating habits. This makes it all the more mysterious to them when one of their kind becomes ill and incapable of keeping down food. Vomiting hill giants are seen as vessels of a message from Grolantor.

The clan separates the sickened giant from the others, often trapping the giant in a cage or tying the giant to a post. A priest of Grolantor or chieftain visits the famished giant daily, trying to read portents in the puddles of bile the hill giant retched up. If the sickness soon passes, the hill giant can rejoin society. If not, the hill giant is instead starved to the point of madness so that Grolantor's hunger can be given a mouth in the world.

Starved and Insane. A mouth of Grolantor is so disgraced that it ceases to be an individual and becomes an object. Paradoxically, that object is revered as a holy embodiment of Grolantor's eternal, aching hunger. Unlike a typical thick, sluggish, half-asleep hill giant, a mouth of Grolantor is thin as a whippet, alert like a bird, and constantly twitching around the edges. A mouth of Grolantor is kept perpetually imprisoned or shackled; if it breaks free, it's sure to kill a few hill giants before it's brought down or it sprints away on a killing spree. The only time a mouth of Grolantor is set loose is during a war, a raid against an enemy settlement, or in a last-ditch defense of the tribe's home. When the mouth of Grolantor has slaughtered and eaten its fill of the tribe's enemies, it passes out amid the gory remains of its victims, making it easy to recapture.

MOUTH OF GROLANTOR
Huge giant (hill giant), chaotic evil

Armor Class 14 (natural armor)
Hit Points 105 (10d12 + 40)
Speed 50 ft.

STR	DEX	CON	INT	WIS	CHA
21 (+5)	10 (+0)	18 (+4)	5 (–3)	7 (–2)	5 (–3)

Skills Perception +1
Condition Immunities frightened
Senses passive Perception 11
Languages Giant
Challenge 6 (2,300 XP)

Mouth of Madness. The giant is immune to *confusion* spells and similar magic.

On each of its turns, the giant uses all its movement to move toward the nearest creature or whatever else it might perceive as food. Roll a d10 at the start of each of the giant's turns to determine its action for that turn:

1–3. The giant makes three attacks with its fists against one random target within its reach. If no other creatures are within its reach, the giant flies into a rage and gains advantage on all attack rolls until the end of its next turn.

4–5. The giant makes one attack with its fist against every creature within its reach. If no other creatures are within its reach, the giant makes one fist attack against itself.

6–7. The giant makes one attack with its bite against one random target within its reach. If no other creatures are within its reach, its eyes glaze over and it becomes stunned until the start of its next turn.

8–10. The giant makes three attacks against one random target within its reach: one attack with its bite and two with its fists. If no other creatures are within its reach, the giant flies into a rage and gains advantage on all attack rolls until the end of its next turn.

ACTIONS

Bite. *Melee Weapon Attack:* +8 to hit, reach 5 ft., one creature. *Hit:* 15 (3d6 + 5) piercing damage, and the giant magically regains hit points equal to the damage dealt.

Fist. *Melee Weapon Attack:* +8 to hit, reach 10 ft., one target. *Hit:* 18 (3d8 + 5) bludgeoning damage.

STONE GIANT DREAMWALKER

The surface of the world is an alien realm to stone giants: fluctuating, temporary, exposed to gusting wind and sudden rain. It is as wildly changeable as a dream, and that's how they regard it—as a dream. Nothing there is permanent, so nothing there is real. What happens on the surface doesn't matter. Promises and bargains made there needn't be honored. Life and even art hold less value there.

Dream Dwellers. Stone giants sometimes go on dream quests in the surface world, seeking inspiration for their art, to break a decades-long ennui, or out of simple curiosity. Some who go on these quests let themselves become lost in the dream. Other stone giants are banished to the surface as punishment. Regardless of the reason, if they don't take shelter under stone, such individuals can become dreamwalkers.

Dreamwalkers occupy an odd place of respect outside of stone giant ordning. They are considered outcasts, but their familiarity with the surface world makes them valuable guides, and their insights can help other stone giants grasp the dangers of living in a dream.

Mad Wanderers. Dreamwalkers are driven mad by isolation, shame, and their unendingly alien surroundings, and this madness leeches out into the world around them, affecting other creatures that get too close. Believing that they're living in a dream and that their actions have no real consequences, dreamwalkers act as they please, becoming forces of chaos. As they travel the world, they collect objects and creatures that seem especially significant in their mad minds. Over time, the collected things accrete to their bodies, becoming encased in stone.

STONE GIANT DREAMWALKER

Huge giant (stone giant), chaotic neutral

Armor Class 18 (natural armor)
Hit Points 161 (14d12 + 70)
Speed 40 ft.

STR	DEX	CON	INT	WIS	CHA
23 (+6)	14 (+2)	21 (+5)	10 (+0)	8 (–1)	12 (+1)

Saving Throws Dex +6, Con +9, Wis +3
Skills Athletics +14, Perception +3
Condition Immunities charmed, frightened
Senses darkvision 60 ft., passive Perception 13
Languages Common, Giant
Challenge 10 (5,900 XP)

Dreamwalker's Charm. An enemy that starts its turn within 30 feet of the giant must make a DC 13 Charisma saving throw, provided that the giant isn't incapacitated. On a failed save, the creature is charmed by the giant. A creature charmed in this way can repeat the saving throw at the end of each of its turns, ending the effect on itself on a success. Once it succeeds on the saving throw, the creature is immune to this giant's Dream-walker's Charm for 24 hours.

ACTIONS

Multiattack. The giant makes two attacks with its greatclub.

Greatclub. *Melee Weapon Attack:* +10 to hit, reach 15 ft., one target. *Hit:* 19 (3d8 + 6) bludgeoning damage.

Petrifying Touch. The giant touches one Medium or smaller creature within 10 feet of it that is charmed by it. The target must make a DC 17 Constitution saving throw. On a failed save, the target becomes petrified, and the giant can adhere the target to its stony body. *Greater restoration* spells and other magic that can undo petrification have no effect on a petrified creature on the giant unless the giant is dead, in which case the magic works normally, freeing the petrified creature as well as ending the petrified condition on it.

Rock. *Ranged Weapon Attack:* +10 to hit, range 60/240 ft., one target. *Hit:* 28 (4d10 + 6) bludgeoning damage. If the target is a creature, it must succeed on a DC 17 Strength saving throw or be knocked prone.

STORM GIANT QUINTESSENT

To forestall the inevitable, some storm giants approaching the end of their natural life spans seek an escape from death. They plumb the depths of their powerful connection to the elements and disperse themselves into nature, literally transforming into semiconscious storms. The blizzard that rages unendingly around a mountain peak, the vortex that swirls around a remote island, or the thunderstorm that howls ceaselessly up and down a rugged coastline could, in fact, be the undying form of a storm giant clinging to existence.

Elemental Weapons. A storm giant quintessent sheds its armor and weapons, but gains the power to form makeshift weapons out of thin air. When the giant has no further use of them, or when the giant dies, its elemental weapons disappear.

Forsaken Form. A storm giant quintessent can revert to its true giant form on a whim. The change is temporary but can be maintained long enough for the giant to communicate with a mortal, carry out a short task, or defend its home against aggressors.

A QUINTESSENT'S LAIR

A storm giant quintessent has no need for castles or dungeon lairs. Its lair is usually a secluded region or prominent geographic feature, such as a mountain peak, a great waterfall, a remote island, a fog-shrouded loch, a beautiful coral reef, or a windswept desert bluff. As befits the environment, the storm in which the giant lives could be a blizzard, a typhoon, a thunderstorm, or a sandstorm.

Lair Actions. A storm giant quintessent can use lair actions in giant form and while transformed into a storm. On initiative count 20 (losing initiative ties), the giant can take a lair action to cause one of the following effects; the giant can't use the same effect two rounds in a row:

- The giant creates a thunderclap centered on a point anywhere in its lair. Each creature within 20 feet of that point must succeed on a DC 18 Constitution saving throw or be deafened until the end of its next turn.
- The giant creates a 20-foot-radius sphere of fog (or murky water within water) centered on a point anywhere in its lair. The sphere spreads around corners, and its area is heavily obscured. The fog lasts until the

giant disperses it (no action required), and it can't be dispersed by wind.

- The giant creates a 60-foot-long, 10-foot-wide line of strong wind (or strong current within water) originating from a point anywhere in its lair. Each creature in that line must succeed on a DC 18 Strength saving throw or be pushed 15 feet in the direction the wind is blowing. The gust disperses gas or vapor, and it extinguishes candles, torches, and similar unprotected flames in its area. Protected flames, such as those of lanterns, have a 50 percent chance of being extinguished.

Regional Effects. The region containing a storm giant quintessent's lair is warped by the giant's presence, which creates one or more of the following effects:

- High wind blows within 1 mile of the lair, making it impossible to light a fire unless the location where the fire is lit is protected from the wind.
- Rain, snow, or blowing dust or sand (whichever is most appropriate) is constant within 1 mile of the lair. Rain causes rivers and streams to fill or overflow their banks; snow, dust, or sand form deep drifts or dunes.
- Flashes of lightning and peals of thunder are continual, day and night, within 5 miles of the lair.

If the giant dies, the lightning, thunder, and high wind regional effects end immediately. Rain, snow, and blowing dust abate gradually within 1d8 days.

Storm Giant Quintessent

Huge giant (storm giant), chaotic good

Armor Class 12
Hit Points 230 (20d12 + 100)
Speed 50 ft., fly 50 ft. (hover), swim 50 ft.

STR	DEX	CON	INT	WIS	CHA
29 (+9)	14 (+2)	20 (+5)	17 (+3)	20 (+5)	19 (+4)

Saving Throws Str +14, Con +10, Wis +10, Cha +9
Skills Arcana +8, History +8, Perception +10
Damage Resistances cold; bludgeoning, piercing, and slashing from nonmagical attacks
Damage Immunities lightning, thunder
Senses truesight 60 ft., passive Perception 20
Languages Common, Giant
Challenge 16 (15,000 XP)

Amphibious. The giant can breathe air and water.

Actions

Multiattack. The giant makes two Lightning Sword attacks or uses Wind Javelin twice.

Lightning Sword. *Melee Weapon Attack:* +14 to hit, reach 15 ft., one target. *Hit:* 40 (9d6 + 9) lightning damage.

Wind Javelin. The giant coalesces wind into a javelin-like form and hurls it at a creature it can see within 600 feet of it. The javelin is considered a magic weapon and deals 19 (3d6 + 9) piercing damage to the target, striking unerringly. The javelin disappears after it hits.

Legendary Actions

The giant can take 3 legendary actions, choosing from the options below. Only one legendary action option can be used at a time and only at the end of another creature's turn. The giant regains spent legendary actions at the start of its turn.

Gust. The giant targets a creature it can see within 60 feet of it and creates a magical gust of wind around it. The target must succeed on a DC 18 Strength saving throw or be pushed up to 20 feet in any horizontal direction the giant chooses.

Thunderbolt (2 Actions). The giant hurls a thunderbolt at a creature it can see within 600 feet of it. The target must make a DC 18 Dexterity saving throw, taking 22 (4d10) thunder damage on a failed save, or half as much damage on a successful one.

One with the Storm (3 Actions). The giant vanishes, dispersing itself into the storm surrounding its lair. The giant can end this effect at the start of any of its turns, becoming a giant once more and appearing in any location it chooses within its lair. While dispersed, the giant can't take any actions other than lair actions, and it can't be targeted by attacks, spells, or other effects. The giant can't use this ability outside its lair, nor can it use this ability if another creature is using a *control weather* spell or similar magic to quell the storm.

ZHENTS CLAIM THE BLACK ROAD THE SAFEST PATH ACROSS THE DESERT OF ANAUROCH, BUT THERE'S A STRETCH THAT PASSES NEAR THE SAND-SWALLOWED RUINS OF A ONCE-GREAT ARCH—A PORTAL BUILT BY GIANTS, SOME SAY. A SANDSTORM RAGES ALL AROUND IT, AND IN THE STORM SOME HAVE SEEN A FACE: A GIANT SCOWLING VISAGE.

— ELMINSTER

GIRALLON

A girallon looks like an oversized, four-armed ape with gray skin and white fur. Its fangs and claws set it apart from a normal ape, revealing it to be a monstrous predator.

Forest Hunters. Girallons are most common in temperate or warm forest environments abundant with life. They share the ape's adeptness at climbing, although these half-ton creatures shy away from scaling trees that can't support their bulk. Instead, they stalk the forest floor, lurk in narrow ravines or shallow caves, or hide in ruined sites while waiting for prey to come near. A girallon is surprisingly stealthy, considering its size and its lack of camouflage.

Girallons form loose bands of several individuals and their offspring, usually led by a dominant adult that also tends to be the oldest member of the group. When on the hunt away from their lair, girallons use roars and body language to communicate with one another over distance. Each individual typically hunts alone and widely separated from the others, to ensure that everyone gets adequate fodder. The leader might organize members to work together to make a big kill. If they succeed, everyone in the group shares the spoils, with the best parts going to mothers caring for their young.

Wall Climbers. The ruins of humanoid habitations, especially those found in deep forests and jungles, seem to attract girallons. They move effortlessly along stairs and balconies, as well as on the sloped rooftops and buttresses of such formations. To a girallon, a city's buildings are just another sort of forest—and better yet, one whose uppermost "branches" can easily support the creatures. In such a setting, the girallons take full advantage of their skill in climbing. The creatures can easily scale walls and battlements, and they perch on tower tops and other high vantages to keep an eye on the surrounding area.

Magical Origin. The social habits of wild girallons are unusual for apes, as is their instinctive attraction to humanoid structures. These facts, together with the girallon's appearance, lead sages to believe that girallons were created through magic to serve as guardians for some lost empire. When that empire fell ages ago, girallons turned feral and spread out across the world.

In the time since then, numerous creatures have tried to tame, subjugate, or cooperate with the monsters. For instance, yuan-ti enslave girallons, turning them into border sentinels for their serpent kingdoms. Because girallons are known to be peaceful among their own kind, some humanoids have learned how to approach a group's leader, offering food and other gifts in hopes of establishing an alliance with the creatures.

Girallons that are well treated might be willing to serve as guards, though they lack the intelligence to take on tasks more complicated than attacking strangers that enter their domain. If one is taken young and properly trained, a girallon could end up in a seemingly unlikely place, such as guarding the entrance to a city's thieves' guild. Those who would keep a girallon as a pet must always be wary, because the creature could revert to its predatory nature at any time.

GIRALLON
Large monstrosity, unaligned

Armor Class 13
Hit Points 59 (7d10 + 21)
Speed 40 ft., climb 40 ft.

STR	DEX	CON	INT	WIS	CHA
18 (+4)	16 (+3)	16 (+3)	5 (–3)	12 (+1)	7 (–2)

Skills Perception +3, Stealth +5
Senses darkvision 60 ft., passive Perception 13
Languages —
Challenge 4 (1,100 XP)

Aggressive. As a bonus action, the girallon can move up to its speed toward a hostile creature that it can see.

Keen Smell. The girallon has advantage on Wisdom (Perception) checks that rely on smell.

ACTIONS

Multiattack. The girallon makes five attacks: one with its bite and four with its claws.

Bite. *Melee Weapon Attack:* +6 to hit, reach 5 ft., one creature. *Hit:* 7 (1d6 + 4) piercing damage.

Claw. *Melee Weapon Attack:* +6 to hit, reach 10 ft., one target. *Hit:* 7 (1d6 + 4) slashing damage.

G

FLIND

Medium humanoid (gnoll), chaotic evil

Armor Class 16 (chain mail)
Hit Points 127 (15d8 + 60)
Speed 30 ft.

STR	DEX	CON	INT	WIS	CHA
20 (+5)	10 (+0)	19 (+4)	11 (+0)	13 (+1)	12 (+1)

Saving Throws Con +8, Wis +5
Skills Intimidate +5, Perception +5
Senses darkvision 60 ft., passive Perception 15
Languages Gnoll, Abyssal
Challenge 9 (5,000 XP)

Aura of Blood Thirst. If the flind isn't incapacitated, any creature with the Rampage trait can make a bite attack as a bonus action while within 10 feet of the flind.

ACTIONS

Multiattack. The flind makes three attacks: one with each of its different flail attacks or three with its longbow.

Flail of Madness. *Melee Weapon Attack:* +9 to hit, reach 5 ft., one target. *Hit:* 10 (1d10 + 5) bludgeoning damage, and the target must make a DC 16 Wisdom saving throw. On a failed save, the target must make a melee attack against a random target within its reach on its next turn. If it has no targets within its reach even after moving, it loses its action on that turn.

Flail of Pain. *Melee Weapon Attack:* +9 to hit, reach 5 ft., one target. *Hit:* 10 (1d10 + 5) bludgeoning damage plus 22 (4d10) psychic damage.

Flail of Paralysis. *Melee Weapon Attack:* +9 to hit, reach 5 ft., one target. *Hit:* 10 (1d10 + 5) bludgeoning damage, and the target must succeed on a DC 16 Constitution saving throw or be paralyzed until the end of its next turn.

Longbow. *Ranged Weapon Attack:* +4 to hit, range 150/600 ft., one target. *Hit:* 4 (1d8) piercing damage.

> WHEN GNOLLS ARE WEAKENED, THEY
> SEEK OUT ISOLATED SETTLEMENTS,
> MAIM AND DISABLE ITS INHABITANTS,
> AND FEED UPON THEM AS THEY REST
> AND REGAIN STRENGTH.
>
> — ELMINSTER

GNOLLS

A gnoll war band might include one or more of the special kinds of gnolls described in this section.

FLIND

A flind is an exceptionally strong and vicious gnoll that commands and directs the war band it is a part of. It wields a flail imbued with powerful magic by Yeenoghu himself.

A war band can have only one flind, and that creature sets a war band's path. Because of its special connection to Yeenoghu, a flind uses god-given omens and demonic insight to guide the gnolls toward weak prey ripe for slaughter.

Unlike other humanoid leaders that might skulk behind their minions, a flind leads the charge in battle. Its flail causes wracking pain, paralysis, and disorientation in those struck by it.

GNOLL FLESH GNAWER

If any group of gnolls could be said to be more feral than the others, that distinction would go to the flesh gnawers. These gnolls eschew the use of ranged weapons in favor of short blades that they wield with speed and efficiency. In the thick of a fight, they are capable of dashing across the field, slashing and snarling as they run down stragglers and finish off wounded foes.

GNOLL HUNTER

Hunters are the stealthiest gnolls in a war band, and they put their talents to use on the battlefield in a number of ways. In the vanguard of a war band, hunters creep around, picking off isolated opposition while clearing the way for the rest of the force to run roughshod over the enemy's territory.

Hunters are particularly skilled with the longbow, and they fire arrows with viciously barbed heads. Even when a hunter doesn't kill its target with its first shot, the arrow strike brings so much pain that the victim is hobbled in its attempt to run away. When a hunter on the prowl finds prey and isn't concerned about remaining stealthy, it sounds a horn crafted from bone that produces a keening wail similar to a banshee's yell.

GNOLL FLESH GNAWER
Medium humanoid (gnoll), chaotic evil

Armor Class 14 (studded leather)
Hit Points 22 (4d8 + 4)
Speed 30 ft.

STR	DEX	CON	INT	WIS	CHA
12 (+1)	14 (+2)	12 (+1)	8 (−1)	10 (+0)	8 (−1)

Saving Throws Dex +4
Senses darkvision 60 ft., passive Perception 10
Languages Gnoll
Challenge 1 (200 XP)

Rampage. When the gnoll reduces a creature to 0 hit points with a melee attack on its turn, the gnoll can take a bonus action to move up to half its speed and make a bite attack.

ACTIONS

Multiattack. The gnoll makes three attacks: one with its bite and two with its shortsword.

Bite. *Melee Weapon Attack:* +4 to hit, reach 5 ft., one target. *Hit:* 4 (1d4 + 2) piercing damage.

Shortsword. *Melee Weapon Attack:* +4 to hit, reach 5 ft., one target. *Hit:* 5 (1d6 + 2) piercing damage.

Sudden Rush. Until the end of the turn, the gnoll's speed increases by 60 feet and it doesn't provoke opportunity attacks.

GNOLL HUNTER
Medium humanoid (gnoll), chaotic evil

Armor Class 13 (leather armor)
Hit Points 22 (4d8 + 4)
Speed 30 ft.

STR	DEX	CON	INT	WIS	CHA
14 (+2)	14 (+2)	12 (+1)	8 (−1)	12 (+1)	8 (−1)

Skills Perception +3, Stealth +4
Senses darkvision 60 ft., passive Perception 13
Languages Gnoll
Challenge 1/2 (100 XP)

Rampage. When the gnoll reduces a creature to 0 hit points with a melee attack on its turn, the gnoll can take a bonus action to move up to half its speed and make a bite attack.

ACTIONS

Multiattack. The gnoll makes two melee attacks with its spear or two ranged attacks with its longbow.

Bite. *Melee Weapon Attack:* +4 to hit, reach 5 ft., one target. *Hit:* 4 (1d4 + 2) piercing damage.

Spear. *Melee or Ranged Weapon Attack:* +4 to hit, reach 5 ft. or range 20/60 ft., one target. *Hit:* 5 (1d6 + 2) piercing damage, or 6 (1d8 + 2) piercing damage when used with two hands to make a melee attack.

Longbow. *Ranged Weapon Attack:* +4 to hit, range 150/600 ft., one target. *Hit:* 6 (1d8 + 2) piercing damage, and the target's speed is reduced by 10 feet until the end of its next turn.

Gnoll Witherling

Sometimes gnolls turn against each other, perhaps to determine who rules a war band or because of extreme starvation. Even under ordinary circumstances, gnolls that are deprived of victims for too long can't control their hunger and violent urges. Eventually, they fight among themselves.

The survivors devour the flesh of their slain comrades but preserve the bones. Then, by invoking rituals to Yeenoghu, they bring the remains back to a semblance of life in the form of a gnoll witherling.

Witherlings act much as gnolls do in life, traveling with their comrades and trying to kill anything in their path. They don't eat and aren't motivated by hunger, leaving more flesh for the rest of the war band. Gnoll witherlings are incapable of wielding any weapon more sophisticated than a simple club.

Undead Nature. A gnoll witherling doesn't require air, food, drink, or sleep.

Gnoll Witherling
Medium undead, chaotic evil

Armor Class 12 (natural armor)
Hit Points 11 (2d8 + 2)
Speed 30 ft.

STR	DEX	CON	INT	WIS	CHA
14 (+2)	8 (−1)	12 (+1)	5 (−3)	5 (−3)	5 (−3)

Damage Immunities poison
Condition Immunities exhaustion, poisoned
Senses darkvision 60 ft., passive Perception 7
Languages understands Gnoll but can't speak
Challenge 1/4 (50 XP)

Rampage. When the witherling reduces a creature to 0 hit points with a melee attack on its turn, it can take a bonus action to move up to half its speed and make a bite attack.

Actions

Multiattack. The witherling makes two attacks: one with its bite and one with its club, or two with its club.

Bite. *Melee Weapon Attack:* +4 to hit, reach 5 ft., one target. *Hit:* 4 (1d4 + 2) piercing damage.

Club. *Melee Weapon Attack:* +4 to hit, reach 5 ft., one target. *Hit:* 4 (1d4 + 2) bludgeoning damage.

Reactions

Vengeful Strike. In response to a gnoll being reduced to 0 hit points within 30 feet of the witherling, the witherling makes a melee attack.

G

GRUNGS

Grungs are aggressive froglike humanoids found in rain forests and tropical jungles. They are fiercely territorial and see themselves as superior to most other creatures.

Tree-Dwelling Amphibians. Grungs live in trees and prefer shade. A grung hatchery is maintained in well-guarded ground-level pools. About three months after hatching, a grung tadpole takes on the shape of an adult. It takes another six to nine months for a grung juvenile to reach maturity.

Castes and Colors. Grung society is a caste system. Each caste lays eggs in a separate hatching pool, and juvenile grungs join their caste upon emergence from the hatchery. All grungs are a dull greenish gray when they are born, but each individual takes on the color of its caste as it grows to adulthood.

Green grungs are the tribe's warriors, hunters, and laborers, and blue grungs work as artisans and in other domestic roles. Supervising and guiding both groups are the purple grungs, which serve as administrators and commanders. (Use the **grung** stat block to represent members of the green, blue, and purple castes.)

Red grungs are the tribe's scholars and magic users. They are superior to purple, blue, and green grungs and given proper respect even by grungs of higher status. (Use the **grung wildling** stat block to represent members of the red caste.)

Higher castes include orange grungs, which are elite warriors that have authority over all lesser grungs, and gold grungs, which hold the highest leadership positions. A tribe's sovereign is always a gold grung. (Use the **grung elite warrior** stat block to represent members of the orange and gold castes.)

A grung normally remains in its caste for life. On rare occasions, an individual that distinguishes itself with great deeds can earn an invitation to join a higher caste. Through a combination of herbal tonics and ritual magic, an elevated grung changes color and is inducted into its new caste in the same way that a juvenile of the

caste would be. From then on, the grung and its progeny are members of the higher caste.

Naturally Toxic. All grungs secrete a substance that is harmless to them but poisonous to other creatures. A grung also uses venom to poison its weapons.

Slavers. Grungs are always on the lookout for creatures they can capture and enslave. Grungs use slaves for all manner of menial tasks, but mostly they just like bossing them around. Slaves are fed mildly poisoned food to keep them lethargic and compliant. A creature afflicted in this way over a long period of time becomes a shell of its former self and can be restored to normalcy only by magic.

Water Dependency. A grung that fails to immerse itself in water for at least 1 hour during a day suffers one level of exhaustion at the end of that day. A grung can recover from this exhaustion only through magic or by immersing itself in water for at least 1 hour.

> *Sentient, poisonous frogs that live in trees. Truly, the gods hate us.*
>
> —Volo

VARIANT: GRUNG POISON

Grung poison loses its potency 1 minute after being removed from a grung. A similar breakdown occurs if the grung dies.

A creature poisoned by a grung can suffer an additional effect that varies depending on the grung's skin color. This effect lasts until the creature is no longer poisoned by the grung.

Green. The poisoned creature can't move except to climb or make standing jumps. If the creature is flying, it can't take any actions or reactions unless it lands.

Blue. The poisoned creature must shout loudly or otherwise make a loud noise at the start and end of its turn.

Purple. The poisoned creature feels a desperate need to soak itself in liquid or mud. It can't take actions or move except to do so or to reach a body of liquid or mud.

Red. The poisoned creature must use its action to eat if food is within reach.

Orange. The poisoned creature is frightened of its allies.

Gold. The poisoned creature is charmed and can speak Grung.

GRUNG

Small humanoid (grung), lawful evil

Armor Class 12
Hit Points 11 (2d6 + 4)
Speed 25 ft., climb 25 ft.

STR	DEX	CON	INT	WIS	CHA
7 (–2)	14 (+2)	15 (+2)	10 (+0)	11 (+0)	10 (+0)

Saving Throws Dex +4
Skills Athletics +2, Perception +2, Stealth +4, Survival +2
Damage Immunities poison
Condition Immunities poisoned
Senses passive Perception 12
Languages Grung
Challenge 1/4 (50 XP)

Amphibious. The grung can breathe air and water.

Poisonous Skin. Any creature that grapples the grung or otherwise comes into direct contact with the grung's skin must succeed on a DC 12 Constitution saving throw or become poisoned for 1 minute. A poisoned creature no longer in direct contact with the grung can repeat the saving throw at the end of each of its turns, ending the effect on itself on a success.

Standing Leap. The grung's long jump is up to 25 feet and its high jump is up to 15 feet, with or without a running start.

ACTIONS

Dagger. *Melee or Ranged Weapon Attack:* +4 to hit, reach 5 ft. or range 20/60 ft., one target. *Hit:* 4 (1d4 + 2) piercing damage, and the target must succeed on a DC 12 Constitution saving throw or take 5 (2d4) poison damage.

GRUNG ELITE WARRIOR

Small humanoid (grung), lawful evil

Armor Class 13
Hit Points 49 (9d6 + 18)
Speed 25 ft., climb 25 ft.

STR	DEX	CON	INT	WIS	CHA
7 (−2)	16 (+3)	15 (+2)	10 (+0)	11 (+0)	12 (+1)

Saving Throws Dex +5
Skills Athletics +2, Perception +2, Stealth +5, Survival +2
Damage Immunities poison
Condition Immunities poisoned
Senses passive Perception 12
Languages Grung
Challenge 2 (450 XP)

Amphibious. The grung can breathe air and water.

Poisonous Skin. Any creature that grapples the grung or otherwise comes into direct contact with the grung's skin must succeed on a DC 12 Constitution saving throw or become poisoned for 1 minute. A poisoned creature no longer in direct contact with the grung can repeat the saving throw at the end of each of its turns, ending the effect on itself on a success.

Standing Leap. The grung's long jump is up to 25 feet and its high jump is up to 15 feet, with or without a running start.

ACTIONS

Dagger. *Melee or Ranged Weapon Attack:* +5 to hit, reach 5 ft. or range 20/60 ft., one target. *Hit:* 5 (1d4 + 3) piercing damage, and the target must succeed on a DC 12 Constitution saving throw or take 5 (2d4) poison damage.

Shortbow. *Ranged Weapon Attack:* +5 to hit, range 80/320 ft., one target. *Hit:* 6 (1d6 + 3) piercing damage, and the target must succeed on a DC 12 Constitution saving throw or take 5 (2d4) poison damage.

Mesmerizing Chirr (Recharge 6). The grung makes a chirring noise to which grungs are immune. Each humanoid or beast that is within 15 feet of the grung and able to hear it must succeed on a DC 12 Wisdom saving throw or be stunned until the end of the grung's next turn.

GRUNG WILDLING

Small humanoid (grung), lawful evil

Armor Class 13 (16 with *barkskin*)
Hit Points 27 (5d6 + 10)
Speed 25 ft., climb 25 ft.

STR	DEX	CON	INT	WIS	CHA
7 (−2)	16 (+3)	15 (+2)	10 (+0)	15 (+2)	11 (+0)

Saving Throws Dex +5
Skills Athletics +2, Perception +4, Stealth +5, Survival +4
Damage Immunities poison
Condition Immunities poisoned
Senses passive Perception 14
Languages Grung
Challenge 1 (200 XP)

Amphibious. The grung can breathe air and water.

Poisonous Skin. Any creature that grapples the grung or otherwise comes into direct contact with the grung's skin must succeed on a DC 12 Constitution saving throw or become poisoned for 1 minute. A poisoned creature no longer in direct contact with the grung can repeat the saving throw at the end of each of its turns, ending the effect on itself on a success.

Spellcasting. The grung is a 9th-level spellcaster. Its spellcasting ability is Wisdom (spell save DC 12, +4 to hit with spell attacks). It knows the following ranger spells:

1st level (4 slots): *cure wounds*, *jump*
2nd level (3 slots): *barkskin*, *spike growth*
3rd level (2 slots): *plant growth*

Standing Leap. The grung's long jump is up to 25 feet and its high jump is up to 15 feet, with or without a running start.

ACTIONS

Dagger. *Melee or Ranged Weapon Attack:* +5 to hit, reach 5 ft. or range 20/60 ft., one target. *Hit:* 5 (1d4 + 3) piercing damage, and the target must succeed on a DC 12 Constitution saving throw or take 5 (2d4) poison damage.

Shortbow. *Ranged Weapon Attack:* +5 to hit, range 80/320 ft., one target. *Hit:* 6 (1d6 + 3) piercing damage, and the target must succeed on a DC 12 Constitution saving throw or take 5 (2d4) poison damage.

GUARD DRAKE

A guard drake is a reptilian creature created out of dragon scales by means of a bizarre and grisly ritual. When trained properly, a drake is obedient, loyal, and territorial, which makes it an excellent watchbeast that can follow simple commands.

Gifts from Dragons. The ritual to create a guard drake was originally devised by the cult of Tiamat, but has spread to other groups that are skilled in arcana and associated with dragons. The cooperation of a dragon is necessary for the ritual to succeed, and a dragon typically provides its help when it wants to reward its allies or worshipers with a valuable servant.

The ritual, which takes several days, requires 10 pounds of fresh dragon scales (donated by the dragon allied with the group), a large amount of fresh meat, and an iron cauldron. When the process is complete, a halfling-sized egg emerges from the cauldron and is ready to hatch within a few hours.

Eager to Learn. A newly hatched guard drake imprints upon the first creature that feeds it (usually the one planning to train it), establishing an aggressive but trusting bond with that individual. A guard drake is fully grown within two to three weeks and can be trained in the same length of time. One is the equivalent of a guard dog in terms of what it can be trained to do.

A guard drake resembles the type of dragon it was created from, but with a wingless, squat, muscular build. A drake can't reproduce, nor can its scales be used to make other guard drakes.

GUARD DRAKE
Medium dragon, unaligned

Armor Class 14 (natural armor)
Hit Points 52 (7d8 + 21)
Speed 30 ft.

STR	DEX	CON	INT	WIS	CHA
16 (+3)	11 (+0)	16 (+3)	4 (−3)	10 (+0)	7 (−2)

Skills Perception +2
Senses darkvision 60 ft., passive Perception 12
Languages understands Draconic but can't speak
Challenge 2 (450 XP)

ACTIONS

Multiattack. The guard drake makes two attacks: one with its bite and one with its tail.

Bite. *Melee Weapon Attack:* +5 to hit, reach 5 ft., one target. *Hit:* 7 (1d8 + 3) piercing damage.

Tail. *Melee Weapon Attack:* +5 to hit, reach 5 ft., one target. *Hit:* 6 (1d6 + 3) bludgeoning damage.

VARIANT: CHROMATIC GUARD DRAKES

Each type of chromatic dragon's scales and blood creates a guard drake that resembles a wingless, stunted version of that type of dragon, with unique abilities related to that type. Each has the special features described below.

Black Guard Drake. A black guard drake is amphibious (it can breathe air or water), has a swimming speed of 30 feet, and has resistance to acid damage.

Blue Guard Drake. A blue guard drake has a burrowing speed of 20 feet and resistance to lightning damage.

Green Guard Drake. A green guard drake is amphibious (it can breathe air or water), has a swimming speed of 30 feet, and has resistance to poison damage.

Red Guard Drake. A red guard drake has climbing speed of 30 feet and resistance to fire damage.

White Guard Drake. A white guard drake has a burrowing speed of 20 feet, a climbing speed of 30 feet, and resistance to cold damage.

Hags

Hags delight in bringing ruin and misery to the world. Malevolence is such a core part of a hag that it shapes her physical form and molds her magical powers.

Annis Hag

Annis hags lair in mountains or hills. Despite being hunchbacked and hump-shouldered, they are the largest and most physically imposing of their kind, standing eight feet tall.

Tormenting the Weak. Although annis hags can easily tear a grown man apart, they love hunting children, preferring their flesh above all others. They use the flayed skin of such victims to make supple leather, and a hag's lair often shows the signs of this industry.

Annis hags leave tokens of their cruelty at the edges of forests and other areas they claim. In this way, they provoke fear and paranoia in nearby villages and settlements. To an annis hag, nothing is sweeter than turning a vibrant community into a place paralyzed with terror, where folk never venture out at night, strangers are met with suspicion and anger, and parents warn their children to "be good, or the annis will get you."

Child Corrupter. When an annis feels especially cruel, she disguises herself as a kindly-looking elderly woman, approaches a child in a remote place, and gives it an iron token that it can use to confide in her. Over time, "Granny" convinces the child that it's okay to have bad thoughts and do bad deeds—starting with breaking things or wandering outside without permission, then graduating to pushing someone down the stairs or setting a house on fire. Sooner or later, the child's family and community become terrified of the "bad seed" and must face the awful decision of whether the child should be punished or exiled.

Tribe Mother. Much in the way that they befriend children in order to corrupt them, annis hags have a tendency for adopting a group of ogres, trolls, or other loutish creatures, ruling them through brute strength, verbal abuse, and superstition.

Covens. An annis hag that is part of a coven (see the "Hag Covens" sidebar in the *Monster Manual*) has a challenge rating of 8 (3,900 XP).

Iron Token

An annis hag can pull out one of her iron teeth or nails and spend 1 minute shaping and polishing it into the form of a coin, a ring, or a tiny mirror. Thereafter, any creature that holds this *iron token* can have a whispered conversation with the hag, provided the creature and the hag are on the same plane of existence and within 10 miles of each other. The holder of the token can hear only the hag's voice, not those of any other creatures or any ambient noise around the hag. Similarly, the hag can hear the holder of the token and not the noise around it.

A hag can have up to three *iron tokens* active at one time. As an action, she can discern the direction and approximate distance to all of her active tokens. She can instantaneously deactivate any of her tokens at any distance (no action required), whereupon the token retains its current form but loses its magical properties.

Annis Hag
Large fey, chaotic evil

Armor Class 17 (natural armor)
Hit Points 75 (10d10 + 20)
Speed 40 ft.

STR	DEX	CON	INT	WIS	CHA
21 (+5)	12 (+1)	14 (+2)	13 (+1)	14 (+2)	15 (+2)

Saving Throws Con +5
Skills Deception +5, Perception +5
Damage Resistances cold; bludgeoning, piercing, and slashing from nonmagical attacks
Senses darkvision 60 ft., passive Perception 15
Languages Common, Giant, Sylvan
Challenge 6 (2,300 XP)

Innate Spellcasting. The hag's innate spellcasting ability is Charisma (spell save DC 13). She can innately cast the following spells:

3/day each: *disguise self* (including the form of a Medium humanoid), *fog cloud*

Actions

Multiattack. The annis makes three attacks: one with her bite and two with her claws.

Bite. *Melee Weapon Attack:* +8 to hit, reach 5 ft., one target. *Hit:* 15 (3d6 + 5) piercing damage.

Claw. *Melee Weapon Attack:* +8 to hit, reach 5 ft., one target. *Hit:* 15 (3d6 + 5) slashing damage.

Crushing Hug. *Melee Weapon Attack:* +8 to hit, reach 5 ft., one target. *Hit:* 36 (9d6 + 5) bludgeoning damage, and the target is grappled (escape DC 15) if it is a Large or smaller creature. Until the grapple ends, the target takes 36 (9d6 + 5) bludgeoning damage at the start of each of the hag's turns. The hag can't make attacks while grappling a creature in this way.

she often forgoes a direct attack on her remaining enemies and instead takes a moment to feed on the corpse, dismembering it and tearing meat from bone. The sight of this savagery is enough to render witnesses temporarily insane.

Covens. A bheur hag that is part of a coven (see the "Hag Covens" sidebar in the *Monster Manual*) has a challenge rating of 9 (5,000 XP).

BHEUR HAG

Bheur hags live in wintry lands, favoring snow-covered mountains. They become more active during winter, using their ice and weather magic to make life miserable for nearby settlements.

A bheur hag's skin is blue-white, like that of a person who has frozen to death. Her hair is pale white, and she is emaciated, as if she were a person who had survived winter by eating bark and leather. Her eyes are pale and surrounded by dark, bruise-colored flesh. A bheur carries a twisted gray wooden staff, which she can ride like a flying broom and augments her magical powers.

Cold Hearts. Bheur hags are attracted to selfish actions justified by deadly cold, such as murdering a traveler for a winter coat, chopping down a dryad's grove for firewood, and so on. These actions are especially sweet to a bheur if they are unwarranted, such as a greedy merchant hoarding more food for the winter than he could possibly eat while others starve. Bheurs love to seed such ideas and thoughts in mortals. They use their ability to manipulate weather to batter villages with snow and freezing cold, hoping to instill despair that turns the villagers against each other.

A bheur hag loves watching unprepared people suffer and die for their mistakes during the winter. She is delighted when mortals make petty, pathetic attempts to survive, such as eating boots and leather scraps when no real food is to be found.

Awful to Behold. When a bheur hag is fully in the throes of combat and has recently slain one of her foes,

---

BHEUR HAG

Medium fey, chaotic evil

Armor Class 17 (natural armor)
Hit Points 91 (14d8 + 28)
Speed 30 ft.

STR	DEX	CON	INT	WIS	CHA
13 (+1)	16 (+3)	14 (+2)	12 (+1)	13 (+1)	16 (+3)

Saving Throws Wis +4
Skills Nature +4, Perception +4, Stealth +6, Survival +4
Damage Immunities cold
Senses darkvision 60 ft., passive Perception 14
Languages Auran, Common, Giant
Challenge 7 (2,900 XP)

Graystaff Magic. The hag carries a *graystaff*, a length of gray wood that is a focus for her inner power. She can ride the staff as if it were a *broom of flying*. While holding the staff, she can cast additional spells with her Innate Spellcasting trait (these spells are marked with an asterisk). If the staff is lost or destroyed, the hag must craft another, which takes a year and a day. Only a bheur hag can use a *graystaff*.

Ice Walk. The hag can move across and climb icy surfaces without needing to make an ability check. Additionally, difficult terrain composed of ice or snow doesn't cost her extra moment.

Innate Spellcasting. The hag's innate spellcasting ability is Charisma (spell save DC 14, +6 to hit with spell attacks). She can innately cast the following spells, requiring no material components:

At will: *hold person,* ray of frost*
3/day each: *cone of cold,* ice storm,* wall of ice**
1/day each: *control weather*

ACTIONS

Slam. *Melee Weapon Attack:* +4 to hit, reach 5 ft., one target. *Hit:* 10 (2d8 + 1) bludgeoning damage plus 3 (1d6) cold damage.

Maddening Feast. The hag feasts on the corpse of one enemy within 5 feet of her that died within the past minute. Each creature of the hag's choice that is within 60 feet of her and able to see her must succeed on a DC 15 Wisdom saving throw or be frightened of her for 1 minute. While frightened in this way, a creature is incapacitated, can't understand what others say, can't read, and speaks only in gibberish; the DM controls the creature's movement, which is erratic. A creature can repeat the saving throw at the end of each of its turns, ending the effect on itself on a success. If a creature's saving throw is successful or the effect ends for it, the creature is immune to the hag's Maddening Feast for the next 24 hours.

Hobgoblins

Hobgoblins of the cruelest bent gain admittance to elite organizations that provide special training above and beyond what military service has to offer. The Academy of Devastation and the Iron Shadows are two such organizations, and their graduates are feared among the ranks of goblinkind.

Hobgoblin Devastator

In hobgoblin society, the Academy of Devastation identifies hobgoblins with a talent for magic and puts them through a grueling training regimen that endows them with the ability to call down fireballs and other destructive magic on the host's behalf. A hobgoblin devastator on the battlefield is simultaneously a boon to all its allies and a threat to every foe around it.

Into the Fray. While other cultures treat their wizards as cloistered academics, hobgoblins expect their spellcasters to fight. Devastators learn the basics of weapon use, and they measure their deeds by the enemies defeated though their magic.

Devastators have the respect of other members of the host, and they receive obedience and deference from many quarters. Their ability to lay waste to entire formations with a single use of magic allows them to gain far more glory in battle than a single warrior.

Other cultures might view the use of such abilities as a short cut to glory, but to hobgoblins a gift for magic is as valued and useful as a strong sword arm or brilliance in tactics. They are all boons from Maglubiyet that must be cultivated and unleashed upon the enemy.

Only Results Matter. Devastators study a simplified form of evocation magic. Their training lacks the theory and context that other folk study, making them skilled in battle but relatively illiterate on the finer points of how and why their magic works.

The Academy of Devastation believes that an academic approach to magic is a sign of weakness and inefficiency. A warrior doesn't need to know about metallurgy to wield a blade, so why should a wizard care about where magic comes from? Devastators love to prove their superiority in battle by seeking out enemy spellcasters and destroying them.

HOBGOBLIN DEVASTATOR
Medium humanoid (goblinoid), lawful evil

Armor Class 13 (studded leather)
Hit Points 45 (7d8 + 14)
Speed 30 ft.

STR	DEX	CON	INT	WIS	CHA
13 (+1)	12 (+1)	14 (+2)	16 (+3)	13 (+1)	11 (+0)

Skills Arcana +5
Senses darkvision 60 ft., passive Perception 11
Languages Common, Goblin
Challenge 4 (1,100 XP)

Arcane Advantage. Once per turn, the hobgoblin can deal an extra 7 (2d6) damage to a creature it hits with a damaging spell attack if that target is within 5 feet of an ally of the hobgoblin and that ally isn't incapacitated.

Army Arcana. When the hobgoblin casts a spell that causes damage or that forces other creatures to make a saving throw, it can choose itself and any number of allies to be immune to the damage caused by the spell and to succeed on the required saving throw.

Spellcasting. The hobgoblin is a 7th-level spellcaster. Its spellcasting ability is Intelligence (spell save DC 13, +5 to hit with spell attacks). It has the following wizard spells prepared:

Cantrips (at will): *acid splash, fire bolt, ray of frost, shocking grasp*
1st level (4 slots): *fog cloud, magic missile, thunderwave*
2nd level (3 slots): *gust of wind, Melf's acid arrow, scorching ray*
3rd level (3 slots): *fireball, fly, lightning bolt*
4th level (1 slot): *ice storm*

Actions

Quarterstaff. *Melee Weapon Attack:* +3 to hit, reach 5 ft., one target. *Hit:* 4 (1d6 + 1) bludgeoning damage, or 5 (1d8 + 1) bludgeoning damage if used with two hands.

HOBGOBLIN IRON SHADOW

The Iron Shadows are hobgoblin monks that serve as secret police, scouts, and assassins. Among other hobgoblins, they spy to ferret out treachery, rebellion, and betrayal.

Trained in Secret. Iron Shadows are recruited from across the hobgoblin ranks. Each member keeps her eyes open for potential recruits, those whose agility and stamina are matched only by an ironclad commitment to Maglubiyet's will.

A candidate for admission undergoes a series of tests designed to reveal any potential for treachery. Those who fail are slain, while those who pass receive secret training in the magical and martial arts. This indoctrination is a slow and arduous process; many aspirants don't finish it, and years might go by during which the Iron Shadows welcome no new members into their ranks. While a recruit is in training, it serves the Iron Shadows by looking for and reporting suspicious behavior.

Masters of Shadow and Fist. When a recruit's training is complete, she is ready to wield a deadly combination of unarmed fighting techniques and shadow magic to deceive and defeat her foes. She continues to spy on other hobgoblins, but is now also empowered to conduct assassinations and spy missions, both against enemies and among goblinoids. These missions are ordained by the clerics of Maglubiyet, who keep a careful eye on the goblinoid community to ensure that it functions according to Maglubiyet's will.

Masked Devils. Iron Shadows on a secret mission wear masks crafted to resemble devils, both to conceal their identities and to strike fear into their foes.

Their masks also signify the supposed origin of their fighting techniques. The priests of Maglubiyet teach that the Great One stole the secrets of shadows from an archdevil, allowing his followers to conceal their identities, walk between shadows, and craft illusions to confuse and confound their enemies.

HOBGOBLIN IRON SHADOW
Medium humanoid (goblinoid), lawful evil

Armor Class 15
Hit Points 32 (5d8 + 10)
Speed 40 ft.

STR	DEX	CON	INT	WIS	CHA
14 (+2)	16 (+3)	15 (+2)	14 (+2)	15 (+2)	11 (+0)

Skills Acrobatics +5, Athletics +4, Stealth +5
Senses darkvision 60 ft., passive Perception 12
Languages Common, Goblin
Challenge 2 (450 XP)

Spellcasting. The hobgoblin is a 2nd-level spellcaster. Its spellcasting ability is Intelligence (spell save DC 12, +4 to hit with spell attacks). It has the following wizard spells prepared:

Cantrips (at will): *minor illusion, prestidigitation, true strike*
1st level (3 slots): *charm person, disguise self, expeditious retreat, silent image*

Unarmored Defense. While the hobgoblin is wearing no armor and wielding no shield, its AC includes its Wisdom modifier.

ACTIONS

Multiattack. The hobgoblin makes four attacks, each of which can be an unarmed strike or a dart attack. It can also use Shadow Jaunt once, either before or after one of the attacks.

Unarmed Strike. *Melee Weapon Attack:* +5 to hit, reach 5 ft., one target. *Hit:* 5 (1d4 + 3) bludgeoning damage.

Dart. *Ranged Weapon Attack.* +5 to hit, range 20/60 ft., one target. *Hit:* 5 (1d4 + 3) piercing damage.

Shadow Jaunt. The hobgoblin magically teleports, along with any equipment it is wearing or carrying, up to 30 feet to an unoccupied space it can see. Both the space it is leaving and its destination must be in dim light or darkness.

Ki-rin

Ki-rins are noble, celestial creatures. In the Outer Planes, ki-rins in service to benevolent deities take a direct role in the eternal struggle between good and evil. In the mortal world, a ki-rin is celebrated far and wide as a harbinger of destiny, a guardian of the sacred, and a counterbalance to the forces of evil.

Good Personified. Ki-rins are the embodiment of good, and simply beholding one can evoke fear or awe in an observer. A typical ki-rin looks like a muscular stag the size of an elephant, covered in golden scales lined in some places with golden fur. It has a dark gold mane and tail, coppery cloven hooves, and a spiral-shaped coppery horn just above and between its luminous violet eyes. In a breeze or when aloft, the creature's scales and hair can create the impression that the ki-rin is ablaze with a holy, golden fire.

Beyond their coloration, ki-rins vary in appearance, based on the deity each one reveres and the function it typically performs in service to that god. Some are horse-shaped, looking like gigantic unicorns, and are often used as guardians. Others have draconic features and tend to be aggressive foes of evil. One horn is most common, but a ki-rin of fierce demeanor might have two horns or a set of antlers like those of a great stag.

Bringers of Boons. Common folk consider ki-rins to be rare and remote heralds of good fortune. Seeing a ki-rin fly overhead is a blessing, and events that happen on such a day are especially auspicious. If a ki-rin alights during a ceremony, such as a birth announcement or a coronation, everyone present understands that the creature is telling them great good could be in the offing. The ki-rin conveys its gifts and omens, then rises back into the sky. Ki-rins have also been known to appear at the sites of great battles to inspire and strengthen the side of good, or to rescue heroes from certain death.

A ki-rin in the world claims a territory to watch over, and one ki-rin might safeguard an area that encompasses several nations. On other planes, ki-rins that serve good deities go wherever they are commanded, which could include coming to the Material Plane on a mission. A ki-rin disciple in the world usually serves its deity as a scout, a messenger, or a spy.

Ki-rins are attracted to the worship of deities of courage, loyalty, selflessness, and truth, as well as the advancement of just societies. For instance, in Faerûn, ki-rins rally mostly to Torm, although ki-rins also serve his allies Tyr and Ilmater.

Objects of Adoration. Because a ki-rin is renowned for its wisdom, other creatures would naturally seek it out with questions and requests if they could. For that reason among others, the creature makes its lair atop a forbidding mountain peak or in some other equally inaccessible location. Only those that have the tenacity to

Ki-rin

Huge celestial, lawful good

Armor Class 20 (natural armor)
Hit Points 152 (16d12 + 48)
Speed 60 ft., fly 120 ft. (hover)

STR	DEX	CON	INT	WIS	CHA
21 (+5)	16 (+3)	16 (+3)	19 (+4)	20 (+5)	20 (+5)

Skills Perception +9, Insight +9, Religion +8
Damage Immunities poison
Condition Immunities poisoned
Senses blindsight 30 ft., darkvision 120 ft., passive Perception 19
Languages all, telepathy 120 ft.
Challenge 12 (8,400 XP)

Innate Spellcasting. The ki-rin's innate spellcasting ability is Charisma (spell save DC 17). The ki-rin can innately cast the following spells, requiring no material components:

At will: *gaseous form, major image* (6th-level version), *wind walk*
1/day: *create food and water*

Legendary Resistance (3/Day). If the ki-rin fails a saving throw, it can choose to succeed instead.

Magic Resistance. The ki-rin has advantage on saving throws against spells and other magical effects.

Magic Weapons. The ki-rin's weapon attacks are magical.

Spellcasting. The ki-rin is a 18th-level spellcaster. Its spellcasting ability is Wisdom (spell save DC 17, +9 to hit with spell attacks). It has the following cleric spells prepared:

Cantrips (at will): *light, mending, sacred flame, spare the dying, thaumaturgy*
1st level (4 slots): *command, cure wounds, detect evil and good, protection from evil and good, sanctuary*
2nd level (3 slots): *calm emotions, lesser restoration, silence*
3rd level (3 slots): *dispel magic, remove curse, sending*
4th level (3 slots): *banishment, freedom of movement, guardian of faith*
5th level (3 slots): *greater restoration, mass cure wounds, scrying*
6th level (1 slot): *heroes' feast, true seeing*
7th level (1 slot): *etherealness, plane shift*
8th level (1 slot): *control weather*
9th level (1 slot): *true resurrection*

Actions

Multiattack. The ki-rin makes three attacks: two with its hooves and one with its horn.

Hoof. *Melee Weapon Attack:* +9 to hit, reach 15 ft., one target. *Hit:* 10 (2d4 + 5) bludgeoning damage.

Horn. *Melee Weapon Attack:* +9 to hit, reach 5 ft., one target. *Hit:* 14 (2d8 + 5) piercing damage.

Legendary Actions

The ki-rin can take 3 legendary actions, choosing from the options below. Only one legendary action option can be used at a time and only at the end of another creature's turn. The ki-rin regains spent legendary actions at the start of its turn.

Detect. The ki-rin makes a Wisdom (Perception) check or a Wisdom (Insight) check.
Smite. The ki-rin makes a hoof attack or casts *sacred flame*.
Move. The ki-rin moves up to its half speed without provoking opportunity attacks.

K

I was awed to tears at the mere sight of my first ki-rin, and I've met gods.

—Volo

complete the daunting journey to a ki-rin's lair can prove themselves worthy of speaking with its occupant.

Many who seek a ki-rin's guidance end up pledging service to the creature. They study as monks under its tutelage and serve as its agents in the world. The followers of a ki-rin might travel incognito across the land, seeking news of growing evil and working behind the scenes, or might be champions of their master's cause, out to defeat villainy wherever it is found.

Lair of Luxury

On the celestial planes, ki-rins reside in lofty, elegant aeries filled with luxurious objects. In the world, a ki-rin chooses a similar location, such as atop a tall pinnacle or within a cloud solidified by the ki-rin's magic. When viewed from the outside, a ki-rin's lair is indistinguishable from a natural site, and the entrance is difficult for visitors to find and reach. Inside, the lair is a serene and comfortable place, its ambiance a mix between palace and temple. If the ki-rin has taken creatures into its service, its lair doubles as a sacred site wherein the ki-rin not only rests, but also teaches of holy mysteries.

Inside its lair, a ki-rin has the power to conjure objects up to three times per day, using each of the following versions of the power once. One version permanently creates enough objects made of soft, plant-based material—including manufactured objects such as cloth, pillows, rope, blankets, and clothing—to fill a cube 20 feet on a side. The second version permanently creates enough objects made of wood, or similarly hard plant-based material, to fill a cube 10 feet on a side. The third version creates enough objects made of stone or metal to fill a cube 2 feet on a side, but any materials created in this way last for only 1 hour.

Regional Effects

The ki-rin's celestial nature transforms the region around its lair. Any of the following magical effects is possible for travelers to encounter in the vicinity:

- Water flows pure within 3 miles of a ki-rin's lair. Any purposeful corruption of the water lasts for no longer than 3 minutes.
- Animals, plants, and good creatures within 3 miles of the ki-rin's lair gain vigor as they evolve toward an idealized form. Such creatures are rarely aggressive toward others that aren't normally prey. Evil creatures can't tolerate the holy atmosphere within the same distance, and usually choose to live much farther from the domain of a ki-rin.
- Curses, diseases, and poisons affecting good-aligned creatures are suppressed when those creatures are within 3 miles of the lair.
- A ki-rin can cast *control weather* while it is within 3 miles of its lair. The spell's point of origin is always the point outdoors closest to the center of its lair. The ki-rin doesn't need to maintain a clear path to the sky or to concentrate for the change in weather to persist.
- Within 3 miles of the lair, winds buoy non-evil creatures that fall due to no act of the ki-rin or its allies. Such creatures descend at a rate of 60 feet per round and take no falling damage.

When the ki-rin dies, all these effects disappear immediately, although the invigorating effect on flora and fauna remains for 3 years.

Kobolds

Some kobolds have gifts bequeathed to them by dragons or gods, enabling them to rise above their peers. Others are born with a cruel inventiveness that few can match.

Kobold Dragonshield

A kobold dragonshield is a champion of its race. Almost all dragonshields begin life as normal kobolds, then are chosen by a dragon and invested with great powers for the purpose of protecting the dragon's eggs, but once every few years a kobold hatches with an innate version of the dragonshield's abilities. Accomplished at hand-to-hand combat, it bears many scars from desperate fights and carries a shield made out of cast-off dragon scales.

Uncommon Courage. A dragonshield knows that it has a place of honor in the tribe, but—being kobolds at heart—most of them feel unworthy of their status and thus desperate to prove themselves deserving of it. A dragonshield's natural kobold cowardice is still present in its makeup, and thus it might still run away from a threat. But it also has the ability to rally in the face of certain death, inspiring other kobolds to follow it in a charge against the invaders of their warren.

Kobold Inventor

A kobold inventor, crafty and with quick hands, builds improvised weapons in the hope of gaining some new advantage in combat. An inventor captures bugs, scoops up exotic dungeon slimes, and claims the best stolen goods as ingredients in its experiments. Its creations are sometimes comical in appearance, but—like kobolds' traps—they work a lot better than their materials would suggest.

Good While They Last. An inventor's new weapons last for only one or two attacks before they break, but might be surprisingly effective in the meantime. Most inventors are skilled enough that their improvised weapons don't backfire on them, but other users might not be so lucky. The weapons don't have to be lethal—in many cases one serves its purpose if it distracts, scares, or confuses a creature long enough for other kobolds to kill the enemy. In any particular encounter, an inventor usually has one or two improvised weapons at its disposal.

Kobold Scale Sorcerer

A kobold scale sorcerer has an innate talent for arcane magic, making it a highly valuable member of the tribe for several reasons. Because the kobolds' deity remains imprisoned, most tribes lack individuals that can use divine magic, and so the scale sorcerers fill the roles of advisor and historian. In times of peace, they use their spells to fortify and enhance the warren and aid the rest of the tribe. When the tribe is threatened, a scale sorcerer lashes out with fire and poison against enemies, saving a bit of magic for itself in case it needs to flee or take advantage of a captor.

Duty-Bound to a Dragon. In a kobold tribe associated with a dragon, typically one that resides in or near the dragon's lair, the scale sorcerer also serves as diplomat and mouthpiece—anticipating the dragon's needs, issu-

Kobold Dragonshield
Small humanoid (kobold), lawful evil

Armor Class 15 (leather, shield)
Hit Points 44 (8d6 + 16)
Speed 20 ft.

STR	DEX	CON	INT	WIS	CHA
12 (+1)	15 (+2)	14 (+2)	8 (−1)	9 (−1)	10 (+0)

Skills Perception +1
Damage Resistances see Dragon's Resistance below
Senses darkvision 60 ft., passive Perception 11
Languages Common, Draconic
Challenge 1 (200 XP)

Dragon's Resistance. The kobold has resistance to a type of damage based on the color of dragon that invested it with power (choose or roll a d10): 1–2, acid (black); 3–4, cold (white); 5–6, fire (red); 7–8, lightning (blue); 9–10, poison (green).

Heart of the Dragon. If the kobold is frightened or paralyzed by an effect that allows a saving throw, it can repeat the save at the start of its turn to end the effect on itself and all kobolds within 30 feet of it. Any kobold that benefits from this trait (including the dragonshield) has advantage on its next attack roll.

Pack Tactics. The kobold has advantage on an attack roll against a creature if at least one of the kobold's allies is within 5 feet of the creature and the ally isn't incapacitated.

Sunlight Sensitivity. While in sunlight, the kobold has disadvantage on attack rolls, as well as on Wisdom (Perception) checks that rely on sight.

Actions

Multiattack. The kobold makes two melee attacks.

Spear. *Melee or Ranged Weapon Attack:* +3 to hit, reach 5 ft. or range 20/60 ft., one target. *Hit:* 4 (1d6 + 1) piercing damage, or 5 (1d8 + 1) piercing damage if used with two hands to make a melee attack.

K

ing commands to other kobolds on the dragon's behalf, and reporting information back to the dragon. The sorcerer is just as awed by and respectful of dragons as common kobolds are, but it knows that its duty requires it not to fawn over its master at all times. It also understands that its frequent proximity to the dragon means it would probably be the first to die if its master became angry or displeased, and so it frantically maintains a balance between adoration and terror in its behavior toward the dragon.

KOBOLD INVENTOR

Small humanoid (kobold), lawful evil

Armor Class 12
Hit Points 13 (3d6 + 3)
Speed 30 ft.

STR	DEX	CON	INT	WIS	CHA
7 (–2)	15 (+2)	12 (+1)	8 (–1)	7 (–2)	8 (–1)

Skills Perception +0
Senses darkvision 60 ft., passive Perception 10
Languages Common, Draconic
Challenge 1/4 (50 XP)

Pack Tactics. The kobold has advantage on an attack roll against a creature if at least one of the kobold's allies is within 5 feet of the creature and the ally isn't incapacitated.

Sunlight Sensitivity. While in sunlight, the kobold has disadvantage on attack rolls, as well as on Wisdom (Perception) checks that rely on sight.

ACTIONS

Dagger. *Melee or Ranged Weapon Attack:* +4 to hit, reach 5 ft. or range 20/60 ft., one target. *Hit:* 4 (1d4 + 2) piercing damage.

Sling. *Ranged Weapon Attack:* +4 to hit, range 30/120 ft., one target. *Hit:* 4 (1d4 + 2) bludgeoning damage.

Weapon Invention. The kobold uses one of the following options (roll a d8 or choose one); the kobold can use each one no more than once per day:

1. *Acid.* The kobold hurls a flask of acid. *Ranged Weapon Attack:* +4 to hit, range 5/20 ft., one target. *Hit:* 7 (2d6) acid damage.

2. *Alchemist's Fire.* The kobold throws a flask of alchemist's fire. *Ranged Weapon Attack:* +4 to hit, range 5/20 ft., one target. *Hit:* 2 (1d4) fire damage at the start of each of the target's turns. A creature can end this damage by using its action to make a DC 10 Dexterity check to extinguish the flames.

3. *Basket of Centipedes.* The kobold throws a small basket into a 5-foot-square space within 20 feet of it. A **swarm of insects (centipedes)** with 11 hit points emerges from the basket and rolls initiative. At the end of each of the swarm's turns, there's a 50 percent chance that the swarm disperses.

4. *Green Slime Pot.* The kobold throws a clay pot full of green slime at the target, and it breaks open on impact. *Ranged Weapon Attack:* +4 to hit, range 5/20 ft., one target. *Hit:* The target is covered in a patch of green slime (see chapter 5 of the *Dungeon Master's Guide*). *Miss:* A patch of green slime covers a randomly determined 5-foot-square section of wall or floor within 5 feet of the target.

5. *Rot Grub Pot.* The kobold throws a clay pot into a 5-foot-square space within 20 feet of it, and it breaks open on impact. A **swarm of rot grubs** (see appendix A) emerges from the shattered pot and remains a hazard in that square.

6. *Scorpion on a Stick.* The kobold makes a melee attack with a **scorpion** tied to the end of a 5-foot-long pole. *Melee Weapon Attack:* +4 to hit, reach 5 ft., one target. *Hit:* 1 piercing damage, and the target must make a DC 9 Constitution saving throw, taking 4 (1d8) poison damage on a failed save, or half as much damage on a successful one.

7. *Skunk in a Cage.* The kobold releases a skunk into an unoccupied space within 5 feet of it. The skunk has a walking speed of 20 feet, AC 10, 1 hit point, and no effective attacks. It rolls initiative and, on its turn, uses its action to spray musk at a random creature within 5 feet of it. The target must make a DC 9 Constitution saving throw. On a failed save, the target retches and can't take actions for 1 minute. The target can repeat the saving throw at the end of each of its turns, ending the effect on itself on a success. A creature that doesn't need to breathe or is immune to poison automatically succeeds on the saving throw. Once the skunk has sprayed its musk, it can't do so again until it finishes a short or long rest.

8. *Wasp Nest in a Bag.* The kobold throws a small bag into a 5-foot-square space within 20 feet of it. A **swarm of insects (wasps)** with 11 hit points emerges from the bag and rolls initiative. At the end of each of the swarm's turns, there's a 50 percent chance that the swarm disperses.

Never make the mistake of thinking kobolds are stupid or backward just because they're small. Size has nothing to do with it.

—Volo

KOBOLD SCALE SORCERER
Small humanoid (kobold), lawful evil

Armor Class 15 (natural armor)
Hit Points 27 (5d6 + 10)
Speed 30 ft.

STR	DEX	CON	INT	WIS	CHA
7 (−2)	15 (+2)	14 (+2)	10 (+0)	9 (−1)	14 (+2)

Skills Arcana +2, Medicine +1
Senses darkvision 60 ft., passive Perception 9
Languages Common, Draconic
Challenge 1 (200 XP)

Spellcasting. The kobold is a 3rd-level spellcaster. Its spellcasting ability is Charisma (spell save DC 12, +4 to hit with spell attacks). It has the following sorcerer spells prepared:

Cantrips (at will): *fire bolt, mage hand, mending, poison spray*
1st level (4 slots): *charm person, chromatic orb, expeditious retreat*
2nd level (2 slots): *scorching ray*

Sorcery Points. The kobold has 3 sorcery points. It regains all its spent sorcery points when it finishes a long rest. It can spend its sorcery points on the following options:

Heightened Spell: When it casts a spell that forces a creature to make a saving throw to resist the spell's effects, the kobold can spend 3 sorcery points to give one target of the spell disadvantage on its first saving throw against the spell.

Subtle Spell: When the kobold casts a spell, it can spend 1 sorcery point to cast the spell without any somatic or verbal components.

Pack Tactics. The kobold has advantage on an attack roll against a creature if at least one of the kobold's allies is within 5 feet of the creature and the ally isn't incapacitated.

Sunlight Sensitivity. While in sunlight, the kobold has disadvantage on attack rolls, as well as on Wisdom (Perception) checks that rely on sight.

ACTIONS

Dagger. *Melee or Ranged Weapon Attack:* +4 to hit, reach 5 ft. or range 20/60 ft., one target. *Hit:* 4 (1d4 + 2) piercing damage.

K

Korred

Korreds are unpredictable, secretive fey with strong ties to earth and stone. Because of their magical hair and their mystical understanding of minerals, they are sought after by treasure-hunters, dwarves, and others that desire wealth beneath the earth.

Earthy Fey. Korreds prefer to keep their own company and occasionally consort with creatures of elemental earth such as galeb duhr. A tribe of korreds gathers weekly to perform ceremonial dances, beating out rhythms on stone with their hooves and clubs. In the depths of the Material Plane, korreds typically flee from other creatures but become aggressive when they feel insulted or are annoyed by the sounds of mining.

Stone Sympathy. No one knows the ways of stone and earth better than a korred. Korreds can seemingly smell veins of metal or gems. A korred on the surface can feel the rise and fall of bedrock under the earth and where caves lie, and underground it knows the pathways through the stone for miles. Secret doors that lead through stone are as obvious as windows to a korred.

Korreds can hurl boulders far larger than it seems they should be able to, shape stone as though it were clay, swim through rock, and summon earth elementals and other creatures. They also gain supernatural strength just from standing on the ground.

Enchanted Hair. Korreds have hair all over their bodies, but the hair that grows from their heads is magical. When cut, it transforms into whatever material was used to cut it. Korreds use iron shears to cut lengths of their hair, then weave the strands together to create iron ropes that they can manipulate, animating them to bind or snake around creatures and objects. Korreds take great pride in their hair, and equally great offense at anyone who attempts to cut it without permission.

Korred

Small fey, chaotic neutral

Armor Class 17 (natural armor)
Hit Points 102 (12d6 + 60)
Speed 30 ft., burrow 30 ft.

STR	DEX	CON	INT	WIS	CHA
23 (+6)	14 (+2)	20 (+5)	10 (+0)	15 (+2)	9 (−1)

Skills Athletics +9, Perception +5, Stealth +5
Damage Resistances bludgeoning, piercing, and slashing from nonmagical attacks
Senses darkvision 120 ft., tremorsense 120 ft., passive Perception 15
Languages Dwarvish, Gnomish, Sylvan, Terran, Undercommon
Challenge 7 (2,900 XP)

Command Hair. The korred has at least one 50-foot-long rope woven out of its hair. As a bonus action, the korred commands one such rope within 30 feet of it to move up to 20 feet and entangle a Large or smaller creature that the korred can see. The target must succeed on a DC 13 Dexterity saving throw or become grappled by the rope (escape DC 13). Until this grapple ends, the target is restrained. The korred can use a bonus action to release the target, which is also freed if the korred dies or becomes incapacitated.

A rope of korred hair has AC 20 and 20 hit points. It regains 1 hit point at the start of each of the korred's turns while it has at least 1 hit point and the korred is alive. If the rope drops to 0 hit points, it is destroyed.

Innate Spellcasting. The korred's innate spellcasting ability is Wisdom (save DC 13). It can innately cast the following spells, requiring no components:

At will: *commune with nature, meld into stone, stone shape*
1/day each: *conjure elemental* (as 6th-level spell; galeb duhr, gargoyle, earth elemental, or xorn only), *Otto's irresistible dance*

Stone Camouflage. The korred has advantage on Dexterity (Stealth) checks made to hide in rocky terrain.

Stone's Strength. While on the ground, the korred deals 2 extra dice of damage with any weapon attack (included in its attacks).

Actions

Multiattack. The korred makes two attacks with its greatclub or hurls two rocks.

Greatclub. *Melee Weapon Attack:* +9 to hit, reach 5 ft., one target. *Hit:* 10 (1d8 + 6) bludgeoning damage, or 19 (3d8 + 6) bludgeoning damage if the korred is on the ground.

Rock. *Ranged Weapon Attack:* +9 to hit, range 60/120 ft., one target. *Hit:* 15 (2d8 + 6) bludgeoning damage, or 24 (4d8 + 6) bludgeoning damage if the korred is on the ground.

There's a legend about a merchant who tried to cut a korred's hair with golden shears. The korred fed him those shears, from his swallow to his sitter.

—Volo

LEUCROTTA

A leucrotta is what you would get if you took the head of a giant badger, the brain of a person who likes to torture and eat people, the legs of a deer, and the body of a large hyena, put them together, and reanimated them with demon ichor without bothering to cover up the stink of death.

Spawn of Yeenoghu. The first leucrottas came into being alongside the gnolls during Yeenoghu's rampages on the Material Plane. Some of the hyenas that ate Yeenoghu's kills went through different transformations rather than turning into gnolls. Among these bizarre results, leucrottas were the most numerous.

As clever as it is cruel, a leucrotta loves to deceive, torture, and kill. Because leucrottas are smarter and tougher than most gnolls, one could occupy an elevated position within a gnoll tribe. Although a leucrotta is unlikely to lead a group of gnolls, it can influence the leader, and it might even agree to carry a leader into battle and offer advice during the fight.

Gnolls see leucrottas as a form of entertainment, partly because a leucrotta can mimic the squeals of a suffering victim—a sound that always gives gnolls pleasure—even when no victims are to be had. Further, a gnoll is bloodthirsty and sadistic, but unable by its nature to prolong the fun of killing. Most leucrottas are consciously cruel, to the point of being meticulous about their savagery to draw out a kill into better and longer sport. Gnolls enjoy watching a leucrotta work almost as much as they like doing their own killing.

Foulness Embodied. The leucrotta is so loathsome that only gnolls and others of its kind can stand to be around one for long. Its horrific, hodgepodge body oozes a foul stench that pollutes anywhere the creature lairs. This reek is outdone only by the creature's breath, which issues from a maw that drips fluid corrupted with rot and digestive juices. In place of fangs, a leucrotta has bony ridges as hard as steel that can crush bones and lacerate flesh. These plates are so tough that a leucrotta can use them to peel plate armor away from the body of a slain knight.

A leucrotta's stench would normally warn away prey long before the creature could attack. It has two natural capabilities, however, that give it an advantage. First, a leucrotta's tracks are nearly impossible to distinguish from those of common deer. Second, it can duplicate the call or the vocal expressions of just about any creature it has heard. The monster uses its mimicry to lure in potential victims, then attacks when they are confused or unaware of the actual threat.

LEUCROTTA

Large monstrosity, chaotic evil

Armor Class 14 (natural armor)
Hit Points 67 (9d10 + 18)
Speed 50 ft.

STR	DEX	CON	INT	WIS	CHA
18 (+4)	14 (+2)	15 (+2)	9 (−1)	12 (+1)	6 (−2)

Skills Deception +2, Perception +3
Senses darkvision 60 ft., passive Perception 13
Languages Abyssal, Gnoll
Challenge 3 (700 XP)

Keen Smell. The leucrotta has advantage on Wisdom (Perception) checks that rely on smell.

Kicking Retreat. If the leucrotta attacks with its hooves, it can take the Disengage action as a bonus action.

Mimicry. The leucrotta can mimic animal sounds and humanoid voices. A creature that hears the sounds can tell they are imitations with a successful DC 14 Wisdom (Insight) check.

Rampage. When the leucrotta reduces a creature to 0 hit points with a melee attack on its turn, it can take a bonus action to move up to half its speed and make an attack with its hooves.

ACTIONS

Multiattack. The leucrotta makes two attacks: one with its bite and one with its hooves.

Bite. *Melee Weapon Attack:* +6 to hit, reach 5 ft., one target. *Hit:* 8 (1d8 + 4) piercing damage. If the leucrotta scores a critical hit, it rolls the damage dice three times, instead of twice.

Hooves. *Melee Weapon Attack:* +6 to hit, reach 5 ft., one target. *Hit:* 11 (2d6 + 4) bludgeoning damage.

Meenlock

Meenlocks are deformed fey that invoke terror and seek to destroy all that is good, innocent, and beautiful. They primarily live in forests, although they adapt well to urban and subterranean settings.

Fear Incarnate. Meenlocks are spawned by fear. Whenever fear overwhelms a creature in the Feywild, or in any other location where the Feywild's influence is strong, one or more meenlocks might spontaneously arise in the shadows or darkness nearby. If more than one meenlock is born, a lair also magically forms. The earth creaks and moans as narrow, twisting tunnels open up within it. One of these newly formed passageways serves as the lair's only entrance and exit.

Meenlocks give other creatures the creeps and project a supernatural aura that instills terror in those nearby. So evil and twisted are they that a palpable sense of foreboding haunts those who intrude upon a meenlock lair. Inside the warren, black moss covers every surface, muffling sound. A large central chamber serves as the meenlocks' den, where they torment captives.

Dark Dwellers. A meenlock shuns bright light. It can supernaturally sense areas of darkness and shadow in its vicinity and thus is able to teleport from one darkened space to another—enabling it to sneak up on its prey or run away when outmatched.

Telepathic Tormentors. Meenlocks have no form of communication other than telepathy. They can use it to project unsettling hallucinations into the minds of their prey. These hallucinations take the form of terrible whispers or fleeting movements just at the edges of one's peripheral vision.

During the day, meenlocks confine themselves to their dark warrens. At night, they crawl out of their tunnels to torment sleeping prey, particularly those who seem to embody all that is good in the world. Meenlocks like to paralyze creatures with their claws, drag them back to their hidden den, beat them unconscious, and telepathically torture them over a period of hours. A humanoid that succumbs to this psychic torment undergoes a transformation into an evil, full-grown meenlock (see the "Telepathic Torment" sidebar).

Meenlock
Small fey, neutral evil

Armor Class 15 (natural armor)
Hit Points 31 (7d6 + 7)
Speed 30 ft.

STR	DEX	CON	INT	WIS	CHA
7 (−2)	15 (+2)	12 (+1)	11 (+0)	10 (+0)	8 (−1)

Skills Perception +4, Stealth +6, Survival +2
Condition Immunities frightened
Senses darkvision 120 ft., passive Perception 14
Languages telepathy 120 ft.
Challenge 2 (450 XP)

Fear Aura. Any beast or humanoid that starts its turn within 10 feet of the meenlock must succeed on a DC 11 Wisdom saving throw or be frightened until the start of the creature's next turn.

Light Sensitivity. While in bright light, the meenlock has disadvantage on attack rolls, as well as on Wisdom (Perception) checks that rely on sight.

Shadow Teleport (Recharge 5–6). As a bonus action, the meenlock can teleport to an unoccupied space within 30 feet of it, provided that both the space it's teleporting from and its destination are in dim light or darkness. The destination need not be within line of sight.

Actions

Claws. *Melee Weapon Attack:* +4 to hit, reach 5 ft., one target. *Hit:* 7 (2d4 + 2) slashing damage, and the target must succeed on a DC 11 Constitution saving throw or be paralyzed for 1 minute. The target can repeat the saving throw at the end of each of its turns, ending the effect on itself on a success.

TELEPATHIC TORMENT

Up to four meenlocks can telepathically torment one incapacitated creature, filling its mind with disturbing sounds and dreadful imagery. Participating meenlocks can't use their telepathy for any other purpose during this time, though they can move about and take actions and reactions as normal. This torment has no effect on a creature that is immune to the frightened condition. If the creature is susceptible and remains incapacitated for 1 hour, the creature must make a Wisdom saving throw, taking 10 (3d6) psychic damage on a failed save, or half as much damage on a successful one. The save DC is 10 + the number of meenlocks participating in the torment, considering only those that remain within sight of the victim for the entire hour and aren't incapacitated during it. The process can be repeated. A humanoid that drops to 0 hit points as a result of this damage instantly transforms into a meenlock at full health and under the DM's control. Only a *wish* spell or divine intervention can restore a transformed creature to its former state.

M

Mind Flayers

Three members of the horrific illithid family appear here, joining the regular mind flayer in the *Monster Manual*.

Alhoon

Mind flayers that pursue arcane magic are exiled as deviants, and for them no eternal communion with an elder brain is possible. The road to lichdom offers a way to escape the permanency of death, but that path is long and solitary. Alhoons are mind flayers that use a shortcut.

Arcane Temptation. Elder brains forbid mind flayers from pursuing magic power aside from psionics, but it isn't an interdiction they must often enforce. Illithids brook no masters but members of their own kind, so it isn't in their nature to bow to any god or otherworldly patron. However, wizardry remains a rare temptation.

In the pages of a spellbook, an illithid sees a system to acquire authority. Through the writings of the wizard who penned it, the illithid perceives the workings of a highly intelligent mind. Most mind flayers who find a spellbook react with abhorrence or indifference, but for some a spellbook is a gateway to a new way of thinking.

For a time, the study of such forbidden texts can be hidden from other illithids and even from an elder brain. Understanding of wizardry eludes the mind like a living thing. Yet eventually, understanding comes, and a mind flayer arcanist must accept itself as deviant and flee the colony if it is to live.

Existential Fear. Arcanist deviants that taste freedom from the colony react in a variety of ways. Some prize their privacy, others seek to commune with similar minds, and still others seek to dominate a colony, elevating themselves to the position of leadership normally held by an elder brain. Regardless of the arcanist's personal inclinations, it faces the same stark fact: When it dies, it will not join the host of minds in the elder brain. Deviant minds are never accepted as part of the collective. For it, death means oblivion.

Dreadful Deliverance. Lichdom offers salvation and the prospect of being able to pursue knowledge indefinitely. Having feasted on the brains of people when alive, a mind flayer has no compunction about feeding souls to a phylactery. The only hindrance to a mind flayer becoming a lich is the means, which is a secret some mind flayer arcanists stop at nothing to discover. Yet lichdom requires an arcane spellcaster to be at the apex of power, something many mind flayers find is far from their grasps.

Confronting this awful reality, a group of nine mind flayer deviants used their arcane magic and psionics to weave a new truth. These nine called themselves the alhoon, and ever afterward, all those who follow in their footsteps have been referred to by the same name.

A Psionic Secret. Alhoons can cooperate in the creation of a *periapt of mind trapping*, a fist-sized container made of silver, emerald, and amethyst. The process requires at least three mind flayer arcanists and the sacrifice of an equal number of souls from living victims in a three-day-long ritual of spellcasting and psionic com-

munion. Upon its completion, free-willed undeath is conferred on the mind flayers, turning them into alhoons.

Initially, an alhoon can be difficult to distinguish from a normal mind flayer. The most obvious difference is the lack of the mind flayer's ever-present mucus coating. Without that protection, an alhoon's skin becomes dry and cracked. Its eyes might appear shriveled and sunken. Both of these clues are easily missed by someone who hasn't seen a mind flayer. However, in short order, an alhoon's flesh withers away and its empty eye sockets gleam with cold pinpricks of light like other liches.

Precarious Immortality. Unlike with true lichdom, the *periapt of mind trapping* doesn't restore the alhoons to undeath if they are destroyed. Instead, a destroyed alhoon's mind is transferred to the periapt where it remains in communion with any other trapped alhoon minds, as well as the souls of those sacrificed.

The undeath conferred by a *periapt of mind trapping* lasts only so long as the life of the living victim selected. Thus an alhoon who brought a 200-year-old elf to be sacrificed looks forward to a much longer existence than one that sacrifices a 35-year-old person. Alhoons can extend their existence by repeating the ritual with new victims, effectively resetting the clocks for themselves.

Destruction of a *periapt of mind trapping* consigns those trapped within it to oblivion, and thus alhoons often work together to create elaborate protections about the periapt and their preferred ritual site. Sometimes a single alhoon is entrusted with the periapt of mind trapping, but this is a dangerous proposition. Anyone who holds the periapt of mind trapping gains advantage on attacks, saves, and check against the alhoons associated with its creation, and those alhoons in turn suffer disadvantage on attacks, saves, and check against the holder. In addition, the holder of the periapt can telepathically communicate with any sacrificed soul trapped within, and alhoons within the periapt can speak telepathically with the holder. A creature carrying the periapt can't prevent communication from alhoons but can silence trapped souls.

ALHOON
Medium undead, any evil alignment

Armor Class 15 (natural armor)
Hit Points 120 (16d8 + 48)
Speed 30 ft.

STR	DEX	CON	INT	WIS	CHA
11 (+0)	12 (+1)	16 (+3)	19 (+4)	17 (+3)	17 (+3)

Saving Throws Con +7, Int +8, Wis +7, Cha +7
Skills Arcana +8, Deception +7, History +8, Insight +7, Perception +7, Stealth +5
Damage Resistances cold, lightning, necrotic
Damage Immunities poison; bludgeoning, piercing, and slashing from nonmagical attacks
Condition Immunities charmed, exhaustion, frightened, paralyzed, poisoned
Senses truesight 120 ft., passive Perception 17
Languages Deep Speech, Undercommon, telepathy 120 ft.
Challenge 10 (5,900 XP)

Magic Resistance. The alhoon has advantage on saving throws against spells and other magical effects.

Innate Spellcasting (Psionics). The alhoon's innate spellcasting ability is Intelligence (spell save DC 16). It can innately cast the following spells, requiring no components:

At will: *detect thoughts, levitate*
1/day each: *dominate monster, plane shift* (self only)

Spellcasting. The alhoon is a 12th-level spellcaster. Its spellcasting ability is Intelligence (spell save DC 16, +8 to hit with spell attacks). The alhoon has the following wizard spells prepared:

Cantrips (at will): *chill touch, dancing lights, mage hand, prestidigitation, shocking grasp*
1st level (4 slots): *detect magic, disguise self, magic missile, shield*
2nd level (3 slots): *invisibility, mirror image, scorching ray*
3rd level (3 slots): *counterspell, fly, lightning bolt*
4th level (3 slots): *confusion, Evard's black tentacles, phantasmal killer*
5th level (2 slots): *modify memory, wall of force*
6th level (1 slot): *disintegrate, globe of invulnerability*

Turn Resistance. The alhoon has advantage on saving throws against any effect that turns undead.

ACTIONS

Chilling Grasp. *Melee Spell Attack:* +8 to hit, reach 5 ft., one target. *Hit:* 10 (3d6) cold damage.

Mind Blast (Recharge 5–6). The alhoon magically emits psychic energy in a 60-foot cone. Each creature in that area must succeed on a DC 16 Intelligence saving throw or take 22 (4d8 + 4) psychic damage and be stunned for 1 minute. A target can repeat the saving throw at the end of each of its turns, ending the effect on itself on a success.

VARIANT: MIND FLAYER LICH (ILLITHILICH)
The path to true lichdom is something only the most powerful mind flayer mages can pursue, since it requires the ability to craft a phylactery and cast the *imprisonment* spell. A mind flayer lich uses the **lich** stat block (see the *Monster Manual*), with the following changes:

- It has a challenge rating of 22 (41,000 XP).
- It speaks Deep Speech and Undercommon, and has telepathy out to a range of 120 feet.
- It has the Magic Resistance and Innate Spellcasting (Psionics) traits, as well as the Tentacles, Extract Brain, and Mind Blast action options (all described below). So long as a mind flayer lich feeds captured souls to its phylactery, it maintains the muscular power of its tentacles and the ability to extract brains.
- Its suite of legendary actions (described below) is different from that of the normal lich.

Magic Resistance. The lich has advantage on saving throws against spells and other magical effects.

Innate Spellcasting (Psionics). The lich's innate spellcasting ability is Intelligence (spell save DC 20). It can innately cast the following spells, requiring no components.

At will: *detect thoughts, levitate*
1/day each: *dominate monster, plane shift* (self only)

ACTIONS

Tentacles. *Melee Weapon Attack:* +12 to hit, reach 5 ft., one creature. *Hit:* 21 (3d10 + 5) psychic damage. If the target is Large or smaller, it is grappled (escape DC 15) and must succeed on a DC 20 Intelligence saving throw or be stunned until this grapple ends.

Extract Brain. *Melee Weapon Attack:* +12 to hit, reach 5 ft., one incapacitated humanoid grappled by the lich. *Hit:* 55 (10d10) piercing damage. If this damage reduces the target to 0 hit points, the lich kills the target by extracting and devouring its brain.

Mind Blast (Recharge 5–6). The lich magically emits psychic energy in a 60-foot cone. Each creature in that area must succeed on a DC 18 Intelligence saving throw or take 27 (5d8 + 5) psychic damage and be stunned for 1 minute. A creature can repeat the saving throw at the end of each of its turns, ending the effect on itself on a success.

LEGENDARY ACTIONS

The lich gains the following legendary action options, which replace all of the lich's legendary actions.

Tentacles. The lich makes one attack with its tentacles.
Extract Brain (Costs 2 Actions). The lich uses Extract Brain.
Mind Blast (Costs 3 Actions). The lich recharges its Mind Blast and uses it.
Cast Spell (Costs 1–3 Actions). The lich uses a spell slot to cast a 1st-, 2nd-, or 3rd-level spell that it has prepared. Doing so costs 1 legendary action per level of the spell.

ELDER BRAIN

The ultimate expression of illithid domination, an elder brain sprawls within a vat of viscous brine, touching the thoughts of creatures near and far. It scrawls upon the canvas of their minds, rewriting their thoughts and authoring their dreams.

Psychic Infiltrators. When an elder brain infiltrates a mind, it alters the creature's perception and deceives its senses, causing it to see, hear, touch, taste, or feel reality according to the elder brain's intent. From across great distances, it implants subconscious suggestions or subtly influences dreams to compel creatures toward a course of action that benefits its grand plan.

When its insidious suggestions fail to take hold, an elder brain asserts its dominance more directly. It seizes control of a resistant mind and controls the creature's body as it would a puppet. Against the rare, strong-willed stalwart that defies it or attacks it, an elder brain sends a blast of overwhelming psychic force to crush the upstart's mind, rendering the creature a thoughtless, drooling shell.

Devourer of Thoughts. An elder brain sustains itself by consuming the brains of other creatures. When the mind flayer servants that guard and tend to an elder brain don't bring its meals directly to it, the elder brain reaches out with tendrils of thought, mentally compelling creatures to come to it so that it may feed upon them.

When a mind flayer perishes, the elder brain's servants feed the contents of its skull to their master, which absorbs the illithid's brain and all the knowledge and experience contained therein. In this way the elder brain continually increases its knowledge, uniting the thoughts and experiences of the illithid colony into a unified whole. Mind flayers conceive of this "oneness" as a sacred state in the same way that a worshiper of a human deity might view an eternal afterlife in the heavens—for an elder brain can evoke the persona of any illithid it has ever absorbed.

Hive Mind. Non-illithids call this creature an elder brain because it acts as the central communication hub for an entire mind flayer colony just as a brain does for a living body. Linked to the elder brain, the colony acts like a single organism, acting in concert as if each illithid were the digit of a hand.

Ego Unhindered. Each elder brain considers itself and its desires the most important things in the multiverse, the mind flayers in its colony nothing more than extensions of its will. But no two elder brains are alike, and each presides over its colony according to its own unique personality and storehouse of collected knowledge and experience. Some elder brains reign as domineering tyrants, while others serve more benignly as sages, counselors, and repositories of information and lore for the mind flayers that protect and nourish them.

The ambitions of an elder brain are always tempered by its relative immobility. Although its telepathic senses can reach for miles, moving anywhere is always a dangerous proposition. If forced outside its brine pool, an elder brain will swiftly expire, and transporting an elder brain in its pool through confining and tortuous subterranean tunnels frequently proves difficult or impossible.

AN ELDER BRAIN'S LAIR

The lair of an elder brain always lies deep in the heart of a mind flayer colony. The creature dwells in a dimly glowing brine pool, filled with foul and brackish water infused with the elder brain's vital fluids and with psionic energy.

LAIR ACTIONS

When fighting inside its lair, an elder brain can use lair actions. On initiative count 20 (losing initiative ties), an elder brain can take one lair action to cause one of the following effects; the elder brain can't use the same lair action two rounds in a row:

- The elder brain casts *wall of force*.
- The elder brain targets one friendly creature it can sense within 120 feet of it. The target has a flash of inspiration and gains advantage on one attack roll, ability check, or saving throw it makes before the end of its next turn. If the target doesn't or can't use this benefit in that time, the inspiration is lost.
- The elder brain targets one creature it can sense within 120 feet of it and anchors it by sheer force of will. The target must succeed on a DC 18 Charisma saving throw or be unable to leave its current space. It can repeat the saving throw at the end of each of its turns, ending the effect on itself on a success.

REGIONAL EFFECTS

The territory within 5 miles of an elder brain is altered by the creature's psionic presence, which creates one or more of the following effects:

- Creatures within 5 miles of an elder brain feel as if they are being followed, even when they are not.
- The elder brain can overhear any telepathic conversation happening within 5 miles of it. The creature that initiated the telepathic conversation makes a DC 18 Wisdom (Insight) check when telepathic contact is first established. If the check succeeds, the creature is aware that something is eavesdropping on the conversation. The nature of the eavesdropper isn't revealed, and the elder brain can't participate in the telepathic conversation unless it has formed a psychic link with the creature that initiated it.
- Any creature with which the elder brain has formed a psychic link hears faint, incomprehensible whispers in the deepest recesses of its mind. This psychic detritus consists of the elder brain's stray thoughts commingled with those of other creatures to which it is linked.

If the elder brain dies, these effects immediately end.

ELDER BRAIN

Large aberration, lawful evil

Armor Class 10
Hit Points 210 (20d10 + 100)
Speed 5 ft., swim 10 ft.

STR	DEX	CON	INT	WIS	CHA
15 (+2)	10 (+0)	20 (+5)	21 (+5)	19 (+4)	24 (+7)

Saving Throws Int +10, Wis +9, Cha +12
Skills Arcana +10, Deception +12, Insight +14, Intimidation +12, Persuasion +12
Senses blindsight 120 ft., passive Perception 14
Languages understands Common, Deep Speech, and Undercommon but can't speak, telepathy 5 miles
Challenge 14 (11,500 XP)

Creature Sense. The elder brain is aware of the presence of creatures within 5 miles of it that have an Intelligence score of 4 or higher. It knows the distance and direction to each creature, as well as each one's Intelligence score, but can't sense anything else about it. A creature protected by a *mind blank* spell, a *nondetection* spell, or similar magic can't be perceived in this manner.

Innate Spellcasting (Psionics). The elder brain's innate spellcasting ability is Intelligence (spell save DC 18). It can innately cast the following spells, requiring no components:

At will: *detect thoughts, levitate*
1/day each: *dominate monster, plane shift* (self only)

Legendary Resistance (3/Day). If the elder brain fails a saving throw, it can choose to succeed instead.

Magic Resistance. The elder brain has advantage on saving throws against spells and other magical effects.

Telepathic Hub. The elder brain can use its telepathy to initiate and maintain telepathic conversations with up to ten creatures at a time. The elder brain can let those creatures telepathically hear each other while connected in this way.

ACTIONS

Tentacle. *Melee Weapon Attack:* +7 to hit, reach 30 ft., one target. *Hit:* 20 (4d8 + 2) bludgeoning damage. If the target is a Huge or smaller creature, it is grappled (escape DC 15) and takes 9 (1d8 + 5) psychic damage at the start of each of its turns until the grapple ends. The elder brain can have up to four targets grappled at a time.

Mind Blast (Recharge 5–6). The elder brain magically emits psychic energy. Creatures of the elder brain's choice within 60 feet of it must succeed on a DC 18 Intelligence saving throw or take 32 (5d10 + 5) psychic damage and be stunned for 1 minute. A target can repeat the saving throw at the end of each of its turns, ending the effect on itself on a success.

Psychic Link. The elder brain targets one incapacitated creature it can perceive with its Creature Sense trait and establishes a psychic link with that creature. Until the psychic link ends, the elder brain can perceive everything the target senses. The target becomes aware that something is linked to its mind once it is no longer incapacitated, and the elder brain can terminate the link at any time (no action required). The target can use an action on its turn to attempt to break the psychic link, doing so with a successful DC 18 Charisma saving throw. On a successful save, the target takes 10 (3d6) psychic damage. The psychic link also ends if the target and the elder brain are more than 5 miles apart, with no consequences to the target. The elder brain can form psychic links with up to ten creatures at a time.

Sense Thoughts. The elder brain targets a creature with which it has a psychic link. The elder brain gains insight into the target's reasoning, its emotional state, and thoughts that loom large in its mind (including things the target worries about, loves, or hates). The elder brain can also make a Charisma (Deception) check with advantage to deceive the target's mind into thinking it believes one idea or feels a particular emotion. The target contests this attempt with a Wisdom (Insight) check. If the elder brain succeeds, the mind believes the deception for 1 hour or until evidence of the lie is presented to the target.

LEGENDARY ACTIONS

The elder brain can take 3 legendary actions, choosing from the options below. It can take only one legendary action at a time and only at the end of another creature's turn. The elder brain regains spent legendary actions at the start of its turn.

Tentacle. The elder brain makes a tentacle attack.
Break Concentration. The elder brain targets a creature within 120 feet of it with which it has a psychic link. The elder brain breaks the creature's concentration on a spell it has cast. The creature also takes 1d4 psychic damage per level of the spell.
Psychic Pulse. The elder brain targets a creature within 120 feet of it with which it has a psychic link. Enemies of the elder brain within 10 feet of that creature take 10 (3d6) psychic damage.
Sever Psychic Link. The elder brain targets a creature within 120 feet of it with which it has a psychic link. The elder brain ends the link, causing the creature to have disadvantage on all ability checks, attack rolls, and saving throws until the end of the creature's next turn.

ULITHARID

Large aberration, lawful evil

Armor Class 15 (breastplate)
Hit Points 127 (17d10 + 34)
Speed 30 ft.

STR	DEX	CON	INT	WIS	CHA
15 (+2)	12 (+1)	15 (+2)	21 (+5)	19 (+4)	21 (+5)

Saving Throws Int +9, Wis +8, Cha +9
Skills Arcana +9, Insight +8, Perception +8, Stealth +5
Senses darkvision 120 ft., passive Perception 18
Languages Deep Speech, Undercommon, telepathy 2 miles
Challenge 9 (5,000 XP)

Creature Sense. The ulitharid is aware of the presence of creatures within 2 miles of it that have an Intelligence score of 4 or higher. It knows the distance and direction to each creature, as well as each creature's Intelligence score, but can't sense anything else about it. A creature protected by a *mind blank* spell, a *nondetection* spell, or similar magic can't be perceived in this manner.

Magic Resistance. The ulitharid has advantage on saving throws against spells and other magical effects.

Psionic Hub. If an elder brain establishes a psychic link with the ulitharid, the elder brain can form a psychic link with any other creature the ulitharid can detect using its Creature Sense. Any such link ends if the creature falls outside the telepathy ranges of both the ulitharid and the elder brain. The ulitharid can maintain its psychic link with the elder brain regardless of the distance between them, so long as they are both on the same plane of existence. If the ulitharid is more than 5 miles away from the elder brain, it can end the psychic link at any time (no action required).

Innate Spellcasting (Psionics). The ulitharid's innate spellcasting ability is Intelligence (spell save DC 17). It can innately cast the following spells, requiring no components:

At will: *detect thoughts, levitate*
1/day each: *confusion, dominate monster, eyebite, feeblemind, mass suggestion, plane shift* (self only), *project image, scrying, telekinesis*

ACTIONS

Tentacles. *Melee Weapon Attack:* +9 to hit, reach 10 ft., one creature. *Hit:* 27 (4d10 + 5) psychic damage. If the target is Large or smaller, it is grappled (escape DC 14) and must succeed on a DC 17 Intelligence saving throw or be stunned until this grapple ends.

Extract Brain. *Melee Weapon Attack:* +9 to hit, reach 5 ft., one incapacitated humanoid grappled by the ulitharid. *Hit:* 55 (10d10) piercing damage. If this damage reduces the target to 0 hit points, the ulitharid kills the target by extracting and devouring its brain.

Mind Blast (Recharge 5–6). The ulitharid magically emits psychic energy in a 60-foot cone. Each creature in that area must succeed on a DC 17 Intelligence saving throw or take 31 (4d12 + 5) psychic damage and be stunned for 1 minute. A target can repeat the saving throw at the end of each of its turns, ending the effect on itself on a success.

ULITHARID

Very rarely, a tadpole from an elder brain's brine pool transforms an individual into an ulitharid, a larger and more potent mind flayer that boasts six tentacles.

Master Minds. Illithids innately recognize that an ulitharid's survival is more important than their own. An elder brain's reaction to the rise of an ulitharid varies. In most colonies, the ulitharid becomes an elder brain's most favored servant, invested with power and authority. In others, the elder brain perceives an ulitharid as a potential rival for power, and it manipulates or quashes the ulitharid's ambitions accordingly.

Birth of a Colony. When an ulitharid finds sharing leadership with an elder brain to be insufferable, it breaks off from the colony, taking a group of mind flayers with it, and moves to another location to form a new colony. After the death of the ulitharid's body, mind flayers take its brain and place it in a brine pool, where it grows into an elder brain over a few days. This process doesn't work on the brain of an ulitharid that dies a natural death, as a brain that succumbs to old age is too decrepit to be used in the creation of an elder brain.

Extractor Staff. Each ulitharid carries a psionically enhanced staff made of black metal. When the ulitharid is ready to give up its life, it attaches the staff to the back of its head, and the staff cracks open its skull and peels it apart, enabling its brain to be extracted. The brain and the staff are then planted in the ulitharid's corpse, causing it to dissolve into ichor. This psionically potent slime helps to fuel the transformation of the area into a brine pool that surrounds an embryonic elder brain.

Mindwitness

If the beholder can be stunned and brought safely to the brine pool of the elder brain, it can be converted through ceremorphosis into a mindwitness. The process of ceremorphosis transforms four of the beholder's eyestalks into tentacles similar to those of a mind flayer, and alters some of the beholder's eye rays.

Less intelligent than beholders and less liable to endanger the colony, mindwitnesses are psionically imprinted with devotion to the elder brain and submission to illithid commands, making them almost as obedient as intellect devourers.

Telepathic Hub. The primary function of a mindwitness is to improve telepathic communication in a mind flayer colony. A creature in telepathic communication with a mindwitness can converse telepathically through it to as many as seven other creatures the mindwitness can see, allowing the rapid spread of commands and other information.

Solitary Seekers. If separated from its illithid masters, a mindwitness seeks out other telepathic creatures to tell it what to do. Mindwitnesses have been known to ally with flumphs and telepathic planar beings such as demons, shifting their worldview and changing their alignment to match that of their new masters.

Mindwitness
Large aberration, lawful evil

Armor Class 15 (natural armor)
Hit Points 75 (10d10 + 20)
Speed 0 ft., fly 20 ft. (hover)

STR	DEX	CON	INT	WIS	CHA
10 (+0)	14 (+2)	14 (+2)	15 (+2)	15 (+2)	10 (+0)

Saving Throws Int +5, Wis +5
Skills Perception +8
Condition Immunities prone
Senses darkvision 120 ft., passive Perception 18
Languages Deep Speech, Undercommon, telepathy 600 ft.
Challenge 5 (1,800 XP)

Telepathic Hub. When the mindwitness receives a telepathic message, it can telepathically share that message with up to seven other creatures within 600 feet of it that it can see.

Actions

Multiattack. The mindwitness makes two attacks: one with its tentacles and one with its bite.

Bite. *Melee Weapon Attack:* +5 to hit, reach 5 ft., one creature. *Hit:* 16 (4d6 + 2) piercing damage.

Tentacles. *Melee Weapon Attack:* +5 to hit, reach 5 ft., one creature. *Hit:* 20 (4d8 + 2) psychic damage. If the target is Large or smaller, it is grappled (escape DC 13) and must succeed on a DC 13 Intelligence saving throw or be stunned until this grapple ends.

Eye Rays. The mindwitness shoots three of the following magical eye rays at random (reroll duplicates), choosing one to three targets it can see within 120 feet of it:

1. *Aversion Ray.* The targeted creature must make a DC 13 Charisma saving throw. On a failed save, the target has disadvantage on attack rolls for 1 minute. The target can repeat the saving throw at the end of each of its turns, ending the effect on itself on a success.

2. *Fear Ray.* The targeted creature must succeed on a DC 13 Wisdom saving throw or be frightened for 1 minute. The target can repeat the saving throw at the end of each of its turns, ending the effect on itself on a success.

3. *Psychic Ray.* The target must succeed on a DC 13 Intelligence saving throw or take 27 (6d8) psychic damage.

4. *Slowing Ray.* The targeted creature must make a DC 13 Dexterity saving throw. On a failed save, the target's speed is halved for 1 minute. In addition, the creature can't take reactions, and it can take either an action or a bonus action on its turn but not both. The creature can repeat the saving throw at the end of each of its turns, ending the effect on itself on a success.

5. *Stunning Ray.* The targeted creature must succeed on a DC 13 Constitution saving throw or be stunned for 1 minute. The target can repeat the saving throw at the start of each of its turns, ending the effect on itself on a success.

6. *Telekinetic Ray.* If the target is a creature, it must make a DC 13 Strength saving throw. On a failed save, the mindwitness moves it up to 30 feet in any direction, and it is restrained by the ray's telekinetic grip until the start of the mindwitness's next turn or until the mindwitness is incapacitated.

If the target is an object weighing 300 pounds or less that isn't being worn or carried, it is telekinetically moved up to 30 feet in any direction. The mindwitness can also exert fine control on objects with this ray, such as manipulating a simple tool or opening a door or a container.

MORKOTH

Ancient and devious, morkoths are voracious collectors. Each one travels the planes, amassing the valuables, oddities, and castoffs of the multiverse to make its collection ever more complete.

Collectors of everything odd, unusual, and valuable—hopefully not including you.
—Volo

Spawned by a God. Long ago, a deity of greed and strife perished in the battles among the immortals. Its body drifted through the Astral Plane, eventually becoming a petrified husk. This corpse floated up against a pearlescent remnant of celestial matter imbued with life and life-giving magic. The collision shattered both objects and released a storm of chaotic energy. Countless islands of mixed matter spun away into the silvery void. Within some of them, a vein of pearl-like material held a bit of the deity's rejuvenated supernatural vitality, which spontaneously created a habitable environment. On those same islands, bits of the god's petrified flesh came back to life, in the form of tentacled monstrosities brimming with malice and greed. Ever since that time, each morkoth has had an extraplanar island to call home.

No Rhyme or Reason. A morkoth's island has the qualities of a dreamscape in which nature and predictability take a back seat to strangeness and chaos. Upon it is a jumble of objects and a mixture of creatures, some of which date from forgotten times. An island might have natural-looking illumination, but most are shrouded in twilight, and on any of them, mists and shadows can appear without notice. The environment is warm and wet, a subtropical or tropical climate that keeps the morkoth and its "guests" comfortable.

The pearly matter inside an island enables it to glide on planar currents, maintains the island's environment, and keeps the place safe from harmful external effects. A morkoth's island might be found anywhere from the bottom of the ocean to the void of the Astral Plane. One could float in the skies of Avernus in the Nine Hells without being destroyed and without causing harm to its residents. Whatever is on or within a certain distance of a morkoth's isle travels with it in its journey through the planes. Thus, people from lost civilizations and creatures or objects from bygone ages might be found within a morkoth's dominion.

Some islands travel a specific route, arriving at the same destinations regularly over a cycle of years. Others are tied to a particular place or group of locales, and still others move erratically through the cosmos. Rarely, a morkoth learns to control its island's movement, so the island goes wherever its master wishes.

Primeval Hoarders. Morkoths are driven by greed and selfishness, mixed with a yearning for conflict. They desire anything they don't possess, have no scruples about taking what they crave, and endeavor to keep everything they collect.

A morkoth spends its time watching over its collection and plotting to acquire more possessions. The monster hoards vast stores of treasure and knowledge. Its island holds numerous captives, which it considers part of its collection. Some inhabitants, such as descendants of original prisoners, might view the morkoth as a ruler or a god. A morkoth's storehouse of wealth and lore attracts would-be plunderers, of course, as well as those seeking something specific the morkoth has or knows. The creature shows no mercy to those that try to steal from it, but it can be bargained with by a visitor that offers the morkoth something it desires.

No morkoth freely gives away what it owns. Morkoths exist to acquire, and they give up possessions only if doing so helps their hoard grow.

A morkoth knows every object in its collection and can track its possessions through the planes. Someone who dares to steal from a morkoth, or breaks a deal with one, will know no rest until the morkoth is slain or all promises are kept.

A MORKOTH'S LAIR

A morkoth claims dominion over an entire island, and it also maintains a central sanctum on that isle. This lair is most often a twisted network of narrow tunnels that connect several underground chambers, although other structural forms might be incorporated. The morkoth dwells among its most prized possessions in a spacious vault at the core of the warren, where the pearly matter of the island is also located. Sections of the lair and its center might be kept dry to better protect and preserve collected objects and creatures, but most of the lair is underwater.

A morkoth encountered in its lair has a challenge rating of 12 (8,400 XP).

M

MORKOTH

Medium aberration, chaotic evil

Armor Class 17 (natural armor)
Hit Points 130 (20d8 + 40)
Speed 25 ft., swim 50 ft.

STR	DEX	CON	INT	WIS	CHA
14 (+2)	14 (+2)	14 (+2)	20 (+5)	15 (+2)	13 (+1)

Saving Throws Dex +6, Int +9, Wis +6
Skills Arcana +9, History +9, Perception +10, Stealth +6
Damage Resistances bludgeoning, piercing, and slashing from nonmagical attacks
Senses blindsight 30 ft., darkvision 120 ft., passive Perception 20
Languages telepathy 120 ft.
Challenge 11 (7,200 XP)

Amphibious. The morkoth can breathe air and water.

Spellcasting. The morkoth is an 11th-level spellcaster. Its spellcasting ability is Intelligence (save DC 17, +9 to hit with spell attacks). The morkoth has the following wizard spells prepared:

Cantrips (at will): *acid splash, mage hand, mending, ray of frost, shocking grasp*
1st level (4 slots): *detect magic, identify, shield, witch bolt*
2nd level (3 slots): *darkness, detect thoughts, shatter*
3rd level (3 slots): *dispel magic, lightning bolt, sending*
4th level (3 slots): *dimension door, Evard's black tentacles*
5th level (3 slots): *geas, scrying*
6th level (1 slot): *chain lightning*

ACTIONS

Multiattack. The morkoth makes three attacks: two with its bite and one with its tentacles or three with its bite.

Bite. *Melee Weapon Attack:* +6 to hit, reach 5 ft., one target. *Hit:* 9 (2d6 + 2) slashing damage.

Tentacles. *Melee Weapon Attack:* +6 to hit, reach 15 ft., one target. *Hit:* 15 (3d8 + 2) bludgeoning damage, and the target is grappled (escape DC 14) if it is a Large or smaller creature. Until this grapple ends, the target is restrained and takes 15 (3d8 + 2) bludgeoning damage at the start of each of the morkoth's turns, and the morkoth can't use its tentacles on another target.

Hypnosis. The morkoth projects a 30-foot cone of magical energy. Each creature in that area must make a DC 17 Wisdom saving throw. On a failed save, the creature is charmed by the morkoth for 1 minute. While charmed in this way, the target tries to get as close to the morkoth as possible, using its actions to Dash until it is within 5 feet of the morkoth. A charmed target can repeat the saving throw at the end of each of its turns and whenever it takes damage, ending the effect on itself on a success. If a creature's saving throw is successful or the effect ends for it, the creature has advantage on saving throws against the morkoth's Hypnosis for 24 hours.

REACTIONS

Spell Reflection. If the morkoth makes a successful saving throw against a spell, or a spell attack misses it, the morkoth can choose another creature (including the spellcaster) it can see within 120 feet of it. The spell targets the chosen creature instead of the morkoth. If the spell forced a saving throw, the chosen creature makes its own save. If the spell was an attack, the attack roll is rerolled against the chosen creature.

LAIR ACTIONS

When fighting inside its lair, a morkoth can invoke the ambient magic of the island to take lair actions. On initiative count 20 (losing initiative ties), the morkoth takes a lair action to cause one of the effects described below:

- The morkoth uses its Hypnosis action, originating at a point within 120 feet of itself. It doesn't need to see the effect's point of origin.
- The morkoth casts *darkness*, *dispel magic*, or *misty step*, using Intelligence as its spellcasting ability and without expending a spell slot.

REGIONAL EFFECTS

The island surrounding a morkoth's lair is warped by the creature's presence, creating the following effects:

- The morkoth is aware of any new arrival, whether an object or a creature, on its island or in its sanctum. As an action, the morkoth can locate any one creature or object on the island. Visitors to the island feel as though they are being watched, even when they aren't.
- Each time a creature that has been on the island for less than a year finishes a short or long rest, it must make a DC 10 Intelligence (Investigation) check. On a failure, the creature has misplaced one possession (chosen by the player, if the creature is that player's character). The possession remains nearby but concealed for a short time, so it can be recovered with a successful DC 15 Wisdom (Perception) check. An object that is misplaced but not recovered ends up in the morkoth's lair 1 hour later. If the creature later goes to the morkoth's lair, its lost possessions stand out in its perception and are easily recovered.
- Entrances to the morkoth's lair have an enchantment that the morkoth can activate or suppress at any time while it's in its lair and not incapacitated. Any creature within 30 feet of such an entrance and able to see it must make a DC 15 Wisdom saving throw. On a failed save, the creature feels an intense urge to use its movement on each of its turns to enter the lair and to move toward the morkoth's location (the target doesn't realize it's heading toward a creature). The target moves toward the morkoth by the most direct route. As soon as it can see the morkoth, the target can repeat the saving throw, ending the effect on itself on a success. It can also repeat the saving throw at the end of each of its turns and every time it takes damage.
- With a thought (no action required), the morkoth can initiate a change in the water within its lair that takes effect 1 minute later. The water can be as breathable and clear as air, or it can be normal water (ranging in clarity from murky to clear).

If the morkoth dies, these regional effects end immediately.

Neogi

Neogi are hateful slavers that consider most other creatures, even weaker neogi, to be servants and prey. A neogi looks like an outsize spider with an eel's neck and head. The creature can poison the body and the mind of its target, able to subjugate other beings that are otherwise physically superior.

Alien Tyrants. Neogi usually dwell in far-flung locations on the Material Plane, as well as in the Feywild, the Shadowfell, and the Astral and Ethereal Planes. They invaded the world long ago from a remote location on the Material Plane, abandoning their home to conquer and devour creatures in other realms. To meet their need to navigate great distances, the neogi first dominated and assimilated the umber hulks of another lost world. Then, with these slaves providing the physical labor, the neogi designed and built sleek vessels, some capable of traversing the planes, to carry them to their new frontiers. Some neogi groups still create and use such vehicles, which have a distinct spidery aspect.

Some neogi use magic—the result of a pact between the neogi and aberrant entities they met during their journey from their home world. These entities look like stars and embody the essence of evil. They are known by such names as Acamar, Caiphon, Gibbeth, and Hadar.

Nothing about the neogi is more unfathomable than their mentality. Because they have the power to control minds, neogi consider doing so to be entirely appropriate. Their society makes no distinction between individuals, aside from the ability that a given creature has to control others, and they don't comprehend the emotional aspects of existence that humans and similar beings experience. To a neogi, hatred is as foreign a sensation as love, and showing loyalty in the absence of authority is foolishness.

Cycle of Death and Life. A neogi lives about as long as a human, and like a human it faces physical and mental infirmity as it ages. When an individual is rendered weak by advanced age, the other neogi in the group overpower it and inject it with a special poison. The toxin transforms the old neogi into a bloated, helpless mass of flesh called a great old master. Young neogi lay their eggs atop it, and when the hatchlings emerge, they devour the great old master and one another, until only a few of the strongest newborns are left.

Hierarchy of Ownership. Surviving neogi hatchlings begin their lives under the control of adult neogi. They must learn about their society and earn a place in it, and each one starts its training by gaining mastery over a young umber hulk.

Neogi mark themselves and their slaves through the use of dyes, transformational magic, and tattoos intended to signify rank, achievements, and ownership. By these signs, each neogi can identify its betters—and it must defer to those of higher station or risk harsh punishment.

Neogi Hatchling

Tiny aberration, lawful evil

Armor Class 11
Hit Points 7 (3d4)
Speed 20 ft., climb 20 ft.

STR	DEX	CON	INT	WIS	CHA
3 (−4)	13 (+1)	10 (+0)	6 (−2)	10 (+0)	9 (−1)

Senses darkvision 60 ft., passive Perception 10
Languages —
Challenge 1/8 (25 XP)

Mental Fortitude. The hatchling has advantage on saving throws against being charmed or frightened, and magic can't put the hatchling to sleep.

Spider Climb. The hatchling can climb difficult surfaces, including upside down on ceilings, without needing to make an ability check.

Actions

Bite. *Melee Weapon Attack:* +3 to hit, reach 5 ft., one target. *Hit:* 3 (1d4 + 1) piercing damage plus 7 (2d6) poison damage, and the target must succeed on a DC 10 Constitution saving throw or become poisoned for 1 minute. A target can repeat the saving throw at the end of each of its turns, ending the effect on itself on a success.

> Damn eel-spiders want to enslave us all! And no, they don't taste good.
>
> —Volo

Neogi

Small aberration, lawful evil

Armor Class 15 (natural armor)
Hit Points 33 (6d6 + 12)
Speed 30 ft., climb 30 ft.

STR	DEX	CON	INT	WIS	CHA
6 (−2)	16 (+3)	14 (+2)	13 (+1)	12 (+1)	15 (+2)

Skills Intimidation +4, Perception +3
Senses darkvision 60 ft., passive Perception 13
Languages Common, Deep Speech, Undercommon
Challenge 3 (700 XP)

Mental Fortitude. The neogi has advantage on saving throws against being charmed or frightened, and magic can't put the neogi to sleep.

Spider Climb. The neogi can climb difficult surfaces, including upside down on ceilings, without needing to make an ability check.

Actions

Multiattack. The neogi makes two attacks: one with its bite and one with its claws.

Bite. *Melee Weapon Attack:* +5 to hit, reach 5 ft., one target. *Hit:* 6 (1d6 + 3) piercing damage plus 14 (4d6) poison damage, and the target must succeed on a DC 12 Constitution saving throw or become poisoned for 1 minute. A target can repeat the saving throw at the end of each of its turns, ending the effect on itself on a success.

Claws. *Melee Weapon Attack:* +5 to hit, reach 5 ft., one target. *Hit:* 8 (2d4 + 3) slashing damage.

Enslave (Recharges after a Short or Long Rest). The neogi targets one creature it can see within 30 feet of it. The target must succeed on a DC 14 Wisdom saving throw or be magically charmed by the neogi for 1 day, or until the neogi dies or is more than 1 mile from the target. The charmed target obeys the neogi's commands and can't take reactions, and the neogi and the target can communicate telepathically with each other at a distance of up to 1 mile. Whenever the charmed target takes damage, it can repeat the saving throw, ending the effect on itself on a success.

Outside the obligations of a servant to its master, neogi are willing to engage in any activity that profits them, and they are as devious as devils when doing so. Neogi buy and sell, but they pose a grave risk to potential patrons that might instead be easily enslaved, so their customers generally consist of desperate or evil individuals, or creatures that are formidable enough to treat with the neogi as equals. Neogi traders might set up shop in a planar bazaar, on the edge of a drow city, or near a mind flayer enclave. In other locations, the natives are more likely to join together to destroy a neogi caravan than to allow it safe conduct and trading privileges.

Neogi Master

Medium aberration, lawful evil

Armor Class 15 (natural armor)
Hit Points 71 (11d8 + 22)
Speed 30 ft., climb 30 ft.

STR	DEX	CON	INT	WIS	CHA
6 (−2)	16 (+3)	14 (+2)	16 (+3)	12 (+1)	18 (+4)

Saving Throws Wis +3
Skills Arcana +5, Deception +6, Intimidation +6, Perception +3, Persuasion +6
Senses darkvision 120 ft. (penetrates magical darkness), passive Perception 13
Languages Common, Deep Speech, Undercommon, telepathy 30 ft.
Challenge 4 (1,100 XP)

Mental Fortitude. The neogi has advantage on saving throws against being charmed or frightened, and magic can't put the neogi to sleep.

Spellcasting. The neogi is a 7th-level spellcaster. Its spellcasting ability is Charisma (spell save DC 14, +6 to hit with spell attacks). It regains its expended spell slots when it finishes a short or long rest. It knows the following warlock spells:

Cantrips (at will): *eldritch blast* (range 300 ft., +4 bonus to each damage roll), *guidance, mage hand, minor illusion, prestidigitation, vicious mockery*
1st–4th level (2 4th-level slots): *arms of Hadar, counterspell, dimension door, fear, hold person, hunger of Hadar, invisibility, unseen servant*

Spider Climb. The neogi can climb difficult surfaces, including upside down on ceilings, without needing to make an ability check.

Actions

Multiattack. The neogi makes two attacks: one with its bite and one with its claws.

Bite. *Melee Weapon Attack:* +5 to hit, reach 5 ft., one target. *Hit:* 6 (1d6 + 3) piercing damage plus 14 (4d6) poison damage, and the target must succeed on a DC 12 Constitution saving throw or become poisoned for 1 minute. A target can repeat the saving throw at the end of each of its turns, ending the effect on itself on a success.

Claws. *Melee Weapon Attack:* +5 to hit, reach 5 ft., one target. *Hit:* 8 (2d4 + 3) piercing damage.

Enslave (Recharges after a Short or Long Rest). The neogi targets one creature it can see within 30 feet of it. The target must succeed on a DC 14 Wisdom saving throw or be magically charmed by the neogi for 1 day, or until the neogi dies or is more than 1 mile from the target. The charmed target obeys the neogi's commands and can't take reactions, and the neogi and the target can communicate telepathically with each other at a distance of up to 1 mile. Whenever the charmed target takes damage, it can repeat the saving throw, ending the effect on itself on a success.

Neothelid

A slime-covered worm of immense size, a neothelid is the result of the mind flayer reproductive cycle gone horribly wrong. On rare occasions, an illithid colony collapses, typically after an external assault, and the elder brain is killed. When that happens, the colony's tadpoles are suddenly freed from their fate. They no longer serve as food, and in turn are no longer fed by their caretakers. Driven by hunger, they turn to devouring one another. Only one tadpole survives out of the thousands in the colony's pool, and it emerges as a neothelid.

Abhorrent to Illithids. Among the strongest taboos in illithid society is the idea of allowing a mature tadpole to survive without implanting it into a donor brain. Under normal circumstances, any tadpole that grows larger than a few inches in length is killed by the elder brain to be food for it or for less mature tadpoles. Any tadpole that survives beyond that state is perceived as a threat to the colony, and the mind flayers organize hunting parties to exterminate the abomination. Lacking enough intelligence to be detected by an elder brain's power to sense thoughts, neothelids warrant such precautions.

Savage Behemoth. As a feral thing, a neothelid knows nothing beyond the predatory existence it has lived so far and struggles to comprehend its new psionic abilities. Neothelids prowl subterranean passages in search of more brains to sate their constant hunger, growing ever more vicious. These creatures can spray tissue-dissolving enzymes from their tentacle ducts, reducing victims to a puddle of slime and leaving only the pulsing brain unharmed. They have no knowledge of their link to illithids, so they're just as likely to prey on mind flayers as on anything else.

Neothelid

Gargantuan aberration, chaotic evil

Armor Class 16 (natural armor)
Hit Points 325 (21d20 + 105)
Speed 30 ft.

STR	DEX	CON	INT	WIS	CHA
27 (+8)	7 (−2)	21 (+5)	3 (−4)	16 (+3)	12 (+1)

Saving Throws Int +1, Wis +8, Cha +6
Senses blindsight 120 ft., passive Perception 13
Languages —
Challenge 13 (10,000 XP)

Creature Sense. The neothelid is aware of the presence of creatures within 1 mile of it that have an Intelligence score of 4 or higher. It knows the distance and direction to each creature, as well as each creature's Intelligence score, but can't sense anything else about it. A creature protected by a *mind blank* spell, a *nondetection* spell, or similar magic can't be perceived in this manner.

Innate Spellcasting (Psionics). The neothelid's innate spellcasting ability is Wisdom (spell save DC 16). It can innately cast the following spells, requiring no components:

At will: *levitate*
1/day each: *confusion*, *feeblemind*, *telekinesis*

Magic Resistance. The neothelid has advantage on saving throws against spells and other magical effects.

Actions

Tentacles. *Melee Weapon Attack:* +13 to hit, reach 15 ft., one target. *Hit:* 21 (3d8 + 8) bludgeoning damage plus 13 (3d8) psychic damage. If the target is a Large or smaller creature, it must succeed on a DC 18 Strength saving throw or be swallowed by the neothelid. A swallowed creature is blinded and restrained, it has total cover against attacks and other effects outside the neothelid, and it takes 35 (10d6) acid damage at the start of each of the neothelid's turns.

If the neothelid takes 30 damage or more on a single turn from a creature inside it, the neothelid must succeed on a DC 18 Constitution saving throw at the end of that turn or regurgitate all swallowed creatures, which fall prone in a space within 10 feet of the neothelid. If the neothelid dies, a swallowed creature is no longer restrained by it and can escape from the corpse by using 20 feet of movement, exiting prone.

Acid Breath (Recharge 5–6). The neothelid exhales acid in a 60-foot cone. Each creature in that area must make a DC 18 Dexterity saving throw, taking 35 (10d6) acid damage on a failed save, or half as much damage on a successful one.

Nilbog

When Maglubiyet conquered the goblin gods, he intended to leave only Khurgorbaeyag alive as a harsh overseer who would keep the goblins under heel. But the goblins' pantheon included a trickster deity who was determined to get the last laugh. Although its essence was shattered by Maglubiyet, this trickster god survives in splintered form as a possessing spirit that arises when goblinoids form a host, causing disorder in the ranks unless it is appeased. Goblins have no name for this deity and dare not give it one, lest Maglubiyet use its name to ensnare and crush it as he did their other deities. They call the possessing spirit, and the goblin possessed by it, a nilbog ("goblin" spelled backward), and they revel in the fear that a nilbog sows among the ranks of the bugbears and hobgoblins in the host.

Goblins' Revenge. When goblinoids form a host, there is a chance that a goblin will become possessed by a nilbog, particularly if the goblin has been mistreated by its betters. This possession turns the goblin into a wise-cracking, impish creature fearless of reprisal. It gives the goblin strange powers that drive others to do the opposite of what they desire. Attacking a goblin possessed by a nilbog is foolhardy, and killing the creature just prompts the spirit to possess another goblin. The only way to keep a nilbog from wreaking havoc is to treat it well and give it respect and praise.

No Joking Matter. The possible presence of a nilbog in a host has given rise to a practice among goblinoids that each host include at least one goblin jester. This jester is allowed to go anywhere and do whatever it pleases. The position of jester is a much sought-after one among the goblins, because even if the jester is obviously not a nilbog, hobgoblins and bugbears indulge its manic behavior.

Nilbog

Small humanoid (goblinoid), chaotic evil

Armor Class 13 (leather armor)
Hit Points 7 (2d6)
Speed 30 ft.

STR	DEX	CON	INT	WIS	CHA
8 (−1)	14 (+2)	10 (+0)	10 (+0)	8 (−1)	15 (+2)

Skills Stealth +6
Senses darkvision 60 ft., passive Perception 9
Languages Common, Goblin
Challenge 1 (200 XP)

Innate Spellcasting. The nilbog's innate spellcasting ability is Charisma (spell save DC 12). It can innately cast the following spells, requiring no material components:

At will: *mage hand, Tasha's hideous laughter, vicious mockery*
1/day: *confusion*

Nilbogism. Any creature that attempts to damage the nilbog must first succeed on a DC 12 Charisma saving throw or be charmed until the end of the creature's next turn. A creature charmed in this way must use its action praising the nilbog.

The nilbog can't regain hit points, including through magical healing, except through its Reversal of Fortune reaction.

Nimble Escape. The nilbog can take the Disengage or Hide action as a bonus action on each of its turns.

Actions

Fool's Scepter. *Melee Weapon Attack:* +4 to hit, reach 5 ft., one target. *Hit:* 5 (1d6 + 2) bludgeoning damage.

Shortbow. *Ranged Weapon Attack:* +4 to hit, range 80/320 ft., one target. *Hit:* 5 (1d6 + 2) piercing damage.

Reactions

Reversal of Fortune. In response to another creature dealing damage to the nilbog, the nilbog reduces the damage to 0 and regains 1d6 hit points.

Nilbogism

A nilbog is an invisible spirit that possesses only goblins. Bereft of a host, the spirit has a flying speed of 30 feet and can't speak or be attacked. The only action it can take is to attempt to possess a goblin within 5 feet of it.

A goblin targeted by the spirit must succeed on a DC 15 Charisma saving throw or become possessed. While possessed by the spirit, the goblin's alignment becomes chaotic evil, its Charisma becomes 15 (unless it was already higher), and it gains the nilbog's Innate Spellcasting and Nilbogism traits, as well as its Reversal of Fortune reaction. If the save succeeds, the spirit can't possess that goblin for 24 hours. If its host is killed or the possession is ended by a spell such as *hallow, magic circle,* or *protection from evil and good*, the spirit searches for another goblin to possess. The spirit can leave its host at any time, but it won't do so willingly unless it knows there's another potential host nearby. A goblin stripped of its nilbog spirit reverts to its normal statistics and loses the traits it gained while possessed.

ORCS

To the common folk of the world, an orc is an orc. They know that any one of these savages can tear an ordinary person to pieces, so no further distinction is necessary.

Orcs know better. Different groups of orcs exist within a tribe, the actions of each dictated by the deity they pay homage to. To complement the various kinds of warriors that spill forth to ravage the countryside, each tribe has members that remain deep inside the lair, seldom if ever seeing what lies outside the darkness of their den.

In addition, orcs have special relationships with two creatures that are sometimes found in their company: the aurochs, a great bull that serves as a mount for warriors that revere Bahgtru, and the tanarukk, a demon-orc crossbreed that is so depraved and destructive that even orcs seek to kill it. The aurochs is described in appendix A. The tanarukk is described below.

ORC BLADE OF ILNEVAL

Ilneval is Gruumsh's battle captain, a devious strategist who directs Gruumsh's soldiers with boldness. Among orcs, warriors that venerate Ilneval emulate their deity. Such orcs learn to command their fellows in ways that are unpredictable but help to ensure victory.

ORC BLADE OF ILNEVAL
Medium humanoid (orc), chaotic evil

Armor Class 18 (chain mail, shield)
Hit Points 60 (8d8 + 24)
Speed 30 ft.

STR	DEX	CON	INT	WIS	CHA
17 (+3)	11 (+0)	17 (+3)	10 (+0)	12 (+1)	14 (+2)

Saving Throws Wis +3
Skills Perception +3, Insight +3, Intimidation +4
Senses darkvision 60 ft., passive Perception 13
Languages Common, Orc
Challenge 4 (1,100 XP)

Aggressive. As a bonus action, the orc can move up to its speed toward a hostile creature that it can see.

Foe Smiter of Ilneval. The orc deals an extra die of damage when it hits with a longsword attack (included in the attack).

ACTIONS

Multiattack. The orc makes two melee attacks with its longsword or two ranged attacks with its javelins. If Ilneval's Command is available to use, the orc can use it after these attacks.

Longsword. *Melee Weapon Attack:* +5 to hit, reach 5 ft., one target. *Hit:* 12 (2d8 + 3) slashing damage, or 14 (2d10 + 3) slashing damage when used with two hands.

Javelin. *Melee or Ranged Weapon Attack:* +5 to hit, reach 5 ft. or range 30/120 ft., one target. *Hit:* 6 (1d6 + 3) piercing damage.

Ilneval's Command (Recharge 4–6). Up to three allied orcs within 120 feet of this orc that can hear it can use their reactions to each make one weapon attack.

ORC CLAW OF LUTHIC
Medium humanoid (orc), chaotic evil

Armor Class 14 (hide armor)
Hit Points 45 (6d8 + 18)
Speed 30 ft.

STR	DEX	CON	INT	WIS	CHA
14 (+2)	15 (+2)	16 (+3)	10 (+0)	15 (+2)	11 (+0)

Skills Intimidation +2, Medicine +4, Survival +4
Senses darkvision 60 ft., passive Perception 12
Languages Common, Orc
Challenge 2 (450 XP)

Aggressive. As a bonus action, the orc can move up to its speed toward a hostile creature that it can see.

Spellcasting. The orc is a 5th-level spellcaster. Its spellcasting ability is Wisdom (spell save DC 12, +4 to hit with spell attacks). The orc has the following cleric spells prepared:

Cantrips (at will): *guidance, mending, resistance, thaumaturgy*
1st level (4 slots): *bane, cure wounds, guiding bolt*
2nd level (3 slots): *augury, warding bond*
3rd level (2 slots): *bestow curse, create food and water*

ACTIONS

Multiattack. The orc makes two claw attacks, or four claw attacks if it has fewer than half of its hit points remaining.

Claw. *Melee Weapon Attack:* +4 to hit, reach 5 ft., one target. *Hit:* 6 (1d8 + 2) slashing damage.

The wisest among these leaders gain Ilneval's favor and rise to become known as blades, tactical experts who advise their chief in matters of war. Blades lead from the front, wading into combat fearlessly while barking orders at lesser soldiers. A blade knows how to use orcish ferocity to best advantage, and helps the ordinary warriors to work together against their adversaries.

ORC CLAW OF LUTHIC

Luthic is Gruumsh's wife and the paragon of maternity to all orcs. She is the Cave Mother, a fierce dweller in the darkness who raises new broods of orcs to be vicious and strong. Her symbol is the cave bear, and orc females raise such bears alongside orc whelps. Females particularly attracted to Luthic grow long nails and lacquer them, learning to use these claws as weapons much as Luthic uses her own.

Orc females devoted to Luthic are in charge of fortifying and maintaining an orc stronghold. They help to guarantee the survival of the tribe, and most are skilled in the healing arts. The most powerful among Luthic's disciples are the claws of Luthic, which can use the Cave Mother's magic to heal, protect, and curse.

ORC NURTURED ONE OF YURTRUS

Medium humanoid (orc), chaotic evil

Armor Class 9
Hit Points 30 (4d8 + 12)
Speed 30 ft.

STR	DEX	CON	INT	WIS	CHA
15 (+2)	8 (−1)	16 (+3)	7 (−2)	11 (+0)	7 (−2)

Senses darkvision 60 ft., passive Perception 10
Languages Common, Orc
Challenge 1/2 (100 XP)

Aggressive. As a bonus action, the orc can move up to its speed toward a hostile creature that it can see.

Corrupted Carrier. When the orc is reduced to 0 hit points, it explodes, and any creature within 10 feet of it must make a DC 13 Constitution saving throw. On a failed save, the creature takes 14 (4d6) poison damage and becomes poisoned. On a success, the creature takes half as much damage and isn't poisoned. A creature poisoned by this effect can repeat the save at the end of each of its turn, ending the effect on itself on a success. While poisoned by this effect, a creature can't regain hit points.

Nurtured One of Yurtrus. The orc has advantage on saving throws against poison and disease.

ACTIONS

Claws. *Melee Weapon Attack:* +4 to hit, reach 5 ft., one target. *Hit:* 4 (1d4 + 2) slashing damage plus 2 (1d4) necrotic damage.

Corrupted Vengeance. The orc reduces itself to 0 hit points, triggering its Corrupted Carrier trait.

ORC HAND OF YURTRUS

Medium humanoid (orc), chaotic evil

Armor Class 12 (hide armor)
Hit Points 30 (4d8 + 12)
Speed 30 ft.

STR	DEX	CON	INT	WIS	CHA
12 (+1)	11 (+0)	16 (+3)	11 (+0)	14 (+2)	9 (−1)

Skills Arcana +2, Intimidation +1, Medicine +4, Religion +2
Senses darkvision 60 ft., passive Perception 12
Languages understands Common and Orc but can't speak
Challenge 2 (450 XP)

Aggressive. As a bonus action, the orc can move up to its speed toward a hostile creature that it can see.

Spellcasting. The orc is a 4th-level spellcaster. Its spellcasting ability is Wisdom (spell save DC 12, +4 to hit with spell attacks). It requires no verbal components to cast its spells. The orc has the following cleric spells prepared:

Cantrips (at-will): *guidance, mending, resistance, thaumaturgy*
1st level (4 slots): *bane, detect magic, inflict wounds, protection from evil and good*
2nd level (3 slots): *blindness/deafness, silence*

ACTIONS

Touch of the White Hand. *Melee Weapon Attack:* +3 to hit, reach 5 ft., one target. *Hit:* 9 (2d8) necrotic damage.

As befits followers of a god who doesn't speak, hands of Yurtrus remove their tongues to emulate their deity, for a reason similar to why an eye of Gruumsh puts out one of its eyes.

Orc Nurtured One of Yurtrus

When plague strikes a tribe, the hands of Yurtrus isolate the sick. The priests then minister to those who can be saved but not healed. The hands cultivate the sickness of these nurtured ones, turning them into instruments of defense and weapons of war. When orcs go to battle, a band of nurtured ones might charge in first—to give themselves up while softening up the enemy by spreading Yurtrus's vile blessing in its ranks.

Orc Red Fang of Shargaas

Shargaas is the orc deity of deep darkness and sneakiness, a murderous god who hates anything that lives that isn't an orc. Orcs consider Shargaas to be a divinity suited to pariahs and weaklings, all of them unfit for

---

Orc Red Fang of Shargaas

Medium humanoid (orc), chaotic evil

Armor Class 15 (studded leather)
Hit Points 52 (8d8 + 16)
Speed 30 ft.

STR	DEX	CON	INT	WIS	CHA
11 (+0)	16 (+3)	15 (+2)	9 (−1)	11 (+0)	9 (−1)

Skills Intimidation +1, Perception +2, Stealth +5
Senses darkvision 60 ft., passive Perception 12
Languages Common, Orc
Challenge 3 (700 XP)

Cunning Action. On each of its turns, the orc can use a bonus action to take the Dash, Disengage, or Hide action.

Hand of Shargaas. The orc deals an 2 extra dice of damage when it hits a target with a weapon attack (included in its attacks).

Shargaas's Sight. Magical darkness doesn't impede the orc's darkvision.

Slayer. In the first round of a combat, the orc has advantage on attack rolls against any creature that hasn't taken a turn yet. If the orc hits a creature that round who was surprised, the hit is automatically a critical hit.

Actions

Multiattack. The orc makes two scimitar or dart attacks.

Scimitar. *Melee Weapon Attack:* +5 to hit, reach 5 ft., one target. *Hit:* 13 (3d6 + 3) slashing damage.

Dart. *Ranged Weapon Attack:* +5 to hit, range 20/60 ft., one target. *Hit:* 10 (3d4 + 3) piercing damage.

Veil of Shargaas (Recharges after a Short or Long Rest). The orc casts *darkness* without any components. Wisdom is its spellcasting ability.

Orc Hand of Yurtrus

Yurtrus is the orc god of death and disease. He is a horrifying abomination covered in rot and infection, except for his perfect, smooth white hands.

Orc priests that oversee the line between life and death are known by the others in the tribe as hands of Yurtrus. They dwell on the fringes of an orc lair, usually communing with other orcs through the auspices of those who follow Luthic. The hands of Yurtrus wear pale gloves made of the bleached skin of other humanoids (preferably elves), symbolizing their connection with Yurtrus, and are sometimes called "white hands" as a result.

Every orc knows that the hands of Yurtrus are the tribe's gateway to the ancestors. Orcs who die having served the tribe well go on to rituals meant to send them to Gruumsh's realm.

through the tribe, attempting to take over by force. Most such coups fail, but at great cost to the tribe. If a tanarukk does seize the leadership of a tribe, reckless war is the course it inevitably chooses.

If a tanarukk manages to breed, its blood taints numerous subsequent generations, so its female descendants randomly produce tanarukks. Rather than risk raising a natural-born tanarukk, most tribes slay such abominations.

true roles in tribal life. These outsiders live in the most remote, deepest parts of the tribe's domain.

The elite among Shargaas's followers are the assassins and thieves that follow the cult of the Red Fang. They perform assassinations, stealthy raids, and other covert operations on the tribe's behalf. They rely on a mix of intense training and magic granted to them by Shargaas.

Most Red Fang enclaves keep and nurture giant bats, creatures that are sacred to Shargaas. Red Fangs ride these bats into battle or on secret raids and assassination missions into enemy territory.

TANARUKK

When demonic corruption taints a tribe's leadership, orcs might turn to abyssal magic to make tanarukks. Evil humans who control orcs also use such power to bolster their followers' strength.

The demon lord Baphomet gladly shares the secret of creating tanarukks with those who entreat him for power. The process corrupts an unborn orc of the tribe, transforming it at birth into a creature much more savage than an orc.

Although tanarukks are fearsome fighters, they are a threat to their allies off the battlefield. Within the tribe's lair, a tanarukk is destructive and volatile, and best kept imprisoned. Sooner or later, a free tanarukk rampages

TANARUKK
Medium fiend (demon, orc), chaotic evil

Armor Class 14 (natural armor)
Hit Points 95 (10d8 + 50)
Speed 30 ft.

STR	DEX	CON	INT	WIS	CHA
18 (+4)	13 (+1)	20 (+5)	9 (−1)	9 (−1)	9 (−1)

Skills Intimidation +2, Perception +2
Damage Resistances fire, poison
Senses darkvision 60 ft., passive Perception 12
Languages Abyssal, Common, Orc
Challenge 5 (1,800 XP)

Aggressive. As a bonus action, the tanarukk can move up to its speed toward a hostile creature that it can see.

Magic Resistance. The tanarukk has advantage on saving throws against spells and other magical effects.

ACTIONS

Multiattack. The tanarukk makes two attacks: one with its bite and one with its greatsword.

Bite. *Melee Weapon Attack:* +7 to hit, reach 5 ft., one target. *Hit:* 8 (1d8 + 4) piercing damage.

Greatsword. *Melee Weapon Attack:* +7 to hit, reach 5 ft., one target. *Hit:* 11 (2d6 + 4) slashing damage.

REACTIONS

Unbridled Fury. In response to being hit by a melee attack, the tanarukk can make one melee weapon attack with advantage against the attacker.

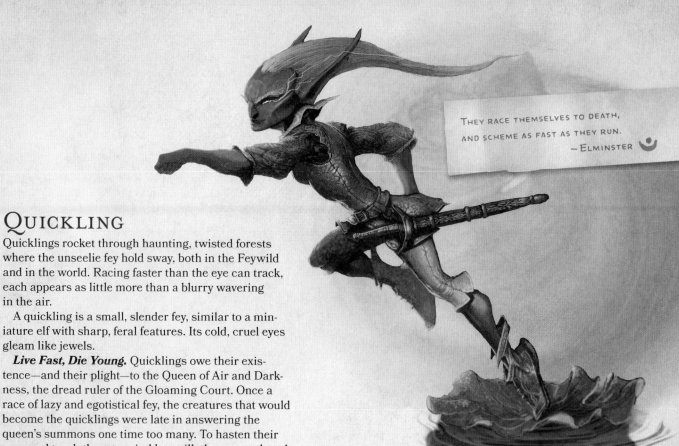

QUICKLING

Quicklings rocket through haunting, twisted forests where the unseelie fey hold sway, both in the Feywild and in the world. Racing faster than the eye can track, each appears as little more than a blurry wavering in the air.

A quickling is a small, slender fey, similar to a miniature elf with sharp, feral features. Its cold, cruel eyes gleam like jewels.

Live Fast, Die Young. Quicklings owe their existence—and their plight—to the Queen of Air and Darkness, the dread ruler of the Gloaming Court. Once a race of lazy and egotistical fey, the creatures that would become the quicklings were late in answering the queen's summons one time too many. To hasten their pace and teach them to mind her will, the queen shrank their stature and sped up their internal clocks. The queen's curse gave quicklings their amazing speed but also accelerated their passage through life—no quickling lives longer than fifteen years.

Too Fast for Words. The mortal realm is a ponderous place to a quickling's eye: a hurricane creeps gradually across the sky, a torrent of rain drifts earthward like lazy snowflakes, lightning crawls in a meandering path from cloud to cloud. The slow and boring world seems to be populated by torpid creatures whose deep, mooing speech lacks meaning.

To other creatures, a quickling seems blindingly fast, vanishing into an indistinct blur as it moves. Its cruel laughter is a burst of rapid staccato sounds, its speech a shrill squeal. Only when a quickling deliberately slows down, which it prefers not to do, can other beings properly see, hear, and comprehend it. Never truly at rest, a "stationary" quickling constantly paces and shifts in place, as though it can't wait to be off again.

Mischief, Not Murder. Quicklings have a capricious nature that goes well with their energy level: they think as fast as they run, and they are always up to something. A quickling spends most of its time perpetrating acts of mischief on slower creatures. One rarely passes up an opportunity to tie a person's bootlaces together, move the stool a creature is about to sit on, or unbuckle a saddle while no one's looking.

Tricks of that sort are hardly the limit of their artful malice, however. They don't commit outright murder, but quicklings can ruin lives in plenty of other ways: stealing an important letter, swiping coins collected for the poor, planting a stolen item in someone's bag. Quicklings enjoy causing suffering that transcends mere mischief, especially when the blame for their actions falls on other creatures and creates discord.

QUICKLING
Tiny fey, chaotic evil

Armor Class 16
Hit Points 10 (3d4 + 3)
Speed 120 ft.

STR	DEX	CON	INT	WIS	CHA
4 (−3)	23 (+6)	13 (+1)	10 (+0)	12 (+1)	7 (−2)

Skills Acrobatics +8, Sleight of Hand +8, Stealth +8, Perception +5
Senses darkvision 60 ft., passive Perception 15
Languages Common, Sylvan
Challenge 1 (200 XP)

Blurred Movement. Attack rolls against the quickling have disadvantage unless the quickling is incapacitated or restrained.

Evasion. If the quickling is subjected to an effect that allows it to make a Dexterity saving throw to take only half damage, it instead takes no damage if it succeeds on the saving throw, and only half damage if it fails.

ACTIONS

Multiattack. The quickling makes three dagger attacks.

Dagger. *Melee or Ranged Weapon Attack:* +8 to hit, reach 5 ft. or range 20/60 ft., one target. *Hit:* 8 (1d4 + 6) piercing damage.

REDCAP

A redcap is a homicidal fey creature born of blood lust. Redcaps, although small, have formidable strength, which they use to hunt and kill without hesitation or regret.

Blood Lust Personified. In the Feywild, or where that plane touches the world at a fey crossing, if a sentient creature acts on an intense desire for bloodshed, one or more redcaps might appear where the blood of a slain person soaks the ground. At first, new redcaps look like tiny bloodstained mushrooms just pushing their caps out of the soil. When moonlight shines on one of these caps, a creature that looks like a wizened and undersized gnome with a hunched back and a sinewy frame springs from the earth. The creature has a pointed leather cap, pants of similar material, heavy iron boots, and a heavy bladed weapon. From the moment it awakens, a redcap desires only murder and carnage, and it sets out to satisfy these cravings.

Redcaps lack subtlety. They live for direct confrontation and the mayhem of mortal combat. Even if a redcap wanted to be stealthy, its iron boots force it to take ponderous, thunderous steps. When a redcap is near to potential prey, though, it can close the distance quickly and get in a vicious swing of its weapon before the target can react.

Steeped in Slaughter. To sustain its unnatural existence, a redcap has to soak its hat in the fresh blood of its victims. When a redcap is born, its hat is coated with wet blood, and it knows that if the blood isn't replenished at least once every three days, the redcap vanishes as if it had never been. A redcap's desire to slay is rooted in its will to survive.

Bloodthirsty Mercenaries. Redcaps don't usually operate in groups, but in some circumstances they might be fond in the employ of hags and dark mages that know methods to call redcaps out of the Feywild and put them to work as grisly servants.

Also, some redcaps can sense the being whose murderous acts led to their birth. A redcap might use this innate connection to find its creator and make that creature its first victim. Others seek out their maker to enjoy proximity to a kindred spirit. An individual responsible for the creation of multiple redcaps at the same site could attract the entire group to serve as cohorts, emulating that creature's murderous handiwork.

In any case, if a redcap works with another being, the redcap demands to be paid in victims. A patron who tries to stifle a redcap's natural and necessary urge for blood risks becoming the redcap's next target.

As subtle as a
flung battleaxe.
—Volo

REDCAP

Small fey, chaotic evil

Armor Class 13 (natural armor)
Hit Points 45 (6d6 + 24)
Speed 25 ft.

STR	DEX	CON	INT	WIS	CHA
18 (+4)	13 (+1)	18 (+4)	10 (+0)	12 (+1)	9 (−1)

Skills Athletics +6, Perception +3
Senses darkvision 60 ft., passive Perception 13
Languages Common, Sylvan
Challenge 3 (700 XP)

Iron Boots. While moving, the redcap has disadvantage on Dexterity (Stealth) checks.

Outsize Strength. While grappling, the redcap is considered to be Medium. Also, wielding a heavy weapon doesn't impose disadvantage on its attack rolls.

ACTIONS

Multiattack. The redcap makes three attacks with its wicked sickle.

Wicked Sickle. *Melee Weapon Attack:* +6 to hit, reach 5 ft., one target. *Hit:* 9 (2d4 + 4) slashing damage.

Ironbound Pursuit. The redcap moves up to its speed to a creature it can see and kicks with its iron boots. The target must succeed on a DC 14 Dexterity saving throw or take 20 (3d10 + 4) bludgeoning damage and be knocked prone.

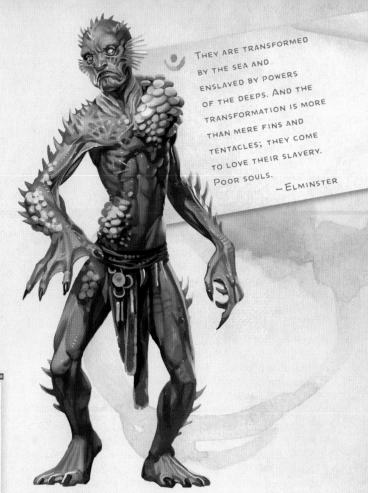

They are transformed by the sea and enslaved by powers of the deeps. And the transformation is more than mere fins and tentacles; they come to love their slavery. Poor souls.

—Elminster

SEA SPAWN

Medium humanoid, neutral evil

Armor Class 11 (natural armor)
Hit Points 32 (5d8 + 10)
Speed 20 ft., swim 30 ft.

STR	DEX	CON	INT	WIS	CHA
15 (+2)	8 (–1)	15 (+2)	6 (–2)	10 (+0)	8 (–1)

Senses darkvision 120 ft., passive Perception 10
Languages understands Aquan and Common but can't speak
Challenge 1 (200 XP)

Limited Amphibiousness. The sea spawn can breathe air and water, but needs to be submerged in the sea at least once a day for 1 minute to avoid suffocating.

ACTIONS

Multiattack. The sea spawn makes three attacks: two unarmed strikes and one with its Piscine Anatomy.

Unarmed Strike. *Melee Weapon Attack:* +4 to hit, reach 5 ft., one target. *Hit:* 4 (1d4 + 2) bludgeoning damage.

Piscine Anatomy. The sea spawn has one or more of the following attack options, provided it has the appropriate anatomy:

Bite. *Melee Weapon Attack:* +5 to hit, reach 5 ft., one target. *Hit:* 4 (1d4 + 2) piercing damage.

Poison Quills. *Melee Weapon Attack:* +5 to hit, reach 5 ft., one creature. *Hit:* 3 (1d6) poison damage, and the target must succeed on a DC 12 Constitution saving throw or be poisoned for 1 minute. The target can repeat the saving throw at the end of each of its turns, ending the effect on itself on a success.

Tentacle. *Melee Weapon Attack:* +5 to hit, reach 10 ft., one target. *Hit:* 5 (1d6 + 2) bludgeoning damage, and the target is grappled (escape DC 12) if it is a Medium or smaller creature. Until this grapple ends, the sea spawn can't use this tentacle on another target.

SEA SPAWN

Many of the stories sung as sea shanties and passed on as tales in dockside taverns tell of people lost to the sea—but not merely drowned and gone. These unfortunates are taken by the ocean and live on as sea spawn, haunting the waves like tortured reflections of their former selves. Coral encrusts them. Barnacles cling to their cold skin. Lungs that once filled with air can now breathe in water as well.

Tales provide myriad reasons for these strange transformations. "Be wary of falling in love with a sea elf or a merfolk," some say. "Return to port before a storm, no matter how tempting the catch." "Honor the sea gods as they demand, but never promise them your heart." Such cautionary tales disguise the deeper truth: things lurk beneath the waves that strive to claim the hearts and minds of land dwellers.

Deep Thralls. Krakens, morkoths, sea hags, marids, storm giants, dragon turtles—all of these sea creatures and more can mark mortals as their own and claim them as minions. Such people might become beholden to their master through a bleak bargain, or they might find themselves cursed by such creatures. Once warped into a fishlike form, the person can't leave the sea for long without courting death.

Anatomical Diversity. Sea spawn come in a wide variety of forms. An individual might have a tentacle for an arm, the jaws of a shark, a sea urchin's spines, a whale's fin, octopus eyes, seaweed hair, or any combination of such qualities. Some sea spawn have piscine body parts that provide them with special abilities beyond those of an ordinary humanoid.

Shadow Mastiff

These black hounds of the Shadowfell move invisibly through the shadows, always on the hunt. In gloomy places where the veil between the Shadowfell and the Material Plane is thinnest, they can cross over into the dark realms of the world.

Ravenous Lurkers. Shadow mastiffs hunt in packs on the Shadowfell, so when one of them enters a rift between the planes, several more are sure to follow. Each pack is led by an alpha (male or female) that is the smartest and toughest one of the group. The alpha must remain sharp to keep the rest of the pack in line, lest it be killed and replaced.

When a shadow mastiff pack is hungry and senses prey nearby, the alpha lets loose a howl that strikes fear into the hearts of nearby beasts and humanoids. Its howl is also a signal to the rest of the pack to move in for the kill. Gloom provides a shadow mastiff with supernatural protection, granting it resistance to nonmagical weapons while in dim light or darkness. Shadow mastiffs can tolerate bright light, but they shun sunlight.

Summoned for Service. Some faiths devoted to deities of gloom and night, such as Shar in the Forgotten Realms, perform unholy rites to summon shadow mastiffs from the Shadowfell and then put them to work as temple sentinels, bodyguards, and punishers of nonbelievers, heretics, and apostates. The method for bringing shadow mastiffs into the world is also known by other strong-willed and evil-minded individuals, who find use for the hounds as guards in their strongholds.

Ethereal Sight. In addition to its other capabilities, a shadow mastiff can see creatures and objects on the Ethereal Plane. This extraplanar perception makes a mastiff an especially skilled guardian, especially in situations when magical or spiritual incursion is likely.

Shadow Mastiff

Medium monstrosity, neutral evil

Armor Class 12
Hit Points 33 (6d8 + 6)
Speed 40 ft.

STR	DEX	CON	INT	WIS	CHA
16 (+3)	14 (+2)	13 (+1)	5 (−3)	12 (+1)	5 (−3)

Skills Perception +3, Stealth +6
Damage Resistances bludgeoning, piercing, and slashing from nonmagical attacks while in dim light or darkness
Senses darkvision 60 ft., passive Perception 13
Languages —
Challenge 2 (450 XP)

Ethereal Awareness. The shadow mastiff can see ethereal creatures and objects.

Keen Hearing and Smell. The shadow mastiff has advantage on Wisdom (Perception) checks that rely on hearing or smell.

Shadow Blend. While in dim light or darkness, the shadow mastiff can use a bonus action to become invisible, along with anything it is wearing or carrying. The invisibility lasts until the shadow mastiff uses a bonus action to end it or until the shadow mastiff attacks, is in bright light, or is incapacitated.

Sunlight Weakness. While in bright light created by sunlight, the shadow mastiff has disadvantage on attack rolls, ability checks, and saving throws.

Actions

Bite. *Melee Weapon Attack:* +5 to hit, reach 5 ft., one target. *Hit:* 10 (2d6 + 3) piercing damage. If the target is a creature, it must succeed on a DC 13 Strength saving throw or be knocked prone.

Shadow Mastiff Alpha

A shadow mastiff alpha has the statistics of a normal shadow mastiff, with the following modifications:

- The alpha has above average (42–54) hit points.
- It has an Intelligence of 6 (−2).
- It has the Terrifying Howl action option described below.

Terrifying Howl. The shadow mastiff howls. Any beast or humanoid within 300 feet of the mastiff and able to hear its howl must succeed on a DC 11 Wisdom saving throw or be frightened for 1 minute. A frightened target can repeat the saving throw at the end of each of its turns, ending the effect on itself on a success. If a target's saving throw is successful or the effect ends for it, the target is immune to any shadow mastiff's Terrifying Howl for the next 24 hours.

SLITHERING TRACKER

Medium ooze, chaotic evil

Armor Class 14
Hit Points 32 (5d8 + 10)
Speed 30 ft., climb 30 ft., swim 30 ft.

STR	DEX	CON	INT	WIS	CHA
16 (+3)	19 (+4)	15 (+2)	10 (+0)	14 (+2)	11 (+0)

Skills Stealth +8
Damage Vulnerabilities cold, fire
Damage Resistances bludgeoning, piercing, and slashing from nonmagical attacks
Condition Immunities blinded, deafened, exhaustion, grappled, paralyzed, petrified, prone, restrained, unconscious
Senses blindsight 120 ft., passive Perception 12
Languages understands languages it knew in its previous form but can't speak
Challenge 3 (700 XP)

Ambusher. In the first round of a combat, the slithering tracker has advantage on attack rolls against any creature it surprised.

Damage Transfer. While grappling a creature, the slithering tracker takes only half the damage dealt to it, and the creature it is grappling takes the other half.

False Appearance. While the slithering tracker remains motionless, it is indistinguishable from a puddle, unless an observer succeeds on a DC 18 Intelligence (Investigation) check.

Keen Tracker. The slithering tracker has advantage on Wisdom checks to track prey.

Liquid Form. The slithering tracker can enter an enemy's space and stop there. It can also move through a space as narrow as 1 inch wide without squeezing.

Spider Climb. The slithering tracker can climb difficult surfaces, including upside down on ceilings, without needing to make an ability check.

Watery Stealth. While underwater, the slithering tracker has advantage on Dexterity (Stealth) checks made to hide, and it can take the Hide action as a bonus action.

ACTIONS

Slam. *Melee Weapon Attack:* +5 to hit, reach 5 ft., one target. *Hit:* 8 (1d10 + 3) bludgeoning damage.

Life Leech. One Large or smaller creature that the slithering tracker can see within 5 feet of it must succeed on a DC 13 Dexterity saving throw or be grappled (escape DC 13). Until this grapple ends, the target is restrained and unable to breathe unless it can breathe water. In addition, the grappled target takes 16 (3d10) necrotic damage at the start of each of its turns. The slithering tracker can grapple only one target at a time.

SLITHERING TRACKER

The quest for revenge sometimes leads one to undergo a ritual whereby they transform into a body of semiliquid sentience known as a slithering tracker. Innocuous and insidious at the same time, a tracker flows into places where a normal creature can't go and brings its own brand of watery death down upon its quarry.

Vengeance at Any Cost. The ritual for creating a slithering tracker is known to hags, liches, and priests who worship gods of vengeance. It can only be performed on a willing creature that hungers for revenge. The ritual sucks all the moisture from the person's body, killing it. Yet the mind lives on in the puddle of liquid that issues forth from the remains, and so too does the subject's insatiable need for retribution.

Stealthy Assassins. A slithering tracker tastes the ground it courses over, seeking any trace of its prey. To kill, a slithering tracker rises up and enshrouds a creature, attempting to drown the prey while also draining it of blood. A slithering tracker that has killed in this fashion becomes much easier to locate for a time, since its liquid form becomes tinged with blood and its body leaves a visible trail of the stuff behind it.

Descent into Madness. Achieving revenge against its target doesn't end a slithering tracker's existence, nor its hunger for blood. Some slithering trackers remain aware of their purpose and extend their quest for vengeance to others, such as anyone who supported or befriended the original target. Most of the time, though, a tracker's mind can't cope with being trapped in liquid form, unable to communicate, and driven by the desire for blood: after a tracker fulfills its duty, insanity takes over the creature, and it attacks indiscriminately until it is destroyed.

SPAWN OF KYUSS

Medium undead, chaotic evil

Armor Class 10
Hit Points 76 (9d8 + 36)
Speed 30 ft.

STR	DEX	CON	INT	WIS	CHA
16 (+3)	11 (+0)	18 (+4)	5 (−3)	7 (−2)	3 (−4)

Saving Throws Wis +1
Damage Immunities poison
Condition Immunities exhaustion, poisoned
Senses darkvision 60 ft., passive Perception 8
Languages understands the languages it knew in life but can't speak
Challenge 5 (1,800 XP)

Regeneration. The spawn of Kyuss regains 10 hit points at the start of its turn if it has at least 1 hit point and isn't in sunlight or a body of running water. If the spawn takes acid, fire, or radiant damage, this trait doesn't function at the start of the spawn's next turn. The spawn is destroyed only if it starts its turn with 0 hit points and doesn't regenerate.

Worms. If the spawn of Kyuss is targeted by an effect that cures disease or removes a curse, all the worms infesting it wither away, and it loses its Burrowing Worm action.

ACTIONS

Multiattack. The spawn of Kyuss makes two attacks with its claws and uses Burrowing Worm.

Burrowing Worm. A worm launches from the spawn of Kyuss at one humanoid that the spawn can see within 10 feet of it. The worm latches onto the target's skin unless the target succeeds on a DC 11 Dexterity saving throw. The worm is a Tiny undead with AC 6, 1 hit point, a 2 (−4) in every ability score, and a speed of 1 foot. While on the target's skin, the worm can be killed by normal means or scraped off using an action (the spawn can use this action to launch a scraped-off worm at a humanoid it can see within 10 feet of the worm). Otherwise, the worm burrows under the target's skin at the end of the target's next turn, dealing 1 piercing damage to it. At the end of each of its turns thereafter, the target takes 7 (2d6) necrotic damage per worm infesting it (maximum of 10d6). A worm-infested target dies if it drops to 0 hit points, then rises 10 minutes later as a spawn of Kyuss. If a worm-infested creature is targeted by an effect that cures disease or removes a curse, all the worms infesting it wither away.

Claw. Melee Weapon Attack: +6 to hit, reach 5 ft., one target. Hit: 6 (1d6 + 3) slashing damage plus 7 (2d6) necrotic damage.

SOME WORMS ARE GOOD EATING. NOT THESE.

—ELMINSTER

SPAWN OF KYUSS

Kyuss was a high priest of Orcus who plundered corpses from necropolises to create the first spawn of Kyuss. Even centuries after Kyuss's death, his mad disciples continue performing the horrific rites he perfected.

Plague of Worms. From a distance or in poor light, a spawn of Kyuss looks like an ordinary zombie. As it comes into clearer view, one can see scores of little green worms crawling in and out of it. These worms jump onto nearby humanoids and burrow into their flesh. A worm that penetrates a humanoid body makes its way to the creature's brain. Once inside the brain, the worm kills its host and animates the corpse, transforming it into a spawn of Kyuss that breeds more worms. The dead humanoid's soul remains trapped inside the corpse, preventing the individual from being raised or resurrected until the undead body is destroyed. The horror of being a soul imprisoned in an undead body drives a spawn of Kyuss insane.

Corruption Without End. Spawn of Kyuss are expressions of Orcus's intent to replace all life with undeath. Left to its own devices, a solitary spawn of Kyuss travels aimlessly. If it stumbles across a living creature, the spawn attacks with the sole intent of creating more spawn. Whether they are dispersed or clustered, spawn reproduce exponentially if nothing stops them.

Undead Nature. Spawn of Kyuss require no air, food, drink, or sleep.

TLINCALLI

Tlincallis, also called scorpion folk, are chitin-covered creatures, humanoid from the waist up with the lower body of an enormous scorpion, complete with a stinger at the end of a long tail.

Desert Nomads. Tlincallis live austerely. They range across arid lands, hunting at dawn and dusk. In the hours between, they wait out the day's heat or the night's cold by burying themselves in loose sand or earth or, if the terrain proves too inflexible, lurking in ruins or shallow caves. A tribe of tlincallis stays in one place for only as long as the hunting is good in the immediate area, though they might visit the same way stations over and over during their wanderings. The tribe also settles down temporarily whenever it's time to lay eggs and hatch a new brood of young.

Poisonous Eggs. Tlincallis deposit their eggs in warm places out of direct sunlight, often amid a stand of cacti near their present encampment. There the eggs lie protected by hard shells coated in paralytic poison similar to that produced by their stingers. A would-be predator that dares to break an egg is defenseless against the tlincallis that come to investigate.

Horrid Kidnappers. Tlincallis eat what they kill, but they also take some of their prey alive when they have new mouths to feed. After using their stingers to paralyze victims and their spiked chains to bind them, tlincallis take these prisoners back to their encampment and tie them to cactus or rock formations. There, victims wait until the sun sets and the newly hatched young emerge from the lair to eat them alive.

Prideful Hunters. Tlincallis see themselves as great hunters. If a tlincalli tribe encounters a more powerful hunter, such as a blue dragon, the tribe's leader must decide whether the group becomes obedient to the superior hunter, moves on, or fights to the death to defeat it.

Makeshift Weapons and Objects. Tlincallis are uncivilized and don't build cities, make clothing, or mine metals. Instead, they scavenge what they need or want. They do, however, know how to melt down scavenged metal to forge crude weapons and tools.

TLINCALLI
Large monstrosity, neutral evil

Armor Class 15 (natural armor)
Hit Points 85 (10d10 + 30)
Speed 40 ft.

STR	DEX	CON	INT	WIS	CHA
16 (+3)	13 (+1)	16 (+3)	8 (−1)	12 (+1)	8 (−1)

Skills Perception +4, Stealth +4, Survival +4
Senses darkvision 60 ft., passive Perception 13
Languages Tlincalli
Challenge 5 (1,800 XP)

ACTIONS

Multiattack. The tlincalli makes two attacks: one with its longsword or spiked chain, and one with its sting.

Longsword. *Melee Weapon Attack:* +6 to hit, reach 5 ft., one target. *Hit:* 7 (1d8 + 3) slashing damage, or 8 (1d10 + 3) slashing damage if used with two hands.

Spiked Chain. *Melee Weapon Attack:* +6 to hit, reach 10 ft., one target. *Hit:* 6 (1d6 + 3) piercing damage, and the target is grappled (escape DC 11) if it is a Large or smaller creature. Until this grapple ends, the target is restrained, and the tlincalli can't use the spiked chain against another target.

Sting. *Melee Weapon Attack:* +6 to hit, reach 5 ft., one creature. *Hit:* 6 (1d6 + 3) piercing damage plus 14 (4d6) poison damage, and the target must succeed on a DC 14 Constitution saving throw or be poisoned for 1 minute. If it fails the saving throw by 5 or more, the target is also paralyzed while poisoned. The target can repeat the saving throw at the end of each of its turns, ending the effect on itself on a success.

TRAPPER

A trapper is a manta-like creature that lurks in subterranean and natural environments. It can change the color and texture of its tough, outward-facing side to help it blend in with its surroundings, while its soft, inward-facing side clings to the floor, wall, or ceiling in its hunting territory. It remains motionless as it waits for prey to come close. When a target is within its reach, it peels itself away from the surface and wraps around its prey, crushing, smothering, and then digesting it.

Versatile Camouflage. A trapper can alter the color and texture of its outer side to match its surroundings. It can blend in with any surface made of stone, earth, or wood, masking its presence to any but the most rigorous scrutiny. It can't change its texture to that of a grassy or snow-covered surface, but it can change its color to match and then conceal itself under a thin layer of vegetation or actual snow.

Stationary Hunters. A trapper needs to eat about a halfling-sized meal once a week to remain sated. It is content to stay in one place, given a steady supply of food, and thus trappers are a threat along any well-traveled dungeon corridor and on routes through the wilderness that see a lot of traffic. When prey is scarce, a trapper enters a state of hibernation that can last for months, though it is still aware when prey comes near. A trapper on the verge of starvation might defy its instincts and begin creeping along, abandoning its old territory in search of better hunting.

Beware of Leftovers. When its prey is dead, a trapper dissolves and absorbs the fleshy parts, leaving a scattering of bones, metal, treasure, and other indigestible bits in the place where the creature had been. A trapper that lurks on the floor of its hunting grounds can cover these remains with own body, making them look like irregularities in the surface. The creature might also attach itself to a wall or a ceiling close to a recent kill, effectively using the remnants as bait: a creature that stops to investigate the bones for valuables stands a good chance of becoming the trapper's next meal.

TRAPPER

Large monstrosity, unaligned

Armor Class 13 (natural armor)
Hit Points 85 (10d10 + 30)
Speed 10 ft., climb 10 ft.

STR	DEX	CON	INT	WIS	CHA
17 (+3)	10 (+0)	17 (+3)	2 (−4)	13 (+1)	4 (−3)

Skills Stealth +2
Senses blindsight 30 ft., darkvision 60 ft., passive Perception 11
Languages —
Challenge 3 (700 XP)

False Appearance. While the trapper is attached to a ceiling, floor, or wall and remains motionless, it is almost indistinguishable from an ordinary section of ceiling, floor, or wall. A creature that can see it and succeeds on a DC 20 Intelligence (Investigation) or Intelligence (Nature) check can discern its presence.

Spider Climb. The trapper can climb difficult surfaces, including upside down on ceilings, without needing to make an ability check.

ACTIONS

Smother. One Large or smaller creature within 5 feet of the trapper must succeed on a DC 14 Dexterity saving throw or be grappled (escape DC 14). Until the grapple ends, the target takes 17 (4d6 + 3) bludgeoning damage plus 3 (1d6) acid damage at the start of each of its turns. While grappled in this way, the target is restrained, blinded, and at risk of suffocating. The trapper can smother only one creature at a time.

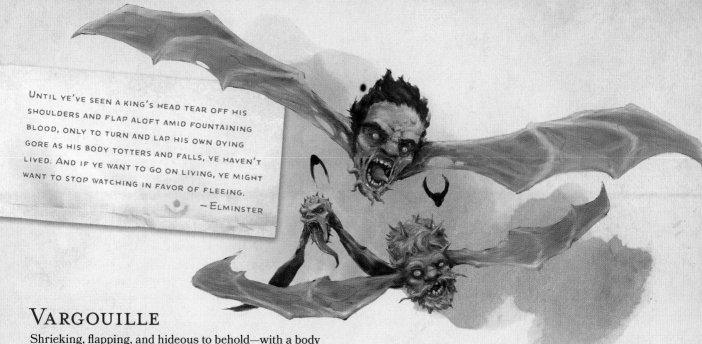

VARGOUILLE

Shrieking, flapping, and hideous to behold—with a body like a severed head and bat-like wings in place of ears—vargouilles boil out of the Abyss to infest other planes of existence, such as Carceri, where they are a menace. Each vargouille carries a disease that creates more of its kind; a flock of vargouilles on the wing is a plague of chaos and evil waiting to happen.

Abyssal Nuisances. Swarms of vargouilles flap through the caverns and skies of the Abyss. They are given little regard by powerful and intelligent demons since vargouilles can do them no harm. Even the weakest demon, such as a manes or a dretch, fears vargouilles only if they appear in great numbers. In the Lower Planes, vargouilles rarely get the chance to eat live prey other than vermin. More often, they lap up the ichor left behind when one fiend kills another.

The World Awaits. Because of their instinctive hunger for living prey, vargouilles are eager to escape the Lower Planes. On rare occasions, the summoning of a demon to another plane can bring a vargouille along for the ride, attaching itself like a tick. The precautions a mortal takes to contain and control a summoned demon rarely account for a stowaway, and thus a vargouille enters the world unbidden.

Ghastly Reproduction. Vargouilles that roam free on the Material Plane are a dire threat to all creatures, especially humanoids. Their awful shrieking can paralyze other creatures with fear, and such victims are helpless to resist a vargouille's accursed kiss.

The kiss of a vargouille infects a humanoid with a fiendish curse. If allowed to run its course, the curse brings about a gruesome transformation as an abyssal spirit invades the person's body. Over a period of hours, the victim's head takes on fiendish aspects such as fangs, tentacles, and horns. At the same time, the person's ears grow larger, expanding and transforming into wing-like appendages. In the final moments, the victim's head tears away from the body in a fountain of blood, becoming another vargouille, which often then eagerly laps up its own life fluids. Sunlight or the brilliant illumination of a *daylight* spell can delay this transformation, and vargouilles instinctively shun bright light as a result.

VARGOUILLE
Tiny fiend, chaotic evil

Armor Class 12
Hit Points 13 (3d4 + 6)
Speed 5 ft., fly 40 ft.

STR	DEX	CON	INT	WIS	CHA
6 (–2)	14 (+2)	14 (+2)	4 (–3)	7 (–2)	2 (–4)

Damage Resistances cold, fire, lightning
Damage Immunities poison
Condition Immunities poisoned
Senses darkvision 60 ft., passive Perception 8
Languages understands Abyssal, Infernal, and any languages it knew before becoming a vargouille but can't speak
Challenge 1 (200 XP)

ACTIONS

Bite. *Melee Weapon Attack:* +4 to hit, reach 5 ft., one target. *Hit:* 5 (1d6 + 2) piercing damage plus 10 (3d6) poison damage.

Kiss. The vargouille kisses one incapacitated humanoid within 5 feet of it. The target must succeed on a DC 12 Charisma saving throw or become cursed. The cursed target loses 1 point of Charisma after each hour, as its head takes on fiendish aspects. The curse doesn't advance while the target is in sunlight or the area of a *daylight* spell; don't count that time. When the cursed target's Charisma becomes 2, it dies, and its head tears from its body and becomes a new vargouille. Casting *remove curse*, *greater restoration*, or a similar spell on the target before the transformation is complete can end the curse. Doing so undoes the changes made to the target by the curse.

Stunning Shriek. The vargouille shrieks. Each humanoid and beast within 30 feet of the vargouille and able to hear it must succeed on a DC 12 Wisdom saving throw or be frightened until the end of the vargouille's next turn. While frightened in this way, a target is stunned. If a target's saving throw is successful or the effect ends for it, the target is immune to the Stunning Shriek of all vargouilles for 1 hour.

Vegepygmies

Vegepygmies are fungus creatures that live in simple tribal units, hunting for sustenance and spreading the spores from which they reproduce.

Primitive Plants. Vegepygmies, also called mold folk or moldies, inhabit dark areas that are warm and wet, so they are most commonly found underground or in dense forests where little sunlight penetrates. A vegepygmy instinctively feels kinship with other plant and fungus creatures, and thus vegepygmy tribes coexist well with creatures such as myconids, shriekers, and violet fungi.

Although they prefer to eat fresh meat, bone, and blood, vegepygmies can absorb nutrients from soil and many sorts of organic matter, meaning that they rarely go hungry. A vegepygmy can hiss and make other noises by forcing air through its mouth, but it can't speak in a conventional sense. Among themselves, vegepygmies communicate by hissing, gestures, and rhythmic tapping on the body. Vegepygmies build and craft little; any gear they have is acquired from other creatures or built by copying simple construction they have witnessed.

Russet Mold

The fungus known as russet mold is reddish-brown in color and found only in places that are dark, warm, and wet. Russet mold that spreads out across a metal object can be mistaken for natural rust, and a successful DC 15 Intelligence (Nature) or Wisdom (Survival) check is required to identify it accurately by sight in such a case.

Any creature that comes within 5 feet of russet mold must make a DC 13 Constitution saving throw as the mold emits a puff of spores. On a failed save, the creature becomes poisoned. While poisoned in this way, the creature takes 7 (2d6) poison damage at the start of each of its turns, sprouting mold as it takes damage. The creature can repeat the saving throw at the end of each of its turns, ending the effect on itself on a success. Any magic that neutralizes poison or cures disease kills the infestation. A creature reduced to 0 hit points by the mold's poison damage dies. If the dead creature is a beast, a giant, or a humanoid, one or more newborn vegepygmies emerge from its body 24 hours later: one newborn from a Small corpse, two from a Medium corpse, four from a Large corpse, eight from a Huge corpse, or sixteen from a Gargantuan corpse.

Russet mold can be hard to kill, since weapons and most types of damage do it no harm. Effects that deal acid, necrotic, or radiant damage kill 1 square foot of russet mold per 1 damage dealt. A pound of salt, a gallon of alcohol, or a magical effect that cures disease kills russet mold in a square area that is 10 feet on a side. Sunlight kills any russet mold in the light's area.

Mold Begets Mold. Vegepygmies originate from the remains left behind when a humanoid or a giant is killed by russet mold. One or more vegepygmies emerge from the corpse a day later. If a beast such as a dog or a bear dies from russet mold, the result is a bestial moldie called a thorny result instead of a humanoid-shaped vegepygmy. Thornies are less intelligent than vegepygmies, but have greater size and ferocity, as well as a thorn-covered body.

As a vegepygmy ages, it grows tougher and develops spore clusters on its body. Spore-bearing vegepygmies are deferred to by other vegepygmies, so outsiders refer to such vegepygmies as chiefs. A chief can expel its spores in a burst, infecting nearby creatures. If a creature dies while infected, its corpse produces vegepygmies the same way russet mold does.

No one knows for sure where russet mold came from. One historical account tells of adventurers in a forbidding mountain range discovering russet mold and vegepygmies in a peculiar metal dungeon full of strange life. Another story says that explorers found russet mold in a crater left by a falling star, with vegepygmies infesting the dense jungle nearby.

Vegepygmy
Small plant, neutral

Armor Class 13 (natural armor)
Hit Points 9 (2d6 + 2)
Speed 30 ft.

STR	DEX	CON	INT	WIS	CHA
7 (−2)	14 (+2)	13 (+1)	6 (−2)	11 (+0)	7 (−2)

Skills Perception +2, Stealth +4
Damage Resistances lightning, piercing
Senses darkvision 60 ft., passive Perception 12
Languages Vegepygmy
Challenge 1/4 (50 XP)

Plant Camouflage. The vegepygmy has advantage on Dexterity (Stealth) checks it makes in any terrain with ample obscuring plant life.

Regeneration. The vegepygmy regains 3 hit points at the start of its turn. If it takes cold, fire, or necrotic damage, this trait doesn't function at the start of the vegepygmy's next turn. The vegepygmy dies only if it starts its turn with 0 hit points and doesn't regenerate.

Actions

Claws. *Melee Weapon Attack:* +4 to hit, reach 5 ft., one target. *Hit:* 5 (1d6 + 2) slashing damage.

Sling. *Ranged Weapon Attack:* +4 to hit, range 30/120 ft., one target. *Hit:* 4 (1d4 + 2) bludgeoning damage.

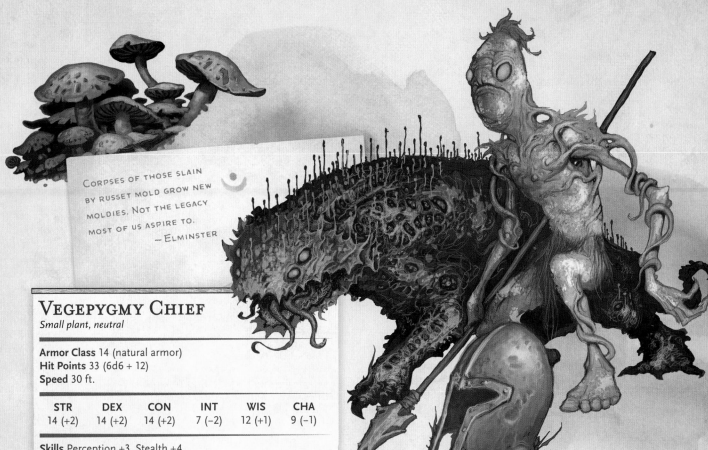

> CORPSES OF THOSE SLAIN
> BY RUSSET MOLD GROW NEW
> MOLDIES. NOT THE LEGACY
> MOST OF US ASPIRE TO.
> —ELMINSTER

VEGEPYGMY CHIEF

Small plant, neutral

Armor Class 14 (natural armor)
Hit Points 33 (6d6 + 12)
Speed 30 ft.

STR	DEX	CON	INT	WIS	CHA
14 (+2)	14 (+2)	14 (+2)	7 (–2)	12 (+1)	9 (–1)

Skills Perception +3, Stealth +4
Damage Resistances lightning, piercing
Senses darkvision 60 ft., passive Perception 13
Languages Vegepygmy
Challenge 2 (450 XP)

Plant Camouflage. The vegepygmy has advantage on Dexterity (Stealth) checks it makes in any terrain with ample obscuring plant life.

Regeneration. The vegepygmy regains 5 hit points at the start of its turn. If it takes cold, fire, or necrotic damage, this trait doesn't function at the start of the vegepygmy's next turn. The vegepygmy dies only if it starts its turn with 0 hit points and doesn't regenerate.

ACTIONS

Multiattack. The vegepygmy makes two attacks with its claws or two melee attacks with its spear.

Claws. *Melee Weapon Attack:* +4 to hit, reach 5 ft., one target. *Hit:* 5 (1d6 + 2) slashing damage.

Spear. *Melee or Ranged Weapon Attack:* +4 to hit, reach 5 ft. or range 20/60 ft., one target. *Hit:* 5 (1d6 + 2) piercing damage, or 6 (1d8 + 2) piercing damage if used with two hands to make a melee attack.

Spores (1/Day). A 15-foot-radius cloud of toxic spores extends out from the vegepygmy. The spores spread around corners. Each creature in that area that isn't a plant must succeed on a DC 12 Constitution saving throw or be poisoned. While poisoned in this way, a target takes 9 (2d8) poison damage at the start of each of its turns. A target can repeat the saving throw at the end of each of its turns, ending the effect on itself on a success.

THORNY

Medium plant, neutral

Armor Class 14 (natural armor)
Hit Points 27 (5d8 + 5)
Speed 30 ft.

STR	DEX	CON	INT	WIS	CHA
13 (+1)	12 (+1)	13 (+1)	2 (–4)	10 (+0)	6 (–2)

Skills Perception +4, Stealth +3
Damage Resistances lightning, piercing
Senses darkvision 60 ft., passive Perception 14
Languages —
Challenge 1 (200 XP)

Plant Camouflage. The thorny has advantage on Dexterity (Stealth) checks it makes in any terrain with ample obscuring plant life.

Regeneration. The thorny regains 5 hit points at the start of its turn. If it takes cold, fire, or necrotic damage, this trait doesn't function at the start of the thorny's next turn. The thorny dies only if it starts its turn with 0 hit points and doesn't regenerate.

Thorny Body. At the start of its turn, the thorny deals 2 (1d4) piercing damage to any creature grappling it.

ACTIONS

Bite. *Melee Weapon Attack:* +3 to hit, reach 5 ft., one target. *Hit:* 8 (2d6 + 1) piercing damage.

WOOD WOAD

A wood woad is a powerful plant in humanoid form invested with the soul of someone who gave up life to become an eternal guardian.

Born of Sacrifice. The ritual to create a wood woad is a primeval secret passed down through generations of savage societies and dark druid circles. Performing the ritual isn't necessarily an act of evil, if the victim-to-be has entered into a bargain that requires it to be a willing sacrifice.

In the ritual a living person's chest is pierced and the heart removed. A seed is then pushed into the heart, and it is placed in a tree. Any hollow or crook will do, but often a special cavity is carved out of the trunk. The tree is then bathed and watered with the blood of the sacrificed victim, and the body is buried among the tree's roots. After three days, a sprout emerges from the ground at the base of the tree and swiftly grows into a humanoid form.

This new body, armored in tough bark and bearing a gnarled club and shield, is at once ready to perform its duty. The one who performed the ritual sets the wood woad to its task, and the creature follows those orders unceasingly.

Pitiless Protectors. A wood woad has a hole where its heart would be, just as does the body of its former self, buried in the earth. Those who become wood woads trade their free will and all sense of sentiment for supernatural strength and a deathless duty. They exist only to protect woodlands and the people who tend them. A wood woad's face is void and expressionless, except for the motes of light that swim about in its eye sockets. Wood woads speak little, and when not being called upon to take action, they root themselves in the earth and silently take sustenance from it.

Uprooted by Immortality. Like a tree, a wood woad needs only sunlight, air, and nutrients from the earth to go on living. Because they are undying, some wood woads outlive their original purpose. The site a wood woad guards might lose its power or significance over time, or those whom it was assigned to guard might themselves die. If it is freed from its specific duties, a wood woad might roam to find another place of natural beauty or fey influence to watch over.

Wood woads are drawn to creatures that have close ties to nature, and that protect and respect the land, such as druids and treants. Some treants have wood woad servants by virtue of age-old pacts with druids or fey that performed the rituals, while others acquire the services of freed wood woads that find renewed purpose in the domain of a kindred guardian.

WOOD WOAD
Medium plant, lawful neutral

Armor Class 18 (natural armor, shield)
Hit Points 75 (10d8 + 30)
Speed 30 ft., climb 30 ft.

STR	DEX	CON	INT	WIS	CHA
18 (+4)	12 (+1)	16 (+3)	10 (+0)	13 (+1)	8 (−1)

Skills Athletics +7, Perception +4, Stealth +4
Damage Vulnerabilities fire
Damage Resistances bludgeoning, piercing
Condition Immunities charmed, frightened
Senses darkvision 60 ft., passive Perception 14
Languages Sylvan
Challenge 5 (1,800 XP)

Magic Club. In the wood woad's hand, its club is magical and deals 7 (3d4) extra damage (included in its attacks).

Plant Camouflage. The wood woad has advantage on Dexterity (Stealth) checks it makes in any terrain with ample obscuring plant life.

Regeneration. The wood woad regains 10 hit points at the start of its turn if it is in contact with the ground. If the wood woad takes fire damage, this trait doesn't function at the start of the wood woad's next turn. The wood woad dies only if it starts its turn with 0 hit points and doesn't regenerate.

Tree Stride. Once on each of its turns, the wood woad can use 10 feet of its movement to step magically into one living tree within 5 feet of it and emerge from a second living tree within 60 feet of it that it can see, appearing in an unoccupied space within 5 feet of the second tree. Both trees must be Large or bigger.

ACTIONS

Multiattack. The wood woad makes two attacks with its club.

Club. *Melee Weapon Attack:* +7 to hit, reach 5 ft., one target. *Hit:* 14 (4d4 + 4) bludgeoning damage.

Xvarts

Xvarts are cruel, cowardly humanoids spawned by a cowardly, renegade demigod. They have blue skin, vivid orange eyes, and receding hairlines, mirroring their creator's appearance. They stand about 3 feet tall.

Xvarts live in remote hills, forests, and caves. Each tribe is led by a speaker, who is usually the brightest one among them. The speaker serves as the tribe's ambassador, and often dons short wooden stilts and heavy robes to look taller and more imperious. The rest of the tribe hunts for food, plundering crops and livestock from nearby farms if the hunt goes poorly. Xvarts aren't much of a threat to civilized locations because they are somewhat fearful of humans, dwarves, and elves.

Raxivort's Betrayal. All xvarts are the degenerate offspring of an entity named Raxivort, who once served Graz'zt the Dark Prince as treasurer. Raxivort spent long centuries watching over the treasury, and in time he grew to lust after his master's riches. In one bold move, he plundered a treasure vault and fled to the Material Plane. One of the treasures he stole was the Infinity Spindle, a crystalline shard from the early days of the multiverse that could transform even a creature as low as Raxivort into a demigod.

After he ascended to godhood, Raxivort forged a realm called the Black Sewers, within Pandesmos, the topmost layer of Pandemonium. He enjoyed his divine ascension only briefly, though, before Graz'zt unleashed his vengeance. The demon prince had no need to regain the Infinity Spindle, since he already possessed power greater than what it could grant. Instead, he dispatched agents far and wide to spread news of what the spindle could do and the puny, pathetic creature that claimed its ownership. Soon enough, Raxivort was pursued by a variety of enemies, all eager to claim the Spindle as their own.

In the face of his imminent destruction, Raxivort hatched a plan. Fleeing to the Material Plane, he wandered across a variety of worlds and spawned creatures that were his exact duplicate. These are the xvarts, creatures that not only look identical to Raxivort in appearance but also foil any magic used to track him down. Spells, rituals, and other effects that could reveal Raxivort's location instead point to the nearest xvart.

Although the initial rush of enemies against him has subsided, Raxivort knows that the planar powers are patient. He remains in hiding, a wretch of a demigod who does little more than wander the planes, spawning ever more xvarts to ensure his continued safety.

Greedy Thugs. Xvarts have all of their creator's flaws and few redeeming qualities. They lack the physical equipment to reproduce, as well as the inclination to do so. They are greedy, conniving, and obsessed with the acquisition of valuables—the more ornate or bizarre, the better. They know they are flawed, and this minor amount of self-awareness only magnifies their other deficiencies. They hate almost any creature they perceive as better than they are, which includes almost anyone, but they lack the courage or wherewithal to act on their hatred most of the time. Their fear has led them to dwell either in gloomy places on the far fringes of civilized

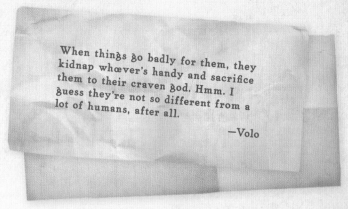

When things go badly for them, they kidnap whoever's handy and sacrifice them to their craven god. Hmm. I guess they're not so different from a lot of humans, after all.

—Volo

lands or in areas neglected or forgotten by mightier creatures. In other words, xvarts usually live in places where normal vermin might flourish.

Despite their muddled nature, all xvarts have an unshakable devotion to Raxivort. The desire to please Raxivort weighs heavily on all their decisions. When things aren't going well for them, xvarts naturally assume that Raxivort is angry. To appease their troubled lord, they stage kidnappings. They fashion nets to capture their enemies, which are dragged back to the lair and sacrificed on a makeshift altar. Raxivort can hear their supplications, but he's too afraid to come out of hiding most of the time. Occasionally, he does appear before a tribe of worshipers as a 9-foot-tall xvart carrying an empty sack. In every such instance, Raxivort takes all of the treasure that the tribe has accumulated, stuffs it in his sack, and disappears, leaving nothing behind as compensation.

Vermin Masters. Rats and bats (including giant-sized specimens) are naturally attracted to xvarts, and xvarts domesticate such beasts for food and battle. Xvarts also form alliances with wererats, although the lycanthropes are dominant in any such arrangement. This relationship traces back to Raxivort's divine nature. Even though the xvarts inherited Raxivort's greed and cowardice, they also gained his ability to form bonds with such creatures.

Xvart Warlocks. A xvart can forge a pact with Raxivort by stealing an item of such great value that the demigod himself appears before the xvart to claim it. After surrendering the item to Raxivort, the xvart asks for magical power so that it can find and deliver more great treasures into Raxivort's custody. If the demigod feels so inclined, he imbues the xvart with greater wisdom and charisma and grants it the spellcasting abilities of a warlock before returning to the howling chaos of Pandemonium. Raxivort's warlocks are respected and feared in xvart society, but they have little interest in political power. They scour the wilderness, old ruins, and dungeons for treasures, often with a handful of xvart sycophants and giant rat bodyguards in tow.

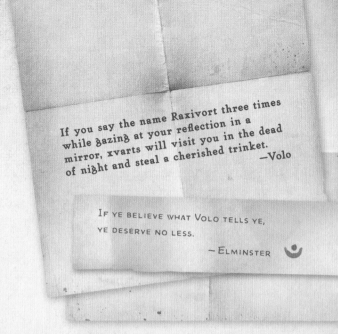

If you say the name Raxivort three times while gazing at your reflection in a mirror, xvarts will visit you in the dead of night and steal a cherished trinket. —Volo

IF YE BELIEVE WHAT VOLO TELLS YE, YE DESERVE NO LESS.

—ELMINSTER

XVART

Small humanoid (xvart), chaotic evil

Armor Class 13 (leather armor)
Hit Points 7 (2d6)
Speed 30 ft.

STR	DEX	CON	INT	WIS	CHA
8 (−1)	14 (+2)	10 (+0)	8 (−1)	7 (−2)	7 (−2)

Skills Stealth +4
Senses darkvision 30 ft., passive Perception 8
Languages Abyssal
Challenge 1/8 (25 XP)

Low Cunning. The xvart can take the Disengage action as a bonus action on each of its turns.

Overbearing Pack. The xvart has advantage on Strength (Athletics) checks to shove a creature if at least one of the xvart's allies is within 5 feet of the target and the ally isn't incapacitated.

Raxivort's Tongue. The xvart can communicate with ordinary bats and rats, as well as giant bats and giant rats.

ACTIONS

Shortsword. *Melee Weapon Attack:* +4 to hit, reach 5 ft., one target. *Hit:* 5 (1d6 + 2) piercing damage.

Sling. *Ranged Weapon Attack:* +4 to hit, range 30/120 ft., one target. *Hit:* 4 (1d4 + 2) bludgeoning damage.

XVART WARLOCK OF RAXIVORT

Small humanoid (xvart), chaotic evil

Armor Class 12 (15 with *mage armor*)
Hit Points 22 (5d6 + 5)
Speed 30 ft.

STR	DEX	CON	INT	WIS	CHA
8 (−1)	14 (+2)	12 (+1)	8 (−1)	11 (+0)	12 (+1)

Skills Stealth +3
Senses darkvision 30 ft., passive Perception 10
Languages Abyssal
Challenge 1 (200 XP)

Innate Spellcasting. The xvart's innate spellcasting ability is Charisma. It can innately cast the following spells, requiring no material components:

At will: *detect magic, mage armor* (self only)

Spellcasting. The xvart is a 3rd-level spellcaster. Its spellcasting ability is Charisma (spell save DC 11, +3 to hit with spell attacks). It regains its expended spell slots when it finishes a short or long rest. It knows the following warlock spells:

Cantrips (at will): *eldritch blast, mage hand, minor illusion, poison spray, prestidigitation*
1st–2nd level (2 2nd-level slots): *burning hands, expeditious retreat, invisibility, scorching ray*

Low Cunning. The xvart can take the Disengage action as a bonus action on each of its turns.

Raxivort's Blessing. When the xvart reduces an enemy to 0 hit points, the xvart gains 4 temporary hit points.

Raxivort's Tongue. The xvart can communicate with ordinary bats and rats, as well as giant bats and giant rats.

ACTIONS

Scimitar. *Melee Weapon Attack:* +4 to hit, reach 5 ft., one target. *Hit:* 5 (1d6 + 2) slashing damage.

Foiled by Sunlight. Yeth hounds can't stand sunlight. A pack never willingly prolongs a hunt beyond the night hours and always seeks to return to its dark den before the first rays of dawn. No amount of coercion by a pack's master can deter this behavior. If a yeth hound is exposed to natural sunlight, it fades away, vanishing into the Ethereal Plane, from where its master can retrieve it only after the sun has set.

YETH HOUND

Granted by powerful fey to individuals who please them, yeth hounds serve evil masters like hunting dogs. Yeth hounds fly in pursuit of their prey, often waiting until it is too exhausted to fight back. Only the threat of dawn drives the pack back into hiding.

Minions of a Dark Master. A pack of yeth hounds can be created by powerful fey such as the Queen of Air and Darkness. Once it is brought into existence, a pack must have a master, who is often someone the creator wishes to reward. The master can telepathically communicate with its yeth hounds to give them commands from afar. If the master of a pack is killed, the hounds seek and choose a new master, typically an individual of great evil such as a vampire, a necromancer, or a hag.

A yeth hound stands about 5 feet tall at the shoulder and weighs around 400 pounds. Often all that can be seen of one in the darkness is the red glow of its eyes against its night-black fur. The head of a yeth hound has a human-like face, held up by a neck more flexible than a dog's. The creature gives off an odor like smoke.

Sound of Looming Death. Yeth hounds make a ghastly baying sound that can be heard all around. Creatures that can see a hound when it bays are filled with supernatural fear and usually flee in terror. When a victim tries to run away, a hound delights in chasing after it and tormenting it before bringing the hunt to a close.

Those that stand their ground and fight back discover that mundane weapons partially pass through the hound as if it was made of fog, but magic weapons and silvered weapons can strike true.

YETH HOUND

Large fey, neutral evil

Armor Class 14 (natural armor)
Hit Points 51 (6d10 + 18)
Speed 40 ft., fly 40 ft. (hover)

STR	DEX	CON	INT	WIS	CHA
18 (+4)	17 (+3)	16 (+3)	5 (−3)	12 (+1)	7 (−2)

Damage Immunities bludgeoning, piercing, and slashing from nonmagical attacks not made with silvered weapons
Condition Immunities charmed, exhaustion, frightened
Senses darkvision 60 ft., passive Perception 11
Languages understands Common, Elvish, and Sylvan but can't speak
Challenge 4 (1,100 XP)

Keen Hearing and Smell. The yeth hound has advantage on Wisdom (Perception) checks that rely on hearing or smell.

Sunlight Banishment. If the yeth hound starts its turn in sunlight, it is transported to the Ethereal Plane. While sunlight shines on the spot from which it vanished, the hound must remain in the Deep Ethereal. After sunset, it returns to the Border Ethereal at the same spot, whereupon it typically sets out to find its pack or its master. The hound is visible on the Material Plane while it is in the Border Ethereal, and vice versa, but it can't affect or be affected by anything on the other plane. Once it is adjacent to its master or a pack mate that is on the Material Plane, a yeth hound in the Border Ethereal can return to the Material Plane as an action.

Telepathic Bond. While the yeth hound is on the same plane of existence as its master, it can magically convey what it senses to its master, and the two can communicate telepathically with each other.

ACTIONS

Bite. *Melee Weapon Attack:* +6 to hit, reach 5 ft., one target. *Hit:* 11 (2d6 + 4) piercing damage, plus 14 (4d6) psychic damage if the target is frightened.

Baleful Baying. The yeth hound bays magically. Every enemy within 300 feet of the hound that can hear it must succeed on a DC 13 Wisdom saving throw or be frightened until the end of the hound's next turn or until the hound is incapacitated. A frightened target that starts its turn within 30 feet of the hound must use all its movement on that turn to get as far from the hound as possible, must finish the move before taking an action, and must take the most direct route, even if hazards lie that way. A target that successfully saves is immune to the baying of all yeth hounds for the next 24 hours.

YUAN-TI

Yuan-ti malisons who become priestly devotees of a particular god—be it Sseth, Dendar the Night Serpent, or Merrshaulk—often rise through the ranks to become spiritual leaders among the serpent folk. These priests perform sacrificial rites to appease their vile gods.

Also described here are the degenerate yuan-ti brood-guard and the horrifying yuan-ti anathema.

YUAN-TI ANATHEMA

A yuan-ti abomination's quest for godhood might lead it to perform a ritual that, if successful, transforms it into an even greater form: a yuan-ti anathema. This ritual demands the sacrifice of hundreds of snakes and requires the abomination to bathe in the blood of its enemies. The transformation is quick yet painful.

Not all yuan-ti are eager to see one of their own become an anathema, since anathemas brutally subjugate their lessers for their own evil ends.

Not Quite Divine. An anathema considers itself a demigod on the path to greater divinity. It demands obeisance from weaker yuan-ti and uses every resource at

YUAN-TI ANATHEMA
Huge monstrosity (shapechanger, yuan-ti), neutral evil

Armor Class 16 (natural armor)
Hit Points 189 (18d12 + 72)
Speed 40 ft., climb 30 ft., swim 30 ft.

STR	DEX	CON	INT	WIS	CHA
23 (+6)	13 (+1)	19 (+4)	19 (+4)	17 (+3)	20 (+5)

Skills Perception +7, Stealth +5
Damage Resistances acid, fire, lightning
Damage Immunities poison
Condition Immunities poisoned
Senses blindsight 30 ft., darkvision 60 ft., passive Perception 17
Languages Abyssal, Common, Draconic
Challenge 12 (8,400 XP)

Innate Spellcasting (Anathema Form Only). The anathema's innate spellcasting ability is Charisma (spell save DC 17). It can innately cast the following spells, requiring no material components:

At will: *animal friendship* (snakes only)
3/day each: *darkness, entangle, fear, haste, suggestion, polymorph*
1/day: *divine word*

Magic Resistance. The anathema has advantage on saving throws against spells and other magical effects.

Ophidiophobia Aura. Any creature of the anathema's choice, other than a snake or a yuan-ti, that starts its turn within 30 feet of the anathema and can see or hear it must succeed on a DC 17 Wisdom saving throw or become frightened of snakes and yuan-ti. A frightened target can repeat the saving throw at the end of each of its turns, ending the effect on itself on a success. If a target's saving throw is successful or the effect ends for it, the target is immune to this aura for the next 24 hours.

Shapechanger. The anathema can use its action to polymorph into a Huge **giant constrictor snake**, or back into its true form. Its statistics are the same in each form. Any equipment it is wearing or carrying isn't transformed.

Six Heads. The anathema has advantage on Wisdom (Perception) checks and on saving throws against being blinded, charmed, deafened, frightened, stunned, or knocked unconscious.

ACTIONS

Multiattack (Anathema Form Only). The anathema makes two claw attacks, one constrict attack, and one Flurry of Bites attack.

Claw (Anathema Form Only). *Melee Weapon Attack:* +10 to hit, reach 10 ft., one target. *Hit:* 13 (2d6 + 6) slashing damage.

Constrict. *Melee Weapon Attack:* +10 to hit, reach 15 ft., one Large or smaller creature. *Hit:* 16 (3d6 + 6) bludgeoning damage plus 7 (2d6) acid damage, and the target is grappled (escape DC 16). Until this grapple ends, the target is restrained and takes 16 (3d6 + 6) bludgeoning damage plus 7 (2d6) acid damage at the start of each of its turns, and the anathema can't constrict another target.

Flurry of Bites. *Melee Weapon Attack:* +10 to hit, reach 10 ft., one creature. *Hit:* 27 (6d6 + 6) piercing damage plus 14 (4d6) poison damage.

its disposal to launch small-scale wars against its neighbors. Each conquest brings new slaves and sacrifices, as well as glory and riches, that the anathema thinks it needs to achieve true divinity.

An anathema's most loyal yuan-ti followers see it as the pinnacle of the serpentine form, an unbelievable improvement on the nearly perfect abomination. Its devoted human followers think of it as "divine flesh in a mortal body," and cultists serving an anathema tend to be more bloodthirsty and self-sacrificing in its presence.

Immortal. Anathemas don't age, allowing them to pursue their goals until the end of days. Truly powerful ones can grow to rule multiple yuan-ti cities and bring entire regions, including humanoid realms, under yuan-ti control.

YUAN-TI BROODGUARD

Broodguards are humanoids transformed by yuan-ti into simple-minded, scaly creatures that do their masters' bidding. The transformation process warps not only a subject's body but also its mind, making it instinctively obey any yuan-ti and filling it with a seething rage that rises at the sight of non-reptilian creatures.

Although broodguards have low intelligence, they are able to perform simple yet important tasks in the community, such as guarding eggs or patrolling for intruders. The yuan-ti refer to broodguards as "histachii," which means "egg-watchers."

Human No More. Most broodguards are made from human prisoners forced to consume a magical brew that renders them helpless and unable to fight off the inevitable. A human transformed into a broodguard loses all semblance of who it once was, and even its human origin is barely discernible. A broodguard is hairless and emaciated, with yellow-green, scaly skin. It has beady, bloodshot eyes and a forked tongue, and smells faintly of rotting meat. Broodguards can speak but rarely do so, preferring to use snake-like hisses and guttural noises.

YUAN-TI MIND WHISPERER

Mind whisperers are malison spellcasters that enter into a pact with the serpent god Sseth, the Sibilant Death. They use their abilities to convert others to their faith, increase their personal power, and befuddle the minds of their enemies.

A mind whisperer is elusive, manipulative, unpredictable, and willing to cheat or kill comrades and rivals alike if doing so benefits it. The worshipers of Sseth have their hands in many schemes, often plying the

---

YUAN-TI BROODGUARD

Medium humanoid (yuan-ti), neutral evil

Armor Class 14 (natural armor)
Hit Points 45 (7d8 + 14)
Speed 30 ft.

STR	DEX	CON	INT	WIS	CHA
15 (+2)	14 (+2)	14 (+2)	6 (−2)	11 (+0)	4 (−3)

Saving Throws Str +4, Dex +4, Wis +2
Skills Perception +2
Damage Immunities poison
Condition Immunities poisoned
Senses darkvision 60 ft., passive Perception 12
Languages Abyssal, Common, Draconic
Challenge 2 (450 XP)

Mental Resistance. The broodguard has advantage on saving throws against being charmed, and magic can't paralyze it.

Reckless. At the start of its turn, the broodguard can gain advantage on all melee weapon attack rolls it makes during that turn, but attack rolls against it have advantage until the start of its next turn.

ACTIONS

Multiattack. The broodguard makes three attacks: one with its bite and two with its claws.

Bite. *Melee Weapon Attack:* +4 to hit, reach 5 ft., one target. *Hit:* 6 (1d8 + 2) piercing damage.

Claws. *Melee Weapon Attack:* +4 to hit, reach 5 ft., one target. *Hit:* 5 (1d6 + 2) slashing damage.

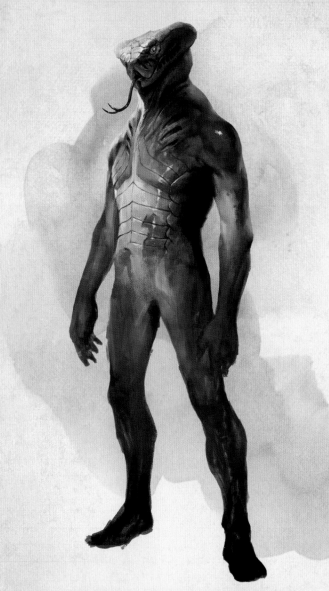

YUAN-TI MIND WHISPERER

Medium monstrosity (shapechanger, yuan-ti), neutral evil

Armor Class 14 (natural armor)
Hit Points 71 (13d8 + 13)
Speed 30 ft.

STR	DEX	CON	INT	WIS	CHA
16 (+3)	14 (+2)	13 (+1)	14 (+2)	14 (+2)	16 (+3)

Saving Throws Wis +4, Cha +5
Skills Deception +5, Stealth +4
Damage Immunities poison
Condition Immunities poisoned
Senses darkvision 120 ft. (penetrates magical darkness),
    passive Perception 12
Languages Abyssal, Common, Draconic
Challenge 4 (1,100 XP)

Shapechanger. The yuan-ti can use its action to polymorph into a Medium snake or back into its true form. Its statistics are the same in each form. Any equipment it is wearing or carrying isn't transformed. If it dies, it stays in its current form.

Innate Spellcasting (Yuan-ti Form Only). The yuan-ti's innate spellcasting ability is Charisma (spell save DC 13). The yuan-ti can innately cast the following spells, requiring no material components:

At will: *animal friendship* (snakes only)
3/day: *suggestion*

Magic Resistance. The yuan-ti has advantage on saving throws against spells and other magical effects.

Mind Fangs (2/Day). The first time the yuan-ti hits with a melee attack on its turn, it can deal an extra 16 (3d10) psychic damage to the target.

Spellcasting (Yuan-ti Form Only). The yuan-ti is a 6th-level spellcaster. Its spellcasting ability is Charisma (spell save DC 13, +5 to hit with spell attacks). It regains its expended spell slots when it finishes a short or long rest. It knows the following warlock spells:

Cantrips (at will): *eldritch blast* (range 300 ft., +3 bonus to each damage roll), *friends, message, minor illusion, poison spray, prestidigitation*
1st–3rd level (2 3rd-level slots): *charm person, crown of madness, detect thoughts, expeditious retreat, fly, hypnotic pattern, illusory script*

Sseth's Blessing. When the yuan-ti reduces an enemy to 0 hit points, the yuan-ti gains 9 temporary hit points.

ACTIONS

Multiattack (Yuan-ti Form Only). The yuan-ti makes one bite attack and one scimitar attack.

Bite. *Melee Weapon Attack:* +5 to hit, reach 5 ft., one target. *Hit:* 5 (1d4 + 3) piercing damage plus 7 (2d6) poison damage.

Scimitar (Yuan-ti Form Only). *Melee Weapon Attack:* +5 to hit, reach 5 ft., one target. *Hit:* 6 (1d6 + 3) slashing damage.

---

middle ground between two factions, and thus spend a lot of energy making sure neither of their allies learn of their conflicting connections. Even among yuan-ti, mind whisperers are known for being self-important, sneaky, and prone to flee at the first sign of trouble.

This malison is the type that has a human body and a snake head.

YUAN-TI NIGHTMARE SPEAKER

Nightmare speakers are female yuan-ti malison priests that make a pact with the Dendar the Night Serpent to feed their deity the fears and nightmares of their victims in exchange for power in the mortal world. The priestesses receive nightmarish visions from Dendar, which they interpret as prophecies, and then use their magic and influence to make these visions come true.

The cruelest of all yuan-ti, nightmare speakers revel in torturing prisoners and slaves, leaving them in a constant state of fear and dread. They prefer to terrify rather than kill their opponents. They manipulate humanoid communities for the purpose of acquiring more victims, and enjoy the company of undead.

This malison is the type that has a human head and upper body with a serpentine lower body instead of legs.

I'm the explorer who likes to travel on roads and spend my evenings in cozy inns, not hacking through jungles or trudging across deserts through blinding sand to learn the secrets of the serpent folk. I've met a few purebloods and broodguards in my day, but if I had met a yuan-ti pit master, I'm quite sure I'd not be here to tell the tale!

—Volo

YUAN-TI NIGHTMARE SPEAKER

Medium monstrosity (shapechanger, yuan-ti), neutral evil

Armor Class 14 (natural armor)
Hit Points 71 (13d8 + 13)
Speed 30 ft.

STR	DEX	CON	INT	WIS	CHA
16 (+3)	14 (+2)	13 (+1)	14 (+2)	12 (+1)	16 (+3)

Saving Throws Wis +3, Cha +5
Skills Deception +5, Stealth +4
Damage Immunities poison
Condition Immunities poisoned
Senses darkvision 120 ft. (penetrates magical darkness),
passive Perception 11
Languages Abyssal, Common, Draconic
Challenge 4 (1,100 XP)

Shapechanger. The yuan-ti can use its action to polymorph into a Medium snake or back into its true form. Its statistics are the same in each form. Any equipment it is wearing or carrying isn't transformed. If it dies, it stays in its current form.

Death Fangs (2/Day). The first time the yuan-ti hits with a melee attack on its turn, it can deal an extra 16 (3d10) necrotic damage to the target.

Innate Spellcasting (Yuan-ti Form Only). The yuan-ti's innate spellcasting ability is Charisma (spell save DC 13). The yuan-ti can innately cast the following spells, requiring no material components:

At will: *animal friendship* (snakes only)
3/day: *suggestion*

Magic Resistance. The yuan-ti has advantage on saving throws against spells and other magical effects.

Spellcasting (Yuan-ti Form Only). The yuan-ti is a 6th-level spellcaster. Its spellcasting ability is Charisma (spell save DC 13, +5 to hit with spell attacks). It regains its expended spell slots when it finishes a short or long rest. It knows the following warlock spells:

Cantrip (at will): *chill touch*, *eldritch blast* (range 300 ft., +3 bonus to each damage roll), *mage hand*, *message*, *poison spray*, *prestidigitation*
1st–3rd level (2 3rd-level slots): *arms of Hadar*, *darkness*, *fear*, *hex*, *hold person*, *hunger of Hadar*, *witch bolt*

ACTIONS

Multiattack (Yuan-ti Form Only). The yuan-ti makes one constrict attack and one scimitar attack.

Constrict. *Melee Weapon Attack:* +5 to hit, reach 10 ft., one target. *Hit:* 10 (2d6 + 3) bludgeoning damage, and the target is grappled (escape DC 14) if it is a Large or smaller creature. Until this grapple ends, the target is restrained, and the yuan-ti can't constrict another target.

Scimitar (Yuan-ti Form Only). *Melee Weapon Attack:* +5 to hit, reach 5 ft., one target. *Hit:* 6 (1d6 + 3) slashing damage.

Invoke Nightmare (Recharges after a Short or Long Rest). The yuan-ti taps into the nightmares of a creature it can see within 60 feet of it and creates an illusory, immobile manifestation of the creature's deepest fears, visible only to that creature. The target must make a DC 13 Intelligence saving throw. On a failed save, the target takes 11 (2d10) psychic damage and is frightened of the manifestation, believing it to be real. The yuan-ti must concentrate to maintain the illusion (as if concentrating on a spell), which lasts for up to 1 minute and can't be harmed. The target can repeat the saving throw at the end of each of its turns, ending the illusion on a success, or taking 11 (2d10) psychic damage on a failure.

YUAN-TI PIT MASTER

Pit masters are yuan-ti malison priests that have made a pact with the god Merrshaulk and seek to rouse him from his slumber by sacrificing humanoids to him. They are the most traditionalist in attitude among yuan-ti and believe that they are best equipped to achieve the goals of their people.

Pit masters are deeply involved in the race's long-term plan to take over humanoid governments, as well as in the ongoing effort to protect their cities from discovery or attacks by hostiles. They oppose reckless behavior and argue for a slow, cautious approach in all matters.

This malison is the type that has a human head and body and snakes for arms.

YUAN-TI PIT MASTER
Medium monstrosity (shapechanger, yuan-ti), neutral evil

Armor Class 14 (natural armor)
Hit Points 88 (16d8 + 16)
Speed 30 ft.

STR	DEX	CON	INT	WIS	CHA
16 (+3)	14 (+2)	13 (+1)	14 (+2)	12 (+1)	16 (+3)

Saving Throws Wis +3, Cha +5
Skills Deception +5, Stealth +4
Damage Immunities poison
Condition Immunities poisoned
Senses darkvision 120 ft. (penetrates magical darkness), passive Perception 11
Languages Abyssal, Common, Draconic
Challenge 5 (1,800 XP)

Shapechanger. The yuan-ti can use its action to polymorph into a Medium snake or back into its true form. Its statistics are the same in each form. Any equipment it is wearing or carrying isn't transformed. It doesn't change form if it dies.

Innate Spellcasting (Yuan-ti Form Only). The yuan-ti's innate spellcasting ability is Charisma (spell save DC 13). The yuan-ti can innately cast the following spells, requiring no material components:

At will: *animal friendship* (snakes only)
3/day: *suggestion*

Magic Resistance. The yuan-ti has advantage on saving throws against spells and other magical effects.

Poison's Disciple (2/Day). The first time the yuan-ti hits with a melee attack on its turn, it can deal an extra 16 (3d10) poison damage to the target.

Spellcasting (Yuan-ti Form Only). The yuan-ti is a 6th-level spellcaster. Its spellcasting ability is Charisma (spell save DC 13, +5 to hit with spell attacks). It regains its expended spell slots when it finishes a short or long rest. It knows the following warlock spells:

Cantrips (at will): *eldritch blast* (range 300 ft., +3 bonus to each damage roll), *friends, guidance, mage hand, message, poison spray*
1st–3rd level (2 3rd-level slots): *command, counterspell, hellish rebuke, invisibility, misty step, unseen servant, vampiric touch*

ACTIONS

Multiattack (Yuan-ti Form Only). The yuan-ti makes two bite attacks using its snake arms.

Bite. *Melee Weapon Attack:* +5 to hit, reach 5 ft., one target. *Hit:* 5 (1d4 + 3) piercing damage plus 7 (2d6) poison damage.

Merrshaulk's Slumber (1/Day). The yuan-ti targets up to five creatures that it can see within 60 feet of it. Each target must succeed on a DC 13 Constitution saving throw or fall into a magical sleep and be unconscious for 10 minutes. A sleeping target awakens if it takes damage or if someone uses an action to shake or slap it awake. This magical sleep has no effect on a creature immune to being charmed.

Appendix A: Assorted Beasts

This appendix contains statistics for various beasts, expanding on appendix A of the *Monster Manual*.

Aurochs

Bahgtru, son of Gruumsh and Luthic, is the orc deity of unbridled strength. Legend says Bahgtru needed a mount as fierce as him for making war, so he sought a mighty aurochs, subjugated the creature with his bare hands, and hauled it to Nishrek, Gruumsh's realm. Bahgtru named the beast Kazaht, or "Bull" in Orc. On Kazaht's bare back, Bahgtru charges into battle, ramming into an enemy host and leaping over the aurochs's horns to land in the midst of his foes.

Orcs that revere Bahgtru might tend a stable of war bulls that carry them into combat. Trained to be fierce mounts from a young age, aurochs are sacred symbols of Bahgtru. No orc will eat such creatures, which are treated as honored warriors when they perish.

Cattle

There are many kinds of cattle, from common oxen to more unusual, magical variants. Use the cow stat block to represent them, with the changes noted below.

AUROCHS

Aurochs

Large beast, unaligned

Armor Class 11 (natural armor)
Hit Points 38 (4d10 + 16)
Speed 50 ft.

STR	DEX	CON	INT	WIS	CHA
20 (+5)	10 (+0)	19 (+4)	2 (−4)	12 (+1)	5 (−3)

Senses passive Perception 11
Languages —
Challenge 2 (450 XP)

Charge. If the aurochs moves at least 20 feet straight toward a target and then hits it with a gore attack on the same turn, the target takes an extra 9 (2d8) piercing damage. If the target is a creature, it must succeed on a DC 15 Strength saving throw or be knocked prone.

Actions

Gore. *Melee Weapon Attack:* +7 to hit, reach 5 ft., one target. *Hit:* 14 (2d8 + 5) piercing damage.

Cow

Large beast, unaligned

Armor Class 10
Hit Points 15 (2d10 + 4)
Speed 30 ft.

STR	DEX	CON	INT	WIS	CHA
18 (+4)	10 (+0)	14 (+2)	2 (−4)	10 (+0)	4 (−3)

Senses passive Perception 10
Languages —
Challenge 1/4 (50 XP)

Charge. If the cow moves at least 20 feet straight toward a target and then hits it with a gore attack on the same turn, the target takes an extra 7 (2d6) piercing damage.

Actions

Gore. *Melee Weapon Attack:* +6 to hit, reach 5 ft., one target. *Hit:* 7 (1d6 + 4) piercing damage.

Ox

An ox is mainly used for draft work rather than meat or milk. Oxen have the following additional trait:

Beast of Burden. The oxen is considered to be a Huge animal for the purpose of determining its carrying capacity.

Rothé

Ordinary rothé resemble musk oxen and have darkvision out to a range of 30 feet.

Deep rothé are stunted Underdark variants of rothé. They are Medium instead of Large, have 13 (2d8 + 4) hit points, and communicate with each other by using magical flashing lights. They have darkvision out to a range of 60 feet and the following additional trait:

Innate Spellcasting. The deep rothé's spellcasting ability is Charisma. It can innately cast *dancing lights* at will, requiring no components.

Stench Kow

These orange and green misshapen bison are native to the Lower Planes. They have resistance to cold, fire, and poison damage, darkvision out to a range of 60 feet, and the following additional trait:

Stench. Any creature other than a stench kow that starts its turn within 5 feet of the stench kow must succeed on a DC 12 Constitution saving throw or be poisoned until the start of the creature's next turn. On a successful saving throw, the creature is immune to the stench of all stench kows for 1 hour.

Dolphin

Dolphins are clever, social marine mammals that feed on small fish and squid. An adult specimen is between 5 and 6 feet long.

DOLPHIN
Medium beast, unaligned

Armor Class 12 (natural armor)
Hit Points 11 (2d8 + 2)
Speed 0 ft., swim 60 ft.

STR	DEX	CON	INT	WIS	CHA
14 (+2)	13 (+1)	13 (+1)	6 (−2)	12 (+1)	7 (−2)

Skills Perception +3
Senses blindsight 60 ft., passive Perception 13
Languages —
Challenge 1/8 (25 XP)

Charge. If the dolphin moves at least 30 feet straight toward a target and then hits it with a slam attack on the same turn, the target takes an extra 3 (1d6) bludgeoning damage.

Hold Breath. The dolphin can hold its breath for 20 minutes.

ACTIONS

Slam. *Melee Weapon Attack:* +4 to hit, reach 5 ft., one target. *Hit:* 5 (1d6 + 2) bludgeoning damage.

Swarm of Rot Grubs

Rot grubs are finger-sized maggots that eat living or dead flesh, although they can survive on plant matter. They infest corpses and piles of decaying matter and attack living creatures that disturb them. After burrowing into the flesh of a living creature, a rot grub instinctively chews its way toward the heart in order to kill its host.

Rot grubs pose a threat both singly and as a swarm. See the accompanying stat block for the mechanics of a swarm of rot grubs. A single rot grub has no stat block. Any creature that comes into contact with it must make a DC 10 Dexterity saving throw. On a failed save, the rot grub burrows into the creature's flesh and deals 3 (1d6) piercing damage at the start of each of the host creature's turns. Applying fire to the wound before the end of the host creature's next turn deals 1 fire damage to the host and kills the infesting rot grub. After this time, the rot grub is too far under the host creature's skin to be burned. If a creature infested by one or more rot grubs ends its turn with 0 hit points, it dies as the grubs burrow into its heart and kill it. Any effect that cures disease kills all rot grubs infesting the target. Burning a body kills any rot grubs infesting it.

SWARM OF ROT GRUBS
Medium swarm of Tiny beasts, unaligned

Armor Class 8
Hit Points 22 (5d8)
Speed 5 ft., climb 5 ft.

STR	DEX	CON	INT	WIS	CHA
2 (−4)	7 (−2)	10 (+0)	1 (−5)	2 (−4)	1 (−5)

Damage Resistances piercing, slashing
Condition Immunities charmed, frightened, grappled, paralyzed, petrified, prone, restrained
Senses blindsight 10 ft., passive Perception 6
Languages —
Challenge 1/2 (100 XP)

Swarm. The swarm can occupy another creature's space and vice versa, and the swarm can move through any opening large enough for a Tiny maggot. The swarm can't regain hit points or gain temporary hit points.

ACTIONS

Bites. *Melee Weapon Attack:* +0 to hit, reach 0 ft., one creature in the swarm's space. *Hit:* The target is infested by 1d4 rot grubs. At the start of each of the target's turns, the target takes 1d6 piercing damage per rot grub infesting it. Applying fire to the bite wound before the end of the target's next turn deals 1 fire damage to the target and kills these rot grubs. After this time, these rot grubs are too far under the skin to be burned.

If a target infested by rot grubs ends its turn with 0 hit points, it dies as the rot grubs burrow into its heart and kill it. Any effect that cures disease kills all rot grubs infesting the target.

Appendix B: Nonplayer Characters

This appendix contains statistics for various humanoid nonplayer characters (NPCs)—whether friend or foe—expanding on appendix B of the *Monster Manual*. These stat blocks can represent human and nonhuman NPCs, and you can add racial traits to further customize them.

Abjurer

Abjurers are specialist wizards who feel secure when warded by layers of magical power. Kings, nobles, and other wealthy individuals commonly hire abjurers to cast protective spells on their homes and vaults.

Apprentice Wizard

Apprentices are novice arcane spellcasters who serve more experienced wizards or attend school. They perform menial work such as cooking and cleaning in exchange for education in the ways of magic.

Abjurer

Medium humanoid (any race), any alignment

Armor Class 12 (15 with *mage armor*)
Hit Points 84 (13d8 + 26)
Speed 30 ft.

STR	DEX	CON	INT	WIS	CHA
9 (−1)	14 (+2)	14 (+2)	18 (+4)	12 (+1)	11 (+0)

Saving Throws Int +8, Wis +5
Skills Arcana +8, History +8
Senses passive Perception 11
Languages any four languages
Challenge 9 (5,000 XP)

Spellcasting. The abjurer is a 13th-level spellcaster. Its spellcasting ability is Intelligence (spell save DC 16, +8 to hit with spell attacks). The abjurer has the following wizard spells prepared:

Cantrips (at will): *blade ward, dancing lights, mending, message, ray of frost*
1st level (4 slots): *alarm,* mage armor,* magic missile, shield**
2nd level (3 slots): *arcane lock,* invisibility*
3rd level (3 slots): *counterspell,* dispel magic,* fireball*
4th level (3 slots): *banishment,* stoneskin**
5th level (2 slots): *cone of cold, wall of force*
6th level (1 slot): *flesh to stone, globe of invulnerability**
7th level (1 slot): *symbol,* teleport*
*Abjuration spell of 1st level or higher

Arcane Ward. The abjurer has a magical ward that has 30 hit points. Whenever the abjurer takes damage, the ward takes the damage instead. If the ward is reduced to 0 hit points, the abjurer takes any remaining damage. When the abjurer casts an abjuration spell of 1st level or higher, the ward regains a number of hit points equal to twice the level of the spell.

Actions

Quarterstaff. *Melee Weapon Attack:* +3 to hit, reach 5 ft., one target. *Hit:* 2 (1d6 − 1) bludgeoning damage, or 3 (1d8 − 1) bludgeoning damage if used with two hands.

Apprentice Wizard

Medium humanoid (any race), any alignment

Armor Class 10
Hit Points 9 (2d8)
Speed 30 ft.

STR	DEX	CON	INT	WIS	CHA
10 (+0)	10 (+0)	10 (+0)	14 (+2)	10 (+0)	11 (+0)

Skills Arcana +4, History +4
Senses passive Perception 10
Languages any one language (usually Common)
Challenge 1/4 (50 XP)

Spellcasting. The apprentice is a 1st-level spellcaster. Its spellcasting ability is Intelligence (spell save DC 12, +4 to hit with spell attacks). It has the following wizard spells prepared:

Cantrips (at will): *fire bolt, mending, prestidigitation*
1st level (2 slots): *burning hands, disguise self, shield*

Actions

Dagger. *Melee or Ranged Weapon Attack:* +2 to hit, reach 5 ft. or range 20/60 ft., one target. *Hit:* 2 (1d4) piercing damage.

ARCHDRUID

Archdruids watch over the natural wonders of their domains. They seldom interact with civilized folk unless there is a great threat to the natural order. An archdruid typically has one or more pupils who are **druids** (see the *Monster Manual* for statistics), and the archdruid's lair is usually guarded by loyal beasts and fey creatures.

ARCHDRUID

Medium humanoid (any race), any alignment

Armor Class 16 (hide armor, shield)
Hit Points 132 (24d8 + 24)
Speed 30 ft.

STR	DEX	CON	INT	WIS	CHA
10 (+0)	14 (+2)	12 (+1)	12 (+1)	20 (+5)	11 (+0)

Saving Throws Int +5, Wis +9
Skills Medicine +9, Nature +5, Perception +9
Senses passive Perception 19
Languages Druidic plus any two languages
Challenge 12 (8,400 XP)

Spellcasting. The archdruid is an 18th-level spellcaster. Its spellcasting ability is Wisdom (spell save DC 17, +9 to hit with spell attacks). It has the following druid spells prepared:

Cantrips (at will): *druidcraft, mending, poison spray, produce flame*
1st level (4 slots): *cure wounds, entangle, faerie fire, speak with animals*
2nd level (3 slots): *animal messenger, beast sense, hold person*
3rd level (3 slots): *conjure animals, meld into stone, water breathing*
4th level (3 slots): *dominate beast, locate creature, stoneskin, wall of fire*
5th level (3 slots): *commune with nature, mass cure wounds, tree stride*
6th level (1 slot): *heal, heroes' feast, sunbeam*
7th level (1 slot): *fire storm*
8th level (1 slot): *animal shapes*
9th level (1 slot): *foresight*

ACTIONS

Scimitar. *Melee Weapon Attack:* +6 to hit, reach 5 ft., one target. *Hit:* 5 (1d6 + 2) slashing damage.

Change Shape (2/Day). The archdruid magically polymorphs into a beast or elemental with a challenge rating of 6 or less, and can remain in this form for up to 9 hours. The archdruid can choose whether its equipment falls to the ground, melds with its new form, or is worn by the new form. The archdruid reverts to its true form if it dies or falls unconscious. The archdruid can revert to its true form using a bonus action on its turn.

While in a new form, the archdruid retains its game statistics and ability to speak, but its AC, movement modes, Strength, and Dexterity are replaced by those of the new form, and it gains any special senses, proficiencies, traits, actions, and reactions (except class features, legendary actions, and lair actions) that the new form has but that it lacks. It can cast its spells with verbal or somatic components in its new form.

The new form's attacks count as magical for the purpose of overcoming resistances and immunity to nonmagical attacks.

ARCHER

Archers defend castles, hunt wild game on the fringes of civilization, serve as artillery in military units, and occasionally make good coin as brigands or caravan guards.

ARCHER

Medium humanoid (any race), any alignment

Armor Class 16 (studded leather)
Hit Points 75 (10d8 + 30)
Speed 30 ft.

STR	DEX	CON	INT	WIS	CHA
11 (+0)	18 (+4)	16 (+3)	11 (+0)	13 (+1)	10 (+0)

Skills Acrobatics +6, Perception +5
Senses passive Perception 15
Languages any one language (usually Common)
Challenge 3 (700 XP)

Archer's Eye (3/Day). As a bonus action, the archer can add 1d10 to its next attack or damage roll with a longbow or shortbow.

ACTIONS

Multiattack. The archer makes two attacks with its longbow.

Shortsword. *Melee Weapon Attack:* +6 to hit, reach 5 ft., one target. *Hit:* 7 (1d6 + 4) piercing damage.

Longbow. *Ranged Weapon Attack:* +6 to hit, range 150/600 ft., one target. *Hit:* 8 (1d8 + 4) piercing damage.

BARD

Bards are gifted poets, storytellers, and entertainers who travel far and wide, but are commonly found in taverns or in the company of jolly bands of adventurers, rough-and-tumble mercenaries, and wealthy patrons.

BLACKGUARD

Blackguards are paladins who broke their sacred oaths and now indulge their own dark ambitions. They consort with fiends and undead, and they reject all goodly things from their former lives.

BARD

Medium humanoid (any race), any alignment

Armor Class 15 (chain shirt)
Hit Points 44 (8d8 + 8)
Speed 30 ft.

STR	DEX	CON	INT	WIS	CHA
11 (+0)	14 (+2)	12 (+1)	10 (+0)	13 (+1)	14 (+2)

Saving Throws Dex +4, Wis +3
Skills Acrobatics +4, Perception +5, Performance +6
Senses passive Perception 15
Languages any two languages
Challenge 2 (450 XP)

Spellcasting. The bard is a 4th-level spellcaster. Its spellcasting ability is Charisma (spell save DC 12, +4 to hit with spell attacks). It has the following bard spells prepared:

Cantrips (at will): *friends, mage hand, vicious mockery*
1st level (4 slots): *charm person, healing word, heroism, sleep, thunderwave*
2nd level (3 slots): *invisibility, shatter*

Song of Rest. The bard can perform a song while taking a short rest. Any ally who hears the song regains an extra 1d6 hit points if it spends any Hit Dice to regain hit points at the end of that rest. The bard can confer this benefit on itself as well.

Taunt (2/Day). The bard can use a bonus action on its turn to target one creature within 30 feet of it. If the target can hear the bard, the target must succeed on a DC 12 Charisma saving throw or have disadvantage on ability checks, attack rolls, and saving throws until the start of the bard's next turn.

ACTIONS

Shortsword. *Melee Weapon Attack:* +4 to hit, reach 5 ft., one target. *Hit:* 5 (1d6 + 2) piercing damage.

Shortbow. *Ranged Weapon Attack:* +4 to hit, range 80/320 ft., one target. *Hit:* 5 (1d6 + 2) piercing damage.

BLACKGUARD

Medium humanoid (any race), any non-good alignment

Armor Class 18 (plate)
Hit Points 153 (18d8 + 72)
Speed 30 ft.

STR	DEX	CON	INT	WIS	CHA
18 (+4)	11 (+0)	18 (+4)	11 (+0)	14 (+2)	15 (+2)

Saving Throws Wis +5, Cha +5
Skills Athletics +7, Deception +5, Intimidation +5
Senses passive Perception 12
Languages any one language (usually Common)
Challenge 8 (3,900 XP)

Spellcasting. The blackguard is a 10th-level spellcaster. Its spellcasting ability is Charisma (spell save DC 13, +5 to hit with spell attacks). It has the following paladin spells prepared:

1st level (4 slots): *command, protection from evil and good, thunderous smite*
2nd level (3 slots): *branding smite, find steed*
3rd level (2 slots): *blinding smite, dispel magic*

ACTIONS

Multiattack. The blackguard makes three attacks with its glaive or its shortbow.

Glaive. *Melee Weapon Attack:* +7 to hit, reach 10 ft., one target. *Hit:* 9 (1d10 + 4) slashing damage.

Shortbow. *Ranged Weapon Attack:* +3 to hit, range 80/320 ft., one target. *Hit:* 5 (1d6 + 2) piercing damage.

Dreadful Aspect (Recharges after a Short or Long Rest). The blackguard exudes magical menace. Each enemy within 30 feet of the blackguard must succeed on a DC 13 Wisdom saving throw or be frightened for 1 minute. If a frightened target ends its turn more than 30 feet away from the blackguard, the target can repeat the saving throw, ending the effect on itself on a success.

CHAMPION

Champions are mighty warriors who honed their fighting skills in wars or gladiatorial pits. To soldiers and other people who fight for a living, champions are as influential as nobles, and their presence is courted as a sign of status among rulers.

CONJURER

Conjurers are specialist wizards who summon creatures from other planes and create materials out of thin air. Some conjurers use their magic to bolster armies or destroy enemies on battlefields, while others use summoned creatures to guard their lairs.

CONJURER
Medium humanoid (any race), any alignment

Armor Class 12 (15 with *mage armor*)
Hit Points 40 (9d8)
Speed 30 ft.

STR	DEX	CON	INT	WIS	CHA
9 (–1)	14 (+2)	11 (+0)	17 (+3)	12 (+1)	11 (+0)

Saving Throws Int +6, Wis +4
Skills Arcana +6, History +6
Senses passive Perception 11
Languages any four languages
Challenge 6 (2,300 XP)

Spellcasting. The conjurer is a 9th-level spellcaster. Its spellcasting ability is Intelligence (spell save DC 14, +6 to hit with spell attacks). The conjurer has the following wizard spells prepared:

Cantrips (at will): *acid splash, mage hand, poison spray, prestidigitation*
1st level (4 slots): *mage armor, magic missile, unseen servant**
2nd level (3 slots): *cloud of daggers,* misty step,* web**
3rd level (3 slots): *fireball, stinking cloud**
4th level (3 slots): *Evard's black tentacles,* stoneskin*
5th level (2 slots): *cloudkill,* conjure elemental**
*Conjuration spell of 1st level or higher

Benign Transportation (Recharges after the Conjurer Casts a Conjuration Spell of 1st Level or Higher). As a bonus action, the conjurer teleports up to 30 feet to an unoccupied space that it can see. If it instead chooses a space within range that is occupied by a willing Small or Medium creature, they both teleport, swapping places.

ACTIONS

Dagger. *Melee or Ranged Weapon Attack:* +5 to hit, reach 5 ft. or range 20/60 ft., one target. *Hit:* 4 (1d4 + 2) piercing damage.

CHAMPION
Medium humanoid (any race), any alignment

Armor Class 18 (plate)
Hit Points 143 (22d8 + 44)
Speed 30 ft.

STR	DEX	CON	INT	WIS	CHA
20 (+5)	15 (+2)	14 (+2)	10 (+0)	14 (+2)	12 (+1)

Saving Throws Str +9, Con +6
Skills Athletics +9, Intimidation +5, Perception +6
Senses passive Perception 16
Languages any one language (usually Common)
Challenge 9 (5,000 XP)

Indomitable (2/Day). The champion rerolls a failed saving throw.

Second Wind (Recharges after a Short or Long Rest). As a bonus action, the champion can regain 20 hit points.

ACTIONS

Multiattack. The champion makes three attacks with its greatsword or its shortbow.

Greatsword. *Melee Weapon Attack:* +9 to hit, reach 5 ft., one target. *Hit:* 12 (2d6 + 5) slashing damage, plus 7 (2d6) slashing damage if the champion has more than half of its total hit points remaining.

Shortbow. *Ranged Weapon Attack:* +6 to hit, range 80/320 ft., one target. *Hit:* 5 (1d6 + 2) piercing damage, plus 7 (2d6) piercing damage if the champion has more than half of its total hit points remaining.

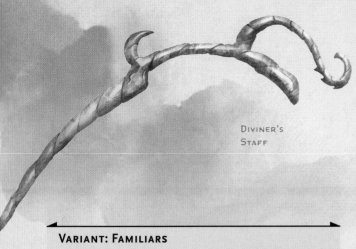

DIVINER

Diviners are specialist wizards who know that knowledge is power. They might act aloof and mysterious, hinting at omens and secrets, or they might be know-it-alls, spilling secrets and insights to advance their own status or reputation.

ENCHANTER

Enchanters are specialist wizards who understand how to alter and control minds using magic. They might be personable and interesting, using magic to manipulate people only when banter and conventional persuasion fails, or they might be rude and demanding, using and relying on charmed, obedient minions.

VARIANT: FAMILIARS

Any spellcaster that can cast the *find familiar* spell (such as an apprentice, warlock, or wizard) is likely to have a familiar. The familiar can be one of the creatures described in the spell (see the *Player's Handbook*) or some other Tiny monster, such as a cranium rat, a crawling claw, a gazer, an imp, a pseudodragon, or a quasit.

DIVINER
Medium humanoid (any race), any alignment

Armor Class 12 (15 with *mage armor*)
Hit Points 67 (15d8)
Speed 30 ft.

STR	DEX	CON	INT	WIS	CHA
9 (−1)	14 (+2)	11 (+0)	18 (+4)	12 (+1)	11 (+0)

Saving Throws Int +7, Wis +4
Skills Arcana +7, History +7
Senses passive Perception 11
Languages any four languages
Challenge 8 (3,900 XP)

Spellcasting. The diviner is a 15th-level spellcaster. Its spellcasting ability is Intelligence (spell save DC 15, +7 to hit with spell attacks). The diviner has the following wizard spells prepared:

Cantrips (at will): *fire bolt, light, mage hand, message, true strike*
1st level (4 slots): *detect magic,* feather fall, mage armor*
2nd level (3 slots): *detect thoughts,* locate object,* scorching ray*
3rd level (3 slots): *clairvoyance,* fly, fireball*
4th level (3 slots): *arcane eye,* ice storm, stoneskin*
5th level (2 slots): *Rary's telepathic bond,* scrying**
6th level (1 slot): *mass suggestion, true seeing**
7th level (1 slot): *delayed blast fireball, teleport*
8th level (1 slot): *maze*
*Divination spell of 1st level or higher

Portent (Recharges after the Diviner Casts a Divination Spell of 1st Level or Higher). When the diviner or a creature it can see makes an attack roll, a saving throw, or an ability check, the diviner can roll a d20 and choose to use this roll in place of the attack roll, saving throw, or ability check.

ACTIONS

Quarterstaff. *Melee Weapon Attack:* +2 to hit, reach 5 ft., one target. *Hit:* 2 (1d6 − 1) bludgeoning damage, or 3 (1d8 − 1) bludgeoning damage if used with two hands.

ENCHANTER
Medium humanoid (any race), any alignment

Armor Class 12 (15 with *mage armor*)
Hit Points 40 (9d8)
Speed 30 ft.

STR	DEX	CON	INT	WIS	CHA
9 (−1)	14 (+2)	11 (+0)	17 (+3)	12 (+1)	11 (+0)

Saving Throws Int +6, Wis +4
Skills Arcana +6, History +6
Senses passive Perception 11
Languages any four languages
Challenge 5 (1,800 XP)

Spellcasting. The enchanter is a 9th-level spellcaster. Its spellcasting ability is Intelligence (spell save DC 14, +6 to hit with spell attacks). The enchanter has the following wizard spells prepared:

Cantrips (at will): *friends, mage hand, mending, message*
1st level (4 slots): *charm person,* mage armor, magic missile*
2nd level (3 slots): *hold person,* invisibility, suggestion**
3rd level (3 slots): *fireball, haste, tongues*
4th level (3 slots): *dominate beast,* stoneskin*
5th level (2 slots): *hold monster**
*Enchantment spell of 1st level or higher

ACTIONS

Quarterstaff. *Melee Weapon Attack:* +2 to hit, reach 5 ft., one target. *Hit:* 2 (1d6 − 1) bludgeoning damage, or 3 (1d8 − 1) bludgeoning damage if used with two hands.

REACTIONS

Instinctive Charm (Recharges after the Enchanter Casts an Enchantment Spell of 1st Level or Higher). The enchanter tries to magically divert an attack made against it, provided that the attacker is within 30 feet of it and visible to it. The enchanter must decide to do so before the attack hits or misses.

The attacker must make a DC 14 Wisdom saving throw. On a failed save, the attacker targets the creature closest to it, other than the enchanter or itself. If multiple creatures are closest, the attacker chooses which one to target.

APPENDIX B | NONPLAYER CHARACTERS

213

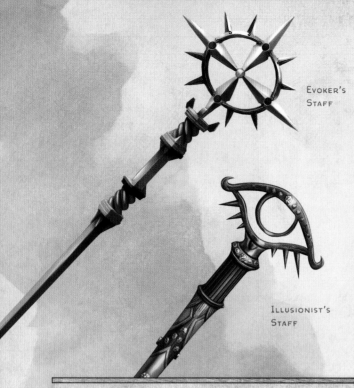

EVOKER'S STAFF

ILLUSIONIST'S STAFF

EVOKER

Evokers are specialist wizards who harness magical energy and elemental forces to destroy. Many tend to be hotheaded and aggressive. Others are cold and reserved, unleashing their power at just the right moment to exploit an opponent's weakness.

ILLUSIONIST

Illusionists are specialist wizards who twist light, sound, shadow, and even minds to create false and quasi-real effects. They can be flamboyant and use their powers in spectacular and obvious ways, or quiet and subtle, using their magic to conceal the truth.

ILLUSIONIST

Medium humanoid (any race), any alignment

Armor Class 12 (15 with *mage armor*)
Hit Points 38 (7d8 + 7)
Speed 30 ft.

STR	DEX	CON	INT	WIS	CHA
9 (−1)	14 (+2)	13 (+1)	16 (+3)	11 (+0)	12 (+1)

Saving Throws Int +5, Wis +2
Skills Arcana +5, History +5
Senses passive Perception 10
Languages any four languages
Challenge 3 (700 XP)

Spellcasting. The illusionist is a 7th-level spellcaster. Its spellcasting ability is Intelligence (spell save DC 13, +5 to hit with spell attacks). The illusionist has the following wizard spells prepared:

Cantrips (at will): *dancing lights, mage hand, minor illusion, poison spray*
1st level (4 slots): *color spray,* disguise self,* mage armor, magic missile*
2nd level (3 slots): *invisibility,* mirror image,* phantasmal force**
3rd level (3 slots): *major image,* phantom steed**
4th level (1 slot): *phantasmal killer**
*Illusion spell of 1st level or higher

Displacement (Recharges after the Illusionist Casts an Illusion Spell of 1st Level or Higher). As a bonus action, the illusionist projects an illusion that makes the illusionist appear to be standing in a place a few inches from its actual location, causing any creature to have disadvantage on attack rolls against the illusionist. The effect ends if the illusionist takes damage, it is incapacitated, or its speed becomes 0.

ACTIONS

Quarterstaff. *Melee Weapon Attack:* +1 to hit, reach 5 ft., one target. *Hit:* 2 (1d6 − 1) bludgeoning damage, or 3 (1d8 − 1) bludgeoning damage if used with two hands.

EVOKER

Medium humanoid (any race), any alignment

Armor Class 12 (15 with *mage armor*)
Hit Points 66 (12d8 + 12)
Speed 30 ft.

STR	DEX	CON	INT	WIS	CHA
9 (−1)	14 (+2)	12 (+1)	17 (+3)	12 (+1)	11 (+0)

Saving Throws Int +7, Wis +5
Skills Arcana +7, History +7
Senses passive Perception 11
Languages any four languages
Challenge 9 (5,000 XP)

Spellcasting. The evoker is a 12th-level spellcaster. Its spellcasting ability is Intelligence (spell save DC 15, +7 to hit with spell attacks). The evoker has the following wizard spells prepared:

Cantrips (at will): *fire bolt,* light,* prestidigitation, ray of frost**
1st level (4 slots): *burning hands,* mage armor, magic missile**
2nd level (3 slots): *mirror image, misty step, shatter**
3rd level (3 slots): *counterspell, fireball,* lightning bolt**
4th level (3 slots): *ice storm,* stoneskin*
5th level (2 slots): *Bigby's hand,* cone of cold**
6th level (1 slot): *chain lightning,* wall of ice**
*Evocation spell

Sculpt Spells. When the evoker casts an evocation spell that forces other creatures it can see to make a saving throw, it can choose a number of them equal to 1 + the spell's level. These creatures automatically succeed on their saves against the spell. If a successful save means a chosen creature would take half damage from the spell, it instead takes no damage from it.

ACTIONS

Quarterstaff. *Melee Weapon Attack:* +3 to hit, reach 5 ft., one target. *Hit:* 2 (1d6 − 1) bludgeoning damage, or 3 (1d8 − 1) bludgeoning damage if used with two hands.

KRAKEN PRIEST

A kraken can seem godlike to folk who have witnessed its fury. Those who mistake its might for divine power and those who seek to appease the monster through veneration are sometimes rewarded with power, to serve thereafter as kraken priests.

The kraken can make itself dimly aware of a kraken priest's thoughts if the two are on the same plane of existence, and it can then push aside the priest's personality and control it. Kraken priests can thereby act as eyes and ears for their masters, and when the kraken has something to say, the priest becomes its mouthpiece.

Every kraken priest undergoes a change in appearance that reflects the kraken's influence, although each one differs in how its reverence is displayed. One kraken priest might have ink-black eyes and a suckered tentacle for a tongue, while another has a featureless face and a body covered in eyes and mouths that dribble seawater. These horrific manifestations intensify when the kraken possesses its minion to utter its dire pronouncements.

KRAKEN PRIEST
Medium humanoid (any race), any evil alignment

Armor Class 10
Hit Points 75 (10d8 + 30)
Speed 30 ft., swim 30 ft.

STR	DEX	CON	INT	WIS	CHA
12 (+1)	10 (+0)	16 (+3)	10 (+0)	15 (+2)	14 (+2)

Skills Perception +5
Damage Resistances bludgeoning, piercing, and slashing from nonmagical attacks
Senses passive Perception 15
Languages any two languages
Challenge 5 (1,800 XP)

Amphibious. The priest can breathe air and water.

Innate Spellcasting. The priest's spellcasting ability is Wisdom (spell save DC 13, +5 to hit with spell attacks). It can innately cast the following spells, requiring no material components:

At will: *command, create or destroy water*
3/day each: *control water, darkness, water breathing, water walk*
1/day each: *call lightning, Evard's black tentacles*

ACTIONS

Thunderous Touch. *Melee Spell Attack:* +5 to hit, reach 5 ft., one creature. *Hit:* 27 (5d10) thunder damage.

Voice of the Kraken (Recharges after a Short or Long Rest). A kraken speaks through the priest with a thunderous voice audible within 300 feet. Creatures of the priest's choice that can hear the kraken's words (which are spoken in Abyssal, Infernal, or Primordial) must succeed on a DC 14 Charisma saving throw or be frightened for 1 minute. A frightened target can repeat the saving throw at the end of each of its turns, ending the effect on itself on a success.

Martial Arts Adept

Martial arts adepts are disciplined monks with extensive training in hand-to-hand combat. Some protect monasteries; others travel the world seeking enlightenment or new forms of combat to master. A few become bodyguards, trading their combat prowess and loyalty for food and lodging.

Master Thief

Master thieves are known for perpetrating daring heists. They tend to develop a reputation and a cult of personality. A master thief might "retire" from hands-on work to run a thieves' guild, spearhead some covert enterprise, or enjoy a quiet life of luxury.

Martial Arts Adept

Medium humanoid (any race), any alignment

Armor Class 16
Hit Points 60 (11d8 + 11)
Speed 40 ft.

STR	DEX	CON	INT	WIS	CHA
11 (+0)	17 (+3)	13 (+1)	11 (+0)	16 (+3)	10 (+0)

Skills Acrobatics +5, Insight +5, Stealth +5
Senses passive Perception 13
Languages any one language (usually Common)
Challenge 3 (700 XP)

Unarmored Defense. While the adept is wearing no armor and wielding no shield, its AC includes its Wisdom modifier.

Actions

Multiattack. The adept makes three unarmed strikes or three dart attacks.

Unarmed Strike. *Melee Weapon Attack:* +5 to hit, reach 5 ft., one target. *Hit:* 7 (1d8 + 3) bludgeoning damage. If the target is a creature, the adept can choose one of the following additional effects:

- The target must succeed on a DC 13 Strength saving throw or drop one item it is holding (adept's choice).
- The target must succeed on a DC 13 Dexterity saving throw or be knocked prone.
- The target must succeed on a DC 13 Constitution saving throw or be stunned until the end of the adept's next turn.

Dart. *Ranged Weapon Attack:* +5 to hit, range 20/60 ft., one target. *Hit:* 5 (1d4 + 3) piercing damage.

Reactions

Deflect Missile. In response to being hit by a ranged weapon attack, the adept deflects the missile. The damage it takes from the attack is reduced by 1d10 + 3. If the damage is reduced to 0, the adept catches the missile if it's small enough to hold in one hand and the adept has a hand free.

Master Thief

Medium humanoid (any race), any alignment

Armor Class 16 (studded leather)
Hit Points 84 (13d8 + 26)
Speed 30 ft.

STR	DEX	CON	INT	WIS	CHA
11 (+0)	18 (+4)	14 (+2)	11 (+0)	11 (+0)	12 (+1)

Saving Throws Dex +7, Int +3
Skills Acrobatics +7, Athletics +3, Perception +3, Sleight of Hand +7, Stealth +7
Senses passive Perception 13
Languages any one language (usually Common) plus thieves' cant
Challenge 5 (1,800 XP)

Cunning Action. On each of its turns, the thief can use a bonus action to take the Dash, Disengage, or Hide action.

Evasion. If the thief is subjected to an effect that allows it to make a Dexterity saving throw to take only half damage, the thief instead takes no damage if it succeeds on the saving throw, and only half damage if it fails.

Sneak Attack (1/Turn). The thief deals an extra 14 (4d6) damage when it hits a target with a weapon attack and has advantage on the attack roll, or when the target is within 5 feet of an ally of the thief that isn't incapacitated and the thief doesn't have disadvantage on the attack roll.

Actions

Multiattack. The thief makes three attacks with its shortsword.

Shortsword. *Melee Weapon Attack:* +7 to hit, reach 5 ft., one target. *Hit:* 7 (1d6 + 4) piercing damage.

Light Crossbow. *Ranged Weapon Attack:* +7 to hit, range 80/320 ft., one target. *Hit:* 8 (1d8 + 4) piercing damage.

Reactions

Uncanny Dodge. The thief halves the damage that it takes from an attack that hits it. The thief must be able to see the attacker.

Necromancer

Necromancers are specialist wizards who study the interaction of life, death, and undeath. Some like to dig up corpses to create undead slaves. A few use their powers for good, becoming hunters of the undead and risking their lives to save others.

Swashbuckler

Swashbucklers are charming ne'er-do-wells who live by their own codes of honor. They crave notoriety, often indulge in romantic trysts, and eke out livings as pirates and corsairs, rarely staying in one place for too long.

Necromancer

Medium humanoid (any race), any alignment

Armor Class 12 (15 with *mage armor*)
Hit Points 66 (12d8 + 12)
Speed 30 ft.

STR	DEX	CON	INT	WIS	CHA
9 (−1)	14 (+2)	12 (+1)	17 (+3)	12 (+1)	11 (+0)

Saving Throws Int +7, Wis +5
Skills Arcana +7, History +7
Damage Resistances necrotic
Senses passive Perception 11
Languages any four languages
Challenge 9 (5,000 XP)

Spellcasting. The necromancer is a 12th-level spellcaster. Its spellcasting ability is Intelligence (spell save DC 15, +7 to hit with spell attacks). The necromancer has the following wizard spells prepared:

Cantrips (at will): *chill touch, dancing lights, mage hand, mending*
1st level (4 slots): *false life,* mage armor, ray of sickness**
2nd level (3 slots): *blindness/deafness,* ray of enfeeblement,* web*
3rd level (3 slots): *animate dead,* bestow curse,* vampiric touch**
4th level (3 slots): *blight,* dimension door, stoneskin*
5th level (2 slots): *Bigby's hand, cloudkill*
6th level (1 slot): *circle of death**
*Necromancy spell of 1st level or higher

Grim Harvest (1/Turn). When the necromancer kills a creature that is neither a construct nor undead with a spell of 1st level or higher, the necromancer regains hit points equal to twice the spell's level, or three times if it is a necromancy spell.

Actions

Withering Touch. *Melee Spell Attack:* +7 to hit, reach 5 ft., one creature. *Hit:* 5 (2d4) necrotic damage.

Swashbuckler

Medium humanoid (any race), any non-lawful alignment

Armor Class 17 (leather armor)
Hit Points 66 (12d8 + 12)
Speed 30 ft.

STR	DEX	CON	INT	WIS	CHA
12 (+1)	18 (+4)	12 (+1)	14 (+2)	11 (+0)	15 (+2)

Skills Acrobatics +8, Athletics +5, Persuasion +6
Senses passive Perception 10
Languages any one language (usually Common)
Challenge 3 (700 XP)

Lightfooted. The swashbuckler can take the Dash or Disengage action as a bonus action on each of its turns.

Suave Defense. While the swashbuckler is wearing light or no armor and wielding no shield, its AC includes its Charisma modifier.

Actions

Multiattack. The swashbuckler makes three attacks: one with a dagger and two with its rapier.

Dagger. *Melee or Ranged Weapon Attack:* +6 to hit, reach 5 ft. or range 20/60 ft., one target. *Hit:* 6 (1d4 + 4) piercing damage.

Rapier. *Melee Weapon Attack:* +6 to hit, reach 5 ft., one target. *Hit:* 8 (1d8 + 4) piercing damage.

Transmuter

Transmuters are specialist wizards who embrace change, rail against the status quo, and view magical transmutation as a path to riches, enlightenment, or apotheosis.

War Priest

War priests worship deities of war and combat. They plan tactics, lead soldiers into battle, confront enemy spellcasters, and tend to casualties. A war priest might command an army or serve as a warlord's right hand on the battlefield.

Transmuter

Medium humanoid (any race), any alignment

Armor Class 12 (15 with *mage armor*)
Hit Points 40 (9d8)
Speed 30 ft.

STR	DEX	CON	INT	WIS	CHA
9 (–1)	14 (+2)	11 (+0)	17 (+3)	12 (+1)	11 (+0)

Saving Throws Int +6, Wis +4
Skills Arcana +6, History +6
Senses passive Perception 11
Languages any four languages
Challenge 5 (1,800 XP)

Spellcasting. The transmuter is a 9th-level spellcaster. Its spellcasting ability is Intelligence (spell save DC 14, +6 to hit with spell attacks). The transmuter has the following wizard spells prepared:

Cantrips (at will): *light, mending, prestidigitation, ray of frost*
1st level (4 slots): *chromatic orb, expeditious retreat,* mage armor*
2nd level (3 slots): *alter self,* hold person, knock**
3rd level (3 slots): *blink,* fireball, slow**
4th level (3 slots): *polymorph,* stoneskin*
5th level (1 slot): *telekinesis**
*Transmutation spell of 1st level or higher

Transmuter's Stone. The transmuter carries a magic stone it crafted that grants its bearer one of the following effects:

- Darkvision out to a range of 60 feet
- An extra 10 feet of speed while the bearer is unencumbered
- Proficiency with Constitution saving throws
- Resistance to acid, cold, fire, lightning, or thunder damage (transmuter's choice whenever the transmuter chooses this benefit)

If the transmuter has the stone and casts a transmutation spell of 1st level or higher, it can change the effect of the stone.

Actions

Quarterstaff. *Melee Weapon Attack:* +2 to hit, reach 5 ft., one target. *Hit:* 2 (1d6 – 1) bludgeoning damage, or 3 (1d8 – 1) bludgeoning damage if used with two hands.

War Priest

Medium humanoid (any race), any alignment

Armor Class 18 (plate)
Hit Points 117 (18d8 + 36)
Speed 30 ft.

STR	DEX	CON	INT	WIS	CHA
16 (+3)	10 (+0)	14 (+2)	11 (+0)	17 (+3)	13 (+1)

Saving Throws Con +6, Wis +7
Skills Intimidation +5, Religion +4
Senses passive Perception 13
Languages any two languages
Challenge 9 (5,000 XP)

Spellcasting. The priest is a 9th-level spellcaster. Its spellcasting ability is Wisdom (spell save DC 15, +7 to hit with spell attacks). It has the following cleric spells prepared:

Cantrips (at will): *light, mending, sacred flame, spare the dying*
1st level (4 slots): *divine favor, guiding bolt, healing word, shield of faith*
2nd level (3 slots): *lesser restoration, magic weapon, prayer of healing, silence, spiritual weapon*
3rd level (3 slots): *beacon of hope, crusader's mantle, dispel magic, revivify, spirit guardians, water walk*
4th level (3 slots): *banishment, freedom of movement, guardian of faith, stoneskin*
5th level (1 slot): *flame strike, mass cure wounds, hold monster*

Actions

Multiattack. The priest makes two melee attacks.

Maul. *Melee Weapon Attack:* +7 to hit, reach 5 ft., one target. *Hit:* 10 (2d6 + 3) bludgeoning damage.

Reactions

Guided Strike (Recharges after a Short or Long Rest). The priest grants a +10 bonus to an attack roll made by itself or another creature within 30 feet of it. The priest can make this choice after the roll is made but before it hits or misses..

Warlock of the Archfey

Warlocks of the archfey gain their powers through magical pacts forged with lords of the Feywild. These warlocks commonly associate with lesser fey creatures such as boggles, quicklings, redcaps, satyrs, and sprites.

Warlock of the Fiend

Warlocks of the fiend gain their powers through magical pacts forged with archfiends of the Lower Planes. These warlocks often keep imps or quasits as companions, and they tend toward extremes of behavior: consorting with fiend-worshiping cultists or dedicating their lives to destroying fiendish cults.

Warlock of the Archfey

Medium humanoid (any race), any alignment

Armor Class 11 (14 with *mage armor*)
Hit Points 49 (11d8)
Speed 30 ft.

STR	DEX	CON	INT	WIS	CHA
9 (−1)	13 (+1)	11 (+0)	11 (+0)	12 (+1)	18 (+4)

Saving Throws Wis +3, Cha +6
Skills Arcana +2, Deception +6, Nature +2, Persuasion +6
Condition Immunities charmed
Senses passive Perception 11
Languages any two languages (usually Sylvan)
Challenge 4 (1,100 XP)

Innate Spellcasting. The warlock's innate spellcasting ability is Charisma. It can innately cast the following spells (spell save DC 15), requiring no material components:

At will: *disguise self, mage armor* (self only), *silent image, speak with animals*
1/day: *conjure fey*

Spellcasting. The warlock is a 11th-level spellcaster. Its spellcasting ability is Charisma (spell save DC 14, +6 to hit with spell attacks). It regains its expended spell slots when it finishes a short or long rest. It knows the following warlock spells:

Cantrips (at will): *dancing lights, eldritch blast, friends, mage hand, minor illusion, prestidigitation, vicious mockery*
1st–5th level (3 5th-level slots): *blink, charm person, dimension door, dominate beast, faerie fire, fear, hold monster, misty step, phantasmal force, seeming, sleep*

Actions

Dagger. *Melee or Ranged Weapon Attack:* +3 to hit, reach 5 ft. or range 20/60 ft., one target. *Hit:* 4 (1d4 + 2) piercing damage.

Reactions

Misty Escape (Recharges after a Short or Long Rest). In response to taking damage, the warlock turns invisible and teleports up to 60 feet to an unoccupied space it can see. It remains invisible until the start of its next turn or until it attacks, makes a damage roll, or casts a spell.

Warlock of the Fiend

Medium humanoid (any race), any alignment

Armor Class 12 (15 with *mage armor*)
Hit Points 78 (12d8 + 24)
Speed 30 ft.

STR	DEX	CON	INT	WIS	CHA
10 (+0)	14 (+2)	15 (+2)	12 (+1)	12 (+1)	18 (+4)

Saving Throws Wis +4, Cha +7
Skills Arcana +4, Deception +7, Persuasion +7, Religion +4
Damage Resistances slashing damage from nonmagical attacks not made with silvered weapons
Senses darkvision 60 ft., passive Perception 11
Languages any two languages (usually Abyssal or Infernal)
Challenge 7 (2,900 XP)

Innate Spellcasting. The warlock's innate spellcasting ability is Charisma. It can innately cast the following spells (spell save DC 15), requiring no material components:

At will: *alter self, false life, levitate* (self only), *mage armor* (self only), *silent image*
1/day each: *feeblemind, finger of death, plane shift*

Spellcasting. The warlock is a 17th-level spellcaster. Its spellcasting ability is Charisma (spell save DC 15, +7 to hit with spell attacks). It regains its expended spell slots when it finishes a short or long rest. It knows the following warlock spells:

Cantrips (at will): *eldritch blast, fire bolt, friends, mage hand, minor illusion, prestidigitation, shocking grasp*
1st–5th level (4 5th-level slots): *banishment, burning hands, flame strike, hellish rebuke, magic circle, scorching ray, scrying, stinking cloud, suggestion, wall of fire*

Dark One's Own Luck (Recharges after a Short or Long Rest). When the warlock makes an ability check or saving throw, it can add a d10 to the roll. It can do this after the roll is made but before any of the roll's effects occur.

Actions

Mace. *Melee Weapon Attack:* +3 to hit, reach 5 ft., one target. *Hit:* 3 (1d6) bludgeoning damage plus 10 (3d6) fire damage.

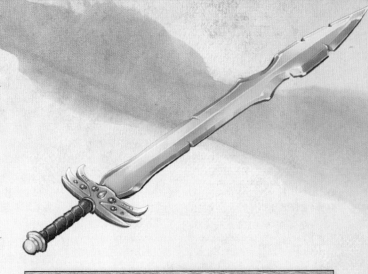

Warlock of the Great Old One

Warlocks of the Great Old One gain their powers through magical pacts forged with eldritch entities from strange and distant realms of existence. Some of these warlocks associate with cultists devoted to these entities, as well as aberrations that share their goals, yet other warlocks of the Great Old One are experts at rooting out the insanity and wickedness inspired by bizarre beings from beyond the stars.

Warlord

Warlords are legendary battlefield commanders whose names are spoken with awe. After a string of decisive victories, a warlord could easily take on the role of monarch or general and attract followers willing to die for his or her banner.

Warlock of the Great Old One

Medium humanoid (any race), any alignment

Armor Class 12 (15 with *mage armor*)
Hit Points 91 (14d8 + 28)
Speed 30 ft.

STR	DEX	CON	INT	WIS	CHA
9 (–1)	14 (+2)	15 (+2)	12 (+1)	12 (+1)	18 (+4)

Saving Throws Wis +4, Cha +7
Skills Arcana +4, History +4
Damage Resistances psychic
Senses darkvision 60 ft., passive Perception 11
Languages any two languages, telepathy 30 ft.
Challenge 6 (2,300 XP)

Innate Spellcasting. The warlock's innate spellcasting ability is Charisma. It can innately cast the following spells (spell save DC 15), requiring no material components:

At will: *detect magic, jump, levitate, mage armor* (self only), *speak with dead*
1/day each: *arcane gate, true seeing*

Spellcasting. The warlock is a 14th-level spellcaster. Its spellcasting ability is Charisma (spell save DC 15, +7 to hit with spell attacks). It regains its expended spell slots when it finishes a short or long rest. It knows the following warlock spells:

Cantrips (at will): *chill touch, eldritch blast, guidance, mage hand, minor illusion, prestidigitation, shocking grasp*
1st–5th level (3 5th-level slots): *armor of Agathys, arms of Hadar, crown of madness, clairvoyance, contact other plane, detect thoughts, dimension door, dissonant whispers, dominate beast, telekinesis, vampiric touch*

Whispering Aura. At the start of each of the warlock's turns, each creature of its choice within 5 feet of it must succeed on a DC 15 Wisdom saving throw or take 10 (3d6) psychic damage, provided that the warlock isn't incapacitated.

Actions

Dagger. *Melee or Ranged Weapon Attack:* +5 to hit, reach 5 ft. or range 20/60 ft., one target. *Hit:* 4 (1d4 + 2) piercing damage.

Warlord

Medium humanoid (any race), any alignment

Armor Class 18 (plate)
Hit Points 229 (27d8 + 108)
Speed 30 ft.

STR	DEX	CON	INT	WIS	CHA
20 (+5)	16 (+3)	18 (+4)	12 (+1)	12 (+1)	18 (+4)

Saving Throws Str +9, Dex +7, Con +8
Skills Athletics +9, Intimidation +8, Perception +5, Persuasion +8
Senses passive Perception 15
Languages any two languages
Challenge 12 (8,400 XP)

Indomitable (3/Day). The warlord can reroll a saving throw it fails. It must use the new roll.

Survivor. The warlord regains 10 hit points at the start of its turn if it has at least 1 hit point but fewer hit points than half its hit point maximum.

Actions

Multiattack. The warlord makes two weapon attacks.

Greatsword. *Melee Weapon Attack:* +9 to hit, reach 5 ft., one target. *Hit:* 12 (2d6 + 5) slashing damage.

Shortbow. *Ranged Weapon Attack:* +7 to hit, range 80/320 ft., one target. *Hit:* 6 (1d6 + 3) piercing damage.

Legendary Actions

The warlord can take 3 legendary actions, choosing from the options below. Only one legendary action option can be used at a time and only at the end of another creature's turn. The warlord regains spent legendary actions at the start of its turn.

Weapon Attack. The warlord makes a weapon attack.
Command Ally. The warlord targets one ally it can see within 30 feet of it. If the target can see and hear the warlord, the target can make one weapon attack as a reaction and gains advantage on the attack roll.
Frighten Foe (Costs 2 Actions). The warlord targets one enemy it can see within 30 feet of it. If the target can see and hear it, the target must succeed on a DC 16 Wisdom saving throw or be frightened until the end of warlord's next turn.

APPENDIX C: MONSTER LISTS

STAT BLOCKS BY CREATURE TYPE

STAT BLOCKS BY CHALLENGE RATING

CREATURES BY ENVIRONMENT

ARCTIC CREATURES

Creatures	Challenge (XP)
Gnoll witherling	1/4 (50 XP)
Gnoll hunter	1/2 (100 XP)
Gnoll flesh gnawer	1 (200 XP)
Guard drake (white)	2 (450 XP)
Warlock of the archfey	4 (1,100 XP)
Warlock of the Great Old One	6 (2,300 XP)
Bheur hag, warlock of the fiend	7 (2,900 XP)
Shoosuva	8 (3,900 XP)
Flind	9 (5,000 XP)
Frost giant everlasting one	12 (8,400 XP)
Storm giant quintessent	16 (15,000 XP)

COASTAL CREATURES

Creatures	Challenge (XP)
Dolphin	1/8 (25 XP)
Dimetrodon	1/4 (50 XP)
Sea spawn	1 (200 XP)
Quetzalcoatlus	2 (450 XP)
Deep scion, swashbuckler	3 (700 XP)
Kraken priest	5 (1,800 XP)
Stone giant dreamwalker	10 (5,900 XP)
Morkoth	11 (7,200 XP)
Frost giant everlasting one, ki-rin	12 (8,400 XP)
Storm giant quintessent	16 (15,000 XP)

Desert Creatures

Creatures	Challenge (XP)
Firenewt	1/2 (100 XP)
Vargouille	1 (200 XP)
Guard drake (blue), yuan-ti broodguard	2 (450 XP)
Leucrotta	3 (700 XP)
Yuan-ti mind whisperer, yuan-ti nightmare speaker	4 (1,100 XP)
Spawn of Kyuss, tlincalli, yuan-ti pit master	5 (1,800 XP)
Warlock of the fiend	7 (2,900 XP)
Champion, necromancer, war priest	9 (5,000 XP)
Ki-rin, yuan-ti anathema	12 (8,400 XP)
Storm giant quintessent	16 (15,000 XP)

Forest Creatures

Creatures	Challenge (XP)
Boggle	1/8 (25 XP)
Gnoll witherling, grung, kobold inventor, vegepygmy, velociraptor	1/4 (50 XP)
Darkling, gnoll hunter, orc Nurtured One of Yurtrus	1/2 (100 XP)
Deinonychus, gnoll flesh gnawer, grung wildling, kobold dragonshield, kobold scale sorcerer, nilbog, quickling, thorny	1 (200 XP)
Darkling elder, grung elite warrior, guard drake (green), hobgoblin Iron Shadow, meenlock, orc Hand of Yurtrus, shadow mastiff, vegepygmy chief, yuan-ti broodguard	2 (450 XP)
Archer, flail snail, orc Red Fang of Shargaas, redcap	3 (700 XP)
Barghest, girallon, hobgoblin devastator, orc Blade of Ilneval, stegosaurus, warlock of the archfey, yeth hound, yuan-ti mind whisperer, yuan-ti nightmare speaker	4 (1,100 XP)
Brontosaurus, wood woad, yuan-ti pit master	5 (1,800 XP)
Korred	7 (2,900 XP)
Shoosuva	8 (3,900 XP)
Flind	9 (5,000 XP)
Archdruid, yuan-ti anathema	12 (8,400 XP)

Grassland Creatures

Creatures	Challenge (XP)
Cow (rothé), gnoll witherling, hadrosaurus, velociraptor	1/4 (50 XP)
Gnoll hunter, orc Nurtured One of Yurtrus	1/2 (100 XP)
Deinonychus, gnoll flesh gnawer	1 (200 XP)
Aurochs, hobgoblin Iron Shadow, orc Hand of Yurtrus	2 (450 XP)
Leucrotta	3 (700 XP)
Barghest, hobgoblin devastator, orc Blade of Ilneval, stegosaurus, yeth hound	4 (1,100 XP)
Brontosaurus	5 (1,800 XP)
Mouth of Grolantor	6 (2,300 XP)
Shoosuva	8 (3,900 XP)
Flind	9 (5,000 XP)
Ki-rin	12 (8,400 XP)

Hill Creatures

Creatures	Challenge (XP)
Boggle, neogi hatchling, xvart	1/8 (25 XP)
Gnoll witherling, kobold inventor	1/4 (50 XP)
Firenewt, gnoll hunter, orc Nurtured One of Yurtrus	1/2 (100 XP)
Deinonychus, firenewt warlock of Imix, giant strider, gnoll flesh gnawer, kobold dragonshield, kobold scale sorcerer, nilbog, xvart warlock of Raxivort	1 (200 XP)
Aurochs, hobgoblin Iron Shadow, orc Hand of Yurtrus, quetzalcoatlus, shadow mastiff	2 (450 XP)
Neogi, orc Red Fang of Shargaas, redcap	3 (700 XP)
Barghest, hobgoblin devastator, neogi master, orc Blade of Ilneval, yeth hound	4 (1,100 XP)
Tanarukk	5 (1,800 XP)
Annis hag, mouth of Grolantor, warlock of the Great Old One	6 (2,300 XP)
Shoosuva	8 (3,900 XP)
Flind	9 (5,000 XP)
Stone giant dreamwalker	10 (5,900 XP)

Mountain Creatures

Creatures	Challenge (XP)
Kobold inventor	1/4 (50 XP)
Firenewt, orc Nurtured One of Yurtrus	1/2 (100 XP)
Firenewt warlock of Imix, giant strider, kobold dragonshield, kobold scale sorcerer	1 (200 XP)
Aurochs, guard drake (red), orc Claw of Luthic, orc Hand of Yurtrus, quetzalcoatlus	2 (450 XP)
Orc Red Fang of Shargaas	3 (700 XP)
Barghest, orc Blade of Ilneval, warlock of the archfey	4 (1,100 XP)
Tanarukk	5 (1,800 XP)
Annis hag, warlock of the Great Old One	6 (2,300 XP)
Stone giant dreamwalker	10 (5,900 XP)
Cloud giant smiling one	11 (7,200 XP)
Archdruid, ki-rin	12 (8,400 XP)
Fire giant dreadnought	14 (11,500 XP)
Storm giant quintessent	16 (15,000 XP)

Swamp Creatures

Creatures	Challenge (XP)
Dimetrodon, hadrosaurus, vegepygmy	1/4 (50 XP)
Darkling, swarm of rot grubs	1/2 (100 XP)
Thorny, vargouille	1 (200 XP)
Darkling elder, guard drake (black), meenlock, shadow mastiff, vegepygmy chief	2 (450 XP)
Flail snail, redcap	3 (700 XP)
Warlock of the archfey	4 (1,100 XP)
Catoblepas	5 (1,800 XP)
Bodak	6 (2,300 XP)
Froghemoth	10 (5,900 XP)
Archdruid	12 (8,400 XP)

UNDERDARK CREATURES

Creatures	Challenge (XP)
Cranium rat	0 (10 XP)
Boggle, neogi hatchling, xvart	1/8 (25 XP)
Cow (deep rothé), kobold inventor	1/4 (50 XP)
Chitine, darkling, firenewt, gazer, orc Nurtured One of Yurtrus, swarm of rot grubs	1/2 (100 XP)
Firenewt warlock of Imix, giant strider, kobold dragonshield, kobold scale sorcerer, maw demon, nilbog, vargouille, xvart warlock of Raxivort	1 (200 XP)
Darkling elder, guard drake (red), orc Claw of Luthic, orc Hand of Yurtrus, yuan-ti broodguard	2 (450 XP)
Cave fisher, choldrith, flail snail, neogi, orc Red Fang of Shargaas, slithering tracker, trapper	3 (700 XP)
Babau, barghest, neogi master, orc Blade of Ilneval, yuan-ti mind whisperer, yuan-ti nightmare speaker	4 (1,100 XP)
Mindwitness, spawn of Kyuss, swarm of cranium rats, tanarukk, yuan-ti pit master	5 (1,800 XP)
Bodak, gauth, warlock of the Great Old One	6 (2,300 XP)
Draegloth, warlock of the fiend	7 (2,900 XP)
Blackguard	8 (3,900 XP)
Ulitharid	9 (5,000 XP)
Alhoon, death kiss, froghemoth	10 (5,900 XP)
Yuan-ti anathema	12 (8,400 XP)
Devourer, neothelid	13 (10,000 XP)
Elder brain, fire giant dreadnought	14 (11,500 XP)
Mind flayer lich (see Alhoon)	22 (41,000 XP)

UNDERWATER CREATURES

Creatures	Challenge (XP)
Dolphin	1/8 (25 XP)
Sea spawn	1 (200 XP)
Deep scion	3 (700 XP)
Kraken priest	5 (1,800 XP)
Morkoth	11 (7,200 XP)
Archdruid	12 (8,400 XP)
Storm giant quintessent	16 (15,000 XP)

URBAN CREATURES

Creatures	Challenge (XP)
Cranium rat	0 (10 XP)
Apprentice, boggle	1/8 (25 XP)
Cow (ox), kobold inventor	1/4 (50 XP)
Darkling	1/2 (100 XP)
Kobold scale sorcerer	1 (200 XP)
Bard, darkling elder, guard drake (any), meenlock	2 (450 XP)
Archer, illusionist, martial arts adept, orc Red Fang of Shargaas, slithering tracker, swashbuckler	3 (700 XP)
Babau, warlock of the archfey	4 (1,100 XP)
Banderhobb, enchanter, master thief, swarm of cranium rats, transmuter	5 (1,800 XP)
Bodak, conjurer, warlock of the Great Old One	6 (2,300 XP)
Warlock of the fiend	7 (2,900 XP)
Blackguard, diviner	8 (3,900 XP)
Abjurer, champion, evoker, necromancer, war priest	9 (5,000 XP)
Warlord	12 (8,400 XP)